Public Relations Writing and Media Techniques

Public Relations Writing and Media Techniques

Dennis L. Wilcox
Professor of Public Relations
San Jose State University

Lawrence W. Nolte
Public Relations Consultant
Hillsborough, California

Foreword by

Patrick Jackson
Senior Counsel, Jackson Jackson & Wagner
and Editor, *pr reporter*

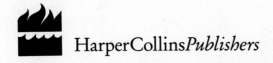
HarperCollins*Publishers*

Sponsoring Editor: Jane E. Kinney
Project Editor: Thomas R. Farrell
Art Direction/Cover Coordinator: Heather A. Ziegler
Cover Design: YIG Studios
Production: Paula Roppolo

PUBLIC RELATIONS WRITING AND MEDIA TECHNIQUES

Library of Congress Cataloging-in-Publication Data

Wilcox, Dennis L.
    Public relations writing and media techniques / Dennis L.
Wilcox, Lawrence W. Nolte.
        p.   cm.
    Includes bibliographical references.
    ISBN 0-06-047105-0
    1. Public relations—United States.   2. Public relations—United
States—Authorship.   I. Nolte, Lawrence W.   II. Title.
HM263.W49   1990   89-38203
659.2—dc20   CIP

90 91 92   9 8 7 6 5 4 3 2

Contents

Foreword

If one book can help us learn to write . . . to think . . . to plan . . . to use various media and methods, obviously that is a superior text. A person who knows and can apply what's in this book is ready for a career in public relations.

This text is the product of several developments in the emerging profession of public relations. First is the subject of writing and media techniques itself. Recent research is emphatic that a majority of people lack sophisticated reading and writing skills necessary to cope with the information explosion. Whether a consumer or a purveyor of goods, services, or information, one's ability to deal effectively with information overload is of paramount importance. Effective media communication skills are more important than ever because only the most targeted and easiest to understand messages will get through to their intended audiences.

Writing is a thought-recovery process. We have thoughts in response to some mental stimulus or to something we observe. Then we capture them at a keyboard or on the back of an envelope on the last flight from Dallas.

What makes this text so valuable is that it goes beyond how to write to examine the reasons why we write. The driving force in effective public relations practice is to see beyond *what* we do (the process) in order to focus on *why* (the expected outcomes).

By analytically teaching why we write, and the strategy and planning that go into persuasive writing, this book helps us to think better. The first step to better writing is better thinking—and the combination leads to better public relations practice.

It is therefore no overstatement that mastering the material covered in this comprehensive book is essential to a career in the field—or even to being able to utilize the principles of public relations as a manager, board member, or committee volunteer. A thorough understanding of this material would significantly enhance most managers' organizational effectiveness and ensure that customer satisfaction would multiply a hundredfold.

Writing and media are not the whole of public relations, of course. The text recognizes this by also illuminating such subjects as events, conferences, meetings of various kinds, presentations, and, most important, *planning*. Still, a public relations practitioner without a thorough understanding of persuasive writing and efficient media networks would be like a doctor without a basic grounding in anatomy or physiology.

Dennis Wilcox, a knowledgeable, questing, and contributing scholar of the field, is a spokesman not only for what public relations is but what it can and ought to be. Larry Nolte, who in his consulting puts into practice the topics of this book, has paved the way for the behavioral science approach widely accepted today. In a society whose very size ensures that communication and relationship-building skills must be recognized as the basis of democracy, these authors demonstrate in this valuable volume the insight students need to succeed.

Patrick Jackson, APR

Senior Counsel, Jackson Jackson & Wagner
and Editor, *pr reporter*

Preface

*. . . the focus is on skills and techniques that cover several closely associated
areas such as writing for public relations, copy dissemination, media use and
media network design. These techniques range across internal and external
media, print, electronic and audiovisual media.*

This statement, from the final report of the Commission on Undergraduate
Public Relations Education, best describes the contents of this book. It was the
commission's belief that a fundamental public relations writing course is essential
to any student planning a career in the field. In the commission's view, "This kind
of knowledge sets public relations communication techniques apart from other
types of written and oral presentations."

Consequently, this book is a practical application of the commission's recommendations. Its emphasis is on teaching students how to write, produce, and distribute a variety of public relations materials—from news releases and public service announcements to brochures, newsletters, slide presentations, and video
news releases.

But a comprehensive writing text cannot stop with the above list. There are
other publicity tools that should be discussed, and this text attempts to address
some areas missed by other writing books. For example, we have included chapters about (1) photography and artwork, (2) audiovisual materials for conferences
and meeting, (3) business letters and memos, (4) advertising, and (5) special-
events planning.

It also differs from other texts in providing a practical context for all public relations writing. Early in the text, for example, the legal and ethical considerations
of writing are discussed. The concluding chapters discuss the organization of an
entire public relations plan—using the variety of publicity tools available—and
how to evaluate overall public relations efforts.

The text is designed for easy reading and comprehension, and a conscious effort was made to take a "nuts and bolts" approach. Every chapter has checklists,

examples from actual public relations efforts, and boxed inserts highlighting key concepts to help students assimilate and retain important information. In addition, there are skill-building exercises at the end of every chapter.

It is impossible, of course, to cover all aspects of public relations writing without producing a text several thousand pages in length. Consequently, we have supplemented the text with a list of suggested readings at the end of every chapter. An effort was made to list materials that students would find practical and informative and that are commonly available in most libraries.

Public Relations Writing and Media Techniques is for the student who wants to learn how to write, prepare, and distribute public relations materials. We hope that it will save the reader many of the scars we acquired as we learned, often by trial and error.

Dennis L. Wilcox

Lawrence W. Nolte

*Public Relations Writing
and Media Techniques*

Chapter
1

The Basics
of Public Relations
Writing

*T*he ability to write is an absolute necessity for work in public relations. Writing is an integral part of the entire public relations process—research, planning, communication, and evaluation—but it is most visible at the third stage, when a program is being implemented and various messages are being communicated to key publics.

Your writing must be planned to attain specific objectives for your client or employer. It must be based on facts; above all, it must be clear, concise, complete, and accurate.

IT'S DIFFERENT FROM JOURNALISM

There was a time when experience in newspaper writing was practically a requirement for a job in public relations. Although this is no longer true, there is still emphasis on use of a journalistic writing style. This is because much of what the public relations writer produces is directed to the news media. A solid understanding of journalistic principles and concepts is needed, but public relations writers should never simply consider themselves "journalists in residence." Public relations writing differs from journalistic writing in its objectives, audiences, and channels.

Objectives

The purpose of a journalist is to inform an audience in the most impartial way possible. Personal bias may affect the choice of words, but in general the reporter tries to maintain an attitude of strict neutrality.

The public relations writer, by definition, is an advocate. His or her purpose is not only to inform but also to persuade and motivate—that is, to make something happen. All public relations writing should begin with the question: How does this help the organization attain its objectives? For example, in choosing subjects for feature stories, a newsletter editor must think about organizational objectives. If one of these is to increase productivity, the editor may decide to run several features about employees who are outstanding workers.

Although a public relations writer carefully chooses facts and story angles that help attain the objectives, this should not be done in a deceptive or misleading way. There is no excuse for writing that is not frank and honest.

Audiences

The journalist writes for one audience—readers, listeners, or viewers of the medium for which he or she works. The composition of this audience is usually well defined. For example, a daily suburban newspaper circulates primarily among people who share a common residential area but have a broad range of backgrounds and interests. By contrast, the readers of a special-interest magazine share a very strong interest in only one particular subject. The newspaper reporter writes about many things for a general audience. The special-interest reporter writes about just one subject for a limited and highly interested audience.

The public relations writer may write for numerous and radically different audiences, such as employees, constituents, customers, businesspeople, homemakers, travelers, bankers, politicians, stockholders, farmers, and many others. Effective public relations writing is based on defining the audience and its composition properly, so you can tailor your information to its interests and concerns. The media must be remembered as an audience too. Their positive response to your writing is what opens the channels.

Channels

The journalist reaches his or her audience through one channel—the medium that publishes or broadcasts his or her writing. Whether this comprises news or features, there is only one channel that conveys the writing to the audience.

The public relations writer, with many audiences to reach, will probably use many channels. Here is a listing of some of the channels of communication that you may use: metropolitan daily newspapers, Sunday newspaper supplements, suburban daily newspapers, weekly newspapers, general magazines, business magazines, trade magazines, special-interest magazines, radio stations, television stations, letters, pamphlets, brochures, newsletters, internal magazines, speeches, audiovisual presentations, posters, direct mail, and telephone calls.

PREPARATION FOR WRITING

In writing for public relations, you need certain basic equipment, references, and files.

Equipment

You will need an electric typewriter or a personal computer to produce written materials of professional quality.

A standard electric typewriter equipped with a high-yield self-correcting ribbon is an economical purchase; thousands of business offices use such machines. A new generation of electronic typewriters, controlled by microcomputers, brings a whole new set of skills to the typing table for much less than the cost of a personal computer.

An electronic typewriter can not only correct mistakes but also tell the typist when a word has been misspelled or even overused. A built-in dictionary can provide correct spellings on a display screen, and a thesaurus can offer alternative words or phrases. The machines can remember and later print out what was typed earlier. Centering and tabulation can be done automatically, eliminating the need to count spaces.

A basic electronic typewriter costs about $200; its internal memory has a capacity of about 7,000 characters. For some $1,500, IBM offers an electronic typewriter that has a 25-line display, a 25-page storage memory, and a host of other functions. The application of laser technology also allows faster printing of documents on electronic typewriters.

Studies by Smith-Corona and Princeton University have found that personal computers are used 70 percent of the time for typing rather than computing functions. Thus, manufacturers of electronic typewriters make the point that it is wasteful to purchase a personal computer if your primary purpose is writing.

The point is well taken, but more powerful word processing is available in

Writing equipment. Word processors and computers are so widely used in all phases of public relations writing that you must know how to use one. This photo is a good example of product publicity. It was widely distributed by Hewlett-Packard Company when it introduced its new HP Vectra personal computer. (*Source:* Hewlett-Packard Company, Palo Alto, CA.)

personal computers. Consequently, more and more professional writers are using them. Personal computers can store large amounts of information, and software programs like WordPerfect and WordStar permit maximum flexibility to write, edit, format, and merge information into one complete document.

One of the most popular word processing programs is WordPerfect. It contains a 115,000-word dictionary that enables you to examine documents for spelling and typographical errors as well as for unintentional double words. The program's thesaurus (10,000 words) can be used to find synonyms and antonyms for specific words in a document or for individual words typed from the keyboard. WordPerfect also allows the writer to incorporate a number of graphic symbols into the text, compile and format statistical tables, vary the size of type, format the document into various column widths, and even automatically insert names and specialized information into standard letters. The ability to do all these things almost instantly with a few instructions on the keyboard significantly increases a writer's productivity.

In addition to a personal computer and the appropriate word processing software, you must also have a printer. A letter-quality dot-matrix printer is more economical than the more expensive laser printers, but advances in technology may bring laser printers down in price and make them the standard. Laser printers have the advantages of exceptionally high speed (an average of eight pages per minute) and extremely high resolution. If you're preparing newsletters and brochures, laser printers allow you to write camera-ready copy complete with large-type headlines. In addition, electronic scanners can input photographs and artwork directly into your computer disk for integration into your newsletter layout. This is further discussed in Chapter 14.

References

A basic library is a must for any writer. First, you should own a dictionary, preferably an unabridged one but at least a collegiate edition. This will answer questions on spelling and also help you select just the right word. A thesaurus (there are several good ones available) will supply synonyms, thus helping you to avoid repeating the same word too often. If you do speech writing, a copy of *Bartlett's Familiar Quotations* will be helpful.

Another necessity is a stylebook. Among the most widely used are the *Associated Press Stylebook and Libel Manual*, the *United Press Stylebook*, and the *New York Times Stylebook.* Of the three, the *Associated Press Stylebook* is used by the most weekly and daily newspapers. A stylebook helps you prepare copy that meets the standards of the media. It tells you how to handle things like titles, acronyms, punctuation, abbreviations, numerals, and so on. If you do any writing for radio or television, you will need the *Associated Press Broadcast Stylebook.*

Other useful volumes on your bookshelf might include a current issue of the *Reader's Digest Almanac,* a Rand McNally world atlas, a *Pocket Guide to the World* (a Facts on File publication), and a *Statistical Abstract of the United States,* published by the U.S. Government Printing Office. These sources are available in paperback, and they often save a hurried trip to a library for basic facts. A visit to the reference section of a large bookstore will help you find other standard references that you may want to own.

Last but not least are media directories and listings of public relations services. If most of your work is geared to the local area, directories of media outlets are often available from the chamber of commerce, United Way, or other civic groups. There are also directories on the state or regional level. *Western Media Contacts,* for example, lists magazines, newspapers, radio stations, and television stations in California, Nevada, Arizona, Washington, and Oregon.

For media listings on the national level, popular sources are *Editor & Publisher Yearbook, Bacon's Publicity Checker,* and *Working Press of the Nation.*

References are necessary. Public relations writers keep a number of references at their fingertips. A good dictionary is a must, and various media directories help pinpoint effective distribution channels. Those shown are just a sample of what might be needed. (*Source:* Photo by James McNay.)

The latter is a five-volume set that contains listings of (1) newspapers, (2) magazines, (3) TV and radio personnel, (4) feature and photography syndicates, and (5) internal publications. Another popular reference source is *Standard Rate and Data*, a six-volume set that contains citations about a media outlet's market, audience demographics, and advertising rates. National media directories can cost several hundred dollars. Therefore an independent freelance writer might find it more economical to use the local library.

For listings of public relations services in photography, printing, distribution, and so on, a standard source is the *Professional's Guide to Public Relations Services*, published by Prentice-Hall. Another good source is O'Dwyer's

PR Services, a monthly publication that contains articles and advertisements about vendors. Advertisements in the monthly publications of Public Relations Society of America (PRSA) and International Association of Business Communicators (IABC)—*Public Relations Journal* and *Communication World*—are also good sources. The national membership directory of each organization contains a section listing companies that specialize in public relations services.

Information Files

You will need to know a lot about the organization for which you work. The key to this is a comprehensive file. You won't be able to remember every pertinent fact, idea, or event, but a good, well-indexed file will help you find what you need. No two writers will need the same system, but the following list should provide some guidance:

1. *Statistics*—about the organization or its industry.
2. *History*—records, reports (annual or special), historical publications.
3. *Publications*—house magazines, newsletters, leaflets, booklets, and so on.
4. *Speeches*—by organization people or by others in the same field.
5. *Releases*—news items and features, plus clippings from those releases.
6. *Clippings*—based on other sources, giving information about the organization or affecting the organization.
7. *Fact sheets*—about the organization.
8. *Position papers*—on issues or situations affecting the organization.
9. *Biographies*—of key personnel.
10. *Photos and art*—see Chapter 7.

Three categories of books can help you become a more professional writer. First, there are those that describe current linguistic usages and give helpful hints about improving your general writing ability. Two of the most popular are *The Elements of Style* by Strunk and White, a book that never seems to go out of style, and the newer *On Writing Well* by William Zinsser. Another outstanding work often used by professional writers is John B. Bremner's *Words on Words: A Dictionary for Writers and Others Who Care About Words.* Having these books on your reference shelf is not enough; you should take the time to read them from cover to cover once a year so as to avoid developing sloppy writing habits.

A superior backgrounder is *The Story of English* by McCrum, Cran, and MacNeil, which offers excellent descriptions of regional variations in vocabulary and pronunciation. As public relations expands to international scope and English becomes more and more an international language, this book should become ever more useful.

Other helpful books on how English is currently used in America are by Rudolph Flesch, who has produced four; Theodore Bernstein, who has also produced four; and Edwin Newman, the television commentator, who has written two.

Books about semantics—the connotative and denotative meaning of words—make up a second category. A knowledge of semantics will help you choose words that will be effective and persuasive and to avoid those that may have negative effects. S. I. Hayakawa has written two classics in semantics: *Language in Thought and Action* and *Through the Communications Barrier.* Mario Pei wrote another, calling it *Weasel Words: The Art of Saying What You Don't Mean.*

Third in the category of educational reading are the classics or semiclassics. Our everyday writing and conversation is liberally sprinkled with phrases and expressions from these books. They are all interesting and many are highly entertaining; any writer who hopes to use the language with skill should read them. Sir Winston Churchill was a master of both spoken and written English. He read voraciously in the classics and freely borrowed ideas and phrases from them.

In addition to books, you should read newspapers and news magazines to learn how *they* use the language. Also, it is imperative to read any publication in which you hope to place news items or features. The purpose is twofold: to learn what kind of material is used and how it is written.

Reading for Information

Writing starts with facts, and reading can supply you with many. Read the daily and weekly news media to know what is going on in the world. Read the trade or professional journals bearing on the organization for which you work, so you will know what is going on in your field. By reading books and booklets on pertinent subjects, you can gain a large amount of information that will help you produce more informative and complete materials.

Another source of current information is the "best-seller." Whenever any book is widely read, it may have a strong influence on the public. Harriet Beecher Stowe's *Uncle Tom's Cabin* was a best-seller in the mid-1800s. It aroused intense feeling against slavery and was, to some degree, responsible for the Civil War. In the 1960s, Rachel Carson's *Silent Spring* first ignited public concern for the environment. And Ralph Nader's *Unsafe at Any Speed* in the 1970s marked the beginning of today's consumer movement. In the 1980s, Allan Bloom's *The Closing of the American Mind* helped to spur public demands for improvements in American liberal arts education.

Listening and Watching

Many people get all their news from television, and the entertainment programs often reflect the attitudes of the viewers. You should know what is being presented to the public. Communications scholars—such as Dr. Max McCombs of the University of Texas—point out that media coverage sets the agenda for people's thinking.

Watching the news will show what kinds of stories are used and how they are handled. The most popular programs will give an indication of the social climate and possible public attitudes. For example, because they are now seen as a threat to health, cigarettes have almost disappeared from the screen.

Listening to radio news will reveal the kinds of items that are used and the way they are presented. An awareness of this will enable you to prepare suitable material. Other programs, especially "talk shows," will show you what sorts of stories get on the air and indicate the kind of audience that listens to such programs.

RESEARCH

Since the purpose of writing is to convey information, the first step is to get the facts. In some cases all the facts will be readily available, but most of the time you'll have to dig for them. For example, an announcement that Jane Smith has been elected president of the school board would not be interesting unless it included some information about her personally.

Research may yield the facts that she is a vice president of a local bank; a graduate of Bryn Mawr, where she majored in American history; the mother of 10-year-old twins named Henry and Philip; the wife of John Smith, a real estate broker; and a member of Soroptimists and the First Presbyterian Church.

Such facts, which make Jane Smith more interesting to the reader, can be gotten from a few phone calls. That's easy. But what if the person is a stranger? Suppose that Dr. James White is to speak at the commencement exercise of Putnam College. Initial information may state that he teaches sociology at Fareastern University, is head of the department, and has written numerous books. These facts won't make a very interesting announcement, but research can provide some meat for these bare bones.

The news bureau of Fareastern University would be the first source to tap. It should provide information about Dr. White's education, experience, family, length of service, the jobs he has held, and what he has written—both books and scholarly papers.

A trip to the library might turn up copies of the books and professional journals that carry some of Dr White's writings. Reading or at least scanning some of these can give you an idea of what Dr. White has said and how others have responded to him. With this backlog of information, you should be able to write an interesting news story that will make the readers want to hear Dr. White.

These illustrations are perhaps oversimplified, but they should indicate the value of research in any kind of writing. In general, research for this purpose is divided into four categories:

1. *Personal inquiry*—asking questions of people who know something about the subject.

2. *Interviews*—detailed questioning of someone who has a thorough knowledge of the subject.
3. *Reading*—systematic reading of available printed material and use of computer data banks like Dialog and Nexis.
4. *Surveys*—planning and conducting a thorough investigation.

Inquiries

Your telephone is one of your best research tools. Call experts in the field or people who are knowledgeable about the subject. Although you may think this is an intrusion, most people will be flattered and pleased to provide information. In addition, they can give you names, places, and examples that will add flavor to your writing.

Interviews

Before the interview, you should look over your information about the subject of the interview. This should reveal what is not known and suggest questions to be asked. You should have a list of specific questions and ask them one at a time. If the answers are not clear, you should continue to probe until they are.

If the interviewee goes off on a tangent, this may contribute information that you hadn't thought of. Pursuing these unexpected leads may yield valuable ideas, so digressions should not be squelched. Taking notes is a must, and a tape recorder can help you keep an accurate account of what was said. As the interview progresses, it is important to watch the interviewee and listen to his or her tone of voice. Tones, facial expressions, and gestures often reveal more than the words alone.

References

The basic references listed at the beginning of this chapter are very general in nature. For detailed information, you will need much more. A good start would be to consult a comprehensive encyclopedia such as the *Brittanica* or *Americana*. The next step is to use a library. A reference librarian can direct you to the proper source if you can be specific about what you want to find out. A vague request for information generally produces unsatisfactory results. When you use books, try to select those published within the last five years; anything older than that tends to be out of date.

You can get much information from newspapers and magazines. To find it, you will need to use one of the periodical indexes. These include the following:

Communications Abstracts—covers major communications-related articles, reports, and books. Indexes include *Public Relations Journal, Public Relations Quarterly, Public Relations Review.*

Dow Jones–Irwin Business Almanac—covers business trends and developments.

Education Index—covers a broad range of subjects relating to man and society.

Facts on File—a fast way to check facts: the date of a public event, the names of national leaders, the circumstances surrounding an issue.

Funk and Scott—information about specific companies. Citations give a brief description of the article contents.

Gallup Opinion Index—a monthly list of polls on political, economic, and cultural issues.

Public Affairs Information Services (PAIS)—indexes books and government documents as well as periodicals.

Reader's Guide to Periodical Literature—the old standard, ideal for high school term papers. Indexes articles in about fifty general circulation publications like *Time, Newsweek, Atlantic, Esquire, New Republic,* and so on.

Social Science Index—periodical articles by author and subject. Covers all aspects of the social sciences, including persuasion and public opinion formation.

Work-Related Abstracts—information from over 250 management, labor, government, and professional publications.

In addition to these indexes, available at most libraries, there are computerized periodical indexes. The *CD-ROM Computer Database* contains *ERIC* (education), *PsychLit* (psychology), *Medline* (health sciences), and *Disclosure* (company information). *Infotrac* is a computerized index to periodicals and some newspapers. For a fee, libraries will also do data searches on *Dialog* and *Nexis,* both large data bases. *Dialog,* for example, has more than 180 data bases and about eighty million entries. *Nexis* includes 8 million full-text articles from more than 125 magazines, newspapers, newsletters, and news services.

A number of major daily newspapers also have their own indexes, available in many libraries. These include the *Christian Science Monitor, Los Angeles Times, New York Times, Wall Street Journal,* and *Washington Post.* A comprehensive newspaper index is *Business NewsBank,* which indexes articles about companies, industries, products, and businesspeople.

Another kind of reference will help you when you have to write about someone of prominence. These are the "Who" reference books. They give detailed information about people—careers, accomplishments, honors, and so on. In addition to *Who's Who in America,* there are several other books that list prominent people by profession or by general area of residence (e.g., *Who's Who in Medicine* or *Who's Who in the West*). These are normally grouped together in the library and, if you can't hit your target in one book, you may do so in another.

Except for a few classified documents, public records of local, state, and national governments are open. The Library of Congress is a large and helpful source. The U.S. Government Printing Office, in Washington, D.C., has publications on thousands of subjects. State and local governments, too, publish bulletins, reports, and statistics that can be helpful.

Other sources of facts and figures include trade and professional associations, trade journals, and pertinent academic departments at colleges and universities. The key to getting at this material is to ask the simple question: Who might know something about this subject?

Surveys

Surveys can produce valuable information, but they are costly and time-consuming. A very simple survey might be conducted without the use of a specialized research firm, but it will usually be necessary to get professional help. Among the things that will be involved in deciding to do a survey are questions like these: What is the objective? (What do we want to find out?) Who will do the survey and how much will it cost? How long will it take? Who will be surveyed and what sort of questions will be asked? How will the questions be asked (by personal interview, mail, or telephone)? See Chapter 18 for further discussion.

Listening

Quotations add interest to news items or feature stories. On one day, a metropolitan newspaper used the word "said" 19 times on its first page. This shows that what people say can be a major factor in the news, and it suggests that you'll do well to use direct quotations whenever possible.

This suggestion is coupled with a warning to be sure that your quotations are accurate. Accuracy is necessary to avoid possible libel, as stated in Chapter 3. It is also necessary to prevent misunderstandings. A misquotation may not lead to legal repercussions, but it can still cause confusion. The only way to make a quotation accurate is to listen carefully. Did the president say "possible" or "probable"? Did the contractor say that the job "would be finished by June 6" or that he "hoped that it would be finished by June 6"? Did the doctor say "epidemic" or "endemic"?

If there is any doubt as to what was said, you must go back to the speaker and ask for clarification. Most people hate to be misquoted and are willing to correct a statement that might be misunderstood. Misquoting is not only inaccurate but also dangerous, because it can mislead the reader and the reaction of the person who has been misquoted can lead to repercussions.

GENERAL GUIDELINES

The first step in writing is to know exactly what idea is to be conveyed. It should be possible to express this in one brief sentence. Once you have this basic idea clearly in mind, all the words you choose should serve to expand and explain the basic message. For example, "The way in which a person drives can make a big difference in the amount of gasoline consumed." This theme could be amplified into a feature article.

The Audience

The message should be aimed at a specific audience. Is it the general public? A group of educators? Hospital administrators? Automobile drivers? Donors to charity? Regardless of who the target audience may be, the message should be couched in words that they will understand. Furthermore, the medium in which the idea is to be conveyed must be considered. *Psychology Today* is quite different from *Popular Mechanics*. The *Wall Street Journal* isn't like the *Toledo Blade*. Radio uses material very differently than a newspaper would. You must not only aim at a specific audience but also tailor your message to the intended medium.

Sentences and Paragraphs

Sentences should be clear and concise. Longer sentences may often be necessary, but a good test is to go back over the material and see how many sentences can be cut down. Don't hesitate to use some sentences of eight or ten words. Mixing long and short sentences improves the rhythm.

The typical paragraph should normally include only one idea. As a general practice, it ought to be no longer than six or eight lines. If necessary, a longer paragraph may be used, but brevity is preferable. Writing that goes on and on without a pause is hard on the reader.

Word Length

Word length is a good measurement of readability, and every writer hopes that his or her writing will be read. In readable writing, most words are short. A message containing an average of 1.5 syllables per word is considered to be very readable. Some states have required this 1.5-syllable average for consumer information about purchase contracts and monetary loans.

For the general public, this guide should be kept in mind. For a more technical audience, it is permissible to use longer words; but even here, brevity is desirable. Whenever there is a choice of two words, it's better to use the shorter one. Don't try to show off your knowledge by using long, complicated words. Remember that Lincoln's Gettysburg Address consisted of 267 words, of which 202 had only one syllable.

Word Choice

In general, the short Anglo-Saxon word is more understandable than the longer one derived from French, Greek, or Latin. "Buy" is better than "purchase." "Home" is better than "residence." "Hire" is better than "employ."

Steps to Effective Writing

USE SHORT SENTENCES

An *average* sentence should contain about fifteen to seventeen words. Avoid compound and run-on sentences.

USE GOOD PARAGRAPHING

A paragraph should express one central idea. For readability, it should not run more than six to eight lines. A lead paragraph to an article or news release should be even shorter.

USE SIMPLE WORDS

Don't use a multisyllable word when a simple word can express the same idea. Be aware of your audience.

USE FAMILIAR WORDS

Don't use jargon from specialized fields and occupations that won't be familiar to the general public.

MAKE YOUR MESSAGE PERSONAL

Use personal pronouns like "you." Tailor the message to the audience's concerns and needs.

ILLUSTRATE CONCEPTS WITH EXAMPLES

A concrete example helps clarify an abstract idea. Make ideas tangible to the reader or listener.

Most readers will react favorably to this kind of writing. In law, education, and science there is a different standard. The language of lawyers is commonly loaded with repetitious and cumbersome words. Educators often seem to love concealing their thoughts behind words that are strange, such as "multi-ethnic individualized learning," and "continuum."

Scientific writing, too, is loaded with esoteric words. To make them understandable to the general public is a difficult task, but it can be done.

Public relations writing should be natural. If it does not sound clear when read out loud, it should be rewritten. Every piece of copy should be reviewed to see if any words can be cut. Active rather than passive language is preferable. "Smith took every possible precaution" is better than "Every possible precaution was taken by Smith."

Keep It Simple

Strike three.
Get your hand off my knee.
You're overdrawn.
Your horse won.
Yes.
No.
You have the account.
Walk.
Don't walk.
Mother's dead.
Basic events
require simple language.
Idiosyncratically euphuistic
eccentricities are the
promulgators of
triturable obfuscation.
What did you do last night?
Enter into a meaningful
romantic involvement
or
fall in love?
What did you have for
breakfast this morning?
The upper part of a hog's
hind leg with two oval
bodies encased in a shell
laid by a female bird
or
ham and eggs?
David Belasco, the great
American theatrical producer,
once said, "If you can't
write your idea on the
back of my calling
card,
you don't have a clear idea."

A United Technologies reprint from *The Wall Street Journal*

Simplicity! Simplicity! Simplicity! This institutional advertisement reprinted from *The Wall Street Journal* cautions the writer not to bury the message in words that don't do anything for the reader. You will hear few complaints that something is "too easy to understand." (*Source:* United Technologies, Hartford, CT.)

Simplicity

In many offices where people are engaged in writing, it is the practice to post a large sign bearing the letters KISS. Underneath, in smaller type, is the definition of this acronym: "Keep It Simple, Stupid."

This is good advice for any writer at any time. It becomes especially important when you must translate technical information into something that lay people will understand. Here the sign should change from KISS to MISS and the words beneath should read "Make It Simple, Stupid," because there is nothing to keep simple. Instead, there is something complicated that must be *made* simple.

Simplifying a complex idea is hard work. First, you must research the information until you really understand it. It is impossible to explain anything that you do not understand. To gain understanding, you must read the material and question the people who created it.

In explaining a complicated subject, it is important not to overload the reader. He or she should not be given any more than is needed. The language of explanation must be plain English. Jargon has no place here. If possible, there should be no technical terms, but sometimes they must be used because nothing else will serve the purpose. If it is necessary to use technical terms, they should be described in layman's language.

In describing something new and different, use familiar words and go step by step from a base of common understanding. A foolproof test of any writing that is meant to simplify a complex subject is to pretest it. If several people who know nothing about the subject do understand the explanation, it is probably adequate, provided that the experts approve.

If the laity don't understand something, it must be rewritten until they do. And if the experts disapprove, it is probably because the simplification is inaccurate. Here again, a rewrite is called for.

Style

For news items or features to be published, they must conform to the writing style preferred by the mass media. The style books mentioned earlier in this chapter will help you get on the right track. Beyond this, however, you should conform to the style of the specific media for which you write. Some may want hard facts, others may prefer a more breezy approach. Some will accept lengthy material, others insist on terseness. Some use pictures, some don't. If you read what they publish, you will soon learn what to send to them.

Outlining

Before you start writing anything, you should make an outline of what you are going to include in your message. It may be brief (as for a short press release) or comprehensive (as for a large booklet). You will probably modify it as you gather information, but an outline will help to keep your thinking in order.

You may also want to make major changes. For example, this book has been outlined at least nine times in an effort to put the right material into the right chapters, and this chapter has been outlined at least six times in an effort to maximize clarity.

In the simplest terms, an outline is a list of topics to be written about in the order in which they will be presented. Usually an outline has major topics, and within each major topic there are likely to be minor topics. This book is an example of an outline. The book consist of 19 chapters. Each chapter covers one general subject. Within each chapter there are several major topics. Each of these is identified by a major subhead in capital letters. Under each of these major subheads there are minor topics identified by secondary subheads in capital and lowercase letters.

ERRORS TO AVOID

Errors in your writing will brand you as careless, illiterate, or inconsiderate of the reader. Be sure to think about the potential errors.

Spelling

Credibility is sacrificed when spelling errors appear in public relations materials. Media gatekeepers, in particular, are critical of poor grammar and spelling.

Devices for Attaining Clear Writing

EXAMPLE

Say something—and then use an example or a statistic to illustrate it.

DEFINITION

Uncommon words call for a dictionary definition or a simple explanation of what you mean.

COMPARISON

If the reader is unfamiliar with the concept or thing written about, compare it with something familiar.

RESTATEMENT

Say the same thing in different words. This reinforces the concept.

One business editor received the following news release, which contains four spelling errors in two sentences:

> Individuals invest a minimum of $250,000 which is tax *deductable therby* creating out of pocket expenditures of only $125,000. This *deductable* is an outstanding opportunity for the *entreprenuer*. . . . [The misspelled words are in italics.]

Gobbledegook and Jargon

"Gobbledegook" consists of ponderous words and phrases that obscure simple ideas. For example, to the user of gobbledegook, things don't get "finished,"

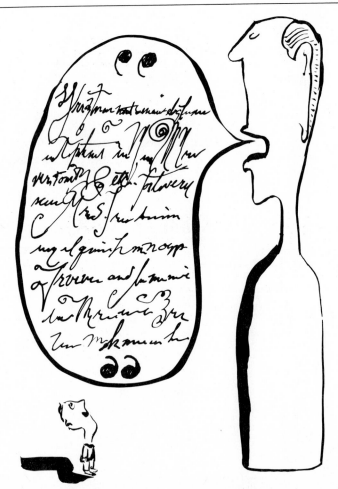

What is that all about? You must use words and symbols that are readily understood by the reader. Don't let your ideas get lost in jargon and gobbledegook. (*Source: Public Relations Journal*, October 1987.)

they get "finalized." Events don't happen "then," they happen "at that point in time." The child isn't "failing," he's "motivationally deprived."

"Jargon" comprises words that are known only, or almost only, to insiders. Some examples: A "four-on-the-floor" is a four-speed hand-shifted automobile transmission. A "no show" is a person who fails to use a ticket for an event or a trip.

Gobbledegook and jargon are often seen in news releases about high-tech products, giving the poor reader a very confusing message. Here is one example:

> Versatec, a Xerox Company, has introduced the Graphics Network Processor—SNA (Model 451). The processor, operating as a 377x RJE station, sends and receives EBCDIC or binary data in IBM system Network Architecture (SNA) networks using Synchronous Data Link Control protocol. . . .

Mixed Metaphors

Metaphors add sparkle and clarity to writing if they are appropriate and conceptually correct. But they can be unintentionally funny when they are made up of incompatible images. A good example of mixed metaphors is this extract from a news release:

> Hitchcock predicted that charter flights and regional airlines might offer lower fares, putting pressure on the major carriers to drop their prices. "It's something of a game of chicken," he said. "The industry has run a fare increase up the flagpole and is now waiting to see if it sticks."

Poor Sentence Structure

The subject and the words that modify it often become separated in a sentence, causing some confusion as to what exactly is being discussed. Here is an example from another news release:

> The proposed budget provides salary increases for faculty and staff performing at a satisfactory level of two percent.

Poor sentence structure can also lead to embarrassment. A company newsletter, detailing the sickness of an employee, once reported the following:

> Jeff was taken to the hospital with what was thought to be thrombus phlebitis. After spending a restless night with a nurse at the hospital, the results were negative. Jeff is now being treated for a secondary infection which caused the swelling in his ankle.

Redundancies

Another gross error in writing is the use of redundant words. It is not necessary to use the word "totally" to modify words like "destroyed" or "completely" to modify "demolished." A lot of writers also say that something is "somewhat" or "very" unique. "Unique," by definition, means one of a kind. Some-thing is either unique or it isn't. The following redundancy appeared in a news release:

> In addition, the company lists $50 million in receivables that it hopes to collect. These are unpaid bills, largely from customers, that have yet to be paid.

Wrong Figures

Another common error is the misuse of percentages. The price or value of anything can be expressed in clear figures. The price can go up 10 percent, 150 percent, or 1,000 percent. It cannot go down more than 100 percent. Even if the price has gone up 1,000 percent from a given base, the new price becomes a new base. If the price then goes down to nothing, it has gone down only 100 percent of that new base. There can be no greater loss than 100 percent. In spite of this, writers may say something like this: "The price is now 327 percent less than it was ten years ago." What they mean is the price ten years ago was 327 percent higher than it is today.

Stereotypes

A couple of generations ago, it was a common practice in writing to use stereo-types. Women were frail, Jews avaricious, Scots parsimonious, Negroes lazy, Asians inscrutable, Mexicans indolent, and Indians proud but silent.

Today such stereotyping is certain to provoke violent resentment. Even the designations that were formerly used must be avoided. Now it's "African-American" or "black" instead of "Negro" and "Mexican-American" or "His-panic" instead of "Mexican."

A good way to avoid trouble in this area is to read the following book, sponsored by the International Association of Business Communicators (IABC):

> Pickens, J. et al., *Without Bias: A Guidebook to Nondiscriminatory Communica-tion,* ed. 2. New York: John Wiley & Sons, 1982.

Here are some highlights from *Without Bias:*

Avoid suggesting that all members of any racial, ethnic, or sexual group have the same personal characteristics—ambition, laziness, shrewdness, guile, intelligence, or what have you. Don't suggest that some characteristic sets an individual apart from a stereotyped norm. For instance, it is inappropriate to write, "Although he is black, he has excellent qualifications for the job."

You should avoid racial identification unless it is absolutely necessary. One simple way to check this is to substitute the word "white" whenever you use a racial reference to see if it sounds peculiar. Avoid sexual bias by substi-tuting nonsexual words for sexual ones. That is why airlines now have "flight attendants" instead of "stewardesses," and why there are "mail carriers" in-stead of "mailmen."

The problem of avoiding sexual bias is particularly difficult because so much of our language is geared to use of the word "man" as a generic term for both males and females. Attempts to avoid this lead to such usages as "she/he," "chairperson," "spokesperson," "his/her," and other words or pseudo-words which, being barely understandable, make for difficult reading. There is not yet a good solution for this problem, but try your best to deal with it.

Wrong Words

An Associated Press story once told about a man who had inherited a small scenic railroad from his "descendants," who had started it in the nineteenth century. The writer meant "ancestors," but he used the wrong word. Use of the wrong word may make little difference in some cases, but in many other situations it can change the meaning.

"Sound-alikes"

Some words are so frequently confused that a list is included here. They are not defined because you should hasten to the dictionary and find out what each one means. And in the future, whenever there is the slightest doubt, you should make sure. These are some of the words that are most commonly misused:

> affect, effect
> adapt, adopt
> appraise, apprise
> baited, bated
> canvas, canvass
> comprise, compose
> continual, continuous
> ensure, insure
> flair, flare
> flaunt, flout
> fortunate, fortuitous
> imply, infer
> incredible, incredulous
> magnet, magnate
> negligent, negligible
> peak, peek
> pedal, peddle
> pore, pour
> principal, principle
> rebut, refute
> stationary, stationery

This list is far from complete. There are many other words that sound alike or almost alike but have different spellings and meanings.

Closely related to the misuse of sound-alikes are the errors arising from the transcription of spoken phrases into writing. In cartoons and advertising, we see "gonna" for "going to" and "wanna" for "want to." You are not likely to use these garblings, but one that may trap you, as it has trapped many writers, is this: "would have," "could have," "should have," and "might have" are often pronounced in conversation as "would've," "could've," "should've" and "might've." These abbreviations are permissible, but they should never be written as "would of," "could of," "should of," or "might of."

SUMMARY

1. Public relations writing is different from journalistic writing. It has different objectives, different audiences, and different channels of communication.
2. Public relations writing requires mechanical equipment such as word processors and copiers. It also requires reference sources and information files. It necessitates reading, listening to, and watching the media.
3. Research is imperative. You must gather information before you start to write.
4. Your writing must fit your audience. You must watch sentence and paragraph length. Word length and word choice are always important. Simplicity and correct style must be a constant concern. Everything you write should start with an outline.
5. Errors can destroy the effectiveness of your writing. Be constantly aware of the things that can get you into trouble.

EXERCISES

1. In a magazine or newspaper, find a piece of writing that you think is outstanding. Write a 500-word critique on the style and effectiveness of this piece. What principles and concepts of good writing are illustrated?
2. A company employee asked a manager whether a company-requested early retirement would affect the amount of his pension. Here is the answer he received from the manager:

   > Lack of work in many shops due to decreased programs has caused the Company to ask some employees to take an early retirement. It is regretful that so many people have been hurt—in terms of their career, and in terms of their finances—by the economic stresses we have undergone during the past few years. To maintain a profitable business, however, we cannot afford to keep people on its roll when the jobs are not available. In spite of the unfortunate circumstances which compel the Company to initiate early pensions, it will pay only those benefits to which the employee is eligible under the present contract.

   Rewrite this message making it shorter and clearer. Be tactful; that is, consider the feelings of the employee.
3. Although the content of a message remains the same, the nature of the audience often determines the writing style. A public health agency, for example, wants to

tell people how to avoid winter colds and the flu. It has been decided that three kinds of messages will be prepared:

a. A simple note that can be distributed to children in grade school.
b. A news item in a neighborhood shopper for a general adult audience.
c. An item for a hospital newsletter that provides medical information in lay terms for past, current, and prospective clients of the hospital.

Write a 50- to 75-word article for each of these audiences. To complete this assignment, you may wish to do some additional research.

4. Research is an important factor in public relations writing. Using the various sources cited in this chapter, find the answers to the following questions. For each answer show the source.

a. What is the preferred style of Associated Press—"nationwide" or "nation wide"?
b. What do the acronyms UNESCO, NATO, AFL-CIO, and AIDS stand for?
c. Which of the 50 states has the largest population? What American city has the largest population?
d. What is the world's largest city in terms of population?
e. What percentage of the American population is Hispanic in background?
f. How many sheep are in New Zealand?
g. What is the leading export of Indonesia?
h. What is the population of China?
i. Who is the current prime minister of Japan?
j. What company manufactures and sells the most automobiles worldwide?
k. What were the total worldwide sales of IBM last year? How many employees does IBM have?
l. What is the current age of Lee Iacocca, chairman of Chrysler Corporation?
m. How many personal computers were sold in the United States last year? What percentage of American households now own a personal computer?
n. Who said, "There are two times in a man's life when he should not speculate; when he can't afford it and when he can"?

5. Your company president has been asked to advocate, in a speech to the American Management Association, the idea that companies should provide child-care facilities for their employees. You are asked to do some research on the subject and gather some statistics and information that the president can use in preparing this speech. After gathering your information, write a memo to the president that outlines your findings.

SUGGESTED READINGS

Bachrach, Frank. "Putting All the Information in the World at Your Fingertips." *Communication World*, April 1984, pp. 26–27.

Bivins, Thomas. "The Basics of Grammar" and "The Basics of Style." *Handbook for Public Relations Writing*. Lincolnwood, Ill.: NTC Business Books, 1988, chaps. 7 and 8.

Bremner, John. *Words on Words: A Dictionary for Writers and Others Who Care About Words*. New York: Columbia University Press, 1980.

Curran, John. "How Computer Graphics Can Change Your Workstyle." *Public Relations Journal*, July 1985, pp. 35–36.

Friedman, Stephen. "How to Select and Profit by Word Processors." *Public Relations Journal*, August 1985, p. 31.

Kane, V. "Tomorrow's Library May Be In Your Office Today." *Public Relations Journal*, July 1985, pp. 30–31.

Munter, Mary. *Guide to Management Communication*, ed. 2. Englewood Cliffs, NJ: Prentice-Hall, 1988.

Newsom, Doug, and Carrell, Bob. "Writing Principles," in *Public Relations Writing: Form and Style*. Belmont, Calif.: Wadsworth Publishing, 1986.

Newsom, Doug, and Wollert, James A. *Media Writing: Preparing Information for the Mass Media*. Belmont, Calif.: Wadsworth Publishing, 1989.

Pearson, Ron. "Public Relations Writing Methods by Objectives." *Public Relations Review*, Summer 1987, pp. 14–26.

Pickins, Judy, ed. *A Guidebook to Nondiscriminatory Information*, 2nd ed. New York: John Wiley & Sons, 1982.

Reeves, Anne E. "Romancing the Clock: Time Management Tips for Writers." *Communication World*, February 1988, pp. 18–19.

Rivers, William L., and Harrington, Susan L. *Finding Facts: Research Writing Across the Curriculum*. Englewood Cliffs, NJ.: Prentice-Hall, 1988.

Seitel, Fraser P. "Public Relations Writing Fundamentals." *The Practice of Public Relations*, 3rd ed. Columbus, OH: Merrill Publishing Company, 1987, chap. 7.

Smith, Ron F. "A Comparison of Career Attitudes of News-Editorial and Ad-PR Students." *Journalism Quarterly*, Summer/Autumn 1987, pp. 555–559.

Wakefield, Gay, and Cottone, Laura Perkins. "Knowledge and Skills Required by Public Relations Employers." *Public Relations Review*, Fall 1987, pp. 24–32.

Weiser, Stephen. "Team Writing Made Easier." *Communication World*, October 1987, pp. 32–33, 43, 45.

Wilcox, Dennis L., Ault, Phillip, and Agee, Warren. *Public Relations Strategies and Tactics*. New York: Harper & Row, 1989.

Wright, Donald G. "Where Have All the Writers Gone?" *Communication World*, December 1987, pp. 14–15.

Zinsser, William. *Writing to Learn*. New York: Harper & Row, 1988.

Zinsser, William. *On Writing Well*, 2nd ed. New York: Harper & Row, 1980.

Chapter
2

Persuasive Communication

*T*he basic purpose of public relations writing is to *persuade*. The objective is to create favorable public opinion about an organization—its policies and actions, its goods or services. Edward L. Bernays calls it "Engineering of Consent." Some people consider this manipulative; but regardless of how it is described, the objective *is* to influence people. To be an effective public relations writer, you must understand public opinion, why people have opinions, and how to affect those opinions.

PUBLIC OPINION

Public opinion is not just mass opinion. It is the sum of individual opinions on a subject that affects them. For example, the stockholders of a factory (a public) may favor moving to another location, while the employees (a public) may violently oppose the idea. Meanwhile, the general public may be unaware of the controversy or if aware may be indifferent. The reason for the varying opinions is the variance in attitudes.

Attitudes and Opinions

An opinion is an expression of attitude. It may be expressed by writing, by speaking, by acting, or by not acting. Those who fail to express their opinions may do so because their attitudes are weak or because they don't believe it will do any good.

An attitude is a predisposition to think, speak, or act in a given way about a specific subject. No one is born with an attitude—all are learned. Some attitudes are deeply rooted; when tied into other attitudes, beliefs, and values, they may be very hard to change.

A speech by the President of the United States offers a good example of how attitudes affect opinion. Most members of the President's party will praise it, while most members of the opposing party will criticize it. The opinions differ because the attitudes are different. Nevertheless some members of the President's party may disagree and some of the opponents may agree *on that particular topic.*

In the case of the proposed factory move, the opinion of the stockholders is probably based on an attitude concerned with costs and profits. The opinion of the employees is probably based on a concern for their jobs or the inconvenience of moving to a new environment.

In public relations writing, it is necessary to think constantly about the attitudes of the particular public you are trying to influence. You also need to know how public opinion is built.

Building Public Opinion

Public opinion doesn't really exist until something affects a number of people who have similar or identical attitudes. The people must be aware of the issue or they will not have any opinion about it. Usually the awareness results from some event. When something happens or is likely to happen, the people become concerned—if they know about it. People have to express their opinions to others with similar attitudes. Someone must call for action and the action must be possible. People are much more certain about what they want than they are about how to get it. Public opinion isn't evident unless it can expect to get results. The disagreement about abortion is a good example. Both sides have strong attitudes, and each expresses its opinion vociferously because each really expects, by its actions, to obtain favorable legislation and court decisions.

PRINCIPLES OF COMMUNICATION

To communicate is to make known—to project ideas into the minds of others. This process depends on four elements: a sender, a message, a medium, and a receiver. If all these elements are operating, there will be communication. If any one fails, there will be no communication. Since your purpose is to persuade, you want to communicate your ideas to a particular group of people—those who can help or hinder your organization in attaining its objectives. In describing the process of communication, it is normal to list the elements as sender, message, medium, and receiver; but it may be better to think of them in reverse order. In other words, who to reach, how to reach them, and what to say.

The Receiver

This is the target audience—the people you *must* reach. Throughout this book, you will see the word "audience" many times. You must know that audience and all about that audience. The audience may be hard to reach. Its members may be ignorant, illiterate, indifferent, or inattentive. Some may be misinformed or hostile. Others may be friendly, supportive, and helpful. All are individuals with attitudes.

How do you get to know that target audience? By study! Read anything about it that you can lay your hands on. Go out and get acquainted with some of its members, attend their meetings, participate in their activities. Talk to them, listen to them, ask questions, answer questions. Observe their reactions to events and speeches and things that they read or see on television. Discuss their problems and interests, learn their likes and dislikes. Ultimately you may have to conduct a survey of this audience; but initially, if you make a real effort, you will learn a great deal about them without spending much money.

If you know enough about the audience and its attitudes, you will be able to give information in such a way that the recipients will accept the message, think about it, absorb it, and eventually believe it and act on it.

The Media

The media are the physical channels that carry the message to the receiver. They may include newspapers, magazines, radio, television, letters, speeches, audiovisuals, pictures, newsletters, leaflets, brochures, and the telephone. Every medium has advantages and disadvantages.

Your job is to determine which medium will be most effective in reaching the target audience. You may have to use one, a few, or many. Your budget may prohibit some because of cost. Others may be desirable but impossible (e.g., a personal talk by the chief executive to a specific group that refuses to be the audience).

Your message must reach the audience with enough power and frequency to make an impact. It often takes considerable repetition to plant an idea, and

A Sampler on Persuasion

A number of research studies have contributed to a basic understanding of the persuasion process. Here are some basic ideas from the text *Public Communication Campaigns,* edited by Ronald E. Rice and William J. Paisley (Sage, 1982):

- Positive appeals are generally more effective than negative appeals, both in terms of retention of the message and of actual compliance with it.

- Messages presented on radio and television tend to be more persuasive than those seen in print. If the message is complex, however, better comprehension is achieved through print media.

- The print media are more appropriate for conveying detailed, lengthy information; broadcast channels are best for presenting brief, simple ideas. Television and radio messages tend to be consumed passively, while the print media allow for review and contemplation.

- Strong emotional appeals and the arousal of fear are most effective when the audience has some mimimal concern about or interest in the topic.

- Highly fear-arousing appeals are effective only when some immediate action can be taken to eliminate the threat.

- Logical appeals, using facts and figures, work better than strong emotional appeals with highly educated, sophisticated audiences.

- Altruistic need, like self-interest, can be a strong motivator. Men are more willing to get physical checkups for the sake of their families than for themselves.

- A celebrity or an attractive model is most effective when the audience has low involvement, the theme is simple, and the more personalized broadcast channels are used. An exciting spokesperson attracts attention to a message that would otherwise be ignored.

the greater the impact of any single communication, the more likely it is to be absorbed and remembered.

When your sender is a person (as in speeches, talk shows, and so on), that person must be very persuasive. The criteria for persuasiveness will be covered later in this chapter.

The Message

Planning the message starts with a determination of just what ideas you want your receivers to have: what you want them to think, to believe, to do. Then you must acquire a solid knowledge of what your audience knows and believes. You want to affect attitudes and opinions, you must find out about those that already exist. This calls for research—possibly surveys.

Your message must be applicable, believable, realistic, and convincing. It must be expressed clearly and understandably in familiar words and phrases. Above all, you must convince the receivers that the idea you are presenting can be beneficial to them.

The Sender

The sender is the organization from which the message comes. Every organization has different publics, divergent interests, dissimilar objectives, unique problems, distinctive beliefs, and its own peculiarities. As a writer, you must know and understand the organization so that the messages you prepare will not only be effective but also truly representative of the organization's ethos. In addition, you must be very sure that what you send out is the truth, the whole truth, and nothing but the truth. (See the codes of the PRSA and IABC in Chapter 3.)

THEORIES OF COMMUNICATION

A message can move from the sender through the media, to the receiver, but this does not necessarily do the job of conveying ideas and getting them accepted. Yet ideas do get accepted, and there are several theories about how this is done.

The Two-Step-Flow Theory

This assumes that there is a definite group of "opinion leaders" who get information from the media, analyze and interpret it, and then pass it along to the public. The theory seems to fail on the grounds that there is no permanent group of people who are opinion leaders on all subjects.

The Multistep-Flow Theory

This theory holds that there are opinion leaders on many different subjects and that there are varying levels of influence. Thus Henry Smith may be an opinion leader on waste management and May Jackson may be an opinion leader on education, but both may be influenced by Jane Doe, who is an opinion leader on taxation. Also, Mary Smith may influence Jane Doe because she is better informed than Jane.

The Opinion-Group Theory

This theory has considerable acceptance. It recognizes opinion leaders but does not assume that they are the sole influence on the formation of public opinion.

The basic emphasis is on the function of discussion in crystallizing opinion. People of similar interests discuss mutual problems and arrive at common conclusions. People try to conform to group opinion and to avoid disagreement with the majority. Anyone may belong to several groups—at work, at church, at play. Grouping may be by age, occupation, place of residence, and so on. Whenever there is a common interest, there is formal or informal grouping.

For groups to influence opinion, they must be relatively stable and involved in frequent discussion, although not necessarily with any formality. The group is centered on an opinion leader—a person who is listened to by the others—although he or she may not be identified or recognized as such. This leader is the one who gets information from outside and comments on it to the group.

The Diffusion Theory

This theory was developed by Dr. Everett Rogers of Stanford University. It holds that there are five steps in the process of acquiring new ideas:

1. *Awareness*—the person discovers the idea.
2. *Interest*—the person tries to get more information.
3. *Trial*—the person tries the idea on others.
4. *Evaluation*—the person decides whether the idea is in his or her own self-interest.
5. *Adoption*—the person incorporates the idea into his or her opinion.

Applying Theory to Practice

Most professional communicators recognize the importance of opinion leaders and consider them to be the key to any given public. Reaching the opinion leaders would appear to be very difficult because they are not identified as such. Fortunately, they solve the problem for you because they are the people who seek information and convey it to others. They are the readers, the listeners, the observers—and the talkers.

Another class of people must be considered in this connection—the reporters, editors, commentators, speakers, writers, teachers, columnists, politicians, and other professional communicators. What they say, publish, or broadcast will reach the opinion leaders as well as the general public. What you send to them can influence their opinions and possibly win their support for your efforts.

SELF-INTEREST

These are the two most important words in public relations. The self-interest of your target audience is the foundation of persuasive communication. Visualize each member of that audience as saying to you: What's in it for me? Then you can express your message in such a way that the recipient will have no difficulty in learning how he or she can benefit.

Self-interest isn't always or mainly based on crude selfishness. It has many physical and psychological manifestations, some of which are quite fundamental and others very idealistic. One way to describe self-interest was developed by A. H. Maslow, who listed the various human needs in order, from the lowest to the highest. The assumption is that the lower-order needs must be filled before a person will show interest in the higher-order needs. Maslow's hierarchy of needs, from lowest to highest, is as follows:

1. *Physiological needs.* These are the constituents of self-preservation. They include air, water, food, clothing, shelter, rest, and health—the minimum necessities of life.
2. *Safety needs.* These comprise protection against danger, loss of life or property, restriction of activity, and loss of freedom.
3. *Social needs.* Social needs include acceptance by others, belonging to groups, and enjoying both friendship and love.
4. *Ego needs.* These include self-esteem, self-confidence, accomplishment, status, recognition, appreciation, and the respect of others.
5. *Self-fulfillment needs.* These represent the need to grow to one's full stature—simply as a human being or in terms of some special talent, gift, or interest.

Most public relations activity is aimed at the lower-level needs, since people are generally more concerned about their families, jobs, and homes than they are about more abstract goals. Economics may get the bulk of attention, but don't forget that there are many people who do have noneconomic interests. For example, the Sierra Club has many members who have nothing to gain from their membership but the satisfaction of having helped to protect the environment for the benefit of all.

AMERICAN ATTITUDES

Practitioners of international public relations repeatedly stress the importance of knowing local customs and beliefs, because they differ widely from country to country. America, too, has unique customs and beliefs. To influence American opinions, you should be aware of American attitudes. You may know most or all of these peculiarities; but in case you don't, the list below should remind you of beliefs that can affect your attempts at persuasion. There may, of course, be others as well, of greater or less importance. The sequence is purely random.

1. *Pride.* Americans are generally very proud of their country and to a somewhat lesser degree of their city, county, or state. Texans, for example, are outstanding boosters for their state.
2. *Self-confidence.* The belief in personal competence is widespread— "Of course I can do it."

3. *Voluntarism.* Willingness to work for the common good has been noted by many observers. Some 22,000 national and 500,000 regional and local associations in the United States add proof to these observations.

4. *Optimism.* Americans generally believe that anything can be done if we want to do it. This has many benefits, but it also leads to false expectations of success on problems that are beyond our ability to resolve.

5. *Innovation.* Willingness to accept new ideas is normal, which may be why advertising people claim that "new" is one of the best words to use.

6. *Antiauthority.* Resentment of government controls and restraints is typical. Whether it is speed limits, environmental controls, zoning restrictions, or any other limitation of personal freedom, there will be many who resist.

7. *Equality.* The typical American generally refuses to believe that any individual is superior to him or her as a person. This leads to criticism of special privileges, strong objections to special education for outstanding students, and cries of elitism.

8. *Litigation.* Americans are the most litigious people on earth. Suits for damages may be filed for little reason and often for fantastic sums. The number of such suits is vast and growing.

9. *Suspicion.* Americans are especially willing to believe that people in power are concealing things from the general public. For example, millions are convinced that the government has concealed information about UFOs.

10. *Big is bad.* Big corporations, big government, and big farms are looked upon as against the interests of the people.

Understanding Americans

The unique characteristics of Americans were noted as early as 1782 by S. J. de Crevecoeur. They have since been noted by Alexis de Tocqueville, Harriet Martineau, Frederick Jackson Turner, Charles Dickens, and Rudyard Kipling.

Recently, Dr. Alex Inkeles, of Stanford University, reported that most of these earlier observations are still valid, but that we have become more tolerant, less accepting of the Puritan work ethic, and more doubtful about the ability and responsibility of government.

For additional light on this subject, see *The Closing of the American Mind,* by Allan David Bloom, and *Megatrends,* by John Naisbitt. Also see Ben J. Wattenberg, "The Attitudes Behind American Exceptionalism," *U.S. News & World Report,* August 7, 1989.

11. *Rights versus responsibility.* There is much public interest in peo-
    ple's rights and privileges. Very little is said about duties and respon-
    sibilities.

12. *David versus Goliath.* American sympathies are consistently in fa-
    vor of the "little guy"—for instance, for the small store versus the
    supermarket and the subsistence farm versus the larger and more ef-
    ficient enterprise.

13. *Secrecy.* The American people insist on knowing many things that
    perhaps should be kept secret. England has an Official Secrets Act
    that protects government privacy. We have a Freedom of Information
    Act that does the opposite.

As you try to persuade Americans to adopt your point of view, remember
their special attitudes. Work with those attitudes, not against them. And read
the news regularly, so you will know what attitudes are most current.

INDIVIDUAL ATTITUDES

In addition to the attitudes shared by most human beings and most Americans,
each of us has a considerable number of special attitudes that distinguish us
from others. On any given issue an individual may differ radically from the
norm. Thus the parent of a gifted child will disagree with the majority who
object to elitism. The total number of factors affecting individual attitudes
may be very large. Some are psychological and not evident on the surface, but
there quite a few that are widespread and visible.

The following list includes the most common factors influencing the attitudes of of individuals.

1. *Family.* This is probably the strongest influence of all. People often
   get their religious and political views from their families. Attitudes
   toward education and occupation, too, come from parents or siblings.
   Ambitious parents push their children to strive toward high goals.
   Family members often think alike and talk alike.

2. *Education.* Education has a marked effect on attitudes. A higher level
   of education usually means more liberal views. The *kind* of education is also a factor. Engineers react differently from educators or doctors. The more education a person has, the more easily he or she
   should be able to understand complex issues; but don't assume that
   doctors will understand an engineering problem or that engineers
   will understand the problem of health care.

3. *Economic status.* A persons financial status has a strong effect on his
   attitudes. Many a liberal, for example, has turned conservative upon
   acquiring a substantial sum of money. People with money tend to
   oppose government expenditures; those with limited incomes are
   more likely to favor them.

4. *Membership.* People who belong to organizations tend to have opinions that agree with those of other members, especially on matters affecting the group as a whole. Working with organizations is a necessity in any public relations program.

5. *Experience.* What has happened to a person may have a very great effect on his or her attitudes. An employee who has been mistreated by a supervisor may thereafter think that all supervisors are enemies. A woman who has been sexually harassed may be extremely suspicious of even the most neutral contacts.

6. *Dwelling.* Where a person lives can be very influential on his or her attitudes. Apartment dwellers versus house dwellers; city versus country; rural versus urban; suburb versus inner city—all these affect people's opinions. Even the part of the country in which one lives has an effect. Westerners behave differently than do southerners, easterners, or midwesterners.

7. *Race.* In spite of the efforts in recent years, this factor has become more sensitive. Members of identifiable racial groups are sensitive to the slightest hint of discrimination.

8. *Creed.* Church membership or even informal affiliation can strongly influence attitudes. Religious involvement in social problems is common. Preachers, priests, and rabbis participate actively in political campaigns. Church groups get involved with schoolbooks and curriculums. And the members of religious organizations make major decisions on the basis of their religious beliefs.

9. *National origin.* A generation or two ago, most immigrants tried to Americanize themselves as rapidly as possible. They dropped old customs, learned English, and even changed names in order to be accepted as Americans. Now there is more consciousness of national origin. Theodore Roosevelt castigated "hyphenated Americans," but today many are proud of being "Greek-American," "Mexican-American," or "African-American."

10. *Political party.* Membership in a party is usually reflected in personal attitudes. Democrats and Republicans do have solid differences on many subjects. A knowledge of their party affiliation can help you predict how people will react on many issues.

11. *Occupation.* People tend to group with those of similar occupations. Doctors with doctors, mechanics with mechanics, white collars with white collars, and so on. Members of any such grouping tend to be empathetic with others in their group and neutral or opposed to nonmembers.

12. *Social class.* Most people consider themselves to be members of the middle class. In spite of this, they recognize that even in the middle class, status is relative. A surgeon has more prestige than a barber despite the fact that the two occupations were once the same. Service occupations have less prestige than the professions or management. Public trust of certain occupations varies widely and periodically. In

United States Committee for

unicef

United Nations Children's Fund

A future for every child.

Dear Friend:

In the ten seconds it took you to open and begin to read this letter, three children died from the effects of malnutrition somewhere in the world.

No statistic can express what it's like to see even one child die that way ... to see a mother sitting hour after hour, leaning her child's body against her own ... to watch the small, feeble head movements that expend all the energy a youngster has left ... to see the panic in a dying tot's innocent eyes ... and then to know in a moment that life is gone.

But I'm not writing this letter simply to describe an all-too-common tragedy.

> I'm writing because, after decades of hard work, UNICEF -- the United Nations Children's Fund -- has identified four simple, low-cost techniques which, if applied, have the potential to cut the yearly child mortality rate in half.

These methods don't depend on solving large-scale problems like increasing food supply or cleaning up contaminated water. They can be put into effect before a single additional bushel of wheat is grown, or before a single new well is dug.

They do depend on what you decide to do by the time you finish reading this letter. You see, putting these simple techniques to work requires the support of UNICEF's projects by people around the world. In our country, it means helping the U.S. Committee for UNICEF contribute to that vital work.

> With your help, millions of children will be given the chance of a lifetime -- the chance to live -- to grow up healthy and strong. Without your help, more children will continue to die painfully, slowly and need- lessly -- children like the nine who have died in the past 30 seconds.

The first method is called "oral rehydration." Most children who die

over, please

331 East 38th Street, New York, N.Y. 10016 (212) 686-5522   *An Equal Opportunity Employer*

Emotional appeal. Dramatic and emotional statements are important in persuasive communications. This direct mail letter from UNICEF gets the reader's attention right away. It gives the facts about malnutrition and humanizes the worldwide problem in such a way that readers can identify with it. (*Source:* UNICEF, New York, NY.)

the 1980s, attorneys, particularly trial lawyers, were the focus of much public hostility.

13. _Special interest._ Any individual may have a special interest that outweighs most other influences on attitudes. These people are the demonstrators, agitators, and supporters of causes ranging from pro- or antiabortion to saving whales. They can be the most active helpers

---

Tailoring Messages to American Life-styles

A relatively new form of research, psychographics, is being used increasingly by public relations writers to tailor messages to specific audiences. SRI International, a research organization in Menlo Park, California, has developed a values and life-styles program known as VALS.

Through extensive research, SRI was able to come up with several life-style typologies:

Survivors and sustainers are at the bottom of the hierarchy. Generally they have low incomes, are poorly educated, and are often elderly. These people eat at erratic hours, consume inexpensive foods, and seldom patronize restaurants.

Belongers are highly family-oriented, traditional, and tend to be lower- or middle-income people.

Achievers, at the highest level of the VALS scale, are often college-educated professionals with upper-level incomes. They are also more experimental and willing to try new ideas.

A good example of how public relations writing can be tailored to each group is provided by Burson-Marsteller (a public relations firm), which had the National Turkey Federation as a client. The objective was to increase the consumption of turkey on a year-round basis.

By segmenting the consumer public into various VALS life-styles, Burson-Marsteller was able to select the appropriate media for specific story ideas. An article placed in _True Experience,_ a publication reaching the "survivors and sustainers" group, was headlined "A Terrific Budget-Stretching Meal" and emphasized bargain cuts of turkey. _Better Homes & Gardens_ was used to reach the "belongers" with articles that emphasized tradition, like barbecued turkey as a "summer classic" on the Fourth of July. The "achievers" were reached through _Food and Wine_ magazine and _Gourmet,_ with recipes for turkey salad and turkey tetrazzini.

By identifying the magazines that catered to the three life-style groups and tailoring the information to fit each magazine's demographics, Burson-Marsteller was able to send the right message to each audience. This resulted in expanded turkey sales on a year-round basis.

or hinderers in any public relations program that impinges on their interest.

Recognizing where, when, how, and why your public relations objectives touch upon individual interests will help you to tailor your messages to those attitudes. Messages about sex education will have a good reception among some people and bring violent reactions from others. Restricting imports will be a welcome idea to union members and a red flag to consumers. Sheep men in the West would like to see coyotes killed because some of them kill lambs. Cattlemen might disagree because coyotes eat rodents, which compete with the cattle for grass.

PERSUASION

Knowing who to reach, how to reach them, and the basic message to give to them is the foundation upon which you base your communications. All this can be done in a factual manner, but informing is only part of the job. The receiver may get the message and the the message may be true, but until the receiver is convinced and motivated—until he or she acts—the communication is not successful. Many factors can affect the persuasive process. Some of the most important are credibility of the source, ability of the persuader, pertinence of the idea, clarity of the message, penetration or impact, and the proposed action.

Factors in Persuasive Communications

Source: Is the source credible to the public being reached?

Idea: Is the idea related to the self-interest of the audience?

Meaning: Is the message clear to the audience?

Penetration: Did the message get through to the audience? Messages must be repeated in many different ways through many kinds of channels or mediums.

Proposed action: Recommendations for action must be clear—and the action possible. Don't just tell people to conserve energy—tell them how to do it.

Credibility of Source

There is an old saying that a liar will not be believed even when he speaks the truth. This, of course, presumes that the liar has been identified as such by his past performance. The lesson to be learned from this is that if your message is to be believed, the receiver must have confidence in you and your organization. Rigid adherence to the truth at all times must be the rule.

It takes time to establish a reputation for truthfulness; with most receivers, you won't have that time, so you need to go a step further. You must be credible. The audience may not have a way of testing for the truth, but it may be persuaded that your message is believable simply because it comes from an organization that has established its credibility.

The audience will recognize the self-interest of your organization in any messages you send out. They will accept a message that is reasonable, but they are likely to be skeptical if the message is too obviously self-serving. For example, the Potato Board sent the message that potatoes in themselves are not fattening. This was backed by facts and was accepted and believed. In contrast, the tobacco industry has repeatedly challenged research proving that smoking is harmful. Their challenge has not appreciably swayed public opinion.

Recognizing the public awareness of self-interest, many organizations seek to get the endorsement of people and organizations that are not personally involved. True, it is more persuasive for a message to come from someone who has nothing to gain, but there are pitfalls in this system. Cybill Shepherd was hired to do television commercials for the producers of beef. But Cybill was quoted somewhat later as saying "I don't eat red meat." She was fired.

The testimonial of a supposed neutral is valuable, and some people have even set up organizations for the sole purpose of providing "unbiased and independent" support. This is unethical, it is forbidden by the Code of Professional Standards of the Public Relations Society of America, and it is a stupid thing to do, because the exposure of such an arrangement could demolish the credibility of the organization involved.

The Persuader

Someone once said that the best advertisement in the world was for a satisfied customer to tell a friend. The truth of this goes beyond advertising, since personal communication is the best communication. The more personal you can make your message, the more likely is it to be believed and acted upon.

Person-to-person communication is possible when only a few people must be reached. But when the numbers reach thousands or millions, the problem becomes more difficult. Now one person or a few must communicate with many. Whether the communication takes the form of a speech, an appearance on television or radio, an interview with a newspaper or magazine, or a news release or feature, the objective should be to have the message emanate from the most effective persuader available.

Effective persuasion is based on trust, expertise, and dynamism. Trust of the individual is like trust of the organization—it must be based on credibility. Frankness, friendliness, courtesy, fairness, balance, self-control, and a lack of pomposity are all desirable characteristics. If the audience likes the persuader, it is much more likely to believe the message. People tend to believe those with whom they agree and to disbelieve those with whom they disagree.

Expertise makes the persuader more effective. The person who "knows how" is much more believable than the person who is not so experienced. Expertise comes in many fields and few people are expert in more than one area. Whenever possible, the persuader should be in the field that is most involved in the particular problem at issue. Thus a combustion engineer would be preferred over a construction engineer in dealing with the subject of acid rain.

Another factor in persuasion is dynamism, the projection of personality in a way that moves people to a favorable response. Dynamism is invaluable in a would-be persuader. Lee Iacocca of Chrysler is a good example. He is so dynamic that many have urged him to run for the presidency of the United States.

As long as we are dealing with personal appearances of individuals, the foregoing will apply; but when we come to news releases and feature stories, we lose that personal touch. Nevertheless, we can apply many of the same principles. What you send out should reflect the trustworthiness and expertise of the people in the organization.

Experts should be quoted or cited whenever possible. Dynamism can be conveyed in powerful, memorable phrases. At some point, *you* may have to be the persuader, as in writing a simple one-paragraph news release. Your task is to write it in such a way that the recipient will trust the veracity, rely on the expertise shown in the release, and accept the idea.

Pertinence of the Idea

From time to time someone will calculate the number of advertisements and news items reaching the average citizen, coming up with figures that are astronomical and obviously incorrect. The reason is simple: The messages may be published, but they are not received.

You can prove this to yourself by noting the frequency of shoe advertisements. When you are planning to buy some shoes, there seem to be lots of advertisements; but when you are out of the market, the number of shoe ads appears to drop drastically. The stores aren't scheduling the ads for you, you simply ignore them when you are not interested and you see most of them when you are.

The lesson from this is that if your message is to be persuasive, it must be pertinent to the receiver, and the pertinence must be obvious. It should be expressed in terms that tie in to the attitudes and values of the receiver. It must be easy to understand and the recipient must know exactly how it relates to his or her self-interest. Again, we must think about the "What's in this for me?" or "How does this affect me?" attitude.

Clarity of the Message

An expert on communication has stated that the objective in all communication should be not to create understanding but to prevent misunderstanding.

EVERY BREATH YOU TAKE

Eighteen years
after the passage
of the Clean Air Act,
100 million people in the United
States still live in areas where
the act's health standards
for breathable air are not met.
Air pollution—smog, acid rain
and airborne toxics—threatens
the American public with cancer,
birth defects, lung
disease and other
crippling injuries.

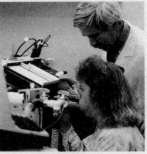

UCSF/David Powers

Persuasion in a few words. This is the cover of a Sierra Club brochure. It summarizes the contents and compels you to read the complete story. In order to affect peoples' opinions, you must first get their attention by arousing their self interest. This booklet would be hard *not* to read. (*Source:* Sierra Club, San Francisco, CA.)

Applying Murphy's law to communication leads to the conclusion that if your message *can* be misunderstood, it *will* be misunderstood.

There are several things you can do to avoid this problem. First, you should work on your writing style and also be sure to read the books listed in Chapter 1. Second, you should use a thesaurus regularly. Many words have numerous synonyms, but each of these has a slightly different effect on the receiver. For example, "youthful" is a favorable word, but "juvenile" has negative connotations. Third, you should test your writing before you inflict it on the public. If at all possible, you should try it out on members of the target audience.

A young public relations practitioner was once called into the office of his boss. "What does this mean?" said the boss, pointing to a garbled paragraph in a proposed booklet. "Oh," replied the beginner, "that means . . ." and launched into an explanation. "Well," said the boss, "are you going to go along with all these booklets and explain that paragraph to every reader?" "No," said the beginner. "I'd better rewrite that paragraph." And he did. Thereafter he wrote more carefully.

Impact

There are several definitions for "impact," but the one most relevant here is "the force and frequency with which a message reaches the receiver." A story on the front page of a newspaper has more impact than one on page 6. A half-page story has more impact than a paragraph. The same message repeated many times has far more impact than the message that is seen or heard only once.

Impact is not complete until the message has been received and noticed. If you will look through any daily newspaper, you will find some articles that interest you and some, or many, that you will ignore. These articles, no matter how big or significant, have no impact on you because you are not concerned. The same point applies to the messages you send out. Bigger, better, and more items may not mean more impact; which is why counting clippings is no true measure of impact. However, if your messages are pertinent to the self-interest of your target audience, they will be noticed, read, believed, and possibly acted on. That is impact.

Feasibility

Since your purpose is to persuade people to do something, that something must be within the power of the receiver. The objective may be to get people to believe. If your message is clear and pertinent, it will be possible for them to do so. If you want people to write letters or answer a questionnaire, that is feasible; but you will get more response if you tell them what to put in the letter and offer a postpaid return envelope.

From time to time we read of political and other fund-raising social events where tickets cost as much as $1000. You can be certain that the invitations to these gatherings are persuasive. You can also be sure that they are sent only to people who can afford the cost. You cannot persuade people to do things that are impossible for them to do.

PERSUASION TACTICS

How you apply the principles of persuasion can help or hinder their effectiveness. There has been much research on the psychology of persuasion, and a study of this subject can materially improve your abilities. Meanwhile, here are a few relevant ideas:

1. *The roots of attitudes.* These should be understood before you appeal to the attitudes. Why is this person an environmentalist? Why is that one a Democrat? Why does this one vote and that one stay at home? Knowing why people have their attitudes will help you persuade them.
2. *Audience views.* The more closely your message comes to the views of the audience, the more effective it will be. Stating these views in your message will promote acceptance.
3. *Positives and negatives.* If your audience is friendly you can ignore the opposing views and concentrate on the positive presentation of your case. If the audience is neutral or hostile, you should tell both sides of the story.
4. *The final word.* The latest message received is likely to have the most influence. If there is opposition, try to get in the last word.
5. *Ask for the Moon.* The more you ask for, the more you are likely to get. Extravagant requests may not be granted, but they may produce a better return than more modest ones.
6. *Fear can be ineffective.* Scaring the receiver won't work unless you can offer a practical way out. If you tell about some threat but don't show how to escape it, people will simply close their minds.
7. *Be precise.* Your audience must know exactly what you propose. Spelling it out in their own language is the certain way to get your message accepted. There is an exception to this. If your audience is *very* intelligent, you may let them draw their own conclusions from the facts you present.

(There are many books on persuasion. Two that you might read are (1) Ruth A. Clark, *Persuasive Messages*, New York: Harper & Row, 1983, and (2) Gary C. Woodward and Robert E. Denton, Jr., *Persuasion and Influence in American Life*, New York: Waveland, 1988.)

PERSUASIVE WRITING

The whole purpose of this chapter is to help you persuade your target audience. Your message may be delivered in one, a few, or many different ways. The media and the ways to get your message through the media will be detailed in succeeding chapters. As you work with the various tools of communication you should remember the principles listed below.

Timing and Context

Your message must arrive at a time when it can conveniently be considered. If it is too early, your audience may not be ready to think about it. April is not the time to talk about winter sports or sports equipment, but October might be just right. Information about income taxes is especially interesting just before the April 15 deadline, but it's "old hat" a few days later. News about a cure for male baldness gets full attention from middle-aged bald-headed men at almost any time. A medicine that would absolutely prevent baldness would undoubtedly also get the attention of young men who had not begun to lose their hair.

Symbols, Slogans, and Acronyms

The Red Cross is the best-known humanitarian organization in the world. The name is totally unenlightening, but the symbol is recognized and associated with the care and help given by the organization. Flags are symbols. Smokey the Bear is a symbol. The Christian cross, the Jewish Star of David, and the Moslem crescent are symbols known to almost everyone. You aren't likely to produce a world-famous symbol, but if at all possible you should try to find something graphic that helps to individualize and identify a given organization. Trademarks and logos are examples, but even unregistered visual symbols can help.

Slogans can be highly persuasive. They, like the following, state something important in a few memorable and easily pronounceable words: "Remember the Alamo," "Remember the Maine," "Don't give up the ship," "Unconditional surrender," "Votes for women," "Equal rights," "No taxation without representation," "Don't shoot until you see the whites of their eyes," "Government of the people, by the people, for the people," "Balanced budget," and so on. If you can coin a slogan that expresses the basic idea of what you are trying to promote, it will help to attain that objective.

Acronyms range from the good and effective to the ridiculous. Coined from the initial letters of the name of some organization or cause, an acronym can in some cases be highly useful. At other times, however, the decision to coin an acronym leads to absurdities. During World War II, the women in the navy were called WAVES, a simple and attractive designation, but the full name was Women Auxiliary Volunteers Enlisted for Service. The Navy's designation for the commander in chief was CINCUS until someone said it aloud: "Sink us."

A good acronym is NOW—National Organization for Women. It is pronounceable, memorable, and makes a succinct political point. These women are striving for equality, and they want it "NOW." Another good reason for acronyms is the shortening of a lengthy name. AIDS is much easier to comprehend and write about than "acquired immune deficiency syndrome."

Semantics

Dictionaries define words—often giving several versions. Thesauruses give synonyms, antonyms, related and contrasting words, and sometimes idiomatic equivalents. These two sources enable the user to be precise and accurate in choosing the right words. A sound knowledge of grammar and syntax would seem to ensure the correct preparation of phrases, sentences, paragraphs, and whole pages of clear, concise, and persuasive messages.

Clear and concise they may be, but to be persuasive there must be another consideration—semantics. Semantics involves the meaning of the words to the receivers. A good example of semantics on a world scale is the word "democracy." To Americans, it means government *by* the people. To the Russian and Chinese, it means government *for* the people.

The term "hiring quota" means opportunity to some and exclusion to others. Knowing what words and phrases mean to your audience can enable you to convey your messages more persuasively.

Dramatization and Imagery

People are motivated by theatrics; they respond to cheerleaders, to demonstrations, to ringing phrases. They are moved by dramatic actions and human drama. Your message should go beyond cold facts or even eloquent phrases. If you can vividly describe what you are talking about—if you can paint a picture—your message will be far more persuasive.

Saying that 3 million Africans are starving isn't as persuasive as actually describing a young mother who is sobbing over the lifeless form of her skeletal baby. Readers and viewers can identify with the mother's loss, which graphically illustrates the need for aid. Large numbers, on the other hand, are cold and impersonal, generating little or no emotional involvement. Think of the receiver—what would appeal to him or her? What words would induce a favorable response? If you know your audience, you will be able to persuade it.

SUMMARY

1. Public opinion is the sum of individual opinions on a subject of importance to those individuals. The purpose of persuasive communication is to sway the opinions of individuals or to motivate them to a specific action.
2. Communication involves four elements: a sender, a medium, a message, and a receiver. All must function if there is to be effective communication.
3. The self-interest of the audience is the basis for persuasion. Self-interest includes physical, social, and psychological needs.
4. American attitudes are unique to the people of this country. If you are to persuade Americans, you must know and understand their attitudes.

5. Individual attitudes are rooted in many factors that influence the way the people think and react to outside influences. A knowledge of why people have certain attitudes is the key to affecting their opinions.

6. Persuasion requires that the source be credible; that the persuader be trusted, expert, and dynamic; that the idea be pertinent; that it be clear; that it be delivered with enough impact; and that it be feasible.

7. The tactics of persuasion are based on psychology. It is vital to understand why your audience thinks as it does, how and when to present your ideas, what to propose, and what to avoid.

8. Writing persuasively requires that your message be delivered at the right time and in the right context. The receivers' minds must be ready and willing to receive the message. The use of symbols, slogans, and acronyms can help make the message effective and memorable. What the words mean to the audience must always be considered. Dramatizing the message and creating visual images adds greatly to its power of persuasion.

EXERCISES

1. Analyze the direct mail literature of a nonprofit or activist group like the American Cancer Society or Greenpeace. What concepts of public opinion and persuasion are being used in the literature? Cite the concepts and use examples from the literature.

2. After five years of limited profits and some losses, your company has had an extremely profitable year. The employee's union, which showed commendable restraint at the bargaining table, is now looking to the company for an increase in wages. Management, however, feels that all available funds must be used to repair equipment and install new and more efficient machinery if the company wants to assure future profitability and survival. The company president asks you to draft a statement to the employees. It must be a persuasive statement explaining why there will be no wage increases this year. What would you write to persuade the employees that the company's decision is a correct one?

3. Review three advertisements in a magazine. In what ways do the advertisements use persuasive concepts to sell the product?

4. The point is made that persuasive communication means the use of words and phrases that paint pictures. Select a magazine article and write down examples of sentences and phrases that the author uses to paint pictures.

5. Knowledge of public opinion and persuasion helps a communicator influence and motivate people. What ethical responsibilities does a persuader have to his or her audiences?

SUGGESTED READINGS

Alsop, Ronald. "Real People Star in Many Ads, But Are They Really Credible?" *Wall Street Journal*, May 23, 1985, p. 37.

Alsop, Ronald. "Firms Play Up Endorsements to Improve Skeptical Shoppers." *Wall Street Journal*, Nov. 20, 1986, p. 29.

Clark, Ruth Anne. *Persuasive Messages.* New York: Harper & Row, 1984.

Davids, Meryl. "Mind Watch: Recent Research in Psychology." *Public Relations Journal*, June 1988, pp. 15–19.

Davids, Meryl. "Believe Me." *Public Relations Journal*, October, 1987, pp. 16–18.

Detwiler, R. M. "The Myths of Persuasion." *Public Relations Journal*, April 1982, pp. 52–54.

Ferguson, Mary Ann, and others. "Using Persuasion Models to Identify Givers." *Public Relations Review*, Fall 1986, pp. 43–50.

Holmes, Peg. "Building Employee Trust." *Communication World*, August 1985, pp. 18–21.

Jowett, Garth S., and O'Donnell, Victoria. *Propaganda and Persuasion.* Newbury Park, CA: Sage Publications, 1986.

Larson, Charles. *Persuasion: Reception and Responsibility.* Belmont, CA: Wadsworth Publishing, 1983.

Lowenstein, Roger. "Many Athletes Have a Tough Time Playing in the Endorsement Game." *Wall Street Journal*, Aug 29, 1986, sec. 2, p. 1.

Lowery, Sharon, and DeFleur, Melvin. *Milestones in Mass Communications Research: Media Effects.* New York: Longman, 1983.

Rice, Ronald E., and Paisley, William J. *Public Communication Campaigns.* Newbury Park, CA: Sage Publications, 1981.

Trippett, Frank. "Slogan Power! Slogan Power!" *Time*, February 12, 1979, p. 102.

Wilcox, Dennis L. "Regis McKenna Sets the Standards in High-Tech PR." *Communication World*, April 1984, pp. 11–12.

Chapter
3

Legal and Ethical Guidelines

*P*ublic relations writing is supposed to produce favorable results, but if the writer is careless, there may be adverse reactions ranging from hurt feelings to suits for damages. There are numerous things to do and to avoid. If you remember the principal pitfalls at all times, you should be able to produce written materials that are safe from the legal standpoint and that conform to the ethical standards of the profession.

RESPONSIBILITY

You represent the management of your organization. What you release is interpreted as the voice of management. You, personally, can be held liable for any statement you make. Usually actions are brought against the top officials of

Imitation isn't flattering to trademark owners

Stockholder information rule in effect Wednesday

Confusion Over Merger-Disclosure Law
Some Attorneys Advise Silence; Others Say Tell All — and Early

PROTECTING TRADE IN 'INTELLECTUAL PROPERTY'

Copyrights Are as Vital as Merchandise

FTC Curbs Bristol-Myers, Sterling Drug On Certain Claims in Pain-Reliever Ads

12 THE WALL STREET JOURNAL TUESDAY, MARCH 26, 1985

High Court to Decide Whether Utilities Can Be Forced to Mail Others' Messages

Pitfalls everywhere. Writers of public relations materials must be aware of numerous laws and governmental regulations that relate to copyright, trademarks, and the release of timely, accurate information. These headlines show a few examples of legal pitfalls. (*Source:* Photo by James McNay.)

an organization, but there have been numerous cases wherein the spokesperson (either an employee or a counseling firm) has been held legally responsible.

Because you may be the target, you must be sure that the facts given you are true and accurate. It is no excuse to say "The boss told me that this was so." In a trial, you must be able to prove that you made a reasonable effort to verify information.

Among the actions for which you might be liable are the following:

1. Disseminating information that a court or regulatory agency finds misleading, untrue, or damaging.
2. Participating in an illegal action.
3. Counseling or guiding policy behind an illegal action.
4. Setting up an organization whose real identity is concealed.

These points are made not to frighten you but to show the importance of studying this chapter thoroughly.

Working with Lawyers

Because of the complexities of the law and the extreme specialization that results, it is probable that no one lawyer can answer every possible question relating to public relations. An expert on libel or slander may know very little about copyrights or trademarks. A specialist on labor may be unqualified to speak on financial relations. It should therefore be evident that when you do have a legal question, you should consult a lawyer who is familiar with the special field.

Your organization may have a legal department, or it may retain a firm of lawyers. If neither includes an expert on your specific problem, you should ask to be referred to a specialist. In any case, your relationship with these consultants must be based on respect and understanding. Lawyers can tell you what to do or not to do; they should not tell you what to say or how to say it. They are experts on the law but not on communication. They don't understand that the media want information *now!* To ensure the best cooperation between the legal and public relations function:

1. Each should have a written definition of its responsibilities.
2. Both should report to the same top executive.
3. Both should be represented on key committees.
4. The legal counsel should keep the public relations staff informed on legal problems involving the organization.
5. The public relations staff should keep legal counsel informed about what it is doing.
6. The two sides should regard each other as allies, not opponents.

Your relations with legal counsel will be more efficient if you keep abreast of new developments. To do this, you should maintain a file of newspaper and magazine articles that report on legal developments and decisions bearing upon public relations. Major lawsuits are often reported on television. Charges and countercharges, cease-and-desist orders, consumer complaints, environmentalist complaints, product recalls, and numerous other items are regularly in the news.

LIBEL AND SLANDER

Any false statement about a person that is printed or broadcast and which tends to bring upon this person public hatred, contempt, or ridicule or to inflict injury on his or her business or occupation may be libel. If the statement is broadcast, it may constitute either libel or slander. If it is made to a third person but neither printed nor broadcast, it may be slander.

Libel

There are both federal and state laws dealing with libel, and they are not identical. There is civil libel, for which the recourse is a suit for damages. There is also criminal libel, which can result in fines or imprisonment.

Any plaintiff in a libel suit must prove four points: (1) that it was published to others by print or broadcast; (2) that the plaintiff was identified or is identifiable; (3) that there was actual injury in the form of money losses, impairment of reputation, humiliation, or mental anguish and suffering; and (4) that the publisher of the statement was malicious or negligent.

With public figures—people in government or politics or who are much in the news—the test is whether the publisher of the statement knew that it was false or had reckless disregard for its truth. The question of who is a public figure cannot be answered arbitrarily, and the courts are inconsistent on this. It often depends on the context.

Although entertainment stars are "public figures," Carol Burnett successfully sued the *National Enquirer* for libel because it published a story saying that she was drunk at a party in Washington, D.C.

With private figures—people who are not officials or prominent in the news—the test is whether the publisher of the statement was negligent in checking the truth of it. In quoting someone, for instance, be sure you state exactly what was said.

Avoiding Libel

These few highlights only hint at the ramifications of libel law. For your protection and for the protection of your organization, you need to dig deeper into this subject.

To understand the nature of libel, you should read the chapter on libel in the *Associated Press Stylebook and Libel Manual.* Another book on this subject is *Synopsis of the Law of Libel and the Right of Privacy*, published by World Almanac Publications.

Since most of your work is planned to create good impressions about some person or thing, you should have no difficulty in avoiding libel. If there is, at some point, a reason to make negative statements, you should consult the libel manual or a lawyer. Generally, such situations arise during political campaigns.

In thinking of libel, you should not confine your precautions to the general media. An item in an organization's newsletter saying that "Jack was feeling no pain" at the office party could be construed as libel. An unflattering picture of a dishevelled employee walking out the door could also be libelous.

Most libel cases arise because someone got careless. Most lawsuits in this area are brought against the media: newspapers, magazines, television stations or networks, and radio stations or networks. However, suits for libel can be brought against other organizations and individuals who are not part of the general media. You, personally, could be sued if you are not careful.

In recent years, several lawsuits have been filed because of news releases. In one case, an ex-employee sued his former employer after a news release announced that he had been let go after having been investigated for accepting kickbacks from suppliers. In another case, a medical center was sued by an-

Legal Ramifications

It is absolutely necessary to know and understand aspects of the law that can affect your work. The following is a short list of recent cases.

An 81-year-old man featured in a United Way advertising poster filed a $100,000 lawsuit against the agency, claiming it used his picture without permission.

Dow Jones & Co. sued McGraw-Hill Company, publisher of *Business Week,* for $20 million because the magazine quoted a speculator that he had advance tips from a *Barron's* columnist on forthcoming stories. Dow Jones claimed that *Business Week* did not check out the quote and, by publishing it, "sullied" the integrity of *Barron's.*

Burroughs Corp. sued Quality Books, Inc., for $1.9 million because the defendant sent out news releases and published advertisements saying that the computer company made an inferior product. Burroughs charged executives of Quality Books with "malicious intent to injure Burroughs and cause loss of sales."

Marineland of Southern California paid $15,000 in civil penalities after the attorney general's office accused the park of issuing misleading publicity about, among other things, the world's tallest Christmas tree, which turned out to be nothing but an observation tower strung with lights.

The National Labor Relations Board threw out a pro-management vote in a union representation election because the company provided beer and liquor 150 feet from the polling area.

The FCC renewed the license of a CBS-owned television station for only one year instead of the normal three years because the network promoted a Las Vegas tennis tournament as offering a "winner take all" $250,000 prize. In fact, all of the players—winners and losers—received substantial amounts of money to play in the tournament.

Three suspended executives of Joseph Schlitz brewing company sued for $3.5 million after the company's public relations firm issued a press statement in which company officials implied that the three were guilty of wrongdoing.

The FTC ruled that the makers of Bayer Aspirin made misleading claims in advertising and product publicity by saying that the product was more effective than any other aspirin.

J. Walter Thompson (JWT) filed a $1 million suit against the former head of its medical advertising division, claiming that he solicited JWT accounts for his new firm while still under contract to JWT.

other medical facility for implying in a news release that the number of patient deaths at the competing medical center was the highest in the region.

Remember that you needn't use a name to commit libel. A recognizable description serves the same purpose. If the subject remains unnamed but the public knows who is being talked about, there may be grounds for a libel case.

Slander

Slander is much like libel except that instead of being written, it is spoken. It can occur in a broadcast, in a speech, or in an informal conversation. In any case it must be heard by a third party. If you call a person a liar or a thief to his face and no one else is present, it is not slander. If anyone else hears it, it may be slander.

You should watch out for slander in speeches that you may prepare and conversations you may have with representatives of the media or the public. A slip of the tongue in an interview with a reporter can make you wind up in court. An off-the-cuff remark that disparages the character or motives of some person can be the basis for a lawsuit for slander.

As with libel, the rule is to avoid saying anything detrimental. You may believe that some person is a crook or that some organization is defrauding the public, but don't say it. Even if it is true and you think that you can prove it, there is no guarantee that a court will agree with you.

INVASION OF PRIVACY

In recent years there has been a great increase in sensitivity to invasion of privacy. Numerous laws have been passed and many lawsuits have been filed in an effort to protect the privacy of individuals. In general, laws and lawsuits strive to prevent anyone from knowing anything about an individual which that individual does not want to be known.

Personnel departments are forbidden to require information about employees that is not directly relevant to their employment. Credit investigations must exclude such information as marital status. Anything about race, color, creed, national origin, or sexual preference is considered private. Marital status and plans for children are also privileged information.

Protection of employee privacy can create problems. People are interested in people and most people are willing to have favorable things said about themselves. The problem is to include the good things and avoid the others. If John Doe is promoted to a new job, he will be pleased if others know about it. He may be willing for considerable personal detail about himself to be revealed.

If Doe has two children, he may approve mention of that fact. If one of them is retarded, he may not want that published. If he is married, he may be willing to have that known. If he is in the middle of a divorce action, he is likely to prefer no mention.

Much information which can make a story interesting can be obtained by asking questions of the people involved. The idea is to get facts that are interesting and favorable. When the story is written, it should be checked with the person mentioned. If he or she objects to anything, take it out. When the material is approved, you should get the subject's signed approval. A simple "OK—John Doe" on the story will do the job.

Implied Consent

If you or a photographer ask an individual or a group of people to pose for a photograph—and you say it is for the employee magazine or distribution to the general media—you do not have to get a signed approval from each person in the picture. By posing, they have given implied consent. If the picture is candid and unposed, however, the safe thing to do is to show the picture to the people involved and ask if it would be all right to publish it. Implied consent also applies to routine news about new employees, promotions, or transfers.

Blanket Releases

News of a personal nature is often covered under a blanket release. In general, the blanket release allows the company to release information about employees as long as it deals exclusively with their jobs.

A blanket release is not acceptable when you plan to use a picture of an employee or his name in advertising copy or product brochures. In such cases, a signed release specifically permitting such use is needed.

The key point about blanket releases is the fact that the information publicized should deal only with the employee and his or her job. If you write a news release about the promotion of an executive and also use such personal information as home address, marital status, civic honors, number of children, and so on, the individual involved should be allowed to read the entire release and sign off on it.

There may be times when a reporter will ask you for information about an employee. In general, most companies have adopted a policy of merely confirming that a person is employed and in what position. You can also tell a reporter the date on which the employee first joined the firm.

Under no circumstances should you take it upon yourself to tell a reporter an employee's home address, marital status, or number of children, nor should you reveal his or her job-performance record. If the reporter wants to know such things, the best approach is to say that you will ask the employee to call him or her. In this way, the employee knows that an inquiry has been made and can determine what information is to be divulged. It also lets you and the company off the hook in terms of protecting the employee's privacy.

Another way that a company can protect itself against employees invasion-of-privacy suits is to have a standard biographical form that each one fills out. At the top of this form there should be a clear-cut statement that the information provided may be utilized in company publicity and employee newsletters.

Increasingly, organizations are getting away from the "personal columns" in employee newsletters. The reporting of employee birthdays, anniversaries, vacations, weddings, and so on are overstepping the thin invasion-of-privacy line and have nothing to do with a person's job.

To summarize: Don't publish anything about anyone unless there is no possibility of objection. You can guarantee this by getting prior approval—in writing. In libel, the truth is a good defense. If you can prove your statement, you are safe; but a court can decide that you did not prove it. So be very careful.

Truth is no defense in a case of invasion of privacy. If Richard Roe once served a term in prison, it may be nonlibelous to release the information; but it may still be an invasion of privacy that can result in a lawsuit.

Individual Releases

When an advertiser wants to use a person's name or picture, it is necessary to secure a signed release that clearly defines the intended use. There is always a fee for such permission.

If the person is prominent, the fee may be large, perhaps thousands of dollars. Fees for less important prople are lower and in some cases purely nominal; $1 is typical. In every case there must be a consideration to make the release a legal contract.

Because much product publicity is planned to promote the sale of something, the use of names and pictures in that connection comes under the same rules as those applying to advertising. You must have a signed release, and all releases should be kept in a well-indexed file. When employees leave the organization, their pictures and releases should be destroyed to make sure that they will no longer be used.

Duration is important in a release; it should be stated in the form. Five to ten years is reasonable. Courts do not recognize that a release can be perpetual. The correct names of both the organization and the person giving permission must be used. With a juvenile, the parent or guardian must sign. It is advisable to indicate that "no other inducements, statements, or promises" were made.

Photo Releases

If a person's picture is to be used in advertising, it may require a complex and detailed release. (An advertising agency is a good source of information about what such a release should include.)

For most public relations purposes, a simple release will probably suffice, and pads of standard photo releases can be purchased at camera stores. Your legal counsel or staff may provide forms tailored to your organization. Or you can use a form like the one here:

LOCKHEED MISSILES & SPACE COMPANY, INC.
A SUBSIDIARY OF LOCKHEED AIRCRAFT CORPORATION
SUNNYVALE, CALIFORNIA

The undersigned, having previously consented to being photographed, does hereby authorize Lockheed Aircraft Corporation and Lockheed Missiles & Space Company, Inc., to use and reproduce the said photograph and copy for Lockheed publicity and promotional purposes.

_____

Date

_____

Name

_____

Address

You do not need a release when the picture records a public event and a considerable number of people are involved. But if that picture is later used for promotional purposes and individuals are identifiable, you should have releases.

DECEPTION

Release of false information is a good way to get into trouble. Government agencies may issue "cease and desist" orders or injunctions. Fines can be levied and much adverse publicity can appear in the media. Also, people who feel that they have been injured or deceived can file lawsuits—and collect damages.

False information can be either flat misrepresentation of facts or information that misleads the recipient into believing something which is not quite true. Deception is most likely to be charged in the areas of financial and marketing information.

Financial Information

You must be especially careful here. Don't take chances or cut corners. The Securities and Exchange Commission (SEC) requires that any information affecting the value of a security be made known to the owners and to the SEC. This is done by filing certain annual and quarterly reports, highlights of which are often included in news releases.

The SEC also requires "Full and Prompt Disclosure" of any changes or developments that might affect the value of securities.

In general, a company whose stock is publicly traded must immediately release the following kinds of news:

1. Dividends or their deletion
2. Annual or quarterly earnings
3. Preliminary but audited interim earnings
4. Stock splits
5. Mergers
6. Changes in top management
7. Major product developments
8. Major expansion plans
9. Change of business purposes
10. Defaults
11. Dispositions of major assets
12. Proxy materials
13. Purchase of own stock

In releasing financial news it is imperative to be accurate. Public relations firms have been held responsible for releasing false information even though they were told by their clients that the supplied facts were correct. The SEC has ruled that anyone releasing financial news is responsible for checking the facts. Do not release *any* financial news unless you know that it is true and accurate. It is your responsibility to check the information given to you. The rules of the SEC change frequently; be sure that you have the latest information.

Marketing Information

The Federal Trade Commission (FTC) deals with "unfair methods of competition in commerce, and unfair acts and practices," all of which are illegal. Both advertising and publicity are subject to FTC scrutiny. Also, false advertising and false publicity may be the subject of lawsuits from individuals who may claim injury or deception.

Any product information you release to the public is subject to FTC scrutiny. At first you may think mainly of news releases and feature stories, but you should also include letters, booklets, leaflets, brochures, pictures, drawings, audiovisual materials, speeches, and any other type of communication that can reach the public.

Among the areas where deception can occur are the following:

1. Unsubstantiated claims—statements that you cannot prove
2. Ambiguous claims—statements that are confusing
3. Fraudulent testimonials—statements that were never actually made
4. Puffery and exaggeration—stretching the truth
5. Deceptive pricing—concealment of true cost
6. Deceptive demonstrations—apparent proof that is not really proof
7. Deceptive surveys—for example, "independent" surveys that you have paid for
8. Unsound surveys—surveys that are not statistically valid
9. Fraudulent contests—contests that were "rigged" in some way

10. Deceptive illustrations—pictures that convey a false impression
11. Nonexistent authority—for example, "Doctors recommend . . ."
12. Nonexistent surveys—interpretation of a few comments as surveys

(If your work deals with any product that is under the jurisdiction of the Food and Drug Administration, you must be familiar with the applicable regulations. Because there are so many rules in this area, it is not feasible to give them here. Instead, consult with the legal authorities in your organization.)

The FTC interpretation of publicity will be based on the "net impression received by the consumer," not just on the bald facts. Among the types of statements that have been found false or deceptive are are these:

1. That the product or service is original or the first in the field
2. That it is approved by a government agency
3. That the product is patented
4. That it was developed in a research laboratory that did not exist
5. That the product contained nutritional substances that were not present
6. That its life or effectiveness was not as claimed
7. That a nonexistent or warped survey proved some point

Warranties

For many years, product liability suits were based on alleged negligence by the manufacturer. Negligence is hard to prove, so now claimants more frequently base suits on breach of warranty. Warranty may be "express" or "implied." An express warranty is a definite statement about the product, such as "This product will not stretch, fade, or shrink." If the product does stretch, fade, or shrink, the buyer can demand and secure a refund. Express warranties may vary considerably in coverage and detail, but they are normally stated in explicit terms.

Implied warranties are not stated. The worry for you is that a statement made in a publicity item may lead some consumer to infer a warranty that is not intended. Anything you say about a product or service should be checked against actual warranties, instruction manuals, and technical specifications. When your item is written, check it for any implied warranty. If you are in doubt, check your statement with legal counsel.

Several years ago, the J. Walter Thompson advertising agency ran afoul of the FTC for writing advertising copy claiming that the Lady Kenmore dishwasher could clean dishes without prior rinsing or scraping when, in fact, the owner's manual and operating instructions stated otherwise. The FTC took the position that the advertising agency had the responsibility to make sure its claims actually matched the ability of the product to perform.

Be sure to avoid disparaging a competitive product or service. If your product or service is demonstrably and provably superior, it may be permissible to compare it with others; but this should be approved by your legal counsel.

Advertisements a few years ago studiously avoided naming competing brands. Today, comparisons are common, but here too the statements are always carefully checked by lawyers before they are released.

Another danger lies in deceiving the public by leading them to believe that your product is actually the product of some other maker. This "look-alike" approach is likely to lead to a lawsuit by the competitor and may also bring consumer suits. For example, a small firm in Los Angeles was served with a cease and desist order after adopting a logo that looked just like the Rolls-Royce symbol. The auto maker claimed that the firm was trying to deceive the consumer by implying a relationship with a prestigious name.

LIABILITY

Activities sponsored by your organization can lead to suits for damages. Open houses, plant tours, meetings, conventions, athletic events, internal or sponsored teams, contests, and parades are the most likely areas of risk. Nevertheless, you must not confine your thinking to the activities listed. Any organizational activity should be carefully planned and controlled to minimize the risk of lawsuits.

Many organizations carry public liability insurance, but this is not enough. All a plaintiff has to do is prove negligence and he or she can collect damages from the insurance company, the organization, or both. Your job is to be certain that there is no negligence.

Open Houses and Plant Tours

In these events, large numbers of people from outside the organization must be moved through the facilities with comfort and safety. Planning for these activities is discussed at length in Chapter 17. From the standpoint of liability, you should pay particular attention to safety. Routing should be clearly marked. Walkways or paths must provide secure footing. Moving equipment and other hazards must be barricaded. Rooms or areas where public access is not wanted must be clearly designated. Parking facilities must be safe and free from moving trucks or other nonpassenger vehicles.

Emergency precautions must be provided. First aid should be available. Guides must know how to call for first aid or an ambulance and how to summon the fire or police departments. Phones should be available along the route so that it will be easy to call for help. Warning signs should be placed wherever needed.

If the event is very large, the local police and fire departments should be warned long before the event. Thus they will know that an unusual number of people will be present at the location and that this may result in a call for assistance.

Meetings and Conventions

When you use the facilities of another organization, it has primary responsibility for the safety of visitors. Nevertheless, you should thoroughly check the entire premises yourself. Even if a visitor sues the hotel in which your organization is meeting, you may incur ill-will for choosing to convene in an unsafe location. Also, the equipment you bring to the meeting can be a hazard for which your organization will be held responsible. If a visitor trips over an electric wire that you have installed or a spotlight falls on a guest, you may be held responsible.

Some organizations provide meeting rooms for outside groups. Savings and loan associations frequently build rooms for this sole purpose and hope to earn goodwill from the community by offering free use of these rooms. Regardless of the type of sponsor, the use of these rooms presents some hazards.

To avoid controversy and prevent legal actions, you should do three things:

1. Be sure that the premises are safe.
2. Have publicly stated rules for use of the facilities.
3. Have a representative of the building on duty or available at all times.

For safety, you should check floors, furniture, and equipment. Entrances and restricted areas should be clearly marked. Electrical outlets, switches, lighting, projectors, coffee makers, and any other things provided for the use of the outsiders must be inspected. Stairs, steps, and doors should be examined to eliminate hazards.

Rules for the use of such facilities should state who can qualify. Usually this is restricted to nonprofit groups. For example, use may be restricted only to groups in the area or city; only members of the United Way or similar communitywide fund-raisers; groups to which a member of the organization belongs; and so on.

It should be clearly stated that granting use of the space does not imply endorsement of the organization. If any charges are to be made—as for light, heat, janitor service, or refreshments—they should be specified. In some situations it may be necessary to escort the visitors through other rooms, to keep them from wandering into restricted areas, or to have a representative of the organization standing by to handle unforeseen problems. Always remember that if you allow outsiders to use your facilities, you will be responsible for their safety.

Contests

Contests can be used to stimulate sales, lend support to a cause or sponsored activity, or build goodwill for the organization conducting the contest. The potential variety is almost limitless. The potential for misunderstanding or legal reaction is also large.

To avoid getting into trouble with a contest, many companies use professional contest management firms. These plan the contest, establish the rules, and judge the entries. If you plan to conduct a contest without professional assistance, you must follow these guidelines: Every entrant must understand exactly what is to be judged; the rules and standards for eligibility must be clearly stated; the judges must be absolutely impartial and preferably unconnected with the organization sponsoring the contest.

If your organization is planning a prize drawing or a raffle, make sure you consult local, state, and federal laws governing such activity. For example, you cannot sell chances for a prize through the mail. If a store is offering prizes at a drawing, the public must be able to register for the drawing without having to make any purchase. Charitable organizations, in particular, must be cognizant of how raffle tickets are sold to the public.

Suggestions

Many organizations have suggestion systems that encourage employees to propose improvements in products, services, or procedures. These systems offer an award, usually money, to the person whose idea is adopted.

These systems have generated many valuable ideas, but they have also created problems. People who think the award is not adequate often sue the organization and sometimes win substantial judgments.

To avoid these lawsuits, it is necessary to have a lawyer prepare a carefully drawn set of rules stating exactly what the employee must do and what the organization will do.

Suggestions from outsiders are particularly dangerous. Determining who first thought of an idea is very difficult, so the safest course is to do as advertising agencies do, refusing to accept, read, or listen to any suggestion from an outsider. You will be well advised to do the same.

CONTRACTS

A contract is a legal agreement that includes three elements: offer and acceptance, time, and consideration. In the simplest terms, this means what will be done, when it will be done, and how much will be paid. If any of these elements is missing, a contract does not exist. Contracts can be verbal, but it is much safer to put them in writing. You may need to make contracts with vendors, with facilities, or with clients.

Vendor Contracts

Vendor contracts are most likely to cover purchases or supplies, equipment or printed materials, and the hiring of photographers or temporary helpers. In buying supplies such as stationery or paper, be sure that the quality as well as the quantity is clearly stated. With equipment, such as a word processor, be certain that you have a clear agreement on warranties and service.

When you purchase printed materials, the specifications you are offered may be very detailed, so check every word. Watch the quantities, because some printers may try to charge for an overrun. That is, on an order for 5000 pieces, the printer may attempt to bill you for 5340 pieces. These may be offered at the original unit price or at a discount, but you must decide whether or not to accept.

Photographer contracts are discussed in Chapter 7, so we will confine ourselves here to the simple warning that you should have a contract with the photographer. In hiring temporary help, you must be sure of the nature of the employment. Are you putting an individual on the organization's payroll, or are you using a personnel service that is the real employer?

Facilities Contracts

Meetings, conventions, meals, and outdoor activities are typical occasions where you will need to negotiate a contract with a restaurant, caterer, or hotel. For your own financial safety, any contract should be written, so that you thoroughly understand basic costs as well as add-on costs.

A restaurant, for example, may quote you $15 per person for a meal but neglect to tell you that this does not include taxes and a 15 percent add-on gratuity for staff. On top of this, you may even find yourself paying a basic rental charge for the banquet room if this isn't clarified in your negotiations. If you want a bar set up, you must also find out if there is a minimum charge. Many restaurants charge a setup fee if the bar does not sell a given volume of drinks.

The financial planning of organizers has also been disrupted by "corkage fees." A prominent public relations man once arranged for a large banquet at a private club, and a winery had donated wine to be served to the guests. The club's waiters served the wine, but the public relations man had failed to ask the charge for this service. Imagine his chagrin—and the organization's financial embarrassment—when the "corkage fee" on the final bill was $500.

In sum, know exactly what you want and how much the restaurant or hotel will charge. Ask a lot of questions and get all price quotations in writing.

Client Contracts

If you are working for or with an agency that provides public relations services to clients or if you are doing the same thing as a freelancer, it is imperative that a formal contract or a letter of agreement cover precisely what is to be done, in what time period, and for what amount of money.

Many people have found themselves in serious trouble because they promised too much, either by direct statement or implication. You cannot guarantee that a particular news release or feature will be published in a specific publication; all you can do is a professional job of writing the material and submitting it to the proper gatekeepers in an appropriate manner. You can guarantee activity but you cannot promise results.

Another pitfall is not specifying costs in a contract or letter of agreement with a client. If you are charging the client for mileage or working by the hour, it should be specified. If you are charging by the job, say, for writing a news release, make sure you specify a fee that will cover your time and energy for several rewrites. A thorough discussion of billing procedures and fees at the beginning of a client relationship will save much agony and recrimination later.

If you are an employee of a public relations firm, be aware of employer contracts. Many agencies, in order to protect themselves, require employees to sign contracts that forbid the following:

1. Divulging information about clients to outsiders
2. Utilizing client information for personal benefit, as in buying stock on the basis of inside information
3. Beginning employment with a client after leaving the agency
4. Leaving the agency and soliciting its clients for new business

Any one of the above could lead to a lawsuit.

TRADEMARKS

A trademark is a valuable asset. Some are valued in the millions of dollars because the logo or trademark (like the Mercedes-Benz symbol) provides instant recognition of a company or a product. Every trademark owner zealously guards the use of it and often maintains a staff of lawyers to make sure that no one infringes on this valuable brand identification. Coca-Cola is reported to have about two hundred full-time lawyers to monitor the use of the word "Coke" throughout the world. The lawyers make sure that it is always capitalized and that a restaurant does not serve another cola drink if "Coke" is ordered by name.

You must know the registered trademarks of your company and how they may be used. For example, at General Foods (GF), the word "Jell-O" is never used alone. Such use would imply that "Jell-O" is a generic product and that others could use the same word. Instead, the usage at GF is always "Jell-O Brand" of gelatin dessert or pudding. Every organization with a trademark has it own rules in terms of placement, context, color, and even size of trademark. Be certain of the rules that apply to the products for which you are responsible.

By the same token, you should be extremely careful not to use another company's trademark. As much as you may like Snoopy, don't put him on posters advertising the company picnic, since this character is owned by United Features Syndicate and you might be sued for copyright and trademark infringement. The student newspaper staff on the Chicago campus of the University of Illinois also found out about trademark infringement when King Features Syndicate, owners of the Superman trademark, took exception to the choice of name for the campus newspaper: *The Daley Planet.*

Don't use any Walt Disney cartoon characters in your materials unless you have written permission from Walt Disney Productions, who license the

Handle with care. Registered trademarks always are capitalized. Companies and organizations, in order to safeguard their trademarked names, often remind writers and journalists with advertisements in magazines like *Editor & Publisher*. A publication not capitalizing a trademark risks legal action. (*Sources:* White Consolidated Industries, Inc.; Weight Watchers International Inc.)

use of the famous figures like Donald Duck and Mickey Mouse. Recently, some universities have even sued manufacturers of beer mugs and ashtrays for using the logos of varsity football teams without first paying a licensing fee to the university in question. There have even been some lawsuits over the use of E.T. as a character, since the movie studio licenses any replica of that friendly creature from space.

Trademarked Names Always Start with a Capital Letter

Trademarked names are like proper nouns; they are always capitalized. Organizations spend a lot of time and money trying to inform journalists, other writers, and the general public that trademarked names need to be capitalized. Here is a list of names that writers often forget to capitalize:

Realtor	Kleenex
Laundromat	Weight Watchers
Xerox	*TV Guide*
Popsicle	Tabasco
Band-Aid	Scotch (tape)
Frigidaire	Technicolor
Vaseline	Deepfreeze
Rolodex	Jockey (underwear)
Formica	Coke
Kodak	Listerine
Pyrex	

The U.S. Olympic Committee zealously guards use of the Olympic logo and the word "Olympics." More than one company has been served with a cease-and-desist order for having used the five-rings logo without paying a licensing fee. When a group tried to stage "The Gay Olympics," they were promptly haled into court.

In the past, it has been assumed that it was permissible to use stock photos of retired or deceased movie actors. The courts have ruled, however, that a company cannot use a picture of W. C. Fields or the Marx Brothers—or even dress up someone to look like them—without first paying the heirs or the movie studios a licensing fee. In sum, don't shortcut creativity by merely adopting a familiar symbol already on the marketplace.

Here are some general guidelines that courts use to determine if there has been trademark infringement:

To all the writers and typists and proofreaders and editors who help us protect our trademark Kleenex® by always starting it with a capital K followed by l-e-e-n-e-x and following it with a proper generic, be it tissue or diapers: Kimberly-Clark says

Ah...

Ah...

Ahh...

Ahhh...

Choo!

"Bless you!"

(Whew!)

Blessed are the careful. Never use a trademarked name to describe a common product like soft tissues. Product news releases often include a statement like this: "IBM is a registered trademark of International Business Machines." (*Source:* Kimberly-Clark Corporation.)

1. Has the defendant used the name as a way of capitalizing on it, and does the defendant benefit from the original company's investment in popularizing the name?
2. Is there a tendency (deliberate or unintentional) to create confusion in the public mind or to imply a connection between the new product and the old product?
3. Has the original company actively protected the trademark by publicizing it and actually continuing to use it on products and services?

COPYRIGHTS

The purpose of a copyright is to secure for the creator of the material all the benefits earned by creating it. Copyrights apply not only to written words but also to illustrations, plays, musical works, motion pictures, sound recordings, graphics, sculptures, pantomimes, and dances. There are two phases of copyright law that concern you: (1) the use of copyrighted material and (2) the protection of the work that you do.

A new federal copyright law that came into effect in 1978 clarifies the whole subject and eliminates the earlier state laws on this matter. It defines "fair use" of material and "infringement of copyright." It also establishes new rules on duration and publication.

Duration

The new copyright law provides protection for the life of the author plus 50 years. This applies to material published during and after the author's lifetime as well as to unpublished material.

If the material is prepared "for hire," the protection runs for 75 years from the first year of publication or the first year of creation, whichever is shorter. Anything you write on the job is considered "for hire," and your client or company is the owner of your work, including the copyright.

Material does not have to be printed or distributed for copyright protection. As soon as it is created in a concrete form, it is protected, particularly if it bears a copyright notice.

Publication

Distributing or offering to distribute copies of a work to the public is considered publication. Such distribution may be free or paid. It may be by rental, lease, or lending.

If you want the strongest possible copyright protection, you should take formal steps to acquire it as soon as any material is published. There is a five-year grace period after publication before formal notice is required. However, this delay should be avoided whenever possible. It is much easier and safer to file the formal notice as soon as your material appears.

To do this, you must place on the material, before publication, any one of three permissible statements:

1. © 19XX
2. Copyright 19XX
3. Copr. 19XX

The actual year shown is the year of publication. Two copies of the copyrighted item must be sent to the Register of Copyrights, Library of Congress, Washington, DC 20559, together with an "Application for Copyright Registration" form and $10. Instructions and the forms can be obtained from the copyright office.

News releases, features, and illustrations accompanying them are not normally copyrighted. Booklets, leaflets, books, and similar publications are usually copyrighted unless there is a desire to allow others to reproduce them. In that case, it is customary to place a notice in the publication stating that reproduction and distribution of copies is permissible without charge.

Infringement and Fair Use

Infringement consists in using copyrighted material in such a way that the infringer reduces the profits that would otherwise be received by the copyright holder.

Fair use for purposes of criticism, comment, news reporting, teaching, scholarship, or research is not infringement. In general, this is a matter of the purpose for which the material is used. If it is not used for profit, if it does not involve a large part of the work, and if it does not have an effect on the income earned from the copyright, there is little chance of infringement.

One special warning should be given here. The holders of musical copyrights do not permit use of *any* part of their compositions without prior written permission. It is forbidden to quote even a part of a lyric or to play only a few bars of a tune. But also keep in mind that most classical music, especially that of the seventeenth and eighteenth centuries, is in the public domain and can be used without permission. In addition, if you need music for a slide presentation, a local radio station might provide the sound for you. Most radio stations have paid a blanket fee to use hundreds of songs from a catalogue, so these songs become the background for ads as well as special shows.

If you are writing something and want to use a quotation from a copyrighted article or book, you may do so as long as you give proper identification to the author and the source. This is called "fair use." If you quote a lengthy passage of several pages, however, it is best to get permission. If you are tempted to use cartoons from publications, remember that cartoons are art and you should get permission from the publication.

Article reprints also require written permission. If your company is profiled in *Business Week*, for example, order reprints from the publisher; if you make your own for widespread distribution, you are violating the copyright of *Business Week*. U.S. government documents, on the other hand, are in the public domain and can be used in whole or in part without permission. You would get in legal trouble, however, if government reports were used out of context to imply endorsement of a product.

REACTION RELEASES

Great care must be taken in releasing information about lawsuits and labor negotiations and responding to charges made against an organization by other organizations or individuals. An error here can magnify the problem and possibly do irreparable damage.

Lawyers generally prefer to say little or nothing in these circumstances. This attitude, and the counsel they give to clients, leads to the familiar "No comment" or "We haven't read the charges" that we so often hear. Another reaction is to refuse to see any media representatives. This leads to reports such as "We were unable to reach anyone at the Blank Organization who would comment."

Charges

An undenied charge is often interpreted by the public as an indication that it is true. Thus, while the lawyers may hope to win in a court of law, they may lose in the court of public opinion. To avoid this result, it is desirable to give a more satisfactory answer than those cited above. Just what to say in any given case depends on many factors, but some sort of statement is better than none at all.

One approach worth trying is to draft a proposed release and submit it to legal counsel for approval. The release should give as much information as possible and be phrased clearly and concisely. The objective in such a release is to convince the public that the organization is not hiding behind legal technicalities.

Labor or Financial Negotiations

These negotiations are often tense. Proposals and counterproposals go back and forth. Tempers may be lost. Each side may strive for public support by releasing news to the media or by staging events that will attract coverage. Conversely, one or both sides of the controversy may want to keep the negotiations or proposed terms of settlement secret. In either case, it is essential that you keep yourself informed on the status of the negotiations. If publicity is desired, anything released must be carefully checked with the head negotiator for both accuracy and implications that may be drawn from what is said.

Lawsuits

Publicity concerning litigation is tricky, and comments about government agencies and their actions may backfire. Two examples point out the dangers of this area:

- In the Imdrim case, the company was charged with false advertising. The FTC asked for an injunction, but the federal district court refused to grant one. The FTC appealed, but while the appeal was pending the company issued a news release about the case. The FTC claimed that the release contained misleading references to the original case and then hit Imdrim with a second case.
- In another case, a company conducted a survey about public attitudes toward government regulations. This started a political uproar, including a demand by one senator that the FTC investigate the company.

To summarize: Be careful.

ETHICS

Your conduct should go beyond the mere avoidance of legal repercussions. It should be honest and honorable. It should be fair and reasonable. It should stay far away from "flackery."

Periodically some journalist blasts public relations people as liars and denigrates them by calling them "flacks." It is unlikely that these opinionated critics will change their tune, but it is your duty to yourself and your work to reject such charges. By following the PRSA and IABC codes of ethics, you will be able to take pride in your work and in yourself.

Code of Professional Standards for the Practice of Public Relations

These articles have been adopted by the Public Relations Society of America to promote and maintain high standards of public service and ethical conduct among its members.

1. A member shall conduct his or her professional life in accord with the **public interest.**

2. A member shall exemplify high standards of **honesty and integrity** while carrying out dual obligations to a client or employer and to the democratic process.

3. A member shall **deal fairly** with the public, with past or present clients or employers, and with fellow practitioners, giving due respect to the ideal of free inquiry and to the opinions of others.

4. A member shall adhere to the highest standards of **accuracy and truth,** avoiding extravagant claims or unfair comparisons and giving credit for ideas and words borrowed from others.

5. A member shall not knowingly disseminate **false or misleading information** and shall act promptly to correct erroneous communications for which he or she is responsible.

6. A member shall not engage in any practice which has the purpose of **corrupting** the integrity of channels of communications or the processes of government.

7. A member shall be prepared to **identify publicly** the name of the client or employer on whose behalf any public communication is made.

8. A member shall not use any individual or organization professing to serve or represent an announced cause, or professing to be independent or unbiased, but actually serving another or **undisclosed interest.**

9. A member shall not **guarantee the achievement** of specified results beyond the member's direct control.

10. A member shall **not represent conflicting** or competing interests without the express consent of those concerned, given after a full disclosure of the facts.

11. A member shall not place himself or herself in a position where the member's **personal interest is or may be in conflict** with an obligation to an employer or client, or others, without full disclosure of such interests to all involved.

12. A member shall **not accept fees, commissions, gifts or any other consideration** from anyone except clients or employers for whom services are performed without their express consent, given after full disclosure of the facts.

13. A member shall scrupulously safeguard the **confidences and privacy rights** of present, former, and prospective clients or employers.

14. A member shall not intentionally **damage the professional reputation** or practice of another practitioner.

15. If a member has evidence that another member has been guilty of unethical, illegal, or unfair practices, including those in violation of this Code, the member is obligated to present the information promptly to the proper authorities of the Society for action in accordance with the procedure set forth in Article XII of the Bylaws.

16. A member called as a witness in a proceeding for enforcement of this Code is obligated to appear, unless excused for sufficient reason by the judicial panel.

17. A member shall, as soon as possible, sever relations with any organization or individual if such relationship requires conduct contrary to the articles of this Code.

Code of Ethics—IABC

The IABC (International Association of Business Communicators) Code of Ethics has been developed to provide IABC members and other communication professionals with guidelines of professional behavior and standards of ethical practice. The Code will be reviewed and revised as necessary by the Ethics Committee and the Executive Board.

Any IABC member who wishes advice and guidance regarding its interpretation and/or application may write or phone IABC headquarters. Questions will be routed to the Executive Board member responsible for the Code.

COMMUNICATION AND INFORMATION DISSEMINATION

1. Communication professionals will uphold the credibility and dignity of their profession by encouraging the practice of honest, candid and timely communication.

    The highest standards of professionalism will be upheld in all communication. Communicators should encourage frequent communication and messages that are honest in their content, candid, accurate and appropriate to the needs of the organization and its audiences.

2. Professional communicators will not use any information that has been generated or appropriately acquired by a business for another business without permission. Further, communicators should attempt to identify the source of information to be used.

    When one is changing employers, information developed at the previous position will not be used without permission from that employer. Acts of plagiarism and copyright infringement are illegal acts; material in the public domain should have its source attributed, if possible. If an organization grants permission to use its information and requests public acknowledgment, it will be made in a place appropriate to the material used. The material will be used only for the purpose for which permission was granted.

STANDARDS OF CONDUCT

3. Communication professionals will abide by the spirit and letter of all laws and regulations governing their professional activities.

    All international, national and local laws and regulations must be observed, with particular attention to those pertaining to communication, such as copyright law. Industry and organizational regulations will also be observed.

4. Communication professionals will not condone any illegal or unethical act related to their professional activity, their organization and its business or the public environment in which it operates.

    It is the personal responsibility of professional communicators to act honestly, fairly and with integrity at all times in all professional activities. Looking the other way while others act illegally tacitly condones such acts whether or not the communicator has committed them. The communicator should speak with the individual involved, his or her supervisor or appropriate authorities—depending on the context of the situation and one's own ethical judgment.

CONFIDENTIALITY/DISCLOSURE

5. Communication professionals will respect the confidentiality and right-to-privacy of all individuals, employers, clients and customers.

    Communicators must determine the ethical balance between right-to-privacy and need-to-know. Unless the situation involves illegal or grossly unethical acts, confidences should be maintained. If there is a conflict between right-to-privacy and need-to-know, a communicator should first talk with the source and negotiate the need for the information to be communicated.

6. Communication professionals will not use any confidential information gained as a result of professional activity for personal benefit or for that of others.

Confidential information can not be used to give inside advantage to stock transactions, gain favors from outsiders, assist a competing company for whom one is going to work, assist companies in developing a marketing advantage, achieve a publishing advantage or otherwise act to the detriment of an organization. Such information must remain confidential during and after one's employment period.

PROFESSIONALISM

7. Communication professionals should uphold IABC's standards for ethical conduct in all professional activity, and should use IABC and its designation of accreditation (ABC) only for purposes that are authorized and fairly represent the organization and its professional standards.

IABC recognizes the need for professional integrity within any organization, including the association. Members should acknowledge that their actions reflect on themselves, their organizations and their profession.

SUMMARY

1. You are personally responsible for the information you release.
2. Libel and slander are easy to avoid: don't write or say negative things.
3. You must be careful not to invade anyone's personal privacy.
4. You must not deceive anyone.
5. You can get your organization, or yourself, sued if you are careless—especially at public events.
6. Contracts always specify what will be done, when it will be done, and what will be paid. Get it in writing.
7. Trademarks are valuable. Protect your own and don't infringe on those of other organizations.
8. Copyrights are simple, easy to get, and dangerous to infringe. Don't plagiarize.
9. Be very careful about releasing information when charges are made against your organization, when labor or financial regotiations are under way, and when lawsuits are involved.
10. Ethics are vital. You must do more than just obey the law. You must be fair and honorable in dealing with the public.

EXERCISES

1. Dry Creek Winery has recently hired a full-time public relations director charged with increasing public awareness of the winery. This also includes an employee and community relations program. The public relations director has decided on the following list of activities for the first year:

a. Open the winery for public tours and sample tastings.

b. Offer a winery meeting room to community groups.

c. Begin a series of advertisements featuring employees at work.

d. Hire a freelance photographer to build up a photo file for promotion, newsletters, and advertising.

e. Reprint various magazine articles that favorably mention Dry Creek wines and distribute the reprints to liquor wholesalers and liquor stores.

f. Cite governmental reports showing that the winery uses a greater percentage of varietal grapes in its wines than do its competitors.

g. Start an employee newsletter with emphasis on employee features and "personals."

h. Sponsor an annual art fair on the winery grounds.

i. Prepare advertising and product publicity saying that the majority of wine writers regularly drink Dry Creek wines.

Prepare a memo outlining the legal and regulatory factors that should be considered in implementing these activities.

2. Conduct an interview with the editor of an employee newspaper or magazine. What is the policy regarding the use of employee personals like birthdays, anniversaries, vacation trips, and so on? What procedures are used to assure that employee privacy is preserved?

3. Conduct an interview with someone in the public relations or human resources department of a company. What policies does the company have regarding the release of employee information to the news media or any other individuals who may request such information?

4. Using the Dow Jones index or another guide to periodicals in business, find some examples of lawsuits stemming from copyright or trademark infringement. In what ways do the cases deal with the production and distribution of public relations and promotion materials?

SUGGESTED READINGS

Abrams, Floyd. "A Chilling Effect on Corporate Speech." *New York Times,* July 6, 1986, Business Section.

Anderson, J. "Off-Air Videotaping: Legal Aspects." *Public Relations Journal,* September 1984, pp. 26–27.

Awad, Joseph F. "Putting a Price on Publicity." *Public Relations Journal,* November 1987, pp. 18–20.

Bates, Don. "Are Practitioners Lazy When It Comes to Ethics?" *Public Relations Journal,* March 1984, pp. 4–5.

Battiata, Mary. "Gray & Co. Faces Justice Inquiry Into Electronic News Releases." *Washington Post,* March 30, 1986, p. 4A.

Bernstein, Jack. "The Deaver Affair—Bad News for Public Relations." *Advertising Age,* May 26, 1987, p. 76.

Burger, Chester, and Wright, Donald. "Ethics and the Real World." *Public Relations Journal,* December 1982, pp. 13–17.

Byrnes, Sondra. "Private Matters." *Public Relations Journal*, August 1987, pp. 7–9.

Corona, D. "The Right of Publicity." *Public Relations Journal*, February 1983, pp. 29–31.

Cutlip, Scott. "Attendant Responsibility." *Public Relations Journal*, January 1985, pp. 26–31.

Delattre, E. "Ethics in the Information Age." *Public Relations Journal*, June 1984, pp. 12–15.

Drechsel, Robert, and Moon, Deborah. "Libel and Business Executives: The Public Figure Problem." *Journalism Quarterly*, Winter 1983, pp. 703–710.

Durant, Sandra, and Isaacs, Audrey. "The Law, Loyalty and Communications." *Communication World*, October 1987, pp. 30–31.

Ecker, Charles R. "Paying the Piper." *Public Relations Journal*, March 1988, pp. 18–19. Using copyrighted music in public relations programs.

Geisler, Dorothy. "How to Avoid Copyright Suits." *Communication World*, June 1984, pp. 34–37.

Hamilton, Seymour. "PR Ethics, from Publicity to Interaction." *Public Relations Quarterly*, Fall 1986, pp. 12–14.

Jackson, Patrick. "Demonstrating Professionalism." *Public Relations Journal*, October 1988, pp. 27–31.

Jurgensen, John H., and Lukaszewski, James. "Ethics: Content Before Conduct." *Public Relations Journal*, March 1988, pp. 47–48.

Killian, Douglas. "Impact of the SEC Rule 10b-5 on Corporate Public Relations." *Journalism Quarterly*, Winter 1986, pp. 735–739, 797.

Lipman, Joanne. "Firm's Outings Pose Liability Dilemma." *Wall Street Journal*, Sept. 14, 1988, p. 35.

Lipman, Joanne. "PR Society Receives Some Very Bad PR From Its Ex-Chief." *Wall Street Journal*, Sept. 26, 1986, pp. 1, 18.

McLean, Deckle. "Recent Privacy Cases Deal With Diverse Issues." *Journalism Quarterly*, Summer 1986, pp. 374–378.

Rome, Edwin, and Roberts, William. *Corporate and Commercial Free Speech: First Amendement Protection of Expression in Business*. Westport, CT: Quorum Books, 1985.

Rosen, Dan. "Coping With Copyright." *Communication World*, December 1986, pp. 18–19.

Rothman, Andrea. "Olympic Committee Sees More Resistance To Its Control Over The Word 'Olympic.'" *Wall Street Journal*, Oct. 28, 1986.

Rubin, Maureen. "Rethinking the Anonymous Source Dilemma." *Public Relations Journal*, November 1988, pp. 12–15, 54.

Ruddell, Tom, and Pettegrew, Loyd. "The Best Companies Have and Heed Codes/Creeds." *Communication World*, September 1988, pp. 30–31.

Shad, John. "Insider Trading Caveat: In the End, Only Ethics Pays." *Wall Street Journal*, Feb. 6, 1987.

"Trademarks." *Editor & Publisher*, Dec. 3, 1988. Annual pull-out section on trademarks.

Traub, James. "Into the Mouths of Babes." *New York Times Magazine,* July 24, 1988, pp. 18–20, 37–38, 52–53.

Turk, Judy VanSlyke. "Pro Visions." *Public Relations Journal,* February 1987, p. 28.

Wilcox, Dennis L., Ault, Phillip, and Agee, Warren. "Ethics and Professionalism." *Public Relations Strategies and Tactics.* New York: Harper & Row, 1989, chap. 6.

Wikleman, Michael. "Soul Searching." *Public Relations Journal,* October 1987, pp. 28–32.

Chapter
4

Finding and Generating News

*I*n public relations, you may write many things that are not specifically aimed at the mass media. Nevertheless, a large part of what is written must contain a substantial element of newness—that is, you must bring something new to the reader. To do this effectively, you need to know the sources of news, what makes news, how to find news, and how to generate news. Most of this chapter deals with news for the mass media, but the basic principles have much wider application.

In every newspaper, magazine, or broadcasting station there are people who decide what information to give their readers, listeners, or viewers. Often they are reporters, editors, or program directors, but for the present we will describe them as "gatekeepers." The gatekeepers examine the information that comes to their attention and use only that which they select. If it is really news, it may be used. If the gatekeeper doesn't think it will interest his or her audience, it won't be used.

Even if the gatekeeper thinks an item is newsworthy, it may not be used. His or her superior may disagree, there may not be space available in a publication, or there may be no air time that can be used. The best way to get your news across is to send to the media the kinds of items they want. To learn what these are, you must read, listen to, and watch what they publish or broadcast.

When your news is published, it becomes "publicity," unpaid and uncontrolled mass communication, which *should* benefit your organization.

THE TWO SOURCES OF NEWS

News is a report on an event or a situation. Usually there is a difference; at times, however, there is considerable overlap, as when a series of events creates a situation.

Events

An event is something that has happened: John Doe has announced his candidacy for election to Congress. Or it may be something that is going to happen: John Doe will announce on May 6 whether or not he will seek the nomination.

Discovery of a new oil field is an event. It may be reported in a news release. The effect of this new oil field on the energy problem may be discussed in a feature story.

Situations

A situation is a relatively permanent or long-lasting issue, condition, or problem. School busing is an issue; the environmental crisis is a condition; the energy shortage is a problem. Situations are usually reported to the public in feature stories—detailed examinations of the entire problem or some part of it.

WHAT MAKES NEWS

There are several ways in which to describe the elements that follow. There is no infallible checklist, but if you keep these topics in mind, you will probably be able to produce news.

Timeliness

Timeliness is possibly the most important characteristic of news. Another way of expressing this is to say "If it isn't new, it isn't news." A morning

Events make news. An old but effective news device: presentation of a giant check to the mayor of San Francisco to symbolize a company's donation to the restoration of a historic landmark. (*Source:* PBN Company, San Francisco, CA.)

newspaper will use the word "yesterday" in nearly every item, because morning newspapers report what happened yesterday. Evening newspapers can use the word "today," and they do so in most of their news items.

Television or radio news will use similar words: "yesterday" in a morning program and "today" in an evening program. In fact, one of the most widely watched daytime television programs is called *Today* because the network knows that people are interested in things that are new and current.

Because of this insistence on newness, you must be sure that whatever you offer the media is sent in as soon as the facts are known.

Another aspect of timeliness is the effect of public interest. If the public is interested in a current situation, a skilled writer will effectively tie news releases into that situation. For example, auto clubs, insurance companies, and the National Safety Council have excellent placement success just before long holiday weekends with articles about safe driving.

Since Christmas is the major season for purchasing children's toys, the media then are receptive to news releases about the toy safety, new toys on the market, and the toys that are setting sales records.

Nieman-Marcus Department Stores always generate much publicity at Christmas time simply by announcing the availability of "his" and "her" gifts, usually extraordinary things like matched Indian elephants or twin Rolls-Royces. Nieman-Marcus's writers have accomplished the objective, over the years, of establishing these stores as expensive ones with a great variety of merchandise.

The lesson from all this is that you should constantly search for ways in which to connect your story to whatever the public is interested in or thinking about at the moment.

Prominence

The news media rarely cover the grand opening of an average store unless a celebrity is involved. For example, an electronics store in a large California city generated a front-page story in the local daily simply because Vanna White, the television personality, was on hand to cut the ribbon. In smaller communities, the mere presence of a beauty queen or an elephant at a commercial event is often enough to attract media coverage.

Another way of looking at prominence is to remember the phrase "Names make news." People are interested in other people. Much of people's everyday conversation is about other people. The success of *People* magazine proves the point.

Try to work personal names into your output, since this increases the interest. (The bigger the name, the greater the interest.) For example, compare these two ways of reporting an energy saving program at Glutz Mfg. Co.: (1) "The Glutz Mfg. Co. announced today that it is installing a new heat exhanger that will save a million barrels of oil a year," or (2) "Henry Glutz, president of The Glutz Mfg. Co., announced today that they are installing. . . ." That the use of names makes a story more interesting is supported by the fact that personal names appeared 61 times on the front page of a suburban daily newspaper in a single day.

Proximity

A number of surveys have shown that the news releases most acceptable to media gatekeepers are those with a local angle. One survey by *Editor & Publisher* of business editors nationwide (March 22, 1986) was summed up in the following statement: "The business journalists stressed their need for a hometown angle in order to justify printing any press release material. If the release has no hometown angle, no local headquarters, plant, dealerships, offices or other outlets, it has no relevance."

Another survey by Brouillard Communications, a division of J. Walter Thompson Co., found that the most common complaint of editors about news releases was lack of relevance and significance to the publication's readers. Poor writing came in as the second most common complaint.

The local angle, or proximity, has strong news value. If Richard Roe is named president of a company in Kansas City, the local newspapers are interested in a news release about him. However, the newspapers in St. Louis, across the state, might well trash this release as being irrelevant to their readers. But these same St. Louis papers *might* be interested in running a small article if the Kansas City firm had a plant in the St. Louis area. In contrast, Richard Roe's success story might be front-page material in the weekly newspaper serving the small town where he went to high school. Trade periodicals serving Roe's industry would also be interested in printing news about his new position. Always keep the local angle, or proximity, in mind when you write a news release. A crucial element is selection of appropriate media. Don't send a local news story to newspapers all over the state.

People are interested in what is close to them. As Mort Rosenblum says, in his book *Coups and Earthquakes,* "A dogfight in Brooklyn makes more news than a civil war in Africa."

Significance

If a situation or event is likely to affect a substantial number of people, it is significant. An increase in the price of heating oil is significant in the Northeast, where many homes are heated by oil. It is not very significant in the West, where most homes are heated by gas. An increase in the price of gasoline is significant wherever people use automobiles. The significance of any event or situation is in direct proportion to the number of people affected.

In judging significance, you must know not only the bare numbers of people affected but also *who* will be affected. A requirement that gasoline stations install equipment to reduce the amount of gasoline vaporized into the atmosphere was of minor interest to the general public. It was significant to environmentalists, however, because it was a symbol of progress, and it was extremely significant to the operators of service stations, since they had to pay for the new nozzles.

Such a story would rate a paragraph in a metropolitan newspaper, a page in an environmental magazine, and probably several pages in the trade magazines read by the operators of service stations.

You should ask the following questions: How many will be affected? Who will be affected? How will they be affected? With the right answers, you should be able to produce the kind of material that will be accepted by the media concerned.

Unusualness

If an ordinary person appears without clothing in a nudist camp, there will be no publicity, since lack of clothing is expected there. If that same person walked down the street of any city, it *would* be news, because there lack of clothing is unusual. Such an action would guarantee an item in the local paper—and on the local television station if the camera crew could get there in time.

A logical offshoot of this is the stunt—any extremely unusual happening

King Kong makes news. This giant inflated replica of King Kong surprised the people of Portland when it appeared one morning in the heart of the city. Planned to increase interest in the new Oregon lottery, the giant figure was placed on a building facing a popular downtown park. The work was done at night and Portlanders were greeted in the morning with the sight and an accompanying sound track that included some of the material from the original score, including Fay Wray's screams. The results were highly successful. The event received national and regional attention: front page photos in newspapers as well as radio and television coverage. Traffic was stalled for blocks, and seven million tickets were sold in the first seven days. (*Source:* Pihas, Schmidt, Westerdahl, Portland, OR.)

---

that is arranged solely for the sake of publicity. Most media are wary of stunts but do often report on them.

Activist groups like Greenpeace and Animal Rights advocates often generate news coverage by staging demonstrations with protestors wearing animal costumes. Antinuclear activists are fond of skeleton suits. But such stunts can become too contrived. A bikini-clad model standing next to a snowman in Minneapolis or a goose on skis at a resort is likely to be bypassed by the press.

Human Interest

People like to read about the lives of other people. Britain's sole ski-jumping entry in the 1988 winter Olympics wasn't a world-class skier—in fact, he finished last—but the media found him interesting and he became a symbol of the Olympics where amateurs could compete in the spirit of international co-operation and understanding. Indeed, many Olympic competitors got world-wide publicity because public relations personnel gave their human interest stories to the media.

Arousing the emotions is an effective way to get attention and to create news. Children, animals, and people are often emotion-arousing subjects. A lost dog that makes its way home across hundreds of miles is a sure-fire story. Children tug at the heartstrings. An editorial entitled "Yes Virginia, there is a Santa Claus" has been reprinted year after year.

Tragedy makes news. The man who lived near Mt. St. Helens and refused to move during its eruption got much attention in the media—and still more of it when he was buried by the ashes.

Comedy makes news. The bank robbers who got away with several thousand dollars were a news item. They were a bigger story when it was discovered that they had dropped all the money.

Mystery makes news. The assassination of President Kennedy continues to make the news because, from time to time, some person claims to have new evidence refuting the Warren Commission's findings. Its report is still distrusted by some because there were several mysterious and apparently unclarified elements in the chain of events.

Conflict

The struggle between the environmentalists and those who hope to develop more sources of energy is an outstanding example of the effect of conflict on news coverage. Proposals to build power plants near Bryce and Zion canyons in Utah resulted in many stories. Both sides got their views presented. Without the conflict, the plants would probably have been built and little would have been published.

Newness

Advertising people say that the two words they find most useful are "new" and "free." You will seldom use "free" but should constantly search for something "new." Any news release announcing a new product or service has a good chance of being published. Every year the automobile companies get major coverage in the media when they announce their new models. New uses for old products are the basis for most food publicity. There is nothing new about potatoes, walnuts, yams, or avocados, yet food editors steadily publish new recipes for these and scores of other foods.

The future suggests newness to an unusual degree; that's why the media publish stories about space travel and colonies on the moon. Predictions of what may or will happen are basically interesting and have a good chance of publication.

Good News and Bad News

Many people say "All news is bad news." There is some basis for this statement, but it is not entirely true. Occasionally you may have to release bad news. A product recall is one example. Yet with careful handling, even bad news can be turned into something beneficial. When Procter & Gamble withdrew Rely tampons, they built goodwill by the speed and frankness with which they acted.

In spite of the large volume of bad news, there is still interest in good news. Some media, in response to public complaints about the nature of the news, have inaugurated special features concentrating on "good" news.

FINDING NEWS

Before you start hunting for news, you should familiarize yourself with the organization for which you are to write. Among the things you should know about are the organization's purpose; whether it is profit or nonprofit; what its products or services are; the nature of its policies or actions and how these may be of concern to one or more publics; the people in the organization and what they do; the organization's place in its community, business, or industry; and its importance in the state or nation. To get this information, you must study the organization closely and keep up with changes.

Internal News Sources

In this situation, your role is that of a reporter. You must move around in the organization, talk to people, ask questions, observe activities—and constantly look for something new or different. News stories don't necessarily come to you. You must come to the stories. Other people may have no awareness of the news value of an event or situation, so you must look for clues and hints as well as hard facts.

A new source of raw material may mean merely costs and quantities to the purchasing agent, but it may lead you to several stories. For example, a new fiber may change the characteristics of a textile, which will be of interest to the users of the textile (clothing manufacturers), wearers of the clothing (consumers), clothing designers, and fashion writers.

A change in work schedules may affect traffic and be important to the community. Personnel changes and promotions may interest editors of business and trade papers. An accident that halts or delays production will interest all the media serving those affected.

External News Sources

You must continually read, listen to, and watch the news for events or situations that may affect your organization. A new ruling by the Environmental

Protection Agency may have a major effect on a public utility. A reduction in federal grants may create budget problems for a city. Changes in rules on Medicare create large problems for hospitals.

Situations, too, can be sources of news. Illegal immigration is a problem that will not readily be solved, but it yields a steady stream of articles in practically all media. Agricultural organizations need labor for work which many Americans shun. Hispanic-Americans protest restrictions on the ground that the proposals are racial, while labor unions object to low-wage competition.

Any situation that affects an organization or that the organization can affect may lead to a story. If an organization finds a new way to conserve energy, if it has been successful in employing handicapped people, or if it has improved service to customers, there is news that will interest someone.

GENERATING NEWS

Action generates news. When the American Association for the Advancement of Science or the American Medical Association holds an annual meeting, the media report on the general nature of the meeting and usually run a considerable number of feature stories based on speeches, discoveries, and statements by the participants. Not many people have the opportunity to serve such large organizations, but anyone may generate news by stimulating activity in the organization that he or she serves.

If you cannot find anything going on, it may be time to make something happen, or to find a problem and a solution for the problem. Making something happen requires that you persuade the principals in the organization to do something that will attract public attention. Solving a problem means that you must identify a difficulty that concerns the public and tell how the organization contributes to the solution.

Special Events

Events can be grouped into two classes; those planned primarily to generate publicity and those that produce publicity as a by-product. Typical of the first class is the "opening." A new branch bank, a new office of a savings and loan association, a new supermarket or shopping center, or even the first day of school can arouse the interest of the local media.

When the Southern Pacific Railroad opened a huge new freight yard in Southern California, it got a large amount of publicity in both the general and trade media. It could have merely started using the yard without saying anything to anybody. Instead, it planned and executed a grand opening and cashed in on the publicity.

Macy's annual Thanksgiving Day parade in New York City is another kind of event. Planned solely to produce publicity for the store, it has become an institution that millions of people look forward to every year.

By contrast, the annual conventions cited in the opening of this section are not planned to produce publicity, but they do generate it. The meetings would be held even if there were no publicity, but they benefit from the by-product.

You must look at every possibility in your organization with an eye to publicity. Can something be done? Can a meeting be held? Can the organization stage an open house, a plant tour, a parade? Can it give an award or scholarship? Can it sponsor a contest or a team? Can it help other organizations, like Junior Achievement or 4-H? Can it help the local schools with guidance counseling? If it is a large organization, can it do any of these things on a national or regional scale?

For any event there can be publicity both before and after. For a continuing event, there may be a stream of publicity throughout it.

Demonstrations for News

Few television stations can resist covering demonstrations. Newspapers, too, generally report them, sometimes extensively. Most demonstrators are activists who want to protest something. Often they represent only a small number of people but, knowing the news principle that action is interesting, they get much media attention.

It doesn't take many people to conduct an effective demonstration. Twenty or thirty of them, carrying placards, can fill a television screen or newspaper picture. Some observers have commented that the news media are suckers for covering such stories, but they do. Also, it has been noted that the sponsors of these events don't start their demonstrations until the television cameras are in place.

There is no reason why any organization cannot benefit from a demonstration. The activists do not have a monopoly. The one thing to remember is that the event must appear to be spontaneous. The president of the XYZ company can't be the center of attention, but the employees can. To get the employees involved, their interests must be explained and their feelings aroused, informally and indirectly.

A situation in which employees generated news with a demonstration was a protest rally in front of a newspaper office after this paper ran a story critical of the company's product and its lack of quality control. Other news media in the city as well as the targeted newspaper covered the rally.

Demonstrations of Fact

In this kind of demonstration, the objective is to prove something. When General Electric demonstrated a new superconductor process, it got nationwide publicity. When Lear demonstrated a new general-service aircraft, there was extensive media coverage telling how new materials had reduced the weight and new design had increased speed to a point where the new plane was remarkably fast and fuel-efficient.

Continental Oil Company got favorable nationwide publicity when it demonstrated that it could extract oil without destroying the habitat of several endangered bird species.

M E M O R A N D U M

TO: Barbara Fenhagen
        Hobart G. Cawood
        Tom Muldoon
        Sam Rogers
        Brian Tierney
        Moe Septee
        Fred Stein

FROM: Margie Segal

DATE: May 27, 1987

RE: Giant balloon flag created for We the People Ceremony

It occurred to me that the giant balloon flag could be a hook for national media coverage in the future.

The July 4th holiday is an important time for our city. We have, without question, the most important historical treasures relating to the celebration of American Independence. The City Representative's Office, the Convention and Visitors Bureau and others already invest a considerable amount of time, energy and money in promoting July 4th.

The balloon flag could become our July 4th signature -- a strong visual that could make Philadelphia a "must" for national television news coverage on that holiday.

Every city has fireworks on July 4, but it could be Philadelphia's balloon flag rising at Independence Hall that could get us on the network news.

I understand that everyone's energies are focused on 1987's We the People celebration, but I think this is an opportunity for 1988 and the future that is worth considering.

Let me know what you think.

attachments

Ideas make news. This internal memo to the staff of a public relations firm outlines an idea that will give an event high visibility and attract television coverage. An effective public relations writer and strategist constantly thinks about how concepts can be translated into high-profile visual symbols. (*Source:* Lewis, Gilman & Kynett, Philadelphia, PA.)

This idea made news. The balloon flag mentioned in the memo opposite became reality at Philadelphia's bicentennial celebration of the U.S. Constitution. The large flag, as large as Independence Hall itself, generated photo and television coverage around the world. (*Source:* Lewis, Gilman & Kynett, Philadelphia, PA.)

The writer who finds something that proves a point has an excellent chance of getting media coverage. The reason is clear. Proof cannot be dismissed as hot air. If you plan a demonstration, be sure that you pretest and rehearse. A demonstration that fails is embarrassing and negative.

Personal Appearances

Two kinds of personal appearances generate news. First is the kind where news is incidental to something else. Second is the appearance where news is the only objective. Most typical of the first type is the situation where someone makes a speech to an organization. If the president of the XYZ company addresses the local chamber of commerce, he will be heard by all who attend the meeting.

Attendance may be increased if the media are notified, by way of either a news release or a telephoned alert. The audience for the speech may be greatly increased if the media are supplied with copies of the speech or a news release summarizing what was said. As a general rule, every public appearance should be considered an opportunity for news both before and after the incident. And, of course, there should always be an effort to get reporters to attend the meeting and get the story themselves.

Appearances where news is the sole objective are typified by television programs such as *Meet the Press* and *Face The Nation*. In these cases the audiences in the studios are very small, but the broadcast audience may number millions. In addition to these nationwide shows, there are a great many local shows, on both TV and radio, where a personal appearance can be arranged. The management of public appearances will be described in a later chapter.

If It's May, It's National Asparagus Month

National organizations and trade associations often designate a week or month to focus on an industry or a product. May is a popular month, with such designations as National Barbecue Month, National Paint Month, National Physical Fitness and Sports Month, National High Blood Pressure Month, National Home Decorating Month, and Correct Posture Month.

The National Asparagus Association selected May because it marks the peak of asparagus production. By promoting the month, the trade group hopes to encourage consumption of its product at home and in restaurants. Surveys show that on Mother's Day more meals are eaten out than any other day, and the Asparagus Association encourages restaurants to use its product.

The warm weather in May also prompts the National Paint & Coating Association to sponsor National Paint Month. As a spokesman says, "It's the time of year when people begin thinking about home improvements, and thus it is the perfect month to alert the public to the 'power of paint.'"

For the past 22 years, the American Chiropractic Association has observed Correct Posture Month during May. Proclamations recognizing May as Good Posture Month are distributed by the association of chiropractors, who submit them for endorsement by local, state, and national officials. This lends the event a shade of governmental legitimacy. Again, the concept of using prominent names often makes such items acceptable to the news media and generates local coverage for chiropractors.

During the month, chiropractors are urged to get involved in community service—including activities such as free spinal checkup clinics—which also generates publicity. During the restoration of the Statue of Liberty, chiropractors donated $1 per patient visit during May toward the landmark's restoration. The association chose this project because, as one spokesperson said, "The Statue of Liberty also had a back problem."

A listing of all the months, weeks, and days designated by all manner of organizations is published annually in *Chase's Annual Events*. By consulting this annual, you will finds that National Kraut and Frankfurter Week is February 13–22. (Many media ignore these special weeks because, in any given calendar week, there may be five or six "weeks.")

News Ideas

Let your imagination run; there are many ways to generate news. Here are a few suggestions to get you started:

1. Tie-ins

    Tie in with news events that are getting public attention.
    Tie in with special days or weeks. They range from Mother's Day to Potato Chip Week.
    Tie in with a holiday, vacation period, back-to-school week, and so on.
    Tie in with a local medium on a public-service project.

2. Announcements

    Announce an appointment, promotion, transfer, or retirement.
    Announce committee appointments.
    Announce a new product, service, or policy.
    Announce organizational accomplishments—earnings, research breakthroughs, sales, construction, moves, openings and closings.

3. Statements

    State the organization's position on a public issue.
    Make a prediction.
    Get involved in a controversy.
    Pass a resolution.

4. Reports

    Issue a report on a survey.
    Interpret national statistics in local terms.
    Report on organizational activities; for example, the employment of minorities.

5. Names

    Use a celebrity.
    Write a letter to a public figure.
    Release a letter from a public figure (with permission).

6. Events

    Hold a meeting or convention.
    Conduct an open house, plant tour, or opening.
    Conduct a contest.
    Make an award.
    Celebrate an anniversary or an accomplishment.
    Stage a debate.

7. Public Appearances

    Schedule speeches.

Better Homes and Gardens ® FAMILY NETWORK

FOR: IMMEDIATE RELEASE   Contacts: Naomi Mintz
                                                   212/536-8832
                                                   Karen Frankel
                                                   212/536-8774

REUNIONS CAPTURE AMERICA'S RENEWED FAMILY SPIRIT

Survey Finds 70% Have Attended Reunions;
Over 1/3 Plan to Hold Them Regularly

America has rediscovered the family -- not just on
Madison Avenue and in prime-time television, but in real life.
From small towns to big cities, the time-honored tradition of the
family reunion is enjoying a renaissance.

The popularity of reunions was gauged recently by a
Better Homes and Gardens Family Network survey. More than 70
percent of respondents said they had attended at least one
reunion, and, on the average, they reported having gone to nearly
four. The future of reunions looks promising as well: One-third
of the respondents hold or plan to hold reunions on a regular
basis.

- more -

1133 AVENUE OF THE AMERICAS • NEW YORK, NY 10036 • (212) 536-8800

Surveys make news. A survey assessing the popularity of family reunions was part of the strategy used by Ketchum Public Relations to help reposition its client, *Better Homes and Gardens,* as a magazine for the entire family. A news release announcing the results of the survey was used by many weekly and daily newspapers throughout the nation. (*Source:* Ketchum Public Relations, New York, NY.)

Appear before governmental bodies—city councils, legislative committees, or public commissions.
Arrange media interviews.

8. Something Different

Look at the way other writers try to catch public attention and think up new ways to do it. For example, a San Francisco jeweler used a giant tarantula to guard his display case. The story was so unique that it made the *New York Times.*

9. Media Coverage

Charged with promoting the *National Geographic* special on PBS television, Ketchum Public Relations scored a major success with "The Great Whales." The program was to air at the time of the annual gray whale migration along the California coast. On a whale-watching expedition that Ketchum arranged, boats carried more than two hundred members of the press out to sea. News coverage was extensive and the special on whales attracted one of the year's largest audiences on PBS.

SUMMARY

1. There are two sources of news: events and situations.
2. The things that make news are timeliness, proximity, prominence, significance, unusualness, human interest, conflict, and newness.
3. Finding news starts with thorough knowledge of your organization. This will help you find news from internal sources and recognize how external events and situations relate to your organization.
4. Generating news requires action: special events, demonstrations for news, demonstrations of fact, personal appearances, and creative thinking.

EXERCISES

1. It is important for public relations writers to know everything about a company or organization in order to determine story angles that may be of interest to the news media. Students should select an organization to research. Things to find out are:
   a. Size of company
   b. Number of plants and where located
   c. Number of employees
   d. Products
   e. Competitive position in the marketplace
   f. Unique aspects of the company
   g. Number of shareholders

    h. Possible medical or safety hazards of the product
    i. Names and background of key executives
    j. Use of trademarks
    k. Key publics
    l. Trends affecting the industry

    A variety of library sources as well as literature from the company can be of help. Once this material is assembled, what timely story angles about the company can be compiled?

2. A Japanese restaurant chain in the United States is celebrating its twenty-fifth anniversary next year. The owners of the chain see this as an opportunity to garner publicity and perhaps motivate more Americans to patronize the local franchise. What activities and special events would you recommend that would attract media coverage?

3. Companies and retail outlets often generate publicity by associating with a special holiday like July 4, Thanksgiving, or even Valentine's Day. Develop some ideas on how a package service like Federal Express or United Parcel Service might tie in to a special holiday.

4. Special events are often organized to generate publicity for an organization. Suggest a special event for each of the following:

    a. A manufacturer of computers
    b. A retail clothing store
    c. A hospital
    d. A charitable agency
    e. An insurance company
    e. A university

5. It is important to localize news if you want coverage in community newspapers. Suggest a way to localize each of the following items:

    a. A national airline has just compiled the number of flights, mileage, and total passengers carried last year.
    b. A computer company has introduced a new portable computer that can be used on a person's lap.
    c. A national manufacturing company with plant sites in 100 different cities has just announced its annual earnings and stock dividend.
    d. A company has just a developed a computerized map system for use in automobiles—a display on the car dash portrays a map and shows the motorist's progress with a red light.
    e. A charitable agency has just released national figures on the number of Americans afflicted with AIDS.

SUGGESTED READINGS

Elfenbein, Dick. "Business Journalists Say If It's Not Local, It's Trashed." *Editor & Publisher*, March 22, 1986, pp. 19, 32–33.

Finn, P. "In-House Research Catches On." *Public Relations Journal*, July 1984, pp. 18–20.

Huey, John. "Quick: Take Me to Your Editor! I'm a Hot Story." *Wall Street Journal*, August 19, 1987, editorial page.

Jeffers, Dennis. "Discovering Media-Value Associations." *Public Relations Review*, Spring 1983, pp. 37–44.

Kessler, Lauren, and McDonald, Duncan. *Mastering the Message: Media Writing with Substance and Style.* Belmont, CA: Wadsworth Publishing, 1989.

Kessler, Lauren, and McDonald, Duncan. *Uncovering the News: A Journalist's Search for Information.* Belmont, CA: Wadsworth Publishing, 1987.

Morton, Linda. "Why Newspapers Choose The Releases They Use." *Public Relations Review*, Fall 1986, pp. 22–27.

Newsom, Doug, and Wollert, James A. "Introduction to Media Writing." *Media Writing: Preparing Information for the Mass Media*, ed. 2. Belmont, CA: Wadsworth Publishing, 1988.

Rumer, Thomas. "Corporate History Can Be Public Relations Gold." *Public Relations Quarterly*, Fall 1984, pp. 19–23.

Stuart, E. "The In-House Interviewer." *Public Relations Journal*, July 1984, pp. 24–27.

Vogel, C. M. "How to Recycle Your Research." *Public Relations Journal*, May 1982, pp. 22–23.

Chapter
5

The News Release

*I*f a news release is to accomplish anything, it must follow a standard format, it must be newsworthy, and it must get to the right person at the right time. Most news releases never get to the printed page because they fail in one of these requirements.

If you write your releases carefully, fill them with news that will interest the readers of the publication, and omit puffery, they *may* be published. If you avoid the shotgun approach and tailor each release to some specific publication, your releases will be much more likely to be published.

Most news releases should be limited to one page. Where there is much detail that is important, as with a new product, it may be necessary to use more space. But remember, long, involved news releases turn off the gatekeepers.

FORMAT

If a release looks as if it was prepared by a professional it has a chance of being used. If it does not conform to a rather standardized format, it is more than likely to end in a wastebasket without being read. Following are the basic guidelines:

Paper

Always use standard $8\frac{1}{2}$- by 11-inch paper; 20-pound bond is preferred. Anything lighter tends to be flimsy and to tear when editors write on it. Never use erasable paper or textured paper. The use of colored paper is controversial. Some people argue that a colored release will stand out from the mass of white paper that piles up in a newsroom. Others, including some editors, think color is gimmicky and not worth the cost.

If color does strike your fancy, use it; but stick to pastel colors like ivory, light blue, light green, or pale yellow. Don't use dark colors; they make the words hard to read. Don't use brilliant colors like shocking pink; the editor wants facts, not a rainbow.

Typing

The copy must be typewritten and should appear on one side of the paper only. Always double space. The typing must be clear and accurate. Always double check what is written. Start your copy about two inches below the heading. Margins should be wide—allow $1\frac{1}{2}$ inches on each side. This allows room for corrections or insertions. Don't place a hyphenated word at the end of a line.

Don't run a one-page release clear to the bottom of the page. Try to leave about two inches of space below the last line. Always show where the release ends. Some people use the old "30" at the bottom center of the page, some use "end," and some use "###." Any of these is satisfactory.

If your release must run to more than one page, be sure to end each page with a complete sentence and insert the word "more" at the bottom center. Multiple-page releases should be stapled together, not clipped. Never send a carbon copy of a release. Letter-quality photocopies are best if you must send several.

Heading

At the top of the page (first page only if there is more than one) there must be something showing the release's origin. Some say that this should be typed on plain paper, but many use a printed heading; there is no evidence that this causes rejection. In fact, if the releases on the printed sheet are consistently good, the heading may help the gatekeeper recognize the source, and this may ensure early attention.

The heading must contain the name and address of the organization and

AMERICAN BAR ASSOCIATION
Division for Communications and Public Affairs
750 North Lake Shore Drive, Chicago, Illinois 60611, (312) 988-5000

ABA

The
Learning
Company

NEWS

SCHLAGE

Part of worldwide Ingersoll-Rand

Schlage Lock Company
2401 Bayshore Blvd.
San Francisco, CA 94134

News Release

Raychem
Racing Team

FOR IMMEDIATE RELEASE

Contact: John Cook
            415/361-2519

RAYCHEM-SPONSORED LOLA TO COMPETE IN ELKHART LAKE RACE

News release letterheads. Many companies and organizations use a standard news release letterhead. These letterheads, shown above, immediately identify the source of the news item to reporters and editors. (*Source:* Photo by James McNay.)

the name and phone number of the person to contact for additional information. This is usually the office number, but it is often advisable to list a night or home number also. (This should be so identified.)

There are three reasons for this: (1) morning newspapers and national wire services have evening staffs, which may need more information after business offices are closed; (2) the news media continue to gather news during weekends, when business offices are shut down; and (3) times zones are different.

Business Wire, a national business news-release service, practically demands a night number on a release. Remember, when it is 3 P.M. in California, it will be 6 P.M. in New York. A West Coast daily calling an East Coast office for information is not likely to get an answer at that time because people will have gone home.

Because they carry no night number and reporters cannot contact anyone, many stories are dumped by the media. If there is any possibility of a request for additional information or clarification, make sure that you can be reached.

Dates

The release should be dated, so that the gatekeeper will know it is current and it can be properly identified at a later day.

Another and even more important date is the release date. This should precede the copy—and the headline if one is used. The release date should specify exactly when the release may be used. There are several ways to do this:

> FOR IMMEDIATE RELEASE. This means that the medium can use it as soon as received. (Most releases are dated this way.)

> FOR RELEASE: Friday, Jan. 16. (This means that the material may not be used before that date.)

> FOR RELEASE: Friday, Jan. 16 or thereafter. (This indicates that the material is still pertinent and usable after the date indicated.)

Radio and television newsrooms get much of their news from AP or UPI, as do newspapers and news magazines. Conversely, the wire services get news from the media as well as from the sources of the news. Accordingly, if you have a story that may be of national interest and want to control the time of publication, you should date it this way:

> FOR RELEASE: 6:30 P.M. est Thursday Jan. 15. (This takes care of morning papers and late-evening newscasts.)

> FOR RELEASE: 6:30 A.M. est Friday Jan. 16. (This permits use in morning newscasts and afternoon papers.)

The purpose of using a specific date for release is to make sure that all media receiving the release can use it at the same time. Without this restriction, one paper might publish the news before another even received it.

If an important person is going to speak at a specific time, the media fre-

FROM: **BLUE SHIELD**
of California

Blue Shield Plaza
Two North Point
San Francisco, CA 94133-1599

FOR MORE INFORMATION: John Rodgers
Office (415) 445-5110
Home (415) 656-4046

RELEASE: IMMEDIATE   May 2, 1988

BLUE SHIELD AWARDED STATE CONTRACT

SAN FRANCISCO--Nearly 200,000 state and local California government employees, retirees and their dependents will be covered under a new $236 million-a-year health benefits program awarded to Blue Shield of California, the Public Employees Retirement System (PERS) announced today.

Effective January 1, 1989, Blue Shield will administer the group's only statewide fee-for-service health coverage option--a self-insured plan called "PERS-CARE." It replaces three fee-for-service/PPO options offered last year to state and contracting public agency employees and retirees.

The PERS Board of Administration said Blue Shield was selected because "it offers the largest preferred provider network and has participated in the PERS program since its inception in 1962."

Citing the fact that Blue Shield is ranked in the top seven PPOs in the nation by "Healthweek," PERS said the Plan's "exclusive focus in California, leverage with providers, and experience in managed care systems will provide valuable assistance to stabilize costs and reduce the differential between the fee-for-service plan and the HMO options."

A spot news release. The format is excellent, and the content is a clear, concise, and complete. The ideal length of a news release is one or two pages, preferably one. (*Source:* Blue Shield of California, San Francisco, CA.)

quently receive advance copies of the speech or a release giving the high-lights of the speech. In either case, a release date is vital. There are two reasons for this: First, you don't want anyone to "scoop" what the speaker said; it might under-cut the speech's impact or even diminish the size of the audience. Second, unplanned things happen. The speaker's plane might be late or an emergency might prevent the speaker from showing up. In such a case, the media would look foolish in reporting a speech that was never made.

A final point about placing specific release dates on news releases: Don't do it unless there is a sound logical reason. In nine cases out of ten, the words "FOR IMMEDIATE RELEASE" are adequate. Also, don't make the mistake of saying something like: "FOR RELEASE in Jan. 16 edition only." Editors don't like to be told when they should print a particular item. *They* are the ones to make that decision.

Headlines

A brief headline at the beginning of the release will tell the gatekeeper what it is about. Some people say that it is presumptuous to write a headline on a news release. However, the headline is not necessarily suggested as a headline to be used. It is simply a summary of the release. Headlines such as the following would certainly seem helpful to editors:

> Outpatient Surgery Cuts Hospital Costs
>
> Apple Reports Results for Fiscal First Quarter
>
> Raychem Celebrates Twenty-fifth Anniversary
>
> Syntex Develops New Drug for Asthma Sufferers

Note that these headlines are all written in the active present tense. Avoid the past tense; it gives the impression that the news item is not timely. If you do use a headline, place it two or three spaces above the first line of the release. This means about two inches below the heading.

Structure

All news releases should be written in the "inverted pyramid" form. This means that the first paragraph or two tell the basic story and succeeding paragraphs add detail.

There are three reasons for this rule. First, if the gatekeeper doesn't find something interesting in the first few lines, he or she won't use the story. Second, editors often cut the length of an item, and they start at the bottom in doing so. If the main part of the story is at the beginning, it will still be understandable after one or more paragraphs are deleted. A third reason for using this structure is that people don't always read all of a news item. If they read only the beginning, they will still get the main facts.

CONTENT

Generations of editors have demanded that reporters include in their stories the five W's and one H: Who, What, When, Where, Why, and How. You should follow the same rule. If a news release answers these six questions, it will probably measure up.

The first step in preparing a news release is to make a brief outline—including the five W's and H—of what it is to contain.

In addition to using the five W's and H, which is done by journalists as well as public relations writers, you should plan the content and tone of a news release to meet the client's or employer's objectives.

The content and tone of a news release are determined by first completing a planning worksheet that answers the following questions:

- What is the subject of the message? What, specifically is the focus of this release?
- Who is this message designed to reach? For example, is it aimed at local citizens, or is it mainly for executives in other companies who read the business page and might order the product?
- What is in it for this particular audience? What are the potential benefits and rewards?
- What goals is the organization pursuing? What is the organization's purpose? Is it, for example, to increase sales of a product? Position the company as a leader in the field? Show company concern for the environment?
- What do you want to achieve with the news release? Is the objective merely to inform, to change attitudes and behavior, or perhaps to increase attendance at a local event?
- What themes should be highlighted in this news release? How can they be tailored to the interests of the audience?

These questions enable you to select and structure the contents of a news release from a public relations perspective. The release can still meet the journalistic goal of presenting information objectively and in proper newspaper or broadcast style, but then it must also be carefully crafted to advance organizational objectives. Otherwise it will only waste your time. Indeed, this kind of planning is the major difference between writing as a journalist and writing as a public relations person.

The Lead

This is the most important part of any release. In one or two paragraphs, it must arouse the interest of the gatekeeper. It must still carry the basic message even if the gatekeeper decides to cut off a large part of it. It must give the hasty reader the essentials of the story. If it is well written, it will encourage the editor to use the whole story and the hasty reader to read more. The lead should give the most newsworthy and important information in a concise and

1100 CENTRAL TRUST TOWER
P.O. BOX 5380
CINCINNATI, OHIO 45201
513 977-3825

CORPORATE COMMUNICATIONS

 **SCRIPPS HOWARD**

NEWS RELEASE

For Immediate Release
August 15, 1988

Contact: Terri Ruggerie
513/977-3825

Ten journalism students from across the country have been
selected as winners in the Roy W. Howard National Writing
Competition in Public Affairs Reporting and will participate in a
public affairs reporting seminar, to be held September 2-3 at
Indiana University, Bloomington, Ind.

The annual award competition and seminar are jointly sponsored
by the Scripps Howard Foundation and the Indiana University
School of Journalism.   The students will each receive $1,000 to
help finance their education.

The ten winners are: Robert Anderson, University of Missouri at
Columbia;   Jennifer Greer, Larry Lee and Steve Liewer, University
of Missouri; Claire Hueholt, Iowa State University at Ames; Blake
Kaplan, Louisiana State University at Baton Rouge; Janelle
Lawrence, Ohio University at Athens; Judy Lundstrom, Kansas
State University at Manhattan; Jeff Opdyke and Delia Taylor,
Louisiana State University.

-more-

An announcement release. This is the first page of a two-page release. The lead really
tells the story, and succeeding copy amplifies it. Note that "-more-" is used at the end
of the page to show that there is a second page. (*Source:* Scripps Howard, Cincinnati,
OH.)

interesting manner. If the release is an announcement, try to use the word "today." This will add to its timeliness.

There are two basic types of leads. First is the summary lead, which includes the key information in a brief statement, like this:

> Work will start today on Hewlett-Packard Company's new 154,000-square-foot engineering laboratory and manufacturing plant.

The second type is the interest lead, which focuses on the most unusual aspect of the item, like this:

> The machine that sparked the current revolution in sophisticated scientific and business calculators $3\frac{1}{2}$ years ago was retired today by Hewlett-Packard Company.

It is often impossible to include the What, Who, Where, When, Why, and How in the lead, as this might make it too long. (As a rule of thumb, it should be no longer than four or five typewritten lines.) One effective device is to start the lead with the most important basic element of the news story. For example:

What: "Fire, Earth, and Water," a major exhibit of pre-Columbian sculpture from the Land Collection, opens Friday. . . ."

Who: "Columbia recording artist Ramsey Lewis will appear at. . . ."

Where: "Jonesville will acquire a major manufacturing plant next year, when. . . ."

When: "November 8 will be the last date for filing claims for flood damage incurred during. . . ."

Why: "A shortage of skilled labor is forcing the Doe Manufacturing Co. to. . . ."

How: "Flex-Time, the system that permits employees to set their own starting and stopping times, has reduced labor turnover at Doe Enterprises by . . . ."

Here are some things to avoid in leads:

Prepositional phrases: "At a meeting held in the . . . ." or "For the first time in the history of. . . ."

Participial phrases: "Meeting in an atmosphere of confidence. . . ."

Dependent clauses: "That all high school students be required to. . . ."

Clutter: "Joe Doakes, veteran retailer and former mayor, at a meeting of the Chamber of Commerce to. . . ."

Following are examples of several different kinds of leads:

1. *Straight news lead* (Who, What, When, Where):
   "The California History Center of De Anza College will open the

school year Sept. 21 with a barbecue at 11 A.M. in Martin Murphy Historical Park, 235 E. California Ave., Sunnyvale."

2. *Modified straight news lead* (stressing a major theme):
"A Chicago thoracic surgeon who plans to focus study on national health insurance programs has been named president of the Cook County Medical Society."

3. *Informal lead* (designed to arouse interest):
"The sky will be ablaze with the crackle of scale-model machine-gun fire this weekend at the Hill Country Air Museum here." (Story about a model airplane exhibit.)

4. *Feature lead* (often used in magazine articles or human interest newspaper features):
"Jan Talbott is into the bike craze in a big way." (Story about a special-order bicycle to accommodate a 6-foot 6-inch man.)

Amplification

Once the lead is written, you must add additional information until the story is complete. There are two ways to do this. It can be done chronologically, as in a report on an athletic event, or it can be done in order of relative importance of the added information (or in the order used in the lead). Many writers tend to overdo the amplification. A good check is to observe how much detail is published on similar stories. If the publication you are writing for generally uses only two or three paragraphs, you should probably try to keep the release brief.

When the release is completed, it should be checked and double checked. Facts, figures, spelling, punctuation, grammar, sentence and paragraph length, clarity, and adherence to approved news style must be considered. Quotations and the spelling of names must be watched with extra care. A certain way to win the ill will of the medium is to issue a release that is inaccurate.

KINDS OF RELEASES

There are several kinds of releases, and each is done in a special way.

Announcements

These include such things as personnel appointments, promotions, and changes; new products or services (if they are really new and interesting); reports of sales, earnings, acquisitions, mergers, events, awards, honors, policy changes, employment opportunities, anniversaries, price changes, hirings, layoffs, construction, openings and closings of facilities, contracts received (or canceled), and legal actions (these, of course, must be checked with the organization's legal counsel).

Editorial wastebaskets throughout the country are filled with announcements that didn't make the grade. One of the most common reasons for this

---

San Mateo County Office of Education

News Release

---

333 Main Street • Redwood City, California 94063
DAVID JON SHEPARD, PUBLIC INFORMATION OFFICER (415) 363-5438

FOR IMMEDIATE RELEASE   October 5, 1988 — No. 6

WESTMOOR HIGH TEACHER NAMED SAN MATEO COUNTY'S TEACHER OF THE YEAR FOR 1989 . . . Janice Gaynor, Fine Arts Department Chairman at Jefferson Union High School District's Westmoor High, has been selected to be San Mateo County's Teacher of the Year for 1989, according to William K. Jennings, County Superintendent of Schools.

Gaynor, a resident of San Mateo, has taught in the Jefferson Union High District for 17 years. She earned her Bachelor of Arts, Secondary Credential, and Master of Arts at San Francisco State University. She has actively supported extracurricular musical activities both on campus and in community theater and community orchestral productions.

The Teacher of the Year competition, which is open to all K-12 teachers, is sponsored by the California State Department of Education, the Council of Chief State School Officers, Encyclopedia Britannica Companies, and Good Housekeeping Magazine.

Gaynor now will represent San Mateo County in the State competition.

* * *

The San Mateo County Office of Education is an intermediate educational agency that provides services to the 23 school districts in the County and to the California State Department of Education. Services to school districts include business services, data processing, administrative and curriculum assistance, professional library, films, videos, and educational technology. The Office conducts classes for students with special needs, vocational training courses through its Regional Occupational Program, and educational programs for wards of the Juvenile Court and County Community Schools.

Local human interest. A good release that did the job. When it reached the *San Mateo Times,* the local interest was obvious so a reporter and photographer were dispatched to interview the teacher. The story was published over six columns and included a large picture of the teacher in the classroom. (*Source:* San Mateo County Office of Education, San Mateo, CA.)

is lack of local interest. If the news is not important or interesting to the readers of the medium, it will not be used.

Tying an announcement into an event is a good way to add interest. Another way to make an announcement more newsworthy is to get some celebrity to deliver it. If a company can get the mayor to announce that it is going to do something, the chances of the story seeing print will be better than if some officer of the company had been the spokesman. Of course, it is important to state clearly just who is doing what.

Spot News

When things that are due to some outside action or influence happen to an organization, a spot news release may be in order. When a storm disrupts the services of a public utility, when a fire or accident stops work, when a flood closes roads, when a strike closes a factory—all these and many other incidents can lead to the issuance of a release that tells what has happened and what effect it is having.

If the affected organization doesn't give the news to the media, reporters will write a story and may do a poor job because they don't have all the facts. In many cases, follow-up stories must be released on later days. These may carry additional detailed information and report on progress in solving the problem.

Reaction Releases

These are used when something is done or said that may harm an organization. Some examples: a charge that a factory has unsafe working conditions, a lawsuit claiming injury, a finding by the Food and Drug Administration that a certain food additive may cause cancer (as with nitrites in bacon).

When a government agency decides to stop funding a particular activity, those affected by the cutback will issue reaction releases proclaiming that the project is essential and that no budget cuts should be made.

Another use of the reaction release is to hitch onto something that, while not harmful to the organization, has some bearing on it. For instance, if the Environmental Protection Agency announces an easing of controls, an affected company might issue a release stating that it will continue its policy of nonpollution and outline how it is doing so.

Bad News

Some organizations still try to suppress news that might reflect badly on them. This is a sure way to make things worse. People will talk, rumors will spread, and investigative reporters will try to get the facts. There will be talk and possibly even news items charging a coverup.

WESTIN
HOTELS & RESORTS
Mexico

News

CONTACT: Victoria Von Arx
         or Donata Maggipinto
         (415) 982-5400

FOR IMMEDIATE RELEASE

CAMINO REAL CANCUN GAUGES HURRICANE DAMAGE, LAUNCHES CLEAN-UP

Cancun, September 21---The Camino Real hotel in Cancun has launched clean-up efforts to offset the effects of Hurricane Gilbert which assaulted this Mexican Caribbean resort September 13th.

According to executives of Camino Real Hotels who recently returned from a site surveying trip to Cancun, the hotel's damages were confined to the first floor and outdoor areas. "The hotel suffered water damage to its first floor guest rooms, food and beverage outlets and offices. In addition, the hurricane's high winds caused broken windows and landscape erosion,"said Nick Van der Kaaij, vice president, operations, for Camino Real Hotels. "However, we are fortunate. The Camino Real fared better than many other hotels in Cancun. Since the damage was limited to the first floor area, our clean-up time will be minimal."

Ogilvy & Mather Public Relations, 10 Lombard Street, San Francisco, CA 94111

Handling bad news. This release went to travel writers shortly after a hurricane damaged many buildings in Mexico. The second page reported that there were no injuries in the hotels and that they were open for business. A timely release like this reassures travelers and reduces cancellations. (*Source:* Ogilvy & Mather Public Relations, San Francisco, CA.)

The only way to make the best of such a situation is to tell the truth. A release giving the facts clearly and completely should be drafted immediately. If reporters ask for information, it should be given to them.

An excellent example of mishandling bad news began when the *Washington Post* got a list of banks that were supposedly having problems. In an effort to check the accuracy of the list, the financial editor of the *Los Angeles Times* called each of the banks. No one would comment. When the *Times* then ran the story, the banks raised hell. If the banks had cooperated with the *Times* or offered a factual release, public reaction would have been much less negative.

Some organizations have a penchant for trying to bury bad news within a story. One such release started out with this lead (names changed to protect the guilty):

> "Joe Doakes, president and chief executive officer of XYZ, a Houston-based specialty apparel firm, Friday announced the key elements developed as a result of intensive strategic planning and market analysis which began two years ago."

In the third paragraph, the firm got around to announcing the closure of seven stores in several states. Four days later, it announced in barely sixty words that the whole chain had been put up for sale. That little detail apparently was not a "key" element in the lead issued four days earlier.

Magazine Releases

Special-interest magazines such as *Motor Trend* and trade magazines like *Chain Store Age* rely heavily on releases for their news content. There are hundreds of national, regional, and local publications of this kind. Some are true magazines and some are newspapers confined to a particular field, such as *Women's Wear Daily*, or local business publications, like *Houston Business Journal*.

All publications of this nature have different standards. In general, however, they will and do use longer releases than regular newspapers do. Again, the key to producing a release that will be used is to read the publication and conform to its pattern. As for content, it must be of interest to the readers. The manager of a store selling women's clothing may be interested in how a new textile fiber will affect the appearance, wearability, and cleanability of a garment. She will not care much about the chemistry involved in producing the fiber. Yet a reader of *Chemical Week* could read about that subject with avidity.

In writing releases for such publications, the writer may be tempted to edge toward a feature article. This should be handled very carefully, because no publication wants to use the same story as one of its competitors—and there are competitors in practically every special field. If a release seems to head this way, it is time for you to cut it down to hard facts and plan to prepare one or more feature articles from the basic material.

Fact Sheets

In some cases it may be desirable to send out a fact sheet rather than a news release. Many editors hate to use anyone's news release and always completely rewrite the stories submitted. One format that has worked well is to list the information in the form of the five W's and H. A fact sheet about a new medical office building gave the following information:

What: A description of the new building.

Who: The name of the builder.

Where: The street address and nearness to hospitals.

When: Date of construction start and expected completion.

Why: The need for more modern buildings with newer equipment.

How: The architects and facilities consultants.

The fact sheet was accompanied by a photo of the architects' rendering. The result was a four-column picture with a long caption carrying all the information in the fact sheet.

Not all fact sheets follow the format described above. Many are quite different, being essentially background information that is not tied to a specific news item. But even these may be sent along with a news release and are nearly always included in press kits. (For details on fact sheets and press kits, see Chapter 10.)

LOCALIZING

Many organizations send out hundreds of releases to hundreds or thousands of publications and wonder why so few are used. The most common reason is that there is no local interest. Editors throughout the country reiterate this complaint, asking "Why don't they give us something that is interesting to *our* readers?"

There are two basic ways to localize. One is to use the names of local people; the other is to use information that is of local significance. Doing this requires an individual release for each publication. With a word processor, it is possible to drop into a basic release the words, sentences, or paragraphs that localize the story. Without a word processor, the task is more laborious but still feasible.

In either case the unit cost is higher but the efficiency is much greater, so that—on the basis of cost per placement—the localized release is cheaper.

Suppose you were trying to publicize a meeting of insurance agents from a particular company. The meeting would be news in the city where the meeting was held, so you would certainly issue a release to the papers in that city. Then, a localized release could go to every city or town from which an agent came. This release would include the name of the agent attending the meeting.

Additional information would add meat to the story. Thus the release

FACT SHEET

PROJECT: RUN AROUND AMERICA
                    10,610 miles

PURPOSE: To raise awareness and encourage participation in
                    physical fitness and to generate funds for the
                    United States Fitness Academy

RUNNER: Sarah Covington Fulcher, age 25
                    Ran 2,727 miles across Australia from Sydney to
                    Perth in 96 days in the fall of 1986 to raise
                    money for world hunger. Graduate of Salem
                    College, North Carolina and a former Marine.

START DATE: July 21, 1987   FINISH DATE: May, 1988 (estimated)

LOCATION: Start and finish at Laguna Hills, California at
                    the site of the United States Fitness Academy.

MAJOR CITIES: Los Angeles, San Francisco, Seattle, Chicago,
                    Detroit, Syracuse, Boston, New York, Philadelphia,
                    Baltimore, Washington, Miami, New Orleans,
                    Houston, San Antonio, Phoenix, San Diego.

ADMINISTRATION: David Buckley (Project Director), Carla Doolittle
                    (Administrative Assistant)

SUPPORT TEAM: Mark Mayers (trainer), Leslie Mayers (trainer),
                    Ann Marlatt (massage therapist), Mark Fulcher
                    (logistics).

SPONSORS: ARCO, Biotune, Bonne Bell

MEDICAL   Dr. John Cates, Ph.D. (UC San Diego), Dr. Gene
ADVISORY TEAM: Profant, M.D. (cardiologist), Dr. Michael
                    Hairston.

CONTACT: Jerry Lenander
                    Jenkins/Mimms/Robbins
                    A Public Relations Company
                    1223 N. Sweetzer
                    Los Angeles, CA 90069
                    (213) 650-7154

BONNE BELL   ARCO ◆   BIO*TUNE*™
                                    The Ultimate Nutritional Enhancer

9601 Jeronimo Road • Irvine, CA 92718 • (714) 859-1011 • El Segundo, (213) 640-0145
Contributions are deductible for income tax purposes

Facts make news. This fact sheet was prepared to give journalists the basic facts regarding an upcoming event. A fact sheet allows reporters to write their own story or keep the information on file for a possible story later. (*Source:* Jenkins, Mimms, Robbins, Studio City, CA.)

might give the length of time the agent had represented the company, as well as the agent's local activities (such as membership in civic organizations and any public service activities in which he or she had participated).

The release might, for example, inform readers that Jane Smith has attended the annual meeting of the Universal Insurance Company in Memphis, that Smith has represented Universal for 15 years, that she has been chairman of the local Chamber of Commerce, and that she is a member of St. Matthew's Church.

The release should also include general information about the company, such as nature of insurance written, total volume of business, and any distinctions the company has earned. Details of the convention might include the number of agents in attendance, names of prominent speakers, and so on.

Details like these make a release interesting. They greatly increase the probability of use and aid the organization by distributing information about it. Getting these details takes work; it may require asking lots of questions; and it takes time. But when the digging is done, the result will be better releases.

Localizing by using material that is locally significant is another way to get releases published. A lumber-company release about the effect of mortgage rates on building construction and its related sales of lumber might reach the business pages of newspapers and trade publications. Details telling how this situation will affect employment in the towns where the lumber is produced would be of great interest in those localities and would probably be published in full.

To get full value out of localizing a news release, you should get the local interest into the lead. The fact that the Universal Insurance Company held a meeting of its sales agents is not likely to strike a spark with the editor of the *Smalltown Sentinel*. But if the story begins with the fact that Jane Smith of Smalltown attended a meeting of agents representing Universal Insurance Company, the editor will probably print the story.

Some trade associations, in order to localize news, will send their members a generic news release containing blanks that are to be filled in with local information. For example, the National Association of Realtors used the following form:

Home resale activity in _____ during the first quarter of this year was
                              (state)
_____% _____ than in the first quarter last year,
              (higher/lower)
_____ reports.
(name of state state organization or spokesman)

In this way, local offices have the structure of the release already set up for them, so they only have to fill in the blanks and send the complete release to the local media. In all cases, however, the local organization should retype the entire news release. Media gatekeepers are always amused (and probably unimpressed) when a local group merely fills in the blanks.

MULTIPLYING

It is possible to produce several different releases from one general story, and these releases may go to a variety of media. If Susan Roe has been appointed executive vice president of the Mammoth Manufacturing Company, the story would go to local news media, the trade magazines serving the industry, magazines of trades using Mammoth's products, towns or cities where Roe lived or grew up, her college alumni publication, and the publications of organizations to which Roe belongs.

In each case the release would be individualized, but all would contain information about the Mammoth Manufacturing Company. Individualizing requires writing the release to fit the medium to which it will be released. For a metropolitan daily, the release should be about one paragraph long—unless the company is of great importance. In that case, it may be longer and give more details. For trade publications, "hometown" papers, and organizational publications, the release may be more lengthy.

PLACEMENT

A news release does no good unless it is published. Getting anything published is called "placement." Placement depends on delivering the story to the right gatekeeper through the right channels at the right time.

The Gatekeepers

You must give the story to the editor or reporter who is most likely to be interested in the particular subject. Thus anything about food would go to the food editor and anything about entertainment would go to the entertainment editor or reporter. Large papers have many editors, while smaller papers often have editors covering several subjects.

You can find their names in the media directories (see Chapter 10). For weekly newspapers and most magazines, your contact is the editor, although some large magazines have a number of specialized editors.

There is much controversy about the practice of sending a news release to more than one person at a paper. If two editors or reporters come up with the same story, each may feel that he or she has been duped. One way to avoid this is to send the release to one gatekeeper and provide copies—marked F.Y.I. (for your information)—to any others who might be interested. The original would show who got copies and copies would show to whom the original was sent.

Delivery Channels

There are several ways to send a news release to a newspaper or broadcast outlet. They include the following:

NEWS RELEASE

RYDER TRUCK RENTAL, INC.   PO BOX 020816   MIAMI FLORIDA 33102-0816

FOR IMMEDIATE RELEASE

Contact: David C. Dawson
          305/593–3210

HOUSTON IS GAINING EDGE ON DALLAS IN HOUSEHOLDS RELOCATING
BETWEEN THE TWO CITIES, RYDER STUDY FINDS

Recent Figures Show Slightly More Households Moving to Houston From
Dallas, Rather Than Vice-versa

HOUSTON, September 3, 1987 — Dallas is the most popular
destination for people relocating from Houston, and also ranks as the top
city from which people are moving to Houston. However, according to
the newest figures, Houston appears to be winning the "tug of war" for
new residents between the two cities. The second most popular
destination for people relocating from Houston is Austin, followed by San
Antonio, Atlanta, Fort Worth and Los Angeles.

These figures were released today by Ryder Truck Rental, the
world's largest truck leasing and rental company, and are based on
information gathered from Ryder's 6,000 truck rental dealers nationwide
as well as statistics from various government sources.

Ryder also noted that this coming Labor Day weekend will be one of
the busiest moving periods of the year, with about 500,000 Americans
moving. About 80 percent will do it themselves, using either a rented or
borrowed vehicle.

Other popular destination cities for people relocating from Houston
include Washington, D.C., Corpus Christi, Longview, Beaumont and
Phoenix.

The second largest source of people moving to the Houston area was
Austin, followed by San Antonio, Fort Worth, Corpus Christi, New
Orleans and Atlanta.

# # #

Localizing makes news. Ryder Truck Rental conducted a national survey and then sent
localized news releases to appropriate newspapers. By taking the time to localize information, a public relations writer can significantly increase the amount of media coverage. (*Source:* Ryder Truck Rental, Inc., Miami, FL.)

Houston, Dallas in a 'tug of war' for new residents

By DIANE FREEMAN
Post Business Writer 4504K

Houstonians are moving to Dallas more than any other city while Houston ranks as the top destination for people relocating from Dallas, truck rental companies say.

Although most of the firms said the numbers are about even, *Ryder Truck Rentals* said Houston appears to be winning the "tug of war" for new residents between the two cities.

The second largest source of people moving to the Houston area was Austin, followed by San Antonio, Fort Worth, Corpus Christi, New Orleans and Atlanta, the firm said.

The information was gathered from Ryder's truck rental dealers as well as statistics from various government sources.

"Between Houston and Dallas, the numbers are about even. I've never seen that happen before," said Diane Boschian, spokeswoman for U-Haul Co. "Nationwide, people aren't moving as much and it's not from state to state," she said. "They move, but

they stay in a close radius."

Hertz Penske Truck Rental also noted the heavy movement between Houston and Dallas as well as Houstonians relocating from San Antonio and other cities in the region.

"There's not nearly as many people leaving Houston as a year ago," said Leonard Schneider, Hertz Penske truck rental manager.

David Dawson, spokesman for Ryder Trucks, said movement out of Houston has stablized. "Last year we couldn't keep a truck in Houston," he said.

"People are moving more regionally, and the length of the average move has dropped off significantly," he said.

Other popular destination cities for people moving out of Houston include Washington D.C., Corpus Christi, Longview, Beaumont and Phoenix, he said.

Ryder noted that this Labor Day weekend will be one of the busiest moving periods of the year, with about 500,000 Americans moving. About 80 percent will do it themselves, using either a rented or borrowed vehicle, the company said.

Localizing pays off. This is what happened to the release on the opposite page. The *Houston Post* reporter called other moving companies for additional information but used most of the material in the release. Ryder's name appeared three times. (*Source: The Houston Post,* copyright © 1987.)

- *First-class mail.* This is the primary delivery method for news releases even in the age of satellites and electronic transmission.
- *Overnight delivery.* This service, offered by the U.S. Postal Service, Federal Express, United Parcel Service, and Airborne—to name only a few—allows overnight delivery of letters and packages to almost any part of the United States. Western Union also offers overnight services and can send hundreds of copies of the same release to various outlets.
- *Messenger or courier services.* Most metropolitan areas have messenger services that can deliver material to a media outlet in the same city or area within hours.
- *Facsimile transmission.* Increasingly, public relations people are transmitting news releases and other documents via telephone lines. All you need is a facsimile machine that converts the document to electronic signals, which are then transmitted over a regular telephone line to another facsimile machine that reproduces the document. A facsimile—or fax, as it is called—can be sent as quickly as you can dial a phone.
- *Computer-to-computer transmission.* Specialized wire services provide transmission of news releases directly into the computers of newspapers, magazines, broadcasters, and news services. Editors then call up the stories on their terminals and select what they want. This is the most significant advance in the development of paperless public relations.
- *Telephone.* You can call a reporter or editor to convey the highlights of a news story over the phone. This works best when you want the newspapers to assign a reporter to the story or when a radio station wants to record a comment from you in what is called "an actuality." (See Chapter 10.)

If you call an editor or reporter, be brief and to the point. Don't open the conversation with banal chat about the weather or his or her state of health. Just identify yourself, your organization, and the nature of the story you have.

The call might be as simple as this: "This is Susan Peabody of Community Hospital. We are going to open a new outpatient clinic on Wednesday that will cut the cost of surgical operations for many patients. The operating suites have state-of-the-art equipment and there are some interesting photo opportunities. Would you be interested in receiving more information or assigning a reporter to cover the event?"

There is no universal rule on how best to deliver a news release to the media. One New York editor says, "I prefer to get information over the phone. Call me first and give me the lead or headline." A number of editors are just as adamant that they *don't* want to be bothered by phone calls and prefer to have news releases mailed to them. Most papers prefer not to have releases delivered by hand.

The key to successful delivery of your news release is to find out from the various media how they would like to receive your material—by first-class mail, overnight delivery, messenger or courier, facsimile, computer-to-computer, or phone.

Timing

News releases must be timely. The media thrive on late-breaking information and want to know about events when they happen, not a week later. If it is not possible to get information distributed right away, a common technique is to make sure there are no references to specific dates in the release. The announcement of a new company president, for example, would not say that he was appointed two weeks ago.

Pre-event releases should be sent to gatekeepers at least four or five days ahead of time, so the editors can process the information and get it into the newspaper in timely fashion. If a major event is planned, editors appreciate as much advance information as possible so that they can plan their "menu" or "budget."

Evening papers go to press about noon. The deadline for news is variable, but usually it is early in the morning. A news story of great importance may get used even if it comes in just before press time, but most stories must be in newsroom well before the "budget" or "menu" meeting. As a general rule, get your stories to the paper one or two days before publication.

Morning papers go to press in the evening, sometimes as late as 10 or 11 o'clock. This late closing enables the paper to cover news up to late afternoon, but you cannot expect consideration of your offerings if they come in late. As a general guide, get your stories to the newsroom by noon at the latest.

Weekly newspapers and magazines have longer deadlines than dailies. For weeklies, you should get your news in a week before the publication date. Occasionally, a hot piece of news may be accepted up to the day before publication, but don't count on it.

Monthly publications need more than a month for preparation, so if you want to make the January issue, the news should get there not later than mid-November.

HOW NOT TO DO IT

In spite of all that has been said by editors about sending usable releases, there are still people who grind out garbage and hope that someone will print it. Here are some horrible examples.

The first, is reprinted from the *Public Relations Journal:*

> editorial production director
> Association Sterline films
> 866x 3rd AvezNYC NY

Typos aside, who would send news releases to the "editorial production director?" And of a film distribution firm at that:

This comedy of errors actually got better (or worse). The first release inside this envelope—which began with double-spaced typing and lapsed into single-spaced lines about halfway down the page—announced: "Veteran Furrier TURNED 'SEASHELL' CREATIVE ARTIST. . . ." The release ended with a note to editors that the furrier was "available with his art work for interviews and radio and tv appearances."

A second release in the packet, this one single-spaced on a 14-inch sheet, announced: "ATTRACTIVE YOUTHFUL HUSBAND AND WIFE TEAM IN APPAREL MANUFACTURING FIELD ACHIEVE THREE MILLION DOLLAR VOLUME IN THREE YEARS. . . ." After a lengthy discussion of the couple's business, the release ended with this note to editors: "X is a top-notch homemaker and gourmet cook—their apartment in Greenwich Village is always full of happy laughter—their children having friends over, etc."

The example points to another rule of successful news-release writing. Stick to the facts. Don't describe the new president of a company as a "charming, witty man with one of the most brilliant minds in American business." If he is all this, it will show up in the listing of his accomplishments.

The following release was sent to the business editor of a small daily. (We give you only the first few lines.)

# # # # #

"FOR IMMEDIATE RELEASE, REPLACES RELEASE OF MAY, 19XX JUNE, 19XX

Internally-Matched GaAs FETs offer 3 watt output over 3.7-4.2 and 5.9-6.4 GHz bands

XXXXX, Inc. Santa Clara, CA is the first American manufacturer to offer internally-matched GaAs FETs for the 3.7-4.2 GHz and 5.9-6.4 GHz communication bands from stock for immediate delivery."

# # # # #

Remember the following don'ts about news-release writing:

1. Don't write lead paragraphs that are 14 lines long and loaded with compound sentences.
2. Don't use flowery adjectives—stick to the facts.
3. Don't place the name of the company or the product all in capital letters, even if it's trademarked that way.
4. Don't use highly technical jargon that only a scientist or engineer would understand.
5. Don't make a news release so commercial that it sounds like an advertisement.

TIPS OF THE TRADE

Remembering these facts will help you do a better job.

1. Your function is not to get a story published just as you wrote it. Your function is to get information to the media.

2. Get acquainted with the gatekeepers, but don't drop in on them when they are up against a deadline. Pick a time when things are relatively quiet.

3. Newspapers operate with skeleton staffs on weekends. You are not likely to reach a gatekeeper by phone on Saturday or Sunday.

4. Sunday papers have more space to fill and more opportunity to use long news items or even features—especially in the Sunday magazine or special sections.

5. Monday papers are usually short of news. That means a greater opportunity for you. Try to get a release for Monday into the newsroom on Saturday.

6. Summer finds many reporters on vacation, but there are still pages to be filled with news. Your news may get published then but omitted if it arrives in October.

7. Holiday weekends and the last week of the year are often short on news.

8. Newspapers are the backbone of publicity campaigns. There are about 1,700 dailies and 6,000 weeklies in the United States, and all need news.

9. Don't overlook magazines: business, trade, special-interest, and professional. Most of them are in need of material.

10. Remember demographics. Just who is reached by any medium? Aim your publicity at the media that reach the people you want to inform or influence.

Tip Sheets

There are several publications containing tips on the kinds of news and feature material wanted by specific media. These sheets are available on a subscription basis. They are not cheap but can be very helpful because they are based on requests from the gatekeepers themselves.

Among the larger tip sheets are the following:

- *PR Aids Party Line* (a weekly roundup of current placement opportunities in all media)
- *Contacts* (a weekly newsletter examining the editorial needs of newspapers, syndicates, and magazines)
- *Trade Media News* (a twice-monthly newsletter outlining the editorial schedules and information needs of editors of trade and professional publications)

SUMMARY

1. A news release must be on white or light-colored $8\frac{1}{2}$- by 11-inch paper. It must be accurately typed and always double spaced. There must be a heading to show where it came from. There must be a date and a

release date. A headline may be used. The pyramidal format is always used.

2. A press release must always tell who, what, when, where, why, and how. The lead is the most important part of the release. It leads the reader into the story. Amplification expands on the lead and completes the story.

3. There are several kinds of releases: announcements, spot news, reaction releases, and bad-news releases. There are also magazine releases, which differ slightly from newspaper releases.

4. Press releases must be localized for the media in which they are to appear.

5. You can multiply your releases by taking one basic news item and modifying it for different publications.

6. If your releases are to be published, they must get to the right gatekeeper.

7. News must be new; your news must get to the publication at the right time.

8. Don't ever send out a release that is full of puffery or technical jargon.

9. Follow the tips of the veterans who *do* get their releases used.

EXERCISES

1. Visit a local newspaper office and collect a number of news releases that the editors have discarded or have used. Write short critiques of at least five of these from the standpoint of writing style and content as discussed in this chapter. Some criteria you might use include (1) general format, (2) length of lead paragraph, (3) local news angles, (4) timeliness, and (5) overall writing style.

2. A news release must not be too commercial or sound like an advertisement for a product. Select an advertisement from a magazine or newspaper about an automobile and, using the same information, write a news release that would be acceptable to a news person.

3. Using the fact sheet about the Run Around America reprinted in this chapter, write a news release targeted to the media in Chicago.

4. Write a news release for your college newspaper about the upcoming meeting of a student organization that has invited a guest speaker.

5. The Balcor Corporation, a diversified commercial real estate company, has a new president. He is Harvey Wilson, formerly executive vice president of Knox Company, a developer of suburban shopping malls. He replaces Adam Smith, president of Balcor for the past 15 years, who has announced his retirement. Wilson's appointment was announced by Balcor's board of directors.

   Wilson's background is as follows:

   - He is 52 years old.
   - He is married and has two children in college.
   - He has been the executive vice president of Knox Company for the past seven years. Prior to this, he served as the chief financial officer of several construction firms including Krupp Company which, builds hotels around the globe.

- He has a B.A. degree in accounting from the University of Washington and an M.B.A. from Stanford University.
- He is a member of the National Accounting Association and was formerly on its board; the Illinois Business Round Table, an organization of business executives; the Chicago Sailing Club; and the Chicago Athletic Club.
- He is respected in the construction and real estate industries for his quiet, efficient management style.
- Presently, he resides in Arlington Heights, Illinois.
- He will assume the presidency of Balcor, headquartered in Atlanta, next month.
- Balcor Corporation owns a number of office parks across the nation and manages 22 other business properties. Total revenue last year was $47 million.

Your assignment is to write a news release announcing Wilson's appointment for the local and national real estate trade press.

6. One way for an organization to get news coverage is to sponsor a poll on a subject that is timely, newsworthy, and related to the organizations's product or service. Magic Pan, a chain of restaurants, took this approach when it commissioned a survey to determine attitudes about women hosting a man at a business lunch.

   The following is a summary of the survey findings. On the basis of the information supplied, write two news releases. One should be written for submission to the business editor of metropolitan daily newspapers. The second should be written for trade newspapers and magazines catering to the restaurant industry. In planning these releases, you might use the worksheet questions mentioned in the discussion of content.

   MAGIC PAN STUDY REVEALS
   WOMEN AND MEN AT EASE
   WHEN WOMEN PAY THE CHECK
   With more than half of all Americans eating one out of three meals away from home, restaurant operators are more eager than ever to identify trends that motivate people and enhance their dining experiences in restaurants. One trend that has been largely unexplored until recently is the dining occasion where the woman is the host and a man is her guest.

   With the evolution of the women's revolution and more than 42 million women employed outside the home, today's woman is becoming at ease in her role of "picking up the tab" when she entertains men for business or social occasions. And so are the men who are being entertained. This general finding emerged from a national survey just released by The Magic Pan Restaurants entitled "The Entertaining Woman . . . at ease in the 80's."

   This independent study was conducted by The Gallup Organization and surveyed men and women, 25 years and older in professional and business or sales occupations. Of all the men and women queried about one-third responded that they had been in a dining situation where the woman paid the check. While it's evident that not everyone is doing it, those who do, report being comfortable about it.

   MAN IS ASSUMED TO BE HOST
   Although men and women are comfortable about the woman paying the check, waiters and waitresses appear to need some direction. Both men and women report that waiters/waitresses assume the man is the host, and this is confirmed by the fact that the man gets the wine list and the check most of the time. Two-thirds of both men and women reported that the man gets the wine list, while about eight in ten reported that the man gets the check.

   The Magic Pan sees this trend becoming more commonplace in the 80's and recognizes the need for speciality restaurants to provide service that will enhance this dining experience for both sexes. Magic Pan, whose guests are principally women (70%), fits the criteria mentioned by both men and women—a definite preference for a restaurant that is quiet and conducive to conversation for business or social occasions.

A closer look at the study reveals some interesting reactions from men and women that relate to the role reversal experience.

WOMEN PAY THE CHECK MORE OFTEN FOR SOCIAL DINING

When a woman takes a man out to lunch or dinner, it is more often for a social occasion than for business. Women don't seem to mind using their disposable income, as opposed to expense accounts, to entertain a man in a restaurant for social enjoyment.

MOST DON'T SQUIRM WHEN SHE PAYS

Although the majority of men say they feel no discomfort or embarrassment in having the woman pay the check, younger men do appear to be more likely than older men to feel at ease. Eighty percent of the women indicate they don't feel uncomfortable about paying the check.

BETTER SERVICE WITH A MAN

Women notice that they get better service when they dine with a man than with a woman or alone. Older women experienced this more often than those under 40. One in five women also thought they were given a better table when they were with a man.

WHO PAYS THE CHECK?

Two-thirds of the women are "allowed" to pay the check. That is, their male guests do not object at all when the woman pays the tab.

But of the one-third who do get objections, nearly one-half of the women "sometimes" let the man pay (48%), while 22% either always or usually let their male guest pick up the check.

WOMEN ASSUME STEAK IS MAN'S PREFERENCE

For business or social dining, women are more inclined to select a steak house when a man is their guest. However, fewer men reported this preference when being invited by a woman for lunch or dinner. Perhaps women are assuming a long held belief that men prefer heavier meals and that a steak type meal would suit their tastes better. Approximately three in ten (26%) of the men reported that they couldn't say what type of restaurant they preferred when being entertained by a woman for a business occasion. Apparently, many of the men don't have a strong preference for a particular type of restaurant for business or social occasions.

Men appear to be making progress in accepting this role reversal experience. Thirty-six percent rarely or never refuse to let the woman pay the check.

Conducting studies and investigating trends like Magic Pan's first survey "The Entertaining Woman . . . at ease in the 80's," will continue to play an important part in restaurant management in the new decade.

According to Magic Pan president James J. Durkin, "We recognize that more women are eating out, that they are willing and able to spend more money for dining. They are very important to our restaurants' business. We are recommending and encouraging our staff to be sensitive and observant to situations where the woman is the host and will pay the check. And we believe that women, just like men, can and should identify their role as host when dining with a man or in a group. This can be done when being seated, when the order is taken—or simply at the end of the meal. 'May I have the check, please?' always gets results!"

SUGGESTED READINGS

Baxter, Bill. "The News Release: An Idea Whose Time Has Gone?" *Public Relations Review*, Spring 1981, pp. 27–31.

Bivens, Thomas. "News Releases and Backgrounders." *Handbook for Public Relations Writing*. Lincolnwood, IL: NTC Business Books, 1988, chap. 1.

DiCostanzo, Frank. "What the Press Thinks of Press Releases." *Public Relations Quarterly*, Winter 1986–87, pp. 22–24.

Elfenbein, Dick. "Business Journalists Say If It's Not Local, It's Trashed." *Public Relations Quarterly*, Summer 1986, pp. 17–19.

Morton, Linda P. "Effectiveness of Camera-Ready Copy in Press Releases." *Public Relations Review*, Summer 1988, pp. 45–49.

Morton, Linda P. "How Newspapers Choose the Releases They Use." *Public Relations Review*, Fall 1986, pp. 22–27.

Newsom, Doug, and Carrell, Bob. "News Releases for Print Media." *Public Relations Writing: Form and Style*. Belmont CA: Wadsworth Publishing, 1986, chap. 7.

Solomon, Julie. "Business Communication in the FAX Age." *Wall Street Journal*, Oct. 27, 1988, p. B1.

Stecker, Elinor. "Make Your Product News Releases Newsworthy." *Communication World*, August 1984, pp. 30–31.

Vermeer, Jans Pons. *For Immediate Release: Candidate Press Releases in American Political Campaigns*. Westport, CT: Greenwood Press, 1982.

Chapter
6

The Feature Story

Writing feature stories is a vital part of public relations work. In many organizations, writing features is far more important than writing news releases.

There are two basic kinds of features. The first is the brief release in "news" format, which is sent to the media without any assurance that it will be used. This is usually sent to a specific section editor—food, fashion, entertainment, travel, and so on. The second is longer, more detailed, and usually written for a specific magazine after the editor has shown interest in publishing it.

PURPOSE

Every feature story must have a purpose: It must convey specific information to a particular audience. Its objective is to create in the minds of the readers, listeners, or viewers a definite attitude about the subject.

A feature on avocados might try to convince nonusers that they should try a recipe that calls for them. A feature telling how a local company disposes of toxic waste might inform citizens about the process and assure them that this is being done effectively.

A feature on tire care might show how to increase tire life and reduce gasoline consumption. Another on variable-rate motgages might show home buyers the advantages and disadvantages of these instruments. A story on a machine for building concrete curbs without using forms might show how contractors could reduce their costs. A feature on a new wrapping material might show how the life of gas pipelines could be extended.

In each of these examples, there is a definite benefit to the sponsor. The company can improve its community relations. The avocado growers may gain increased sales. An oil or tire company might improve its public image. A savings and loan company may get credit for considering the public interest— and get new customers. The machine manufacturer may develop new sales. The maker of the pipeline wrapping material may get new users.

FORMAT

In contrast to a news item, where the lead summarizes the story and the remainder expands on the lead, a feature story does not require a specific format. The writer's purpose is to get the story read in its entirety. Any structure that arouses interest, supplies significant information, and leaves the reader with a definite idea may be used. Subheads are not used in news items, but they may be very important in features, where they serve to highlight different parts of the whole.

Illustrations are common in features. A news item may carry one picture, such as a photograph of the person or thing discussed in the story. Illustrations in a feature may include photographs, charts, diagrams, or anything else that helps to explain the subject.

Feature articles usually run much longer than news items. There is no real guide as to length, but many run to two or three thousand words (six to eight pages). Application features may be considerably shorter, and some depth studies may be much longer. The practical guide is to use enough words to tell the story thoroughly but to stop writing when it is told. Since most features are planned for specific publications, a look at the average length of features in the chosen medium should suggest an appropriate length.

A feature normally consists of three parts: the lead, the body of the story, and a summary. All are important.

The Lead

The purpose of the lead is to attract attention and get the reader interested enough to read the whole article. The lead must promise some sort of reward.

This means that you must know just who you are writing for and why that person should be interested. The feature lead must appeal to the self-interest of the reader. It should arouse curiosity and answer the unspoken question: What's in it for me?

Human interest makes a good lead—as in statements like this: "Ten years ago Juan Garcia started to work for ABC Corporation in the shipping department. Today he is assistant vice-president for customer service. Juan is only one of many Mexican-Americans who have climbed the ladder of success as a result of ABC's training program for minorities."

Excellent examples of the human-interest or personalized lead are often found on the front page of the *Wall Street Journal.*

One story began with this lead: "Gregory Miller is kneeling to repair a fence when, without warning, a 35-pound baboon hurtles through the air and lands on his shoulders. Mr. Miller doesn't flinch, but quietly reaches for his pliers to continue his work." Such a lead does a great deal to arouse reader curiosity; it is much more effective than a straight news lead, merely announcing the establishment of a refuge for exotic animals.

A good lead may focus on the most unusual part of the feature. Thus a lead introducing the machine that builds curbs without forms could start with these words: "The formless curber lays concrete curbs without the use of expensive forms." This statement is factual and true, but the feature would be much more interesting if it started like this: "It's just like squeezing toothpaste out of a tube. In fact, it works on the same principle. By squeezing the concrete through a die shaped like the final curbing, it is possible to lay concrete curbs without the labor and materials needed for forms." This lead should appeal to the contractor who is a prospective buyer of the machine. It is unusual, it is interesting, and it promises the reward of dollar savings.

The pipeline-wrapping feature could start with a matter-of-fact statement, but it would be more attractive to the reader if it started with something like this: "Last year Standard Gas Pipeline Company spent $14 million replacing corroded pipelines, which had lasted an average of 16 years. Now Standard is installing lines that are expected to last 30 years because they are being wrapped in a new corrosion-resistant material."

The Body of the Story

In the body of the story, you must deliver the reward promised in the lead. Here details and facts are essential. This requires research. You must gather the information substantiating the opening statement. You must also use statements and concrete examples; names, places, and direct quotations from people mentioned will help to make the feature believable. As a general guide, you should have much more information than can actually be used. This will allow you to select the most interesting items and guarantee that the article will be loaded with information—not burdened with unnecessary words.

The feature should be clear and logical; that is, the sequence of ideas should lead toward a definite conclusion. This will enable the reader to see how he or she can benefit.

In presenting facts, it may be necessary to offer evidence proving their accuracy. Flat statements may be challenged; however, if they can be supported with information from unbiased sources, they are acceptable. Direct quotes from authorities and citations from official records, prestigious references (such as recognized encyclopedias), or important books will help to confirm the writer's statements.

Another point to keep in mind is the use of parallels. A strange subject will be more understandable if it is explained in familiar terms—as in the toothpaste example. In the amplification of that story, the writer would undoubtedly explain how the concrete is squeezed out of the die by the use of a screw like that in a meat grinder, which extrudes the concrete mix and at the same time pushes the machine away from the newly cast curb.

The Summary

In many cases the summary is the most important part of the feature. It is often quite brief, but it must be complete and clear. Essentially, it is the core of the idea that the writer wants to leave with the reader. A summary of the toxic wastes feature, previously mentioned, could stress that the company's program makes the area's groundwater safer.

KINDS OF FEATURES

There is no formal classification of feature stories and no practical limit to the variety of stories that can be written. Whenever you find something that can be made interesting to some segment of the public, it may be the beginning of a feature. Some ideas may be obvious, but many more can be developed if you hunt for them. Among the most frequently seen features are hitchhikes, case histories, depth studies, application features, and backgrounders. While these do not represent the entire range of possibilities, some familiarity with the more common types will help you to think up ideas.

The Hitchhike or Sidebar

There are two kinds of hitchhikes. One is a new angle on a previously published feature; the other is the feature hooked onto some widely known situation. With both, your problem is to determine the relationship of your organization to the subject and find out what the organization is doing about it.

The new-angle hitchhike must be really new. Gatekeepers who have published a story about how the Brown Corporation is employing used steam from

DOBISKY ASSOCIATES

Media Relations for Higher Education

RFD #1, Box 261D • Keene, NH 03431 • 603 352-8181

America's Top 5 Careers: A Way to Make Them Add Up

Few noticed, but all five of America's top careers in The Jobs Rated Almanac can be won with a math degree, says Edward Connors of the University of Massachusetts at Amherst, who last year coached the first all-women's team to its first national math-competition title.

1) actuary **2)** computer programmer **3)** computer systems analyst **4)** mathematician **5)** statistician -- These, they say, are the cream of the crop when it comes to salary, low-stress, posh working conditions, and lifetime security.

"And each one is a math-related field," Connors says.

Not only can a degree in math land you one of these "pampered" positions, but also may let you write your own ticket well into the 21st century, says Connors, mathematics professor and chair of the American Mathematical Society/ Mathematical Association of America committee on employment & educational policy.

Opportunities abound in these fields, particularly for women and minorities, he says.

Connors, who notes that females currently earn half of all math baccalaureates awarded, adds: "There are plenty of women graduates with math degrees who are well-qualified for these jobs. Blacks, Hispanics and other minorities also are eagerly sought in all five areas."

For students, he advises: "Don't cut short your options in high school by avoiding math. Don't turn off too soon. Give it a chance, stick with it. Once in college, you could find yourself interested in business or science, but be forced to abandon it if you haven't had enough math."

For teachers, especially at the primary level, he calls for a major overhaul: "Math instruction in elementary schools is far inferior than what it should be. Often it's taught by ill-trained teachers who were poor at math themselves. Even in primary grades, math should be taught by math specialists."

Dr. Connors can be reached on campus at 413/545-0982 or 413/545-2762, or at home, 413/527-7072. If I can help put you in touch with him, call 603/352-8181.
                              -0-

Backgrounders generate features. It is not always necessary for the public relations writer to send a complete feature release to media outlets. Many publications prefer to write their own features from background information supplied by public relations personnel. Shown here is a basic "backgrounder" that gives the crux of the story and how the reporter can contact an expert for an interview. (*Source:* Dobisky Associates, Keene, NH.)

its power plant to heat its building are not likely to run a story about how the Green Company is doing the same thing. On the other hand, if the Green Company is selling excess electric power—which it generates—to the local public utility, the story has a new angle.

The situation hitchhike starts with an examination of problems that concern the public. There are many such problems, and they affect most organizations. Corporate social responsibility is an important matter to many people. Say that the Richard Adams Company is giving college scholarships to minority students who would otherwise be unable to continue their schooling. A story about this act of social responsibility would have a good chance of seeing print.

Another example is public concern about technological unemployment. Sensing such public and media interest, one major corporation got extensive exposure for a feature article about the company's efforts to retrain displaced employees for other jobs.

In order to hitchhike on current public concerns, it is absolutely essential that you keep track of the stories running in the media now. Once you see that a topic is on the agenda—be it employment, the economy, worker productivity, or competition from imports—your next step is to think of ways in which your employer or client is related to that issue. Then look for a possible feature story on that subject.

The Case History

The case history is frequently used in product publicity. The story of how some product solved a problem for the user or how a unique service enabled some organization to save money or improve its own service can be important and interesting. Thus, a feature on the use of flexible plastic piping that can be installed without the aid of a plumber could interest many "do-it-yourself" homeowners. A feature about a home cleaning service and how it helps the woman who works full time could interest many working women.

The Depth Study

A depth study on allergy to makeup could provide an opportunity for a company that makes hypoallergenic cosmetics, emphasizing the names and characteristics of its products and registering these with potential users.

A depth study on geothermal power could provide favorable publicity for a public utility that was developing such power. A depth study on the development by insects of resistance to common insecticides could provide a foundation for publicity about newer pesticides—or about biological methods of insect control.

The Application Feature

The application feature tells how to use a new product or a familiar product in a new way. Much food publicity consists of application features—new reci-

DOBISKY ASSOCIATES

Media Relations for Higher Education

RFD #1, Box 261D • Keene, NH 03431 • 603 352-8181

May 25, 1988

Mr. Lloyd Shearer
"Intelligence Report"
<u>Parade</u>
750 Third Avenue
New York, New York 10017

Dear Mr. Shearer:

Few noticed, but all five of America's top careers in <u>The</u> <u>Jobs</u> <u>Rated</u> <u>Almanac</u> can be won with a degree in math.

So says Prof. Edward Connors of the University of Massachusetts at Amherst, who last year coached the first all-women's team to its first national math-competition title. Connors says the top jobs are:

1) actuary **2)** computer programmer **3)** computer systems analyst **4)** mathematician **5)** statistician -- These, they say, are the cream of the crop when it comes to salary, low-stress, posh working conditions, and lifetime security.

"And each one is a <u>math</u>-related field," Connors says.

Not only can a degree in math land you one of these "pampered" positions, but also may let you write your own ticket well into the 21st century, says Connors, mathematics professor and chair of the American Mathematical Society/ Mathematical Association of America committee on employment & educational policy.

Opportunities abound in these fields, particularly for women and minorities, he says.

Connors, who notes that females currently earn half of all math baccalaureates awarded, adds: "There are plenty of

Personalized pitch letters. Background material also can be organized into a personal letter to a specific editor. Notice how the previously given "backgrounder" is adapted for a *Parade* magazine editor. By carefully pinpointing editors and publications that would be most interested in the subject, media coverage dramatically increases. (*Source:* John McLain, Dobisky Associates, Keene, NH.)

PAGE TWO
Mr. Lloyd Shearer
May 25, 1988

women graduates with math degrees who are well-qualified for
these jobs. Blacks, Hispanics and other minorities also are
eagerly sought in all five areas."

    For students, he advises: "Don't cut short your options
in high school by avoiding math. Don't turn off too soon.
Give it a chance, stick with it. Once in college, you could
find yourself interested in business or science, but be
forced to abandon it if you haven't had enough math."

    For teachers, especially at the primary level, he calls
for a major overhaul: "Math instruction in elementary
schools is <u>far</u> inferior than what it should be. Often it's
taught by ill-trained teachers who were poor at math
themselves. Even in primary grades, math should be taught by
math specialists."

    Dr. Connors can be reached at 413/545-0982 or 413/545-
2762. If I can help put you in touch with him, call 603/352-
8181.

                              Regards,

                              John McLain
                              John McLain

    JM/mt

pes or new variations on familiar ones. The food pages of newspapers carry
many such features. Some are published exactly as received; others are rewritten or combined in a longer feature.

    A feature on home maintenance could provide a basis for publicity on a
new kind of paintbrush or paint. Wherever there is a product or service that
serves some useful purpose, there may be an audience for information about
it.

The Backgrounder

There are several kinds of backgrounders. One focuses on a problem and how
it was solved—by an organization or a product. Often there is considerable
historical material and an opportunity for injecting human interest into the
story. One example is a story on the reclamation of stripmined land and how
a coal company restored an area to productive use for farming.

PRUNES
FROM CALIFORNIA

FOR: CALIFORNIA PRUNE BOARD

FROM: KETCHUM PUBLIC RELATIONS
      55 Union Street
      San Francisco, CA   94111
      Susan Mesick (415) 984-6254
      Susan Butenhoff (415) 984-6134

EXCLUSIVE IN YOUR AREA
UNTIL NOVEMBER 1987

<u>PLANTATION HOTCAKES: WARM "DOWN-HOME" TREAT
FOR CHILLY WINTER MORNINGS</u>

      Warm up cold Sunday mornings by treating family and
friends to a taste of down-home cooking. With little advance
preparation, you can create a Southern-style breakfast from your
own "country kitchen."

      Overnight guests will be charmed by old-style
hospitality when you serve a breakfast of Plantation Hotcakes
fresh from the griddle, topped with homemade yogurt and served
with strong, steaming coffee. This mouthwatering yet convenient
menu deliciously combines true Southern hospitality with Yankee
practicality.

(more)

CPB2A1186 The California Prune Board, 55 Union Street San Francisco, CA 94111 (415) 781-9480

An application feature. The food industry often publicizes its products by sending features to food editors about the use of the product in recipes. Ketchum Public Relations developed this application feature for its client, The California Prune Board. Naturally, the recipe for Plantation Hotcakes requires prunes as an ingredient. (*Source:* Ketchum Public Relations, San Francisco, CA.)

Pictures improve media acceptance. A feature accompanied by a photograph often increases media coverage. This photograph accompanied the Prune Board's recipe for Plantation Hotcakes, and food editors were given the choice of a black-and-white photo or a color transparency. Most daily newspaper now have color capability and use extensive color in their specialized sections. (*Source:* Ketchum Public Relations, San Francisco, CA.)

A backgrounder feature. This photo was used in a human-interest feature about the work of a coffee taster. Hills Brothers Coffee Company used this approach to show how its coffee taster ensures the quality of its product. (*Source:* The Leeper Group, San Francisco, CA.)

Another kind of backgrounder explains where a product comes from or how it is made. A manufacturer of woolens might release a feature on sheep farming and the differing characteristics of wool from the various breeds—finally leading up to the excellent products made from that wool.

The Personality Profile

People like to read about people. Within any sizable organization, there may be people about whom interesting stories can be written—and published. How the founder started the business and built it to success; How Joe Donovan got an idea, sold it to management, and improved profits for the firm; how John

LEVI STRAUSS & CO. NEWS

1155 Battery Street, San Francisco, CA 94111

FOR IMMEDIATE RELEASE
FALL, 1988

FOR FURTHER INFORMATION
Kris Kagler 312/836-7295
Dean Christon 415/544-7254

DENIM TREATMENTS REMAIN HOT FOR FALL

Whether stonewashed, bleached or acid washed, your new pair of blue jeans is likely to be finished with a denim treatment, thanks to the explosion of denim "finishes" in the fashion world.

According to Levi Strauss & Co. merchandise manager John Ermatinger, denim fabric treatments will continue to be strong through fall 1988.

"Acid washed denim has paved the way for a host of innovative denim finishes," says Ermatinger. "Finishing gives denim an interesting look and it softens the fabric, which makes it more comfortable."

Levi Strauss & Co. first introduced its acid washed finish, which it has labeled "whitewashed," to 501 jeans in the spring of 1987. Whitewashed jeans are washed with pumice stones soaked in bleach, producing a soft even finish, as if the jeans have been lightly brushed with a coat of paint. The stones soften the jeans while the bleach completes the denim's light finish.

-- more --

Trend feature. The media are interested in trends, whether it be careers or fashion. This was sent to fashion editors of newspapers and magazines. [*Source:* Levi Strauss & Co., San Francisco, CA.]

Smith arrived with nothing but brains and got to his present position through hard work; how Grace Boswell went from junior clerk to president. All these, of course, would be filled with anecdotes, comments from others, and as many specifics as could be obtained.

The Historic Feature

Anniversaries, major changes, centennials, and many other events lend themselves to historic features. Whenever a significant milestone is passed, there may be an opportunity to report on the history of the organization, its facilities, or even some of its people. Stressing the history of an organization lends it an air of stability and permanence. The public can logically deduce that if an organization has lasted "that long," it must have merit.

The hundredth birthday of Sherlock Holmes was the basis of a widely published feature. Another feature story, about the fourth and final supplement of the *Oxford English Dictionary*, started with the words "Yetis, Yuppies, Yabbas, and wimmin." It went on to say that this effort to bring the English language up to date took 29 years and some sixty thousand words.

Both these stories were "news"-type releases that were carried by the wire services.

PLACING FEATURE STORIES

If a feature is to be published, it must be of high quality and be aimed at the right medium. Features are exclusive to one publication, but it is possible to make several placements of a basic idea if it is completely rewritten for each user.

Features may be placed with general magazines, special-interest magazines, business and trade publications, and house magazines. Major newspapers write their own features but occasionally follow through on suggestions from public relations people. Syndicates and freelance writers too may consider suggestions for feature stories.

General Magazines

Although it can be argued that there is no longer any such thing as a "general" magazine (since all periodicals cater to specific audiences of one kind or another), the term is used here to refer to "popular" magazines that reach broad-based audiences. Another way to designate general magazines is to say that they are those—some fifty or more—indexed in the *Reader's Guide to Periodical Literature*. They include magazines like *Time, Newsweek, Esquire, The New Yorker, Better Homes and Gardens, Redbook, Popular Mechanics, Seventeen, National Geographic, Esquire,* and *Reader's Digest*. Although all magazines rely on their own staffs, a number of general magazines do use articles written by freelancers and ideas submitted by public relations people. Thus, in *Seventeen* magazine, there might be an article about the differences between suntan lotions and sunscreens. Most of the information would probably have originated with a suncreen manufacturer who wished to increase sales among female teenagers. Of course, fashion designers also generate a large number of feature ideas and even feature stories for magazines that cater to style-conscious men and women.

Reader's Digest, which has one of the largest circulations in the United States after *TV Guide,* is a prime but very difficult target for the placement of feature stories that benefit companies and industries. A meat tenderizer made by one firm was featured in a *Digest* article about cutting meat costs. And the California wine industry was able to place a highly laudatory article on California wines in the same issue.

The key to placement is finding an idea that fits into the magazine's editorial content. Sunscreens and suntan lotions are a natural for *Seventeen* but not very good for *Popular Mechanics.* Public relations writers often offer basic fact sheets or even a feature article that can be modified by the magazine editors for eventual use. Pride of authorship is not a consideration here. Often, a feature story from a public relations writer will appear almost verbatim but carry the byline of a magazine staffer.

Special-Interest Magazines

There is a special-interest magazine for almost every imaginable field: Coin collecting, stamp collecting, hunting, fishing, yachting, backpacking, jogging, and gardening are just a few of the many possibilities.

Whenever your organization has something bearing upon a special field of interest, there may be a theme for a feature—and it is possible to write more than one feature on the same subject. With a new line of golf clubs, one story might tell how the line was developed under the guidance of a well-known player, another might deal with unusual materials and manufacturing techniques, and a third could feature the experience of several different golfers with the new clubs. Each of these stories might be placed with a different golf magazine.

Business and Trade Magazines

These focus on business in general or on a specific trade. People read these publications to find out what is going on in business overall or in a particular field and to get ideas that can be of help to them.

In many trades, there are numerous competing magazines. This increases the opportunity for the placement of features. It also means that such stories must be individualized. No editor will use a feature that might also be published by a competitor. In general, a feature should not be sent to any publication without a previous expression of interest from the gatekeeper.

Another thing to remember in preparing features for business or trade publications is that a given subject might be of interest in several different fields.

Checklist for Developing Technical Articles

VALUE OF TECHNICAL ARTICLES

They may influence customers and employees.

They impress financial community and editors of trade journals.

They may make a company seem more important because it is mentioned in the trade press.

NATURE OF TECHNICAL ARTICLES

They may describe the technology behind a product (background).

They may explain the utilization of a product (application).

TO FIND AUTHORS

Use people who have written before—engineers, managers, and so on.

Use company speech writers.

Use major customers.

TO MOTIVATE AUTHORS

Offer rewards and recognition.

Offer help in writing, editing, illustrating, placement.

Supply references, information gathering, clerical aid.

TO SELL THE ARTICLE

Choose the right publication.

Submit outline and abstract to editor.

Follow up with phone call.

When idea is accepted, get the writing started.

LONG-TERM STRATEGY

Keep complete records: coverage, inquiries, requests for speakers, and so on.

Get permission to send to foreign publications.

Plan revisions for use in other publications.

Get reprints for direct mail distribution.

Source: Adapted from a product press relations memorandum of Hewlett-Packard, Inc.

ALASKA

From: Alaska Division of Tourism

For more information, contact:
Jared Chaney/Tracey Jones
Carl Byoir & Associates, Inc.
77 Maiden Lane, Suite 300
San Francisco, CA 94108
(415) 433-9333

For Release on Receipt

Note to editors:
See accompanying
line art, photos and
Sitka story

FOLLOWING 19TH CENTURY

RUSSIANS ACROSS ALASKA

by Michael Cooper

Note to Editors: Michael Cooper is a
New York-based freelancer whose stories
have appeared in national publications such
as Travel & Leisure.

Visitors to Alaska who have forgotten their American history are quickly
reminded that the 49th State was once a Russian colony. One reminder is the large
number of Russian names sprinkled across the map, from the Eskimo town of Kotzebue
north of the Arctic Circle to Mitkof Island in the southeastern panhandle.

The Russians began earnestly exploring the islands and mainland of Alaska in
the early eighteenth century. One of the first explorers was a Danish fleet
commander for the Russian navy, Vitus Bering. He and his crew took six years
crossing Siberia on foot, lugging tools, iron, and supplies to build boats after they
reached the coast. Although Bering and many of his men died on their second trip to
Alaska, the survivors returned to Russia with news of an unclaimed land teeming with
fur bearing animals. With that news, a steady flow of trappers began traveling
between Russia and Alaska.

In 1780, to discourage English and Spanish encroachments, the colony was
placed under the governance of a fur trading company that eventually settled on the
name of the Russian American Company. The company not only encouraged trapping, it
also encouraged exploring and surveying to seal Russia's claim to the vast land.
Along the coast and up the tidal rivers, Russian American trappers and surveyors
christened islands, rivers, bays, mountains, and towns with Russian names, while
priests followed planting religion among the Indians.

—more—

A historical feature. This is one of a series of features sent to travel editors by the
Alaska Division of Tourism. Other subjects included camping, a museum of Eskimo
artifacts, and the natural beauty of the Inland Passage. The purpose of the features was
to increase Alaskan tourism. (*Source:* Carl Byoir & Associates, San Francisco, CA.)

The remodeling of a hotel could lead to features for a number of unrelated publications. Engineering magazines could be interested in structural problems and solutions, architectural magazines might use stories about design and decoration, travel publications might use stories about the renaissance of an obsolescent favorite, and hotel-supply magazines might use stories about new carpeting, furniture, kitchen facilities, and so on.

Internal Publications

Many internal publications use material from outside sources. The most likely prospects are those where there is a built-in interest. A feature telling how something produced by your organization is helping another organization has an innate interest. For example, you might have a feature describing exactly how your company makes the special insulating material that the XYZ company is using to produce cold-weather footwear. The newsletter or magazine of the XYZ company might welcome such a piece.

HOW TO PREPARE A FEATURE

You should not start writing a feature until you know exactly which publication or newspaper section you are writing for. Also, you should not start writing a magazine feature until you have an expression of interest from the editor.

To arouse such interest, you must present a proposal—a fairly comprehensive outline of what you intend to write. A good procedure is to phone the editor, outline the subject of the feature, and ask if he or she would be interested. The reason for the phone call is to make sure that there is enough interest to justify writing a proposal. Perhaps the editor has run several features much like the one you have in mind. In that case, he or she may reject your idea immediately and save you a lot of work. On the other hand, the editor may be interested and willing to pursue the matter further. When that happens, you should start writing your proposal. It will consist of the headline, the lead paragraph, and the subheads—including the main points under each subhead—a summary, and a description of the graphics.

The Headline

The headline tells what the article is about. It should be short and direct. A case history could be headlined, "How XYZ Corp. switched from typewriters to word processors."

The Lead Paragraph

The lead paragraph must arouse interest. It sets the stage for what is to follow and gives the reader enough information to encourage further reading. It might go like this:

Jane Doe has been private secretary to the president of XYZ for 11 years. When told that she would have to give up her trusty typewriter and learn to use a word processor, she threatened to quit. Now, after using an IBM word processor for four months, she says "I don't know how I ever got along without one."

The Subheads

The subheads indicate the divisions within the body of the feature. There should be at least one subhead for each printed page. In the feature about word processors, there might be two subheads: "The Training Program" and "The Effect of Word Processors on Office Procedures." In other features, there might be several more subheads.

Each subhead should be followed by a description, about a paragraph in length, of the main points to be included. If paragraphs are required, it may be wise to use secondary subheads to break up the mass of information and highlight individual segments.

Regardless of the possible use of secondary subheads, the main points under each subhead should be stated in the proposal. This is best done with a topic sentence such as "Word processors have made information storage and retrieval much more efficient than the file system, which once frustrated so many people in the office."

The Graphics

If the publication uses graphics, you should indicate exactly what illustrative material—photographs or artwork—is to be provided. Illustrations should be captioned. For a proposal, it might be helpful to send photostats of the illustrations. Of course, when the feature is finished, the illustrations you supply must be original photo prints or good photocopies of the artwork. The copy should be keyed to the illustrative materials (e.g., "See Figure 2").

The Summary

This is a wrap-up of the whole feature. One or two sentences may be enough; a short paragraph should be the maximum.

Acceptance

When your proposal is complete, it should be sent to the editor. If he accepts it, you can start writing. If he rejects your idea, you are free to rewrite the proposal or to try it on a different editor in the same field. Remember also that it might be possible to prepare several different features from the basic information you have collected. In accepting proposals, editors normally specify when they want to receive the article and when it will be published.

Writing

With an approved outline in hand, you can now put the meat on the bones. Your information is available and all you have to do is transform it into words. Be sure that you aim at the publication for which your feature is intended. The use of illustrations, use of subheads, and style of wording should conform to its standards. One editor even suggests that writers work with a copy of his magazine beside the typewriter or console, so their writing will fit into his pages.

SUMMARY

1. Every feature article must have a purpose—to help attain some specific goal by informing or persuading certain people.
2. The format of a feature story is not rigid. There must be an interesting opening lead, an informative body, and a conclusion or summary.
3. There are numerous kinds of features. The most common are hitchhikes or sidebars, case histories, depth studies, application features, backgrounders, personality profiles, and historic features.
4. The publications most likely to use feature stories are general magazines, special-interest magazines, business and trade magazines, and internal publications such as house magazines.
5. The preparation of a feature story starts with sending to the editor a comprehensive outline of what the story will contain.
6. When the editor approves, the writer completes the feature and sends it to the editor.

EXERCISES

1. Feature leads are different in form and tone than straight news leads. Write a feature lead for each of the following story subjects:
    a. The Florida Grapefruit Growers Association has announced that this year's crop is larger than last year's, and greater availability will mean lower prices for the consumer.
    b. IBM has announced a major breakthough in the technology of computer design, which will enable the company to sell its new generation of personal computers at half of the current price.
    c. A Los Angeles company, Map-Guide, has introduced a dashboard computer for cars that will show local maps on a screen and let drivers know exactly where they are at any given time.
    d. Because of the weak Australian dollar, wines from that nation are now good bargains in the United States.
    e. The Denver Livestock Show and Rodeo, a tradition for 75 years, will begin on January 5 and run through January 12.
    f. An Arizona insurance company has cut its utilities bill in half by converting its trash into electrical energy at its headquarters building.

2. The personality profile often appears in the business section of the daily newspaper. It usually outlines how a businessperson became successful or overcame major difficulties to make his or her company profitable again. Select a business executive in your community and write a personality profile about him or her. The feature should be six to eight pages long, typed, and double spaced.

3. A number of university professors are engaged in research projects that increase our understanding of a subject. Select a professor on your campus and write a depth feature about the nature of his or her research and why it is important.

4. The food section of a daily newspaper often carries background features on the origin and contemporary uses of various food products. Do some library research about the introduction of oranges into this country and the current status of the orange-growing industry. Since this feature is for the food section of a daily newspaper, include information that would be helpful to consumers. The objective of the feature story, of course, is to increase the sale of oranges.

5. The historic feature is often written when an organization or even a building reaches a major milestone like its fiftieth or hundredth anniversary. Write a historic feature about a building or academic department on your campus. Or, as an alternative, write a historic feature about something in the community.

6. Contact a local manufacturing company and find out if its product is being used in any new and innovative ways. On the basis of information provided by the company or consumers of the product, write an application feature. Write the feature article for possible use in a trade publication covering a particular industry.

7. Nike, Inc., has just introduced a new running shoe that collects energy released by each step and returns some of it to the wearer. These "high-tech" shoes, made with polyurethane and having compressed air sandwiched in the sole, represent a new "biomechanical design." This new product could lead to a number of feature stories in various general, business, and trade publications. Compile a list of possible publications and name the feature angle that could be used for each one.

SUGGESTED READINGS

Kessler, Lauren, and McDonald, Duncan. "Depth and Context Writing." *Mastering The Message: Media Writing with Substance and Style.* Belmont, CA: Wadsworth Publishing, 1989, sec. III.

Marken, G. A. "How to Place Articles for Company or Product Publicity." *Public Relations Quarterly*, Summer 1987, pp. 28–31.

Nelson, Roy Paul. "The World of Special Publications." *Communication World*, September 1986, pp. 22–27.

Newsom, Doug, and Wollert, James. "Features." *Media Writing: Preparing Information for the Mass Media.* Belmont, CA: Wadsworth Publishing, 1988, chap. 11.

Rosen, Daniel. "An Editorial Snapshot of 15 Customer Magazines." *Communication World*, March 1985, pp. 15–17.

Chapter 7

Photos and Artwork

*I*llustrations—photographs, charts, diagrams, maps, architectural renderings, pictures of scale models, line drawings, cartoons—can perform an important role in public relations. They add interest, introduce variety, and often explain things much better than words alone can do. You should constantly think of ways to use illustrations to supplement or replace regular news releases or to add substance to feature articles.

For example, a good, well-captioned photograph of a supermarket opening would probably get more space than a standard news release. Or, in a release about the planned construction of a skyscraper, a picture of the architect's model would enliven the story. If a company wants to release financial information, a graph or bar chart to go with it would communicate much more than paragraphs full of of numbers.

There is an old saying that "A picture is worth a thousand words"; like most axioms, it has much validity. A picture in a periodical often takes the same space as a thousand words, but it probably has a lot more impact. Any number of readership studies show that illustrations capture a reader's attention as he or she scans a newspaper or magazine page.

NEWSWORTHINESS

As with written releases, the test for an illustration is whether it will appeal to the media gatekeeper. And again as with written releases, one of the first rules is to know the kinds of illustrations that a particular medium uses. The *New York Times, USA Today*, the *Wall Street Journal*, and an increasing number of other newspapers around the country are making extensive use of line drawings in their specialized sections—business, living, sports, editorial, and so on.

Other newspapers have practically banned pictures of the traditional handshaking or check-passing ceremony because these have become so trite. Some publications may have a strong orientation toward human interest or mood pictures. Others, like the *Wall Street Journal*, don't use photographs.

Production and distribution of photos and artwork is an expensive and time-consuming process. People who shotgun pictures all over the country are not only incompetent but are wasting their employers' money. Although it has already been said several times in this text, it cannot be emphasized enough that you should be thoroughly familiar with the media in which you want publicity. Knowing what these outlets use and need makes the difference between success and failure.

Photographs and other illustrations are strong visual symbols, so their newsworthiness is directly related to the traditional news values—timeliness, proximity, prominence, significance, human interest, unusualness, conflict, or just plain newness.

PHOTOGRAPHS

Most publicity illustrations are photographs. Good photographs may see print, but bad ones will fill the gatekeepers' wastebaskets. Accordingly, it is incumbent upon you to know what makes a good picture and what to avoid.

Practical tips and ideas about photography are offered in a monthly column, titled "Photo Critique," by Philip N. Douglis. It runs in *Communication World*, the publication of the International Association of Business Communicators. Douglis discusses how you can improve upon a particular photo or set of photos you may use in public relations.

Quality

Since most of your photographs will be planned for use in some printed publication, the visual quality of the picture is extremely important. The key elements are good contrast and sharp detail so it will reproduce well, even on newsprint. If it is fuzzy or lacking in contrast, it won't reproduce satisfactorily.

For most uses, the pictures should be printed on glossy paper. This produces the best results when it goes through the engraving process for letterpress printing or a negative is made for offset printing. Matte photos, which have a dull finish, do not work well for printing, but they can be used for television. For the print media, you will generally be using black-and-white photographs in either an 8- by 10- or 5- by 7-inch format. Basic head and shoulder pictures (mug shots) can be shot in a 4- by 5-inch format.

It cannot be emphasized enough that photos sent to the media must be of high quality if they are to be considered for use. Never send a snapshot from an Instamatic or Polaroid camera.

Action

Action is important because it projects movement and the idea that something is happening right before the reader's eyes. A picture of someone doing something—talking, gesturing, laughing, running, operating a machine—is more interesting than a picture of people just standing still and looking at the camera.

America's amateur photographers have filled the nation's family albums with pictures of Aunt Minnie and Uncle Oswald in rigid, formal poses staring at the camera, but a quick look through your daily newspaper will not show this kind of shot. A book of prizewinning news photographs also shows that action is the key element in successful photography. A football quarterback throwing a ball makes a better picture than the same player standing on the field during a time out.

With some thinking, an action photo can be taken of almost any situation. Good examples of this will be found in the pictures released by the White House. Instead of a rigidly posed group staring at the camera, the pictures usually show the President and other people in animated discussion or greeting each other. This creates action, spontaneity, and interest.

An announcement in an employee publication of a new hire or promotion can be made into an action picture. Instead of merely showing a head-and-shoulders shot of the employee, why not show him in his working environment—talking on a phone, operating a machine, talking to another new employee, or to his immediate supervisor.

There are, of course, some times when a straight head-and-shoulders portrait is exactly what's needed. For example, a press release announcing a promotion or the new president of a club or organization is often accompanied by just a "mug shot."

You can add interest to a picture of a machine by showing someone examining or operating it. You can generate more reader interest by focusing on just

Dramatize routine pictures. Employee photos can be drab and uninteresting, but an employee productivity campaign with an imaginative theme like "dragon slaying" can result in effective photos for a company newsletter. (*Source:* Advanced Micro Devices, Sunnyvale, CA.)

one part of the machine that has an unusual design or looks interesting. For example, just show the part of the machine where the bottles are being capped or the labels are being applied.

Although buildings cannot show action, you can add interest by placing people in the foreground, either walking by the building or talking together. If you are taking a picture for a restaurant or supermarket, remember that people and activity in the picture convey more than just the picture of the building on a Sunday morning surrounded by an empty parking lot. A publicity photo does not have to show the entire building. In many cases, it is better to focus on an unusual aspect or an area that offers human interest.

You should not conclude, however, that all good pictures must suggest overt action. Some of the greatest photos have been character studies of people whose faces reflected their happiness at having won an award, their intense concentration on a critical issue, or even their sorrow at having lost an election.

Scale

With inanimate objects, it is important to consider the scale. The picture should contain some element of known size so that the viewer can understand how big or small the object is. With large machines, it is common and effective to place a person in the picture. This helps the viewer to estimate the approximate size of the picture's subject.

When smaller things are photographed, the scale guide is even more important. This also offers an opportunity to provide drama and adds the news value of novelty. For example, a transistor has been photographed inside a walnut shell, a miniature radio beside a quarter, and a computer in a wallet.

Camera Angles

Interest can also be achieved through the use of unusual camera angles. Shooting upward at a tall structure makes it look even taller. An aerial shot often gives the viewer a chance to see something that might otherwise be unnoticeable. Telephoto shots can bring an unreachable object close enough to show details that are not visible from a distance. A fish-eye lens can capture a 180-degree image.

Group Pictures

Group pictures nearly always present a problem; with them, it is relatively easy to violate the concepts of newsworthiness, action, and central focus. There is often the danger of showing too many people, and most public relations professionals have adopted the rule that no more than three or four people should be in any one photo.

Such a rule provides for more action, keeps the picture simple, and makes every face easily identifiable. You must realize that an 8- by 10-inch photo is often much reduced in size when it is published. Moreover, a lot of detail is lost on newsprint.

A common mistake is to try to please everyone by having people pose for a group photo. This might mean the entire board of directors, 60 real estate salespeople, 125 college graduates, or even all 250 members of a club. A group photo may be legitimate when you want to give everyone a souvenir of a particular meeting or conference or provide documentation for a specialized publication such as a fraternal or alumni magazine. However, pictures of this kind should never be sent to the mass media. It is may also be unwise to submit them to professional magazines, trade journals, or special-interest publications.

Unusual angles. The media are always looking for a special photo to brighten newspaper layouts. A creative photographer took a routine operation at Parker Pen Company and made it visually interesting. The photo was transmitted via satellite with the caption as part of the photo. (*Source:* Business Wire Photos, New York, NY.)

(NY12-Jan. 28) EYE ON THE BALL--A Technician at the Parker Pen Plant in Janesville, Wisc.--checks some of the millions of textured tungsten-carbide balls that will be used in Parker's roller ball pens. 200 million ball point pens will be purchased in 1985, according to industry forecasters.
(AP Laserphoto)(cjc21000ho)1985

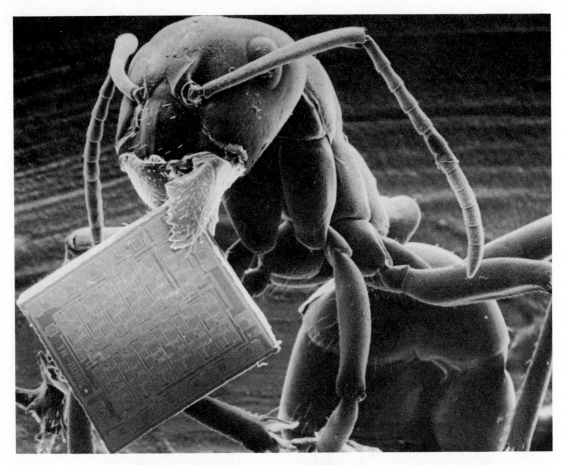

Use size contrast. Everyone knows that microchips are small, but this photo dramatically shows the size by using an ant for contrast. This photo was so unusual that it appeared in publications with a total circulation of 30 million and was even featured in the *National Geographic.* It was outstanding publicity for the microchip's manufacturer. (*Source:* Philips Electronic Instruments, Inc., Mahwah, NJ.)

One way to handle large groups is to take a series of small group pictures of individuals from the same town or company. These then let you multiply the coverage by "localizing" the event for hometown newspapers or employee publications.

In organizing such pictures, you should adhere to all the rules already discussed. Make sure there is activity in the picture; have people talking to each other, looking at a display, or shaking hands with a "notable" in an informal pose. They should not be lined up looking at the camera. A common composition is to show three people all talking or listening to a fourth person who is at the left of the picture. This fourth person may be a keynote speaker, the president of an organization, or someone who has just received an award. Such a composition can provide a central focus.

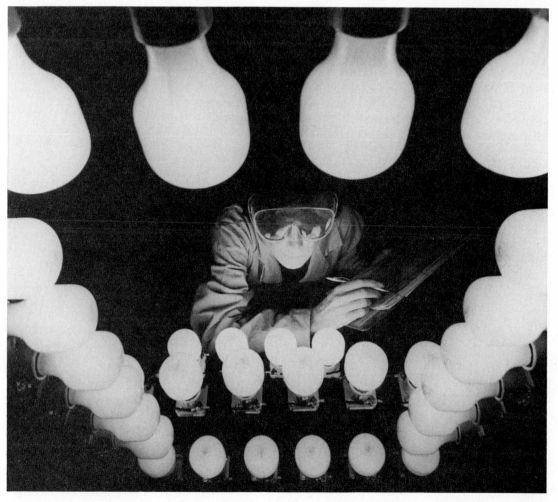

Bright idea. Light bulbs were made newsworthy with this photograph and generated publicity for one of North American Philip Company's product lines. (*Source:* Business Wire Photos, New York, NY.)

A final note. In a group situation, it is extremely important that you take down the names and titles of people as they are photographed. This will make your job much easier later on, when you have to write the caption. Don't rely on your memory or the memories of others several weeks after the event.

Composition

We have already discussed a number of ways to compose photographs of people and things. Inherent in all this is the concept of keeping the photo simple and uncluttered.

A look at the family album will illustrate the point. We have Aunt Minnie and Uncle Oswald looking like underweight pygmies because the family photographer also wanted to include the entire skyline of New York City in the background. Consequently, Aunt Minnie and Uncle Oswald are standing about 35 feet from the camera.

In most cases, the photographer should move into, not away from, the central focus of the picture. If the purpose is to show a busy executive at his or her desk, the picture should be taken close up, so the subject fills most of it. Sufficient background should be included to provide context, but it is really not necessary to show the entire contents of the desk—including the disarray of papers, picture of the wife and kids, and paperweight from the Elks' convention. All this tends to conflict with what the reader is supposed to look at.

Another reason for moving in on the subject and minimizing the background or foreground is to achieve a good composition. That picture of Aunt Minnie and Uncle Oswald also shows the Empire State Building growing out of Uncle Oswald's head.

A number of experts have made the following suggestions about composition and clutter:

1. Get tight shots with minimal background. Concentrate on what you want the reader to get from the picture.
2. Emphasize detail, not whole scenes.
3. Don't use a cluttered background. Pick up stray things that intrude upon the picture.
4. Try to frame the picture.
5. Avoid waste space. A person should be close to the certificate or trophy he or she is receiving; there should not be a large gap between the object and the person's face. In the case of a group picture, have people stand close to teach other.
6. Remove sunglasses from anyone in a group picture.

All this advice is well taken, but there may be times when the background plays an important role. If the picture is to show a group at the opening of some structure, such as a building or a dam, it will be necessary to include it in the background. In doing this, the photographer should place the group in such a position that the background or a portion of it is visible but contrasts with the group.

You may also think of ways to get the client's product or name into the background. A standard procedure is to get the executives of a company in the foreground with the name of the company on a building or sign directly behind them.

Lighting and Timing

If you want a picture of the company's executives in front of their new headquarters and the picture has to be taken in a westward direction, you should schedule the shooting in the morning. Otherwise the glare of the afternoon sun may have a detrimental effect. In general, outdoor pictures taken in the morning or late afternoon are better for contrast than pictures taken at midday. Of course, the photographer can use a flash to lighten dark areas.

Another tip is to take your picture before a planned event like a banquet. Before the keynote speaker and the officials go to the head table, take pictures in an anteroom. This is easier than trying to corral everyone after the banquet is over.

How to Take Product Photos That Get Published

1. Show the product in a scene where it would be logically used. If it's used in an office, show it in an office. Don't fake it.

2. Clean up the area where the picture is to be taken. Remove any litter or extraneous items. Repaint if necessary.

3. If people are in the picture, be sure that they are dressed for the situation. They should wear the kind of clothing—work clothes, uniforms, etc.—that they would wear while they were using the product.

4. Get perspective into the photo so viewers will know how big the item is. Show a hand, a person, a pencil. Don't use items identifiable as being from any particular country. The picture might be used in another.

5. If you need black-and-white pictures, don't rely on making prints from color negatives. They won't be as good.

6. Don't accept anything but the best in photographs. They have a potential shelf life of five years; many may be used by others to illustrate their books or brochures. Give them quality.

7. Take at least two photos—vertical and horizontal—of each new product. This makes them adaptable to a variety of situations. When possible, show the product in use. Application stories need illustrations.

8. If there are other products in the picture, be sure that the new one is in the dominant position. The setting should be realistic, with everything hooked up and ready to go.

9. Every picture must have an identifying caption.

10. Be sure that the background contrasts with the product. Make the product stand out.

11. Check your models. Look at complexions. Is there anything that would ultimately require retouching? Are neckties straight, is hair combed?

Source: Adapted from an internal memo for the product publicity department of Hewlett-Packard.

Selecting the location or setting of a picture is important if you want good, sharp results. For example, if you know that the people involved will be wearing light colors, you should not use a white background. Conversely, don't select a dark background if your photo subjects will be wearing dark clothing.

Color Photos

The vast majority of publicity photographs are produced in black and white because they are economical, versatile, and acceptable to most publications.

Color photographs, on the other hand, are relatively expensive and somewhat limited in application. You may wish to use color, however, in at least three ways: (1) in a leaflet or booklet for an organization, (2) for magazines that publish color photos, and (3) for food, business, sports, or travel section of a newspaper that runs color pages or color supplements.

Everything that has been said about composition and quality should be underlined in relation to color pictures. To be used, they must be outstanding in both interest and technical quality. They must be produced by professionals.

There is some use for color prints, but most magazine and newspaper publishers prefer 8- by 10-inch positive transparencies. There is some use of slides. Transparencies are usually superior in technical quality to prints, and they also give the publisher a head start on the printing process.

In all color printing, it is the practice to make color separations. This is a highly technical process that, in effect, takes each of the primary colors and transfers it to a separate piece of film. From each separation, the engraver makes a plate, which will print one of the primary colors onto the actual page. As each basic color is printed in succession on the same page, a full-color picture comes together.

Some people with substantial budgets regularly offer color separations to certain magazines and newspapers. In food publicity, for example, an editor may use such a set of separations to devote an entire page or spread to a particular product, such as strawberries, peaches, or avocados. This service enables a publication to run a full-color food feature without having to pay for the separations.

Color pictures and separations are always offered as "exclusives" in any media market. Because of their cost, they are not sent unless an editor indicates that he or she would be interested.

Stock Photos

"Stock photos" can be bought from stock photo houses, which exist in every major American city. These photographic libraries catalog almost every con-

Color adds interest. This picture, printed in black and white, was originally a color transparency sent to food editors by Ketchum Public Relations for its client, the California Strawberry Board. Color photos make food items more attractive and make a better impression on readers. (*Source:* Ketchum Public Relations, San Francisco, CA.)

ceivable subject, and some of the larger houses have millions of slides and prints on file. If you are unfamiliar with stock photo houses in your particular city, look in the Yellow Pages or contact a local photo store.

If you want a picture of a charging rhinoceros or a set of organ pipes, a stock house can probably accommodate you at a reasonable fee. Or if you want something more mundane, they can provide photos of people operating computers or ethnic minorities in management situations.

Stock photos should be used *only* in publications *you* produce. Never send a stock photo to any newspaper or magazine.

WORKING WITH PHOTOGRAPHERS

It is important to use a skilled photographer with professional experience. Too many organizations try to cut corners by asking some amateur in the organization to take pictures. The results are, more often than not, disappointing and unacceptable.

It will cost more money to hire a professional photographer, but at least you won't end up with pictures that are unusable. Another reason is that it is better business practice to use a professional. You can give direction to a photographer who is being paid, while it may be awkward to criticize the boss's nephew.

Finding Photographers

You should have a file of photographers, noting their fees and particular expertise. If you have no such file built up, you might consult colleagues to find out if they can make any recommendations. If you are unfamiliar with a photographer's work, ask to see his or her portfolio. This is important, because different photographers are skilled at different things.

A good portrait photographer, for example, may be very bad at photographing special events. A news photographer, on the other hand, may be an expert at special events but unable to take good product photographs. In sum, you should find the special photographer you need for each kind of job.

Photographers' fees vary widely, so it pays to compare prices. If you are on a tight budget, you might also consider using college students who are majoring in photojournalism. They are not quite professional yet, but they have learned most of the basics and may be good enough.

Agreements with Photographers

Any agreement with a photographer should be in writing. A written document does a great deal to avoid misunderstandings about fees, cost of prints, and who retains ownership of the negatives.

A letter of agreement with a photographer should cover the following:

1. The photographer's basic fee for taking pictures and a statement of exactly what this includes (developing the film, making prints, etc.).

2. Costs of prints or transparencies. Most photographers charge for each item ordered.

3. Who will supervise the photographer. Will this be you or someone else in the organization who will help the photographer set up shots?

4. Does the organization pay expenses—mileage and food, or lodging while photographer is on assignment?

5. Who will retain the negatives? In general, photographers want to retain all negatives in their files. This gives them the opportunity to sell you more prints at a later date if some are needed.

6. Nature of use. Does the organization have unrestricted use of the photograph, or does it have to get permission from the photographer?

7. Photographer's use of negatives. Can the photographer sell prints to outside parties, either individuals or other organizations?

The last point can often be a bone of contention and create poor public relations for an organization. It is not uncommon for a photographer to expand

---

Photographer Contract Terms

Professional photographers often use standard contracts with clients, but you should read the fine print carefully to see exactly what you are signing. For example, one standard contract contains the following terms or conditions:

- Except where outright purchase is specified, all photographs and rights not expressly granted . . . remain the exclusive property of Photographer. All editorial use limited to one time in the edition and column contemplated for this assignment. In all cases additional usage by client requires additional compensation and permission for use to be negotiated with Photographer.

- Client agrees to return all unpublished material to Photographer . . . and supply Photographer with two free copies of uses appearing in print.

- Adjacent credit line for Photographer must accompany editorial use, or invoice fee shall be doubled. Absent outright purchase client will provide copyright protection on any use and assign same to Photographer immediately on request without charge.

- Grant of usage is conditioned upon payment. Payment required within 30 days of invoice; $1\frac{1}{2}$ percent per month service charge on unpaid balance. Adjustment of amount must be requested within 10 days of invoice receipt.

- Weather postponements and cancellations 48 hours prior to shooting will be billed at $\frac{1}{2}$ fee. Days put on hold at client or agency request and not canceled within 24 hours will be billed at full fee.

- The agency is responsible for sending an authorized representative to the shooting. If no representative is present, the agency must accept the Photographer's judgment as to the execution of the photograph.

his or her revenues from a photo session by contacting people in the pictures individually and asking them if they want to purchase prints.

Before you hire the photographer you should clearly establish whether it is all right for the photographer to make additional money selling prints to individuals. In many cases, the organization wants exclusive rights to all photographs and their distribution for purposes of its own public relations outreach.

Working with Staff Photographers

The problem of photographer agreements is made much simpler, of course, when the photographer is a regular employee of the company. Under these circumstances, all photographs and negatives automatically belong to the employer. But some problems may still occur.

The most common problem is the extent of a full-time photographer's right to make additional income by selling pictures taken on company time. At one West Coast college, for example, the institution's photographer regularly peddled pictures, ordered by the public relations department, to students and faculty who appeared in the pictures. This sort of "free enterprise" is generally a poor policy because it gives the impression that the college is making money on the faculty and students who willingly cooperated to promote the college. It also undercuts the ability of the public relations department to create goodwill by simply giving photo subjects copies of the pictures.

The best solution is to make sure that photographers clearly understand that they do not have the right to sell photos, even if it is done on their own time and they reimburse the company for film and chemical supplies.

The Photo Session

You will save time and money if you plan ahead.

1. Make a list of the pictures you want. For pictures of people, arrange for a variety of poses.
2. Know who you need, where and when you need them, and what props will be required.
3. Notify people whose pictures are to be taken. Get releases if needed. (See Chapter 3.)
4. Be sure that the location for the photo session is available, clean, orderly, and so on.
5. Consider lighting. Will the photographer have everything needed or should you make preparations?
6. Have everyone and everything at the right place at the right time.
7. Tell the photographer *what* you want. Don't tell him or her *how* to do it.

Retouching and Cropping

When the photographer delivers your proofs, they may be contact sheets showing several pictures in small size on a single sheet of photo print paper. Alternatively, you may get individual proofs, and you can always order these if you choose.

Some of the pictures will be just what you want and some will have faults. If the quality is poor, you won't use the picture. But what happens if you have a good picture that shows some distracting element?

Suppose you have a good group picture that includes, at one side or behind the group, a waiter or some inanimate object intruding on the scene. The photographer can eliminate such things by retouching the negative. Another way to achieve the same result is to have an artist use an airbrush to blank out the element. Airbrushing is normally used only on prints. Still another way to modify a picture is to use a computer. The whole area of computer graphics is growing so rapidly that a new breakthrough occurs every few months. Even the basic techniques of photography involving film and lenses are being rivaled by purely electronic images. If you can conceive of any illustrative material, it may well be possible to execute it entirely by computer (provided that the correct accessories and programs are available). Photography, drawing, and printing as we have known them may be superseded by this new technique.

If you have a picture that has a lot of unfilled space or one that includes distracting or unneeded material at the edges, you can solve the problem by cropping, which means trimming off the edges of the picture. There are two ways to do this. You can change the proportions of the picture in any way you choose. This, however, is done only for your own printed materials. For the mass media you should retain the basic 8- by 10- or 5- by 7-inch format, which is preferred by the gatekeepers.

In cropping, to show the photographer where the new edges of the picture are to be, you use a grease pencil to draw vertical and horizontal lines on a print. Try to retain the proportions of the print; remember that when you cut 2 inches off the width of an 8- by 10-inch picture, you cut the depth by 1.6 inches. Actually, exact measurements are not necessary. A good approximation will enable the photographer to make a new print that shows what you want and omits what you want to leave out.

ARTWORK

Photographs are not the only art form that you can use. Charts, diagrams, maps, renderings, cartoons, line drawings, and clip art can all be of help. Such visuals must be very carefully executed. The lines must be dark, clean, and neat for maximum clarity, and figures must be large enough to remain legible even when the material is later reduced in size when it is printed.

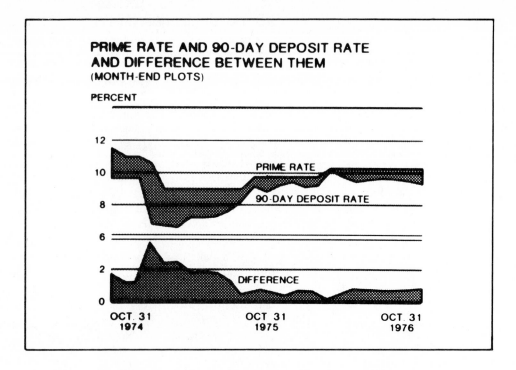

PRIME RATE AND 90-DAY DEPOSIT RATE
AND DIFFERENCE BETWEEN THEM
(MONTH-END PLOTS)

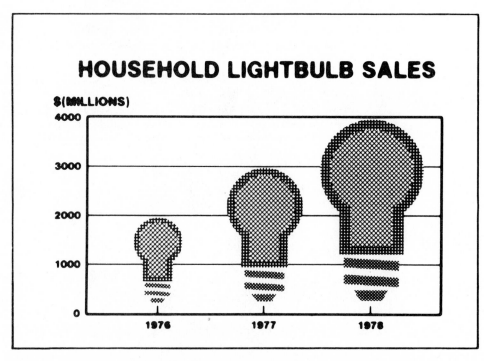

HOUSEHOLD LIGHTBULB SALES

Graphic artists, commercial illustrators, and even art students may all do this type of work. Again, as with photographers, ask to see their portfolios before you commission a particular assignment. In addition, look into computer graphics. The capabilities are increasing every day.

Generally, you will not send artwork to the media. Instead, you will send photographs of the artwork.

Charts

The primary reason for using charts is to make figures understandable. Three basic types of charts are used for this purpose, and each seems to work best for certain kinds of information.

The "pie" chart, which looks like a whole pie cut into uneven slices, is ideal for showing what part of a total is used for each of several different purposes. A pie chart can show that 57 percent of the budget goes for labor, 33 percent for raw materials, 8 percent for taxes, and 2 percent for contingencies. This type of chart is frequently used in trade magazines, news magazines, and in-depth newspaper reports. It is also used by charitable agencies to show how funds are expended.

The "bar" chart, which usually shows several bars side by side, is good for rapid comparisons. It can show, for example, the relative usage of coal, oil, natural gas, and nuclear power as sources of energy. Another use might be to show the numbers of people employed in various occupations. Bar charts can also give yearly comparisons (e.g., the number of widgets sold this year as opposed to five years ago).

The "graph" is frequently used to show year-by-year changes in such things as income, population, sales, prices, and so on. One warning applies especially in the use of graphs. Sometimes, in the interest of saving space, the chart maker may not base the bottom of the chart at zero. If the lowest level of the chart is above that figure, it can create misconceptions. Under this condition, what looks like a big increase may not really be all that large.

The other possible problem with a graph is complexity. It is not wise to have three or four graph lines running at once; this makes the chart difficult to read, particularly if it is in black and white. With all charts, be doubly sure that they do not deceive. It is easy to make charts that exaggerate the facts; don't you do it. (See Huff, Darrell and Geis, Irving: *How to Lie with Statistics* New York. Norton, 1953.)

Computer generated art. Computer graphics can produce many kinds of illustrations, and it is now possible to get computer software programs featuring all kinds of graphic symbols. Many programs, with color capability, can produce overhead projector transparencies, slides, charts, and graphs. (*Source:* Genigraphics Corporation, Liverpool, NY.)

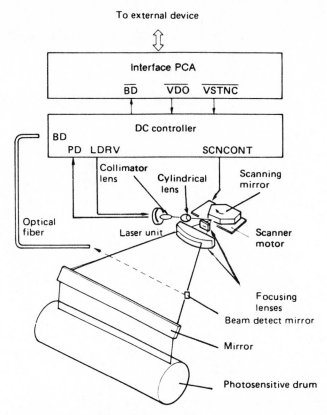

To external device

Interface PCA

BD   VDO   VSTNC

DC controller

BD

PD LDRV   SCNCONT

Collimator
lens   Cylindrical   Scanning
lens   mirror

Optical
fiber   Laser unit   Scanner
motor

Focusing
lenses

Beam detect mirror

Mirror

Photosensitive drum

Drawings can explain. Trade publications often use diagrams and explanatory text to explain how something works. This illustration shows the inner-workings of a laser printer. (*Source:* Hewlett-Packard Company, Palo Alto, CA.)

Diagrams

Diagrams are most valuable in showing how something works. The functioning of an engine, the attachment of some accessory, the use of some product—can all be made clearer with a diagram.

In planning diagrams, you should not only check with the engineers but also pretest the final diagram on potential lay readers for comprehension and understanding. The key to effective artwork, particularly diagrams, is simplicity, simplicity, simplicity.

Avoid waste space. The upper photo has too much irrelevant background. Cropping makes the picture much more interesting at very little cost. Tight cropping is a must in employee publications. (*Source:* Terry Holzemer, Rudolph & Sletten Construction, Inc. Foster City, CA.)

Maps

Maps can show where a road is to be built, how to get to a meeting, how traffic is to be routed, or which street will be closed or opened. They can explain the site of a proposed housing development, the location of a dam, or even the borders of a new lake created by a dam.

Maps for your purposes should, as far as possible, show the details necessary to understand the situation but avoid clutter and irrelevant information. Too much detail makes a map difficult to read.

In preparing a map, it is advisable not to copy a published one. Most of these are copyrighted and permission to use them must be obtained. In addition, most published maps will probably contain too much detail for your purposes. Remember, maps sent to the media are often reduced, so that small type or thin lines may be obscured.

Renderings and Models

A rendering is an architect's drawing that shows how a finished structure will look. A scale model is a three-dimensional mock-up of the finished structure. A rendering or scale model may show either the interior or exterior of a proposed building. In either case, what you give to the media is a professional photograph of the rendering or model.

The use of renderings or scale models enables you to give readers a thorough understanding of what they are reading about. Renderings and models are widely used in news and feature releases about proposed construction or planned modifications of existing structures. The availability of a rendering or a scale model often makes the difference between a major newspaper story or a brief mention; it can also make the difference between a television news story (stations are always seeking ways to present things visually) or just a one-sentence statement by a TV anchor.

Print media will not use extremely high or wide illustrations. If the rendering or model will not fit into a normal 8- by 10-inch picture, you will have to get a new rendering or do some judicious cropping.

Cartoons

Cartoons are capable of packaging information in an interesting manner. They also condense a lot of complex data into very simple concepts. A major electronics firm in the Southwest, for example, used a comic book to explain profit sharing to its many workers who had limited knowledge of English. Utility companies also use the comic book format to tell children, as well as many adults, how electric power is generated.

Single cartoons can also serve many purposes, such as editorial comment. Several years ago, Chrysler Corporation provided the media with cartoons about the auto industry's concern with EPA regulations. Publications that agreed with the cartoon often used them on editorial pages. Cartoons may also be used for easy dissemination of information. The Internal Revenue Service (IRS) regularly distributes a series of cartoons that capsulize basic tax tips in an entertaining manner.

If you send editorial cartoons to news media, be sure that your organization is identified *in* the cartoon. People opposed to the idea may protest or even sue on the grounds that the cartoon's source is concealing its sponsorship.

Line Drawings and Clip Art

Cartoons are a form of line art, but most people think of line art as drawings that explain how something works (diagrams), where something is (maps), or how numerical quantities fit together (charts). These drawings are normally made by artists using paper and ink, but more and more are being produced on computers.

"Clip art" comprises another variety of line drawing; it includes thousands of basic drawings that can be used in advertisements, leaflets, brochures, and newsletter—but *not* in materials sent to the media.

When you need a line drawing, it isn't always necessary to start from scratch and hire an artist to make one for you. In many cases, what you need can be found in what is called a "clip book." The name comes from the fact that the line drawings are camera-ready; all you need do is clip them out and paste them down on the layout being prepared for offset printing.

A clip book may contain line drawings of people talking on the phone,

Clip art has many uses. A number of firms and companies create standardized "clip art" that can be used to brighten up newsletters, brochures, and pamphlets. "Clip art" is routinely used for newspaper advertising because it is cheap and readily available from supplier catalogues and on computer discs. (*Source:* Newspaper Distribution Service, New York, NY.)

standing up, talking to other people, driving cars, or even eating Thanksgiving dinner. Or the line drawings may be of simple objects: a typewriter, a wine bottle, a desk, a light bulb, and so on. Advertising agencies use a great deal of clip art for newspaper display advertising. Examples can be found in any weekly or daily newspaper. The grocery store ad, for example, might show a line drawing of a beef roast, a lobster, or even a butcher cutting meat. Restaurant ads often show clip art of a family being served dinner by a waitress.

A number of companies produce clip books and sell them to printers, advertising agencies, public relations firms, and company publications. Several firms even produce a monthly clip book devoted to upcoming seasons and events like Easter, Labor Day, July 4, Halloween, Thanksgiving, and so on. For names of clip-art vendors, consult a local printer or advertising firm. In addition, trade journals in art and design and public relations often contain advertisements for such firms.

Clip books are still the backbone of camera-ready artwork, but desktop publishing on computers is rapidly changing all this. Today, it is possible to buy software programs that contains thousands of symbols and line drawings on one disk. Used in conjunction with a program like Pagemaker, it is possible to select and even position the line drawing on a page layout before producing the page on a laser printer. As a consequence, even interoffice memos are incorporating clip art to make them more interesting.

CAPTIONS

With the exception of cartoons, which explain themselves, many illustrations need captions. With "mug shots," only the name or name and title may suffice. With other illustrations, the caption should tell the reader what he or she is looking at.

The main idea is to provide context and information that are not readily discernible from the illustration. The caption should not merely summarize; it should complement and explain.

How to Write a Caption

Most captions are short—four to six typewritten lines are usually enough. Follow the rules of good journalistic writing. Insofar as possible give the who, what, how, when, where, and why. Not all of these are necessary in the caption, but between the illustration and the caption the essential should be covered.

Use the present, active tense. Do not say, "The park gates were opened by Mayor Jones." Say, "Mayor Jones opens the park gates."

Don't say, "pictured above . . ." or "This picture shows. . . ." This is obvious to the reader and delays getting to the message.

There is still some argument about the use of writing "from left to right" in a photo caption. To many this seems redundant, since people read copy—and probably photographs—from left to right anyway.

If there are two or three people in the picture, it is assumed that you are identifying them from left to right. You can also indicate identity by the action taking place in the picture. For example, "John Jones presents Nancy South-wick with a $5000 scholarship at the annual awards banquet. . . ."

In general, the most important person in the photograph should be the first person on the left side of the picture. This ensures that this person is mentioned first in the photo caption. On the other hand, the most important person may be in the center of the picture, surrounded by adoring fans. In this case, you can merely write, "Sharon Lewis, the singer, is surrounded by adoring fans after her concert in Denver." Any reader should be able to figure out which person in the picture is Sharon Lewis.

Here are two captions for the same picture, the first poor, the second better:

> From left to right, Hazel Oatley and Les Switzer are shown standing amid sand-bags at a Parker, Arizona resort on the banks of the swollen Colorado River. They are part of a Red Cross team working all night to keep the river from flooding the resort and surrounding residential areas. The water was 5 feet deep and covered the boat dock behind them.

> Hazel Oatley and Les Switzer stand amid sandbags at a Parker, Arizona resort on the banks of the swollen Colorado River. They are part of a Red Cross team working all night to keep the river from flooding the resort and surrounding residential areas. Five feet of water covers the boat dock behind them.

Notice how the second caption retains the present, active tense and eliminates words that slow the reader down.

Format of the Caption

A caption is much like a press release. Some tips:

1. Give identifying information as you would in the heading of a release. This includes your name, telephone number, and organization.
2. You may wish to use a headline—a short phrase in capital letters that indicates the nature of the story.
3. Do not indent. Captions are written flush left for all the lines.
4. Write up to eight lines on a 60-space line. Keep the caption short, concise, and in the present tense as much as possible.
5. Some people use a half page of paper for a caption, others prefer to use a full 8½- by 11-inch page.

In either case, you must type the caption about halfway down the page or half-page, leaving enough blank paper for the next step.

Attaching the Caption

It is important to firmly attach your typewritten caption to the correct photo. As we have previously discussed, you have written your caption about halfway down the page or half-page. This leaves the top half blank. The page is then attached—with rubber cement or tape—to the back of the photo. (Rubber cement is the best bet. If you use tape, be sure that it can be peeled off without tearing the photo.) Never use other kinds of glue, clips, or staples.

You then fold the caption up over the photo. If you use a full-page caption, it will give the photo extra protection from scratches or marring. When the reporter or editor of a publication receives the photo and caption, he or she simply unfolds the paper and can then look at the photo while reading the caption, which, when opened, is directly below the photograph.

Identification of Illustrations

Photos sent to a publication should carry some additional identification besides the typewritten caption. Many organizations use a rubber stamp to print the firm's name, address, and telephone number on the back of every photo sent out. In this way, if the caption is accidently misplaced, the editor can at least call the agency or company to find out what the picture was about.

Some people not only use a rubber stamp but also give the photo a "slug line." For example, "American Cancer Exhibit at the Johnson County Fair, August 1990." This is typed on an adhesive label and attached to the back of the picture. In the case of a head-and-shoulders picture or mug shot, the name and title of the person is attached to the back of the photo.

Never use a pencil or pen to write on the back of a photo; it cracks the finish and causes reproduction problems. A wax or grease pencil—available in any art-supply or stationery store (the same kind of pencil you use for placing crop or scale marks on a photo) can be used if you are careful.

PHOTO AND ART FILE

A properly indexed and rigidly controlled illustration file is a necessity. Without this, negatives or artwork will be lost or the last print will be used and no one will know how to order replacements. Historically important pictures will lose their identity and be useless because everyone who knew what they meant is dead or gone from the organization.

You will probably have two kinds of pictures to deal with: those used in releases to the media and those used in printing in-house materials. (Sometimes a picture will be used for both purposes.)

You may wish to file the news releases—including the captions—separately and maintain a different file for other pictures. In either case, the important thing is to be able to find pictures, know what they mean, and order replacements. A further value of such a file is that it provides a permanent record of which pictures were used for which purpose. It also documents your activity.

Photos (and you may have several prints of each subject, together with their negatives or original artwork) should be placed in file folders with readily identifiable headings. These may be names such as "J. Gladwyn Jones, Chairman" or topical areas such as "19XX Employee Recognition Banquet," "Grand Opening of Lansing Store," or "Scale Model of Springfield Office Bldg." If you do not have the negative, you must mark one print "File Copy" and attach the name and address of the photographer together with his identifying number, so that you can reorder.

It is important to place in the file folder all pertinent data such as date picture was taken, location (if pertinent), photo releases from people portrayed (unless you have a blanket release elsewhere), complete names and titles of people shown, name and address of photographer, and restrictions on use of the picture (if any).

This may seem like overkill in terms of documentation, but you or your successor will appreciate such detail if the picture is taken out of the files five years later or the marketing or advertising department wants to use it in a sales brochure or advertisement. In addition, you can avoid embarrassment to individuals if all photos are dated. If the president of the company is now bald, he will not want you to send an old picture, showing him with a full head of hair, to the media. By dating all photos in your files, you will easily be able to determine whether a given picture is out of date or should be checked.

A final note about the filing of negatives or original artwork. It is important that they be protected from dust and possible scratches. The best bet is to place them in the cellophane sleeves available from any camera store.

SUMMARY

1. Illustrations can greatly increase the effectiveness of your messages. They often accomplish far more than words alone.
2. Illustrations must be newsworthy. They must convey information.
3. Photographs must be of high quality. Remember action, scale, camera angles, composition, lighting, and timing. Be very careful with group pictures.
4. Color photos—as opposed to black and white—add greatly to the visual impact.
5. Stock photos can help you illustrate internal publications economically.
6. Working with photographers requires selection of experts, clear agreement as to what is to be done, and cooperation in the planning and execution of the photo session.
7. Pictures can often be improved by retouching or cropping.
8. Artwork accomplishes many illustrative tasks better than photo-

graphs. Charts, diagrams, maps, renderings and models, cartoons, line drawings, and clip art may be used.

9. A caption must be attached to every illustration you release.
10. Everything you release should also be identified on the back.
11. A good art file is essential.

EXERCISES

1. Illustrative material can include photographs, line drawings, diagrams, models, cartoons, charts, and graphs. Find at least two examples of each from sources such as company newsletters, trade magazines, and newspapers. Mount each example on a single sheet of paper and indicate the context in which it was used.

2. News releases and features, when accompanied by illustrative materials, often stand a better chance of being used. What types of illustrative materials would you recommend for the following news releases? Use your imagination and try to think of as many kinds as possible. Describe in what way each would be applicable.

    a. The appointment of a new company president.
    b. An announcement that a new 15-story hotel will be built.
    c. An announcement of a new digital compact-disk recorder manufactured by Sony.
    d. A news story about the shortage of nurses in local hospitals.
    e. A how-to-do-it feature about planting rosebushes.
    f. A feature story about the rising popularity and sales of a sports car.
    g. A feature story about the growth and suceess of a pizza chain since its beginning five years ago.
    h. A chamber-of-commerce story about the ethnic diversity of a city.

3. A civic organization will be honoring five outstanding citizens at its annual banquet. Describe how you would organize and compose publicity photos of this event that would be acceptable to the photo editor of the local newspaper.

4. A local bank is having a grand opening for its new facilities, including the traditional ribbon cutting by city officials and an open house for the community. Describe what kinds of publicity photos could be taken of this event to ensure media acceptance.

5. Product publicity photos pose a major challenge, since it takes creativity to make a product look interesting and unusual. What kinds of publicity photos would you recommend for the following products?

    a. An electric frying pan
    b. A new tamper-resistant bottle of aspirin
    c. A personal computer
    d. A golf cart
    e. Mrs. Smith's "lite" potato chips
    f. A toy

6. Using the guidelines listed in this chapter, write a photo caption for the following situation: The picture shows two people and two Collie dogs. One person is Dr. Ronald F. Jackson, former president of the American Heartworm Society. The second one is Carolyn Matlack, owner of Teddy and Rose, the two collies. She is giving one dog a newly developed pill recently approved by the FDA to prevent heartworm disease in dogs. This medication, marketed by Merck & Co., is taken once a month.

Prior to its development, the standard prescription was a daily pill. Dr. Jackson is petting one of the dogs.

SUGGESTED READINGS

"Ajhar's Gnomes Hot on Wall Street." *Communication World*, January 1988, pp. 23–26.

Alexander, M. "Picture-Perfect Photographs Help Sell Story Ideas." *Public Relations Journal*, July 1985, pp. 5–7.

Douglis, Philip. *Pictures for Organizations: How and Why They Work as Communication.* Chicago: Ragan Communications, 1982.

"Editorial Cartoonist Brings Life to Word." *Communication World*, December 1987, pp. 23–26.

Hughes, Kathleen. "Why Do Celebrities Jump Through Hoop at Snap of a Camera?" *Wall Street Journal*, December 15, 1986, p. 1.

McDowell, Edwin. "America Is Taking Comic Books Seriously." *New York Times*, July 31, 1988, p. E7.

Morton, Linda P. "Use of Photos in Public Relations Messages." *Public Relations Review*, Winter 1986, pp. 16–21.

"Perils of a Successful Photographer." *Communication World*, October 1987, pp. 24–27.

Rivelli, William. "Photography: The Key to a Successful Annual Report." *Communication World*, December 1984, pp. 32–34.

Sklarewitz, Norman. "Custom Photos for Stock Shots." *Communication World*, February 1987, pp. 23–25.

"Supplier's Directory." *Communication World*, November 1987, pp. 34–38.

Wright, Armand. "Armand Wright: A Photographer Who's Making It on His Own." *Communication World*, February 1988, pp. 23–25.

Chapter
8

Broadcast News and Features

People spend more time watching television than doing anything else other than working or sleeping. Naturally, then, public relations people make great efforts to get their messages on TV—the medium that reaches so many people and does so with such power.

General television stations usually offer different versions of the same sort of news and entertainment. They reach large audiences with material that is supposed to have universal appeal. Public broadcasting system (PBS) stations usually offer more educational, cultural, and intellectual programs; the cable and satellite stations tend to concentrate on specialized topics, with much programming of sports, news, and movies. A few TV stations concentrate on ethnic or linguistic material and do provide direct avenues to certain groups. Recently, two Spanish-language television networks have been established.

Radio stations usually concentrate their programming on one area, such as news, foreign language, ethnic interest, or music, which can range from classical to hard rock. Individual audiences may be small, but listener interest is strong and the total audience for radio is very large.

With broadcast media, it is possible to reach either mass or highly specialized audiences. Knowing just who the stations reach is important and can be learned from the people who sell advertising on the stations. PBS stations don't carry advertising, but they, too, know a lot about their audiences.

Getting your message on TV can be done through the news channels (which involves writing, producing, and delivering news releases to the right gatekeeper) or through feature channels (which requires understanding the many different kinds of programs and the ways to get on them).

RADIO NEWS RELEASES

Because so many radio stations completely rewrite all the news releases they receive, some public relations people just send newspaper-type releases to radio stations. There are, however, numerous radio stations that accept real radio releases, and definite rules apply to these. Radio is based on sound, and every radio release must be so written that it can be easily read by an announcer and clearly understood by a listener.

Format

With one major difference, a radio release follows the form of a press release. Below the release date is the description and time requirement. For example, "RADIO ANNOUNCEMENT: (:30)" or "RADIO ANNOUNCEMENT: (:60)."

This indicates that the release is for radio use and that it runs 30 or 60 seconds. The timing is vital, because broadcasters must fit their messages into a rigid time frame that is measured down to the very second. Most announcers read at a speed of about 150 to 160 words per minute. Because word lengths vary, it is not feasible to set exact word counts for any given length of message. Instead, the general practice is to use a line count. With a typewriter or word processor set for 60 spaces, you will get about 16 lines of copy for every minute. For 10 seconds, you will need a $2\frac{1}{2}$ to 3 lines. For 20 seconds, you will need approximately 5 lines; and for 30 seconds, about 8 lines.

Content

A radio announcement contains the same basic ingredients as a press release, but the information is presented in a different way. Sentences must be short, so that the announcer will have time to draw a breath between them and the listener can better follow what is being said. An average sentence length of 10 words is a good goal.

The first few words are "tune-in" words, words that enable the listener to focus attention of the subject but are not the vital core of the announcement. People need a second or two to adjust their listening and interest to the new topic. If the most important part of the announcement comes in the first few words, it may not be heard. It is better to say, "It was announced today by Mammoth Insurance Company that all its claims arising from the recent earthquake have been settled." If you say, "Mammoth Insurance Company announced today that all its claims arising from the recent earthquake have been settled," many listeners may not get the name of the company.

Another thing to avoid in radio releases is detailed information that is not essential to the story. There isn't much time for amplification in 30 seconds, so the entire announcement is, for all practical purposes, the lead. Even if 60 seconds is used, the announcement must be condensed down to the bare essentials.

If possible, punctuation should be limited to commas and periods. Quotation marks can't be seen by listeners, so if someone is quoted, the copy should say something like this: "Jones said, quote, I will not run, unquote." If uncommon words or names are used, they should be spelled out. If it is necessary to indicate pronunciation, it should be done as in the *AP Broadcast Stylebook*.

Many abbreviations that are suitable for print cannot be used in radio releases. Instead of using symbols like $, %, and &, use the words "dollars," "percent," and "and." Numbers follow the same rule. One thousand, not 1000; five million, not 5,000,000. Time of day should be given as morning or evening, not A.M. or P.M.

Delivery

Because of the immediacy of radio, most stations prefer to receive releases by phone or on audiotape. Written releases that are sent through the mail are often several days old when they arrive. For these reasons, written releases are commonly used only to reach stations that are remote from the organization. Of course, these mailed releases cannot be used for news that has any element of urgency.

AUDIOTAPE NEWS RELEASES

Audiotape sent to a radio station can take two forms: (1) the "actuality" that is recorded by an identified spokesman and, (2) the regular tape recorded by an unidentified announcer. When an actuality is used, it is customary to have an introduction and close that identify the person speaking.

Actualities are better than straight announcements because the message comes from a "real person" rather than a nameless announcer. They are also more acceptable to stations—possibly for the same reasons.

Format

The preferred length for an audiotape is one minute; however, shorter tapes can be used. It is advisable to accompany any sound tape with a cue sheet showing the opening and closing words of the tape and indicating its running time. It is also desirable to send with the cue sheet a complete script of the tape. This enables the news director to judge the value of the tape without having to run it.

Not all sound tapes are limited to one announcement. It is a common practice to record several public service announcements (PSAs) on one tape. They may be of varying length, but they should be accompanied by cue sheets and scripts.

Production

Every audiotape starts with a carefully written and accurately timed script. The next step is to record the words. In doing this, it is imperative to control the quality of the sound. A few large organizations have complete facilities for this; some get help from 'moon lighting' station employees; but most people use a professional recording service.

The recording services have first-class equipment and skilled personnel. They can take a script, edit it, eliminate words or phrases that will not be understandable, record at the proper sound levels, and produce a finished tape suitable for broadcasting. They can find an announcer of whatever type is best suited to the kind of message to be delivered, and they can produce many copies of a tape.

You can find a recording service by asking your colleagues for their recommendations or by looking for "Recording Services" in the Yellow Pages.

Delivery

Tapes can be mailed to stations, but more and more people are relying on the telephone for transmission. Some of the recording services will handle telephone distribution of the tapes they produce. If you do it yourself or have it done by the recording service, the procedure is the same.

Someone phones the station and explains what is available. If the station wants the item, it is then sent over the phone line to the station and recorded there at the same time. If it is news, the item is offered to the news editor. If it is a feature or PSA, it is offered to the proper gatekeeper. Alternatively, it is possible to provide a telephone number that the media can call to pick up a prerecorded message.

Use

Producing sound tape is costly, so this process should be carefully monitored. If tapes are sent to stations and not used, they are a total loss. Some organiza-

**gordon news
and audio visual productions inc.
1557 pine street
san francisco 94109
(415) 776-7484**

FOR: MARSHAL HALE MEMORIAL HOSPITAL
RADIO NEWS ACTUALITY

<u>"EATING DISORDERS PROGRAM"</u>

LEAD: TODAY, A NEW LOCAL CLINIC IS BEING DEDICATED
WHICH EXCLUSIVELY TREATS THE EATING DISORDERS
ANOREXIA AND BULIMIA. HERE'S DR. ERICA GOODE,
MEDICAL DIRECTOR OF THE EATING DISORDERS
PROGRAM AT MARSHAL HALE MEMORIAL HOSPITAL
IN SAN FRANCISCO:

DR. GOODE: WE'VE SEEN A HIGHER INCIDENCE OF ANOREXIA AND
BULIMIA PARTIALLY BECAUSE BODY CONFIRMATION
HAS BECOME AN IMPORTANT PRIORITY IN OUR
SOCIETY. IN OTHER WORDS, MANY PEOPLE,
ESPECIALLY WOMEN, FEEL PRESSURED TO KEEP THEIR
BODIES THIN. HERE AT MARSHAL HALE, WE HAVE A
TREATMENT PORCESS THAT EMPHASIZES
PSYCHOTHERAPY, BODY IMAGE THERAPY, AND A FOOD
AND EATING GROUP. I'M EXCITED ABOUT OUR
PROGRAM BECAUSE WE'RE ABLE TO SEPARATE
ANOREXICS AND BULIMICS FROM PSYCHIATRIC
PATIENTS AND PROVIDE THEM WITH A RELAXING
ATMOSPHERE WHERE MORE HELP CAN BE GIVEN TO
THEM.

CLOSE: THE GOAL OF THE EATING DISORDERS PROGRAM IS TO
NORMALIZE THE PATIENTS' EATING AND BRING BACK
THEIR EMOTIONAL WELL-BEING.

A radio script. This is the written script for an "actuality," an audio tape featuring the
comment of an expert source. The script allows radio announcers to read the lead and
close but use the expert's actual voice as part of the newscast. (Source: Gordon News
and Audio Visual Productions, Inc. San Francisco, CA.)

tions mail tapes to stations and send along a return postcard on which the station can report use. The stations may or may not return the cards, but most users will.

Telephone distribution provides a better measure of utilization. When a forest fire imperiled California's Napa Valley, a large winery featured its president in a topical "actuality." He reported that the fire had not endangered the grape crop and went on to forecast an excellent harvest. When the tape was offered by telephone to some fifty radio stations, almost forty accepted and recorded it for use.

TELEVISION NEWS RELEASES

As with radio, the written release is not as satisfactory as a recording. Nevertheless all television announcements start with a written message that is then turned into an audiovisual presentation.

Format

There is one basic difference between a television release and a radio release. With television, it is necessary to supply not only the words but also the illustrative material. Accordingly, the script will describe the illustrative material (video) on the left side of the page, while the words (audio) are on the right. This script is accompanied by the video material.

The video material may be in the form of 35 mm slides, 16 mm film, or videotape. It must be in color. As with all audiovisual materials, it is vital to coordinate what is seen with what is heard. The words should describe the visuals and the illustrative material must show what is being talked about.

Content

Television relies heavily on action. If at all possible, you should use tape or film to provide the movement that is so essential. If you must use slides, make them active. Show people doing something. Avoid mug shots. Refer to Chapter 7 for guidance on putting life into still pictures.

The objective in any written television release that uses slides is to make it as much like a live action or a videotaped release as is possible. With no actual motion, it must try to provide the illusion of motion. This doesn't suggest optical tricks; it suggests that the still pictures should look like stills from a motion picture.

If you have film or silent videotape to show the action, the problem then is to edit it—by cutting and splicing—to the required length and to have the words keyed to the action. This will ordinarily require the services of a film or tape editor who knows just how many feet provide how many seconds of visual action.

With film or tape, you will have only one piece of visual material to accompany the script. If you are using slides, you must be very sure that they will be sequenced properly. This is done by numbering them and, on the script, indicating each number alongside the description of the slide.

With silent tape, film, or slides, the script indicates the exact time for each scene, so that the operator and the announcer will be coordinating the entire announcement. You should provide at least four copies of the script, so everyone working on the projection of the announcement—director, camera operator, actors, and announcer—will be able to coordinate.

The silent tape or film accompanied by a written news release provides an economical way to localize television announcements. Wells Fargo Bank produced a silent tape of its historic stagecoach carrying a load of happy children. The written release explained that the coach would be in the named city on certain dates and that local children would be given rides. This saved the cost of producing a separate sound track for each city. It also provided great flexibility in scheduling, because the dates could be inserted in the announcement when the exact time had been determined. If a sound track had been used, it might have been necessary to remake the entire tape to accommodate changes in the schedule.

VIDEOTAPE NEWS RELEASES

Videotape has largely displaced film in television news. Accordingly, the best way to get your news used on a television station is to supply a videotape news release (VNR).

Large organizations seeking enhanced recognition for their names, products, or services are the primary clients for VNRs. The high cost of these can more easily be justified if there is potential for national distribution and multiple pickups by television stations. Obviously, the cost is usually too great if the potential for usage is just one local or regional television market.

A VNR may cost between $4,000 and $50,000, according to *PR Services*, an industry publication. Costs for production and distribution vary depending on the number of location shots, special effects, and staff required to produce a high-quality tape comparable to network television news reports. An average high-quality VNR between one and three minutes in length costs about $20,000 to produce and distribute.

Because of the cost, you must carefully analyze the newsworthiness of your information and decide whether an audience of sufficient size and importance will be reached. Another question is whether the information will remain fresh and timely after the six weeks (average) it takes to write the script and produce the news release.

Michael Klepper, chairman of a New York marketing company, wrote in an article for the *Wall Street Journal* that "The only way a video news release will be used is if it contains news."

He said producing a VNR should be considered when:

- The organization is involved in a legitimate medical, health, or scientific breakthrough.
- Visuals can be used as background footage while the reporter or news anchor discusses the pertinent news copy.
- Visuals can be provided that the television stations can't obtain on their own.
- There is an interview segment that television stations can't get on their own.

Klepper gave an example of a well-received VNR: A company gained mass exposure for a new talking doll by producing a video news release about the history of artificial voice synthesis, using the doll as an example of how the technology is incorporated into everyday life. The release was popular with television news editors because it was slanted to new technology and a news trend.

Another example of news interest in technology is a VNR produced by Visa, U.S.A., that discussed the conceptual research of designing a super Visa card with a built-in computer chip and keyboard. The release was used on a number of television news shows, reaching a potential audience of more than 16 million.

Format

Essentially a videotape is a television release converted into a finished tape that can then be broadcast. If it is a news item, it should be about one minute long, though some can run up to 90 seconds. (This length was preferred by 52 percent of TV news directors in one survey.) However, brevity should be the rule. Features, of course, can be longer than news items, sometimes justifying a length of up to two minutes.

Production

The production of a videotape for broadcast use is not a job for amateurs. The entire process is highly technical; moreover, the equipment is costly and can be used only by people who know what they are doing. To find a producer, you can inquire among your colleagues or refer to the telephone directory. The Yellow Pages usually list these under the heading "Motion Picture Producers" or "Television Program Producers."

When you have selected several prospective producers, you may ask them to show you samples of what they have done. It is also advisable to ask their previous customers how well they were satisfied. You should also visit the producer's place of business in order to inspect the facilities and meet the people who would be working on your tapes. In your discussions with producers, you must make sure that each party understands what the other wants, what can be done, how it will be done, and, of course, what it will cost. (Incidentally, Nielsen Media Research surveyed TV news directors and found that 90 percent

**gordon news
and audio visual productions inc.
1557 pine street
san francisco 94109
(415) 776-7484**

FOR: WESTINGHOUSE CORPORATION   # 2157-V
TOTAL TIME: 2:05
                              "SCIENCE SEARCH '87"

SUGGESTED LEAD: This year's Science Talent Search shows a new trend among
                   young scientists...more foreign born science students are
                   developing their talents in the U.S..

SCENES	SECS	NARRATION
WIDE SHOT & VARIOUS MEDIUM SHOTS OF TALENT SEARCH FOREIGN BORN STUDENTS EXPLAIN PROJECTS	:00- :06	The 46th Westinghouse Science Talent Search has a different line-up of winners. Among the top 40 science students who come to Washington for the annual event, seven were born outside the U.S. Last year, four of the top five prize winners were foreign born.
		SOUND ON TAPE: CLAUDIA SANTOSA, FLUSHING, N.Y.
SANTOSA SOT	:19	"Well, I think the first thing I had to tackle was the English language. I came to this country not knowing any English expect for two words--yes and no."
		DAVID KUO, WHITESTONE, NY
KUO SOT	:27	"There's a lot of opportunities here, much, much more such as the Westinghouse Science Talent Search."
"TALENT SEARCH" SIGN CROWD EXAMINES PROJECTS	:34	The Search is the oldest high school science scholarship competition in the U.S. It offers the largest, most prestigious scholarships in the country, including the top prize of $20,000.

A television script. This is the first page of a script for a video news release (VNR) on
behalf of Westinghouse Corporation. Writers preparing a script need to list the visual
elements and a continuous running time in seconds. The third element is the narration.
Once the script is written, the video is produced and sent to television stations. (*Source:*
Gordon News and Audio Visual Productions, Inc. San Francisco, CA.)

preferred to receive three-quarter-inch tapes.) A number of companies now offer both production and distribution of VNRs. The largest firms and the total number of VNRs they produced in a recent year are

Medialink, New York City	425
Pro-Video, Los Angeles	364
DWJ Associates, New York	200
Visnews International, New York	200
West Glen, New York	132
Audio/TV Features, New York	120

In most cases, these firms not only produce the VNRs but also distribute them. Medialink, Pro-Video, Visnews, and Audio/TV features use satellite as a primary method of distribution, but VNRs can also be sent by cassette to television stations. In the case of satellite distribution, stations simply record the VNR off the satellite for later viewing and possible use.

Large public relations firms also produce VNRs for clients. Hill & Knowlton produces about 120 annually and Burson-Marsteller produces about 70. Smaller firms often coordinate the production of a VNR for a client but utilize the services of a production firm as a subcontractor.

Delivery

Except for satellite distribution, tape must be mailed to any station that is not practically at your front door. Tape is costly, and so is postage. For this reason, the use of tapes must be closely monitored. If a station never uses your tapes, you should take if off your mailing list. To monitor use, the general practice is to send with the tape a return card on which the station can tell you when the tape was used. A mailing of 100 tapes may yield a return of twenty-five to thirty cards. Another ten stations may use the tape but fail to report.

With the rapid advance in electronic technology it is conceivable that eventually it will be possible to phone a television station assignment desk, describe the tape, ask if the tape is wanted, and then transmit it electronically to the station, which will record it on its own taping equipment.

Use of VNRs

According to surveys, VNRs are gaining wider acceptance in television newsrooms, particularly among stations in small markets that don't have the staff and facilities to generate their own coverage. Larger news operations in metropolitan areas are also using more VNRs, as stations cut costs and reduce news staff.

One survey of 57 TV news directors, reported in *PR Reporter*, found that 68 percent had used VNRs within the past year. The station's ability to edit

VNRs That Were Used

Medialink reports the following examples of VNRs that were widely used.

- A toothpaste manufacturer gained generic exposure for the importance of anti-plaque toothpaste ingredients by running a well-done anti-plaque health-tip VNR.

- The manufacturer of a magnetic resonance imager—a sort of super x-ray machine—gained national exposure by telling the story of how one man's life was saved using the machine.

- Pan Am recently distributed a video news release about the naming of former Navy Secretary John Lehman as president of the company.

- The American Stock Exchange announced the first listing of a company run by a woman executive.

- Mazda showed off its new Flint, Michigan, auto plant, complete with more than 300 robots.

- IBM produced a five-part series on superconductivity and other important scientific matters.

- Disney announced its new French amusement park, with a joint statement by Disney and French officials.

- A new line of celebrity fragrances produced a feature about the trend, objectively mentioning some of its competitors to give the release more news credence.

- A manufacturer of smokeless tobacco sponsored an interview with A. J. Foyt about racing. There was no commercial message other than Mr. Foyt wearing the same "Copenhagen" cap he normally wears.

- Scott Paper regularly sponsors the Project Orbis flying hospital to Third World countries; it taped a feature on the project, with a secondary mention of Scott's sponsorship.

- Disneyland in California sponsored 44 "State Fair" days at Disneyland with tailored salutes and celebrations to each state that included the Miss America contestants from each state.

was the most important factor in deciding to use a video news release, but TV news directors also evaluated the releases on credibility, objectivity, and video quality. They also preferred getting releases on cassettes instead of by satellite feeds. The most popular VNRs are 60 to 90 seconds in length.

Another survey of 190 news directors by *PR Reporter* reconfirmed that VNRs without voice-over narration and with a B roll (unedited footage) are used twice as often as completely produced, narrated stories. Many stations, for example, prefer to have their own staff members narrate the VNR. This is comparable to the newspaper practice of rewriting news releases.

VNRs are not without controversy, despite their increasing usage. Many critics say they are too expensive in proportion to the audiences actually reached. The media, on the other hand, worry that since they are as well designed as regular news stories, audiences don't know they are produced by special interests. The most recent problem, according to an article in *Public Relations Journal*, is monitoring actual use of VNRs. One technological innovation is to give each VNR a code that can be electronically read by various monitoring services, like Nielson Media Research's SIGMA.

It is important for you to understand the value and purpose of VNRs, even though production and distribution are highly specialized and require the use of outside experts. Before you consult a production company, you must be able to conceptualize and visualize possible VNR topics and how a VNR can contribute to organizational objectives.

STOCK FOOTAGE

Videotape footage doesn't necessarily need to be tailored for each news story. You can supply external and internal scenes to be run as background visuals while the announcer is reading the news item. Such footage, stored at the television station, can be used whenever there is news about the company or a particular product or service. This saves the expense of sending a camera crew to the company whenever something newsworthy occurs. Stock footage is like a newspaper library that keeps photos and biographies of prominent people on file for use whenever there is a story about them.

FILM

The principal use of film is in features. These can be short featurettes of two or three minutes or full length productions that run for half an hour or more. Many organizations produce motion pictures for general use. Some of these, if they are not too commercial, can be placed on television stations. The use can be in established programs such as "magazine" shows or as short fillers to fill out an empty spot in a schedule. Often these films are in videotape form.

Acceptability

A typical listing of films available for use by television stations includes the following:

- *Waltzing Matilda*—a 32-minute travelogue on Australia, sponsored by the Australian Tourist Commission
- *Rethinking Tomorrow*—a 28-minute report on energy conservation, sponsored by the Department of Energy

- *Oil over the Andes*—a 27-minute account of the building of an oil pipe-line, sponsored by Occidental Petroleum Company
- *Noah Was an Amateur*—a 27-minute history of boat building, sponsored by the National Association of Engine and Boat Manufacturers

If your organization has a film suitable for TV use or if it is willing to produce one, this is a real opportunity for exposure.

Delivery and Use

Getting film to a station requires some method of informing the station of its availability (it would be wasteful to send a film without a definite request). You can handle this yourself, but it is better to use a distribution service such as Association Films or Modern Talking Picture Service. These organizations can place your films with television stations, schools, clubs, universities, and civic groups.

A distribution service will get orders, send and recover the film, and report use to you. Some distribution services handle videotape as well. (See Chapter 16 for further information on producing and distributing films and tapes.)

PUBLIC SERVICE ANNOUNCEMENTS

A PSA is defined by the Federal Communications Commission (FCC) as an unpaid announcement that promotes the programs of government or voluntary agencies or that serves the public interest. In general, as part of their responsibility to serve the public interest, radio and TV stations provide free time to charitable and civic organizations. Thus, a PSA may be a message from the American Heart Association about the necessity of regular exercise or an appeal from a civic club for teacher volunteers in a literacy project.

Profit-making organizations rarely receive free broadcast time despite the "public service" nature of their messages, but sometimes an informational campaign by a trade group qualifies. For example, the Aluminum Association did get free air time on a number of stations by producing a PSA about how to recycle aluminum cans. Before the announcement was released, the association received an average of 453 calls a month. Five months after the PSA began appearing, the association had received 9500 calls at its toll-free number. The PSA was used in 46 states, and 244 stations reported 16,464 broadcasts of the announcement.

This example shows the potential effectiveness of PSAs. Remember, however, that others are aware of the potential; therefore many PSAs are available to the stations. Only those that are timely and of high recording quality stand a chance of being used.

Other points to remember about PSAs:

1. Only nonprofit, civic, and voluntary organizations are eligible to use PSAs. Announcements by profit-making organizations are considered

advertisements and stations charge regular advertising rates for carrying them.

2. Since deregulation of the broadcasting industry in the 1980s, stations feel less pressure to provide a community service by running PSAs for nonprofit groups. Although a station's renewal of its license is still based somewhat on serving the community and the public interest, there is no minimum standard for broadcasting PSAs.

3. PSAs, which are broadcast free of charge, are rarely used during periods of peak listening, when a station can run revenue-producing advertisements. Consequently, the PSA about a community health fair may only be heard at 5 A.M. or late Sunday night, when there are fewer ads. Because of this, even nonprofit groups, wishing to reach the largest possible audience, often pay regular advertising rates to get their PSAs on the air.

Use Various PSA Lengths

It is important to furnish a radio station with public service announcements of various lengths. This gives the station the opportunity to vary the announcement and use the appropriate one depending on the time available. The following is an example:

- *10 Seconds:* The San Francisco Fire Department's annual open house is coming up Saturday, October 17, at the Fire Training Center, 19th and Folsom Streets. Doors open at 10 A.M. and admission is free.

- *15 Seconds:* Rescue demonstrations and fire-safety shows are all part of Fire Prevention Day, Saturday, October 17th. The whole family will enjoy events at the Fire Department's Training Center, at 19th and Folsom Streets in San Francisco. Doors open at 10 A.M. and admission is free.

- *20 Seconds:* You can see what really goes on inside fire stations on Saturday, October 17th—Fire Prevention Day—in San Francisco. The fire department will hold its annual open house at the Fire Training Center, 19th and Folsom Streets. See death-defying rescue demonstrations, the latest in equipment and fire prevention techniques. Doors open at 10 A.M. and admission is free.

- *30 Seconds:* The San Francisco Fire Department is holding its annual open house Saturday, October 17th. You won't want to miss the antique fire equipment, daring rescue demonstrations from a seven-story building, and dramatic fire-safety shows.

  It's all part of Fire Prevention Day, and it takes place at the Fire Department's Training Center, at 19th and Folsom Streets in San Francisco. Doors open at 10 A.M. and admission is free. Remember, Fire Prevention Day . . . Saturday, October 19th at the Fire Training Center.

Source: Bay City Public Relations Inc., San Francisco.

Remember, PSAs may be used either on radio or television. They must be prepared for specific time lengths.

Here are samples of some radio public service announcements for Goodwill Industries:

- *10 Seconds* (32 words): A man is no less a craftsman because he sits in a wheelchair. At Goodwill Industries, the disabled are given a chance to keep on working. We hope you'll keep on giving.
- *20 Seconds* (53 words): Men and women who were considered discards by society are now repairing their own lives. On-the-job training has made Goodwill Industries the number-one rehabilitation facility in the country. Goodwill is in the business of helping the handicapped members of our society. Why not make it your business to help Goodwill?
- *30 Seconds* (77 words): Picture a man standing at a table repairing a radio and a woman standing behind a counter working a cash register. Now, picture that man in a wheelchair and that woman on crutches. Is either one any less a craftsman because they have physical handicaps? The people at Goodwill Industries don't think so. At Goodwill it's the ability that counts, not the disability. We hope you'll take another look—and then give your support to Goodwill.

TELEVISION NETWORKS

The networks furnish news and programs to affiliated stations. They are headquartered in New York and most major decisions about news or programs are made there. Most entertainment programs are produced in Hollywood. Feature programs such as *60 Minutes* may be produced anywhere, but the decisions as to what to produce are made at the network headquarters. Network news and programs are generally broadcast from New York or Washington, with some originating in Los Angeles and Chicago.

News

The major networks have large news-gathering departments that cover stories throughout the world. The networks have "bureaus" in most major cities, both domestic and foreign. In addition, a network may pick up a story from an affiliated station or use, with permission, material from another network. Also, the networks get news from the wire services.

To get news onto a network, it must be of great interest. It must be of national importance or have such a strong human interest that it will appeal to practically everyone.

If you are convinced that you have a story worth national exposure, you should telephone the nearest office of each of the networks and ask for the news department. Give the highlights of the story and ask if they are interested. If there is interest, you must then set up a place and time for the news team to cover the story.

Remember that it takes some hours to cover a story, get it to a studio, and edit it for broadcast. If it is hot news, it should get to the networks in the morning so as to have a chance of making the evening broadcast. Morning news may use material from the afternoon of the preceding day.

Features

Network features such as *60 Minutes, 20/20,* and *Yesterday, Today, and Tomorrow* are taped before broadcast, and the content is determined at headquarters by the feature's producer. If you have an idea for inclusion in one of these programs, it should be submitted to the network, but only to one at a time. On things like this, the networks want exclusives.

Interview Shows

Shows like *Meet the Press* and *Face the Nation* want only people of national importance. Generally the participants are political figures, but there are exceptions. A spokesman for a large national corporation or a large nonprofit group may be considered. Placement of a spokesman on one of these shows is done by arrangement with the producer, well in advance of the possible broadcast. The content of these shows is planned weeks or even months ahead.

Another form of interview show on the networks is the morning show, such as *Today* or *Good Morning America,* which combines news and interviews. Getting on one of these shows is done exactly as described for the others, but it may be a little easier. They don't draw such large audiences and hence there is less competition for the spotlight. Also, they lean a little more to the human-interest type of story.

A third type of show in this group is that moderated by some star from the entertainment world. Most of the guests on these shows are entertainers, authors, or celebrities. The point of origin may roam from Hollywood to Las Vegas or even to the East Coast, but arrangements for appearance are generally made through the office where the show is headquartered. These shows are usually taped well in advance. If you have a celebrity who might fit on such a show, you must find a time that is mutually agreeable to the celebrity and to the producer.

Talk Shows

Some of these shows use one guest at a time while others may have a panel of people discussing a given subject. For talk shows, you provide one individual who is the spokesperson for your organization. That spokesperson should be either a celebrity or an expert on the topic you propose. Talk shows generally resist using guests who are employees of the organization represented, because these people tend to seize upon the opportunity to deliver a free commercial.

Nevertheless, it is possible to use your "in-house" expert if he or she is really an expert. For example, the director of consumer relations for your organization might appear on a consumer service show, or a director of home economics could be placed on a cooking show.

Some local stations have talk shows geared to specific audiences. *AM/San Francisco* is an interview show on KGO-TV in that city and is somewhat representative of other such shows across the nation. This particular show defines its audience as nonworking mothers between the ages of 18 and 49. Segments on the one-hour show vary from six to ten minutes. It usually opens with a celebrity guest and then has segments that help its viewers "save money and save time." The show also uses guests from the business community who can comment on money, taxes, the stock market, and similar topics.

Here are some questions you might ask when thinking about what you would like to place on a talk show:

1. Is the topic newsworthy? Can you give a new angle on something in the news?
2. Is the topic timely? Can you tie the idea into some life-style or cultural trend?
3. Is the information useful to the viewers? How-to ideas may be welcomed.
4. Does your spokesperson have viewer appeal? A celebrity may be acceptable, but there must be a logical tie-in to your organization and to the topic to be discussed. An athlete might be plausible in talking about running shoes but out of place in a discussion of education and the importance of reading.
5. Can the spokesperson stay on the track? It is easy for celebrities to get involved in discussions of their personal affairs.
6. Can you keep the speaker from stressing the commercial angle? Most talk-show hosts will allow a brief mention of a brand name or sponsor identification. If your speaker gets too commercial, the entire interview may be deleted—and your organization may land on the list of those who can't come back.

When you know the answers to the foregoing questions, you will be ready to look for a booking—or several. Here are some tips that should help:

1. Be sure that your speaker fits the program. If he or she isn't a fast thinker, avoid shows full of rapid exchanges and loaded questions.
2. Be sure that you know the requirements of the program and the abilities of your spokesperson.
3. Plan to use visuals if possible. Charts, diagrams, samples, and even videotapes may help the producer to decide.
4. Deal with only one person on the program. But you *can* approach producers of other programs on the same station.

5. Be very careful about exclusivity. Some stations will refuse to use a guest who appears on a competing station. Find out before you commit. By committing to one station, you may miss an opportunity to get on several others.

6. Plan variations so that you can offer the same person to different shows or different stations without giving the same thing to each.

7. Don't cancel a booking just because a better opportunity comes up later.

8. Tell the director if you have any special needs, such as lighting, properties, and so on. If you want a copy of the taping, ask in advance. (You should supply the cassette.)

9. Don't make last-minute changes. Be sure that you can deliver your spokesperson on time.

10. Don't let several people get involved in the arrangements. That is a sure way to get things fouled up.

11. Prepare your speaker (see Chapter 15).

Entertainment Programs

A national organization concerned with a social or health issue can propose an episode involving that issue in a dramatic or comedy series. You can assist the program producer by supplying technical information. Such programs do not make overt sales pitches, but the message is inherent in the story line.

In a popular soap opera, for example, a leading female character has to deal with breast cancer. This enables millions of women to get the American Cancer Society's information even though they don't take the time to read the society's brochure. Other popular network series have dealt with such issues as battered wives, alcohol abuse, AIDS, racism, mental depression, suicide, and a host of other societal ills.

Even Nancy Reagan, who was active in the campaign to warn teenagers about the dangers of drug abuse, portrayed herself in an episode of *Different Strokes* centering around her visit to a school classroom to talk about drug abuse.

Mrs. Reagan's appearance—like other story lines about social and health problems—was not accidental. These presentations result from well-organized public relations efforts to convince the producers of entertainment programs that the given issue is a real one and would contribute to a good plot.

"Product Plugs"

Television dramatic and comedy series are also good outlets to enhance a company's products and services. It is not uncommon in a detective show for all the cars used in the various scenes to be from Ford, General Motors, or Chrysler. This, again, happens not by chance but by a carefully planned agreement. Thus the show gets free use of the cars and the manufacturer gets visibility.

The travel industry often gets plugs on TV shows as a trade-off providing transportation and lodging. That is why a viewer may see an Eastern Air Lines or TWA jet landing or taking off as a transition between scenes. But other companies can also get their products mentioned or observed if it fits the script. For example, part of the public relations strategy for introducing Luma's new video telephone to consumers was to place it on the desks of detectives Sonny Crockett and Ricardo Tubbs in episodes of NBC's *Miami Vice.*

In an episode on *The Cosby Show,* Vannessa Huxtable telephones a friend to talk about a forthcoming family trip. "I'm staying at the Hyatt Regency," she says. A few minutes later, Cliff Huxtable (Bill Cosby) remarks that the family will be staying at "a very lovely hotel" that would place fresh fruit and flowers in their rooms.

Again, there was an agreed-upon trade-off. Hyatt Regency provided free lodging for the cast and crew of the show while they were filming that episode in Atlanta. The deal saved the show probably $50,000 in hotel expenses, and in the words of a Hyatt spokesperson to the *Wall Street Journal:* "We believe the Huxtable family's endorsement has much more credibility than a paid ad. Now our name will live forever in reruns and syndication." If the hotel chain had placed a 30-second ad on *The Cosby Show,* it would have cost $380,000.

You should always be alert to possible opportunities for publicity on television. If the company's product or service lends itself to a particular show, contact the show's producer directly or through an agent who specializes in matching company products with the show's needs.

PSAs

The networks allocate some air time to PSAs, but only causes of national interest have a chance. Among the categories that are likely to appear in network PSAs are organizations raising money to combat some disease or those working on famine or flood relief. Messages like "Support the National Guard and Reserves," or "Register and Vote" may also be aired.

Because only a few causes and organizations are eligible for these PSAs, most of them are arranged by large national organizations. The procedure is to contact the public service departments of the networks.

TELEVISION STATIONS

Any television station in your own community may provide opportunities for the placement of news or features. To find and utilize these opportunities, you will need to know who to approach and what to offer.

Gatekeepers

There are on any station a few key executives who determine what is broadcast. The titles may vary, but those given below will usually come close.

WEATHERMAN SEGMENT SUMMARIES

NBC – THE TODAY SHOW   AIR TIME: 7:10 a.m.
NEW YORK   AUDIENCE: 13,710,000
WEATHERMAN: Willard Scott

Since Willard Scott was in Kentucky on the first day of spring, the berries were delivered on Monday, March 24. The segment opened with anchor Jane Pauley apologizing for talking with her mouth full of strawberries. While prominently displaying the basket of berries, Pauley asked Scott where they came from. "The great state of California," replied Scott. Pauley then reached for a berry and commented on the size, while Scott explained how sweet they are. He continued the segment by thanking the growers, and reminding viewers that spring is here and "California strawberries are in, bigger and better than ever."

KSTP   AIR TIME: 6:00 p.m.
MINNEAPOLIS/ST. PAUL   AUDIENCE: 215,000
WEATHERMAN: Dennis Feltgen

Dennis Feltgen devoted a large portion of his broadcast to strawberries. While displaying the "California Grown" flat filled with strawberries, Feltgen began his broadcast with "From the sure sign of spring department, the first fresh fruit of spring -- the strawberry. He explained that the berries came from California and then discussed the number of strawberries Americans consume each year. He lead into the weather by informing his viewers of the large California crop despite the rainy weather.

KGO   AIR TIME: 6:00 p.m.
SAN FRANCISCO, CA   AUDIENCE: 335,000
WEATHERMAN: Pete Giddings

Weatherman Pete Giddings began his broadcast by announcing the arrival of the first day of spring and the first fresh fruit of the season – "strawberries grown in our very own state." While displaying the flat of berries, Giddings and the anchor proceeded to sample some berries before beginning the weather. At the end of the forecast, the anchor and Giddings were still eating the berries, with the anchor commenting on how sweet and beautiful the strawberries were.

WBZ   AIR TIME: 5:30 p.m.
BOSTON, MA   AUDIENCE: 307,000
WEATHERMAN: Bruce Schwoegler

Bruce Schwoegler began his weather broadcast by displaying the flat of strawberries on the weather desk. He then thanked the California Strawberry Advisory Board for sending the berries in celebration of the first day of spring. After warning Bostonians of an impending storm, Schwoegler ended his forecast by picking up a berry and saying "the only medicine for handling the weather is this...a strawberry."

Ideas make news. Ketchum Public Relations, on behalf of the California Strawberry Advisory Board, came up with the idea of sending television weather reporters a crate of strawberries on the first day of spring. The objective was to generate consumer awareness that the first crop of California strawberries was now available, even though many areas of the nation still had cold weather. Weather reporters liked the unusual angle. This is a report showing the idea's "success." (*Source:* Ketchum Public Relations, San Francisco, CA.)

- The general manager. He or she, comparable to the publisher of a newspaper, determines general policy and manages all the departments. It is this person who is charged with the financial success of the station.
- The program director. This person decides which programs to produce and show—including both general entertainment programming and the special continuing programs that are managed by the people in the next group.
- The directors of individual continuing programs. These people moderate the various panel and talk shows and manage the magazine-type shows carried by so many stations.
- The news director. This person manages the entire operation of gathering and producing the news.
- The assignment editor, who works under the news director, is the counterpart of the city editor on a newspaper. He or she assigns the teams that cover the news stories.
- The reporters. This includes both camera operators and the people who get and write the news. They are sent by the assignment editor to cover whatever stories the editor selects. In most cases, the reporter and camera operator work as a team of two, but there are variations. Some reporters appear on the air and some write the stories that others report before the studio cameras.
- The public relations (or public affairs or public service) director. He or she selects the material to be broadcast as a service to the community.

Local News

Every station gathers local news with its own facilities. To get your news story on local television, there are three possible procedures: (1) You can phone the news department, ask for the assignment desk (or assignment editor), and give the highlights of your story; (2) you can send a news release; or (3) you can send a film clip or videotape.

For a station in your own town, the first method is by far the best. For out-of-town stations, the news release with accompanying slides, film, or videotape is the only possibility. Some people have had success with this: When a local station covers a news story, the public relations person arranges for extra videotapes of the item. These are then rushed to the nearby stations in time for their next news programs. For example, a station in Harrisburg might not be able to cover a story in Philadelphia but would possibly use the story if the tape were provided.

Another way to get on the air is applicable if your organization includes some person of great prominence—so prominent that anything he or she says or does is automatically news. In that case it is advisable to provide all stations in your area with color slides of that person for use as a background while a newscaster reads the particular item. This may be your release or a report prepared by the station from information gathered by a reporter.

Whenever you think you have an item worthy of TV coverage, remember the facetious but significant wisecrack made by one expert: "If it wiggles, it's news." Get motion into the story. Talking heads are dull and trite. Remember the visual. Try to get the name of the organization into the background with a poster or a plaque.

If the news is about some event, you must find, before the reporters get there, the part of the event that is most visual and active. Refer back to Chapter 7 and think about camera angles, framing, backgrounds, action, scale, groups, composition, lighting, timing, and so on. Above all, you must do everything possible to help the reporters get the story.

Turning Pitches into Placements

Radio and television news directors, as well as the producers of various talk and interview programs, receive numerous letters offering subject ideas and spokespersons. A good, persuasive query or "pitch" often results in multiple placements.

Unfortunately, too few pitches are well conceived and tailored to the media gatekeeper's needs. Some tips on writing good pitch letters are made by Ketchum Public Relations, New York, in its monthly periodical called *Ketchum Contact*. The following guidelines are adapted from the firm's recommendations:

1. *Keep the pitch down to one page.* If Dan Rather can highlight the essence of a major news story in a few sentences, you can write about a client's product in the same amount of space.

2. *Localize your pitch.* If you're pitching nutrition to a certain segment of the population, then write about that segment of the market. For instance, "The 450,000 women in Boston . . ." or "We estimate one out of four children in Tampa. . . ."

3. *Think trend.* How does your product or program fit into the trends, take a lead in trends, or even buck the trends that have already been noted by the media?

4. *Keep pitch letters informative and lively* to make them more interesting to the reader. Stiff prose won't make a story shine and come alive.

5. *Research your pitch.* Imagine being a news director or talk-show producer and then ask the type of questions these people would want answered. Target marketing, not a shotgun approach, is the name of the game.

6. *Consider alternate dates.* Negotiate with the news director or program producer. If they can't use the idea or your representative this month, how about next month? If they can't interview a person at the studio, how about an over-the-phone interview?

7. *Reach beyond the client and your immediate program.* Offer to help a reporter on stories that may only be indirectly connected to your product or event. You'll make an editorial friend for life.

8. *Take no for an answer,* but get a sense of why the story has been rejected. It may offer you an opportunity to repackage and get a yes on your next pitch.

Local Programs

Television stations broadcast many locally produced programs. A look at *TV Guide* or the weekly television schedule published by your local newspaper will tell you just what shows are being broadcast and which might be an outlet for you. Generally these shows fall into one of two classes: magazine and talk/interview formats. Having identified these prospects, your next step is to watch them as broadcast. Some will be unsuitable, but others may be of such a nature that your ideas and material might be usable.

With a target selected, you must then plan exactly what you want to see on the air. This is presented to the director of the show by letter, giving full details of what you propose and why you think it will be interesting to the viewers of the program. The letter should be followed up with a phone call a few days later. If the idea is accepted, you then make all arrangements for recording the show.

Magazine Shows

These shows appear under many different names but all have feature elements. They are not news shows. They are frequently shot on location and generally show considerable action.

Magazine shows in one city in one week featured such subjects as the one-pound baby who survived, a "used-house" dealer who buys used houses and delivers them to new owners, a treatment for anorexia nervosa, a couple who quit the business world to live on a yacht, a homemaker who went through a complete image makeover before going into the business world, remedies for back pain, bridal fashions, tips on dog training, a community of mentally disturbed people, a black-belt karate expert, blue-collar nervous stress, and several others.

Talk-show opportunities are not limited to your own locality. It is possible, with ample advance planning, to arrange for a whole series of talk-show appearances. There are several useful directories, such as *U.S. Publicity Directory* or *Working Press of the Nation*. Others are separate publications, such as *Television Contacts*, which is published by Larimi Communications Associates, Ltd. Larimi also publishes *Radio Contacts* and *Cable Hotline*.

Program Fillers

Television stations occasionally need small items to fill out a magazine-type programs or longer items to use up a complete 15- or 30-minute time slot. Videotape and film from outside sources is often used for these purposes.

The placement of tape or film is usually done by offering it to the program director through the mail. It is costly to produce these materials, so don't get into this unless there is a chance that a considerable number of stations will use it.

Television Contacts
MONTHLY CHANGE BULLETIN

MAY 1987

NEW PROGRAMS

KTVU-TV, OAKLAND, CA

Independent Station KTVU-TV, Oakland, CA (part of the San Francisco Metropolitan Area), is currently producing a new public affairs program entitled "Studio A." Covering local, regional and sometimes national issues, the program is broadcast Saturday 7:30 - 8:30 a.m. The hosts are Ian Zellick, Cindy Tinsley, Serena Chen, Laura Rodriguez and Johnny Selvin. Interviews on "Studio A" include talks with authors, experts and newsworthy public figures. Contact Cindy Tinsley (415/874-0182) is responsible for booking guests 3 - 4 weeks an advance. Interviews are aired live. Press releases and information on public affairs, consumer issues, science, medicine/health, business, education, behavior/lifestyles, food/fashion/home, women's & minority issues are accepted for usage consideration. Visual aids such as film, tapes slides and black & white photos can also be used.

KTVU-TV also produces a new talk/entertainment program in a magazine format, which airs Monday - Friday 12:00 - 1:00 p.m. The broadcast is entitled "2 At Noon," and features Co-hosts Barbara Simpson and Bob MacKenzie. The program also features hard news and talk on local, regional & national topics. Interviews on "2 At Noon" feature authors, experts, entertainers, politicians, spokespersons and newsworthy public figures. Contact Rich Hall is responsible for booking guests 2 - 3 weeks ahead for live appearances. Press releases and information on public affairs, consumer issues, science/health, business, education, behavior, lifestyles, food/fashion/home, sports and travel/leisure are accepted, as well as film, tapes, slides, black & white photos and new product information.

Also at the station, Caroline Klas-Chang is now program director and Mark Richardson & Tony Bonilla are the assignment editors. CONTACT: KTVU-TV, P.O. Box 22222, Oakland CA 94623 (Stu-

Program opportunities. Specialized directories and monthly supplements help public relations personnel pinpoint what types of information are needed by various radio and television shows. Effective media placement, in large part, depends on public relations personnel doing their "homework." (*Source: Television Contacts,* a publication of Larimi Communications, Inc., New York, NY)

Editorials

Television stations regularly broadcast editorials on topics of public interest. Sometimes the issue is clearly known and sometimes the editorial tries to influence opinion on some subject about which the public knows very little. In every case the editorial is identified as opinion.

It is possible to persuade a station to editorialize. If your topic is noncontroversial, you may be able to propose an editorial by talking to the director of public relations. For example, you might propose an editorial on the need for more Boy Scout or Girl Scout leaders. If the subject is controversial, the station will make the decision at the top level by thoroughly reviewing the pros and cons of the issue.

Rebuttals

When a station runs an editorial on any subject, it usually offers to provide equal time for a rebuttal. Rebuttals are normally accepted only from spokespeople for responsible organizations. If your organization wants to present a rebuttal, you should phone the public relations director, identify yourself and your organization, and explain why you want to present a rebuttal. If the station agrees, you must submit your proposed rebuttal in writing. This allows the station to check for libel, slander, unsuitable language, and length. The length of time may be 20 or 30 seconds. On rare occasions, the permitted length might run to 60 seconds.

When the rebuttal is approved, your contact at the station will tell you when and where your spokesperson or you should appear for the taping. Usually this is in the studio and long before the actual broadcast. It may be necessary to record your rebuttal several times in order to get a good one. This may be aired once or several times, depending on how many times the station airs its editorial. They will try to give both sides equal time.

Controversies

If a story is noncontroversial, it is judged solely on the basis of probable interest to the viewers. If the station thinks that a story has merit, it will be broadcast. With controversial material, the situation is quite different.

The "fairness doctrine" of the Federal Communications Commission requires broadcasters to provide a reasonable amount of time for the discussion and consideration of public issues. The FCC has recently decided that this is unconstitutional. Now the matter is in the courts, but Congress may act to restore the doctrine. Meanwhile, most stations continue to follow the original rules.

A problem arises, however, when a station decides that a given situation is not a public issue. For example, when nurses in San Francisco went on strike against all the hospitals, television stations carried numerous interviews in which nurses were allowed to state their positions. The stations showed the picket lines and in general gave extensive coverage to one side of this controversial story. They did not carry anything about the other side of the issue. When hospital administrators asked for a chance to reply, the stations said that they were reporting news, not discussing a public issue.

On the other hand, when broadcasters decide that a controversy should be covered, both sides are usually given ample opportunity to present their case. In such a situation, every program that could reasonably devote some time to the topic is a prospect.

If your organization is involved in a controversy, your biggest problem may be to get speakers to the programs that ask for them. This means that you must maintain a corps of speakers and an accurate system for keeping track of their appointments. One good way to do this is to prepare a calendar large enough to carry daily listings of stations, programs, times, and speakers. Speakers should be coached and, of course, you must make sure that they get to the right places and at the right times.

Planning Your Approach to Broadcast Media

These guidelines were adapted from a handbook by The Association of Public Service Directors, Bay Area Radio and Television Stations. Check stations in your particular area for such a handbook.

REALISTIC PLANNING

Plan ahead.

Allow four weeks to get your message to the media. This includes preparation, distributing, and broadcast time.

Are you eligible for free public service air time?

If your organization is a nonprofit group, social or civic, and your message is directly related to the activities of your group, it is eligible.

What do you hope to accomplish with your message?

Think carefully about your needs and purposes. Write them down. Then decide upon the most effective method of reaching the public.

What services are offered by stations?

- **Public service announcements.** These are brief messages which describe the activities of your organization. (10, 20, 30 and 60 seconds)

- **Free-speech messages.** Statements of personal opinion on matters of current general public interest.

- **Community calendars.** Announcements listing details of special events of community interest.

- **Public affairs programs.** Interview or discussion programs which provide for in-depth consideration of complex issues.

- **News programs.** Events of wide interest which affect many people often qualify as news items.

What form should your message take?

All stations accept written announcements. Some accept prerecorded messages.

What audience would you like to reach with your message?

Listeners and viewers come in all ages, races, and interests. You must first decide what audience will be most likely to respond to your project or appeal. Select stations which serve that special audience.

Should announcements be prepared in any special form?

All stations prefer copy that is prepared and presented in specified ways. Sample forms and instructions should be studied and followed.

When will your messages be scheduled for broadcast?

Actual days and times of broadcast are determined by the station on the basis of interest, immediacy, balance, and variety. Stations receive numerous public service announcements daily. Submitting your copy early will help in scheduling.

Who do you call for assistance on the preparation of your announcement or materials?

The public service director will be pleased to assist you. You will find that a handbook will answer many of your questions. Please read it carefully before calling.

IN REVIEW

- Plan early.

- Know your purposes.

- Prepare materials properly.

- Select stations carefully.

- Submit your message early.

- Before you start your work, read this handbook carefully.

The National Association of Broadcasters offers a free brochure, called *If You Want Air Time*, to nonprofit organizations. It tells what to do and how to do it.

Free-Speech Messages

Free-speech messages can be classed as guest editorials. They are expressions of opinion presented by an individual or organization on a topic of general public interest. The subject must be timely and the station decides how much time to allot and how many times to air the message. Arrangements are made in the same way as for any other announcement. You provide the spokesperson and the message and record it at the studio.

An individual can present a free-speech message. There is a limitation, however: The speaker must be a responsible person and he or she must present a strong case for the appearance. If the speaker represents a substantial organization, the task is easier.

Community Calendars

These are used to announce events of community interest. The event must be of wide importance. A meeting of the local automobile dealers' association is not of general interest. A meeting of the local school board to consider closing a school is important to the entire community and thus qualifies for listing in the calendar.

These announcements are mailed to the station and read by an announcer. The announcement lists the name of the organization, the time and place of the meeting, and often gives a telephone number that members of the audience may call for further information. If there is a compelling reason, the message can be phoned in to the director of the community calendar; usually, however, all the details of the event are finalized far enough in advance to permit mailing the information. You should mail calendar items to the station at least three or four weeks in advance.

Public Service Programs

In addition to the interview or talk shows previously discussed, many stations regularly produce features devoted to special interests of the community. Among the subjects covered are education; gardening; home repair; problems of the elderly, children, or minorities; foreign-language or ethnic topics; human-interest stories; matters of religion; political forums; documentaries; homemaking; recreation; entertainment; and others.

Getting on one of these programs is handled in the same way as are other station feature programs. A review of the local weekly television schedule will show what might be available.

Station Requirements

To get on the schedules of stations in your area, you must offer things they can use and that they will accept. In many cities, you can get from each station a summary of the kinds of messages it can utilize. These summaries indicate

Champaign — WJTX-AM (Continued)
Profile: Golden Oldies:
T.A.—25-45; W—250

WKIO-FM, 103.9   **(217) 352-1040**
505 S. Locust Street
Champaign, IL 61820   Network: **ABC**
Staff: GM-Jeff Balding
Profile: Rock/AOR; T.A.—18-49;
W—2,300; Guests—Yes;
Release/Scripts

WLRW-FM, 94.5   **(217) 352-4141**
P.O. Box 3369
Champaign, IL 61821   Network: **ABC**
Studio: 2603 West Bradley Avenue,
Champaign, IL, 61821
Staff: GM,SM-Phil Hoover; PD-Matt Mc
Cann; NA,ND-Maureen
Paraventi; PA,PS-Susan
Accardi; PM,MD-John Mc
Keighan; SA-Chuck Hartshorn;
SD-Dave Loane
Profile: Top 40; T.A.—18-49;
W—26,400; News—14
B'casts,80% Staff Prod.;
Guests—Phone;
Release/Scripts

WPGU-FM   **(217) 333-2016**
204 E. Peabody
Champaign, IL 61820   Network: **NBC**
Staff: SM-Melissa Moggio; PD-Thomas
Leslie; NA,ND-Todd Johnson;
PS-Richard Malone; PM-Gary
Lazarski; SA-Mike Bramel;
MD-Stephen O' Day
Profile: Rock/AOR; T.A.—18-34;
W—3,000; News—100% Staff
Prod.; Talk—100% Staff
Prod.;
Guests—Live,Phone,Taped

WRTL-AM, 1460   **(217) 893-1460**
P.O. Box 155
Champaign, IL 61800   Network: **AP**
Staff: GM-David King; ND,FD-John
Soloman; PS-Vicki Jenkins;
SA-Debbie Rowlison
Profile: Adult Contemporary;
T.A.—22-49; W—3,000; Sports
Play-By-Play

WZRO-FM, 98.3   **(309) 928-9876**
P. O. Box 1831
Champaign, IL 61820
Staff: GM-Janet Bro; PD-Mark
Edwards; ND-Steve Hoffman;
SA-Becky Rowe; SD-Brent
Cordes; FD-Alicia Prill
Profile: Country; T.A.—25-49;
W—3,000; News—27
B'casts,25% Staff Prod.;
Sports Play-By-Play

Charleston

WEIC-AM, 1270   **(217) 345-2148**
R.R. 2, Box 185a
Charleston, IL 61920
Staff: GM-Steve Garman; PD,PA-Beth
Surette; ND,FD-Dave
Taylor
Profile: Country; T.A.—25-54;
W—1,000; News—16
B'casts,30% Staff Prod.;
Sports Play-By-Play;
Release/Scripts

Charleston (Continued)

WEIC-FM, 92.1
(See WEIC-AM)
Staff: PD-Steve Stone; ND-Kathy
Tharpe; PA-Sha Carter
Profile: Adult Contemporary;
W—2,200; Guests—Phone

Chicago

WBBM-AM, 780   **(312) 944-6000**
630 N. Mc Clurg Court
Chicago, IL 60611   Network: **CBS-O&O**
Staff: GM-Gregg Peterson;
PD,ND-Chris Witting, Jr.;
NA-Chris Berry; PA,PS-Maria
Munoz; PM-Barbara Di Guido;
SA-Rod Zimmerman; SD-Rich
King; ED-Catherine Cahan
Profile: News; T.A.—Adult;
W—50,000; News—90% Staff
Prod.; Talk—10% Staff Prod.;
Guests—Live,Phone;
Release/Scripts

Program	Contact/Profile
Dave Baum Show	Jane Brouder
Mid-Day	Carleen Mosbach
Interviews	1,2,3,4,5,6,7,8,AM
Money Watch	Len Walter
	1,5,6,PM
Up-To-Date	Carleen Mosbach
	2,5,6,7

WBBM-FM, 96.3
(See WBBM-AM)
Staff: GM-Wayne Jefferson; PD-Buddy
Scott; NA,ND,PS,ED-Karen
Hand; PM-Frank Hanel;
SA-Thomas Matheson; MD-Joe
Bohannon
Profile: Top 40; T.A.—18-49;
News—100% Staff Prod.;
Talk—8% Staff Prod.;
Guests—Live

Program	Contact/Profile
Chicago	Reed Pence
Connection	1,2,3,4,5,6,7,AD

WBEE-AM, 1570   **(312) 726-6842**
35 E. Wacker Drive
Chicago, IL 60601   Network: **IND**
Studio: 15700 Campbell,
Harvey, IL 60426
Staff: GM-Charles R. Sherrell;
SM-Margaret Bell; PD,ND-John
Hill; PA,PS-Nancy Stinson;
SA-Tracy A. Daniel; MD-Mark
Ruffin
Profile: Jazz; T.A.—18-60;
W—1,000

*WBEZ-FM, 91.5   **(312) 890-8225**
1819 W. Pershing Road
Chicago, IL 60609   Network: **NPR,APR**
Staff: GM-Carole Nolan; PD-Ken
Davis; ND-Diane Duvall;
PA-Jerome Mc Donnell;
PS-Merrilee Clark;
PM-Madearia King; SD-Bob
Greenberg
Profile: News, Easy Listening;
T.A.—25-49; W—8,300;
News—25% Staff Prod.;
Talk—100% Staff Prod.;
Guests—Yes;
Release/Scripts
(Continued in Next Column)

Chicago — WBEZ-FM (Continued)

Program	Contact/Profile
About Books &	Ed Morris
Writers	5,6,7,AM
Airplay	Johanna Zorn
	1,2,3,4,5,8,PM
All Things	Diane Divall
Chicago	2,5,6,8,AD
The Flea Market	Jim Hirsch
	3,5,8,PD
Mid Day	Sondra Gair
	2,3,5,PM
Primetime	Carolyn Grisko
	1,2,5,8,PM
Studio A	Linda Paul
	1,2,3,4,5,AM

WCEV-AM, 1450   **(312) 282-6700**
5356 W. Belmont Avenue
Chicago, IL 60641   Network: **IND**
Staff: GM,SM-George Migala;
PD,ND,PA,PS,ED,MD-Lucyna
Migala; PM,SA-Herman Rowe
Profile: T.A.—18+; W—1,000;
News—10 B'casts,20% Staff
Prod.; Sports Play-By-Play;
Guests—Live,Phone,Taped;
Release/Scripts

Program	Contact/Profile
Link-Up	Emil Venutt
	2,3,4,5,7,8,PT
Mosaic	Lucyna Migala
	2,5,7,PT

WCKG-FM, 105.9   **(312) 781-7300**
150 N. Michigan Avenue, #1040
Chicago, IL 60601
Staff: GM-Marc W. Morgan; PD-Tim
Kelly; ND-Brooke Belson;
PA-James Walsh; PM-Don Flood;
SA-Michael G. Disney; SD-Jim
Volkman; MD-Tom Daniels
Profile: Rock/AOR; T.A.—18-49;
W—4,200

WCRW-AM, 1240   **(312) 327-6860**
2756 Pine Grove Avenue
Chicago, IL 60614   Network: **UPI**
Staff: GM-Cherie R. Culler; PS-Clyde
P. Foster
Profile: Spanish; T.A.—18-49;
W—1,000; Guests—Live,Phone;
Release/Scripts

Program	Contact/Profile
The Bitin Flores	Bitin Flores
Show	1,2,3,4,5,7,8,PM

*WCYC-FM, 90.5   **(312) 762-2400**
2801 S. Ridgeway Avenue
Chicago, IL 60623   Network: **NPR**
Staff: GM,SM,PM-Harold R. Kopta;
PD,PS-Jim Strickey
**Profile: Talk, News, Country,
Rock/AOR, Black, Jazz**;
W—8,000

WCZE-AM, 820   **(312) 440-3100**
875 N. Michigan Avenue
Chicago, IL 60611   Network: **IND**
Staff: PD-Gary Parks; ND,PA-Hope
Daniels; PM-Jack Bivans
Profile: Adult Contemporary;
T.A.—32-49; W—5,000

Program	Contact/Profile
Human Nature	Hope Daniels
	2,5,6,7,AM

(Continued on Next Page)

Staff:		Profile:		
GM - General Manager	PS - Public Service Manager	1 - Business/Finance	6 - Releases/Scripts	AM- Morning Hours
SM - Station Manager	PM - Promotion Manager	2 - Public Affairs	7 - Taped	PM- Afternoon Hours
PD - Program Director	SA - Sales Manager	3 - Entertainment	8 - Live	PT - Prime Time
ND - News Director	SD - Sports Director	4 - Sports	9 - Syndicated	LN - Late Night
NA - News Assignment Editor	ED - Editorial Director	5 - Guests	10 - Consumerism	AD - AM Drive Time
PA - Public Affairs Director	FD - Farm Director			PD - PM Drive Time
	MD - Music Director			

Directories are important. Media placement specialists rely on regional and national directories to compile media lists. Media personnel, however, frequently change, and it is important to have up-to-date directories. (*Source: Bacon's Radio/TV Directory.*)

such things as length (10, 20, 30, or 60 seconds), form (film, tape, slide, or live), recording facilities, and subject (free speech, editorials, and public service programs). With one of these guides in hand, you can know just what you can give to each station. Some of these guides are prepared by individual stations and others are prepared by all stations as a joint public service.

CABLE AND SATELLITE TELEVISION

Cable television's main thrust is to offer programs that are not broadcast by the regular stations or networks. Motion pictures, news, sports events, and special-interest topics predominate.

The whole future of television may be changed by this new development. Some predict that the networks will lose a large part of their audiences and that network programming will decline to a new low in quality. What will actually happen is not clear, and the only safe prediction is that in a few years things will be very different. Even as cable threatens the networks, however, it is threatened by satellites. Stations, programming, and receivers are increasing rapidly and unpredictably.

Nevertheless, amid all the confusion, there are opportunities in this new channel. This is especially true for nonprofit organizations. The American Cancer Society has carried a one-hour program on breast cancer into more than a thousand communities, and the American Hospital Association transmitted twenty hours of its annual meeting to hospital people who could not attend.

Most communities that grant franchises for cable systems require that the operators distribute a substantial amount of local, nonentertainment programming. To get your material onto the cable, it is necessary to contact the local franchise holder, stating what you have to offer and why it should be given to the customers. Generally your material will have to be on film or videotape, but in some cases it is possible to get the use of studios and their equipment.

RADIO NETWORKS

ABC, CBS, and NBC operate radio networks in addition to their television networks. The material these stations use is commonly adapted from television material, which is why you will frequently hear a TV anchor on radio. In addition to the big three, there are several others. Mutual (MBS), Black Audio Network (BAN), National Black Network, and Mutual Black Network are the largest, but there are some smaller groups in various parts of the country. National Public Radio (NPR) is a noncommercial network that operates much like television's Public Broadcasting Service (PBS).

The networks associated with the TV nets get most of their news from television, but they gather some on their own. Also, they draw from the Associated Press, United Press International, and affiliated stations. Programming other than news is more like syndicated features than like network programs.

In other words, individual stations may use feature programs on a "pick and choose" basis rather than running a full schedule of network programming.

News

If you have a news story of national importance, you will naturally inform the television networks by calling the nearest office. In addition, it is in order to inform the radio bureau. In some cases both are in one office; in others, the offices are separate. Your telephone directory will give you the number or numbers to call.

The procedure is the same as with television. You identify yourself and your organization, give the highlights of the story, and—if the network asks for it—arrange for the reporter to get the item. In some cases a network may want to take the story over the phone and perhaps record an "actuality." If the network is ethnic, it will be interested primarily in ethnic news. If it is a language network, the news must be pertinent to speakers of that language.

Aside from news, there is little network programming that offers opportunities for the placement of features. Some small regional groups occasionally feed public service programs to affiliates, but there are so many variations that generalization is impossible. If your community is served by one of these small nets, there may be some prospect of placing something in one of its features. The way to find out whether there are any such opportunities is to consult the station nearest you.

RADIO STATIONS

The great diversity in radio-station programming has one advantage for you. It provides a channel for reaching a very specific audience. Most stations have a format appealing to one type of listener and to that type alone.

Every station will have a rather good idea of who listens to its programs. This information will include age, buying power, sex, location, and possibly much more. If you are unsure of a station's demographics, call the station's sales or advertising department and ask for its advertising sales literature. Whenever it is important to reach a particular group, you can probably find a radio station that can deliver your message to them.

Gatekeepers

The key personnel of a radio station are the general manager, the news director, the assignment editor, the program director, the directors of special programs (such as talk shows), and the public relations director. All these people are counterparts of the people on a television station and perform the same function.

News

If a station does broadcast news, it is a prime prospect for your news items. Some stations broadcast nothing *but* news and thus can use a much larger volume of material than others.

There are several ways in which to give news to a radio station: You can mail a release; you can phone the station, ask for the news desk, and give the highlights of the story; or you can send an audio tape.

In many cases, the station may want to take the story over the phone or record an actuality. Occasionally the station will want to send a reporter to get the story. When that happens, you proceed in the same way as with a television reporter, helping him or her get the story.

The telephone call is the best choice for a local station. If the station is out of town, you can send a release or a tape.

Local Programs

Radio stations that are not devoted entirely to music broadcast a great variety of programs. These include talk shows, magazine-type shows, and public service shows. This type of programming is typical for smaller towns and rural areas. The music-only stations tend to serve the larger cities, as do the ethnic stations. Yet there are in all large cities some stations that reach a general audience.

Opportunities for placement on a local program can always be found. Reference to one or more of the directories will indicate the nature of a given station's programming and list specific shows which accept guests. The comprehensive directories—such as *U.S. Publicity Directory* and *Working Press of the Nation*—include a volume on radio stations. In addition, Larimi Communications Associates publishes a book called *Radio Contacts,* which lists the radio talk and interview shows for each station.

These radio shows are handled like the television shows, as described earlier in this chapter. Talk-show tours covering several cities can be planned to include both radio and television appearances on the same day.

Calendars

Radio stations frequently broadcast calendars of community events. The procedure is the same as in television, but there may be more opportunities. There are two reasons for this. First, the radio station calendars may list more events than television calendars do, thus making it easier for any given announcement to be accepted. Second, the specialization of programming creates an outlet for more items of importance to the station's audience.

Ethnic, foreign-language, and special-interest stations all want to build their audiences. By providing services such as calendars listing events of interest, the station can build the size and loyalty of its audience.

Talk shows need guests. There are many radio and television talk shows that give individuals and organizations opportunities for reaching listeners. Every program, however, has a different format and focus. It is the challenge of the public relations expert to be familiar with the programs and the type of guests they are seeking. (*Source:* Ketchum Public Relations, San Francisco, CA.)

Opinion Messages

Many stations provide opportunities for members of the public to express themselves. Not all stations offer the same things, but you should check the opportunities on each thoroughly.

Among the possibilities are editorials and rebuttals, free-speech messages, PSAs, and public service programs. These topics are handled exactly as in television.

In adapting the television procedures, remember that what you say on television is generally aimed at the entire public. What you say on radio may, in the case of special-audience radio, be fine-tuned to the specific audience. A message for an ethnic or foreign-language audience could be expressed in terms that appeal to the audience's unique interests. Blacks have different interests and problems than do whites. Puerto Ricans may need different messages than do Chicanos, even though both may speak Spanish.

SUMMARY

1. The broadcast media are vital channels of communication, but getting on the air requires great skill.
2. Radio releases are similar to press releases, but they require different wording and must be accurately timed.
3. Audiotapes are better than written releases, but they must be well prepared and their distribution must be carefully controlled.
4. TV releases can be written and accompanied by visual material, but the preferred format is videotape.
5. Videotape must be prepared by professionals; it must have great news value and must be sent only to those who are likely to use it.
6. Motion pictures have some acceptance in television. Usually these films are produced for some other audience because their use on television is never certain.
7. In addition to written or taped releases, there are numerous other opportunities for broadcast exposure.
8. The TV networks carry only information of national importance. If you have such a story, it may be used if you direct it to the right gatekeeper.
9. Individual stations usually have a sizable number of news and feature opportunities if what you have to offer is truly interesting to the audience.
10. Cable and satellite TV stations have a big appetite for certain kinds of material. Individual stations vary widely in what they will accept.
11. Radio networks have a very limited capacity for feature material and their news is closely tied to their TV nets. Only news of national importance is carried, but there are some ethnic networks and there may soon be language networks.
12. Radio stations are often highly specialized and thus provide access to intensely interested audiences.

EXERCISES

1. Turn to Chapter 5 and read the sample news release from Ryder Truck Rental. Rewrite it as 30- and 60-second radio news releases, using the guidelines suggested in this chapter.
2. The United States Forest Service wants to alert summer campers about the dangers of forest fires and how to take care of campfires. Write a 10-, 30-, and 60-second PSA for radio use. In addition, write a 30-second PSA for television using the correct format and suggesting visual material.

3. Your client is a book publisher who has just published a book about Japan's economic strength and how the country is pulling ahead of the United States in global economic influence. The book's author is Clyde V. Prestowitz, a professor of economics in the School of Business at Stanford University. The book's title is *Trading Places: How We Allowed Japan to Take the Lead.* Write a persuasive "pitch" letter to the producer of ABC's *Good Morning America* suggesting that the author should be featured on this talk/interview show.

4. A company has just introduced a new line of excercise equipment that is compact and can be used in the home. The primary market comprises middle-aged men and women who want to get more exercise but lead such busy professional lives that they can't make it to a health club very often. Using an appropriate media directory, identify and compile a list of possible television talk/interview shows in Pittsburgh and Philadelphia that might be interested in having a spokesperson from the company demonstrate the equipment. In your listing, indicate the nature of the talk/interview show and why the program director would be interested. A second part of the assignment is to suggest who would be a good spokesperson. The company doesn't have a large budget, so a Hollywood celebrity is out of the question. Many celebrities charge $10,000 to $20,000. Big stars get far more; Bob Hope charges $50,000 and Bill Cosby $100,000. However, if the cause is dear to the heart of the star, a free appearance may be possible.

5. The local YMCA is engaged in a $4 million capital campaign to raise funds for expanding its facilities in an inner-city neighborhood so more youth can be served. Write a 60-second radio editorial encouraging the community to support the campaign.

6. Your public relations firm handles Perrier, the bottled water from France, in the United States. What television entertainment programs might be good outlets for what are called "product plugs"? Name some popular shows and suggest how Perrier could be portrayed.

SUGGESTED READINGS

Alsop, Ronald. "More Prime-Time Shows Plug Airlines, Hotels in Scripts." *Wall Street Journal*, May 28, 1987, p. 29.

Davids, Meryl. "Now You see Them. . . ." *Public Relations Journal*, May 1988, pp. 14–20, 47.

Davids, Meryl. "Doing Well by Doing Good." *Public Relations Journal*, July 1987, p. 17.

Geddie, Tom. "CBS Spends 48 Hours at Parkland Hospital." *Communication World*, March 1988, pp. 27–28.

"Getting Your Message on Television." *Communication World*, December 1987, pp. 32–35.

Getting Your Public Relations Story on TV/Radio. Babylon, NY: Pilot Books, 1986.

Goldsmith, Margie. "Workshop: Developing Topics for VNRs." *Public Relations Journal*, July 1987, p. 29.

Goldsmith, Margie. "Workshop: How to Get Results with PSAs." *Public Relations Journal*, January 1986, pp. 33–34.

Goodman, R. "Selecting Public Service Announcements for Television." *Public Relations Review*, Fall 1981, pp. 25–34.

Grady, Lionel. "How Voice Reports, Actualities Affect Recall of Radio News." *Journalism Quarterly*, Summer/Autumn 1987, pp. 587–590.

Graze, Gregory G. "Anatomy of a Broadcast." *Public Relations Journal*, February 1986, p. 28.

Green, Richard, and Shapiro, Denise. "A Video News Release Primer." *Public Relations Quarterly*, Winter 1987–1988, pp. 10–13.

Helyar, John, and Landro, Laura. "Turner's Plan for Cable Network Draws Large Measure of Skepticism." *Wall Street Journal*, March 30, 1988, p. 21.

Klepper, Michael. "Airing Your Corporate Message on the Evening News." *Wall Street Journal*, Feb. 23, 1987, editorial page.

Klepper, Michael. *Getting Your Message Out: How to Get, Use and Survive Radio & TV Time*. Englewood Cliffs, NJ: Prentice Hall, 1984.

Kneale, Dennis. "Cable Television Channels Emerge as Important Sources of Programs." *Wall Street Journal*, March 16, 1988, p. 29.

Mincer, Richard, and Mincer, Deanne. *Talk Show Book*. New York: Facts on File, 1982.

Moorman, B. "Using Radio? Try Sound?" *Public Relations Journal*, September 1984, pp. 32–33.

Prescott, E. "Behind TV's Morning News." *Public Relations Journal*, November 1983, pp. 16–19.

Rowan, Ford. *Broadcast Fairness: Doctrine, Practice, Prospects*. New York: Longman, 1984.

Saddler, Jeanne. "Public Relations Firms Offer News to TV." *Wall Street Journal*, April 2, 1985, p. 6.

Trufelman, Lloyd. "Workshop: How to Plug In To Cable TV." *Public Relations Journal*, September 1988, pp. 43–44.

"Video News Releases: Hill & Knowlton Claims They're Effective, but TV News Directors Say Few Are Used." *PR Reporter*, March 10, 1986, pp. 1–2.

"VNR—The Video News Release Comes of Age." *PR Week*, April 11–17, 1988, p. 10.

Zaslow, Jeffrey. "Talk-Show Crisis: Too Many Hosts, Too Few Guests." *Wall Street Journal*, Jan. 7, 1987, p. 1.

Chapter
9

Advertising

*T*he four preceding chapters have dealt with materials sent to the media in hope that the gatekeepers will decide they are newsworthy. Reporters, editors, and program directors decide whether to use, how much to use, how much to change, and when and where to use.

In this chapter we deal with materials sent to the media in the expectation that they *will* be used just as you decide. As long as your messages do not violate media standards of acceptability or the occasional whim of some key media mogul, you are the one who determines usage. It is the advertiser who is in control.

Those who think that public relations means publicity often look on it as an alternative to advertising. They cannot understand that advertising can be a public relations tool. This is because there are no widely accepted definitions for the terms involved.

The following admittedly simplistic explanation should help you to understand the relationships of public relations, marketing, advertising, and publicity.

> *Marketing* is the management function that creates goods or services to fill public needs and then persuades the public to buy those goods or services.
>
> *Public relations* is the management function that creates policies and actions to satisfy public needs and then persuades the public to approve those policies and actions.
>
> *Publicity* is unpaid and uncontrolled mass communication. It imparts information, affects attitudes, and may induce action.
>
> *Advertising* is paid and controlled mass communication. Its purpose is to impart information, affect attitudes, and induce action beneficial to the advertiser.

From the foregoing it will be seen that marketing and public relations are parallel functions. Marketing sells goods and services. Public relations "sells" policies and actions. In each case there is a determination of what the public wants or is likely to want. In each case there is an effort to inform and persuade the public. Many tools can be used to inform and persuade, but two of the most important are advertising and publicity.

Advertising and publicity are also parallel functions, but there are important differences. Advertising is paid and controlled, publicity is unpaid and uncontrolled. Each has advantages and disadvantages, but both can have important roles in public relations.

THE USE OF ADVERTISING IN PUBLIC RELATIONS

The primary reason for using advertising as a communications tool is that it is controlled. The advertiser can be certain that the message is delivered to the desired audience in the exact words at the chosen time and as often and as emphatically as desired.

Certain Delivery

An item sent to a medium may or may not be used. The gatekeeper may not like it; there may be more news than can be used at that time. The editor may feel that the subject has been overworked, but as long as the advertising is not obscene, pornographic, blatantly distasteful, or untruthful, it is likely to run just as you want it to run.

Audience Selection

With advertising, you can reach a very specific audience. For example, commercials on language-oriented stations can be fine-tuned to the audience with little regard for any other people. Advertisements in specialized publications can reach their readers with very little exposure to others. Different ideas can be conveyed to different groups and efforts can be concentrated in the most important areas.

For any public relations program, there are usually certain groups or publics that are more important than others. Reaching them may be imperative, while reaching others may be unimportant. To be sure of reaching your key publics, you can rely on advertising.

Control of the Message

Gatekeepers frequently alter or truncate the news or features they receive. Sometimes the changes do little harm, but occasionally the blue pencil ruins the idea or eliminates a really important point. Your communications plan may involve informing the public about subject A before you say anything about subject B, but if a gatekeeper changes the order or eliminates one story, the sequence is destroyed. With advertising, however, you can be sure that your message is reproduced in the exact words you choose and in the sequence you have planned.

Control of Impact

With advertising, you can make your messages as big, frequent, and powerful as you choose. The gatekeeper may think your message is worth a 4-inch space on page 9, but if you think it deserves major treatment, you can buy a whole page. And if you want the idea repeated, you can buy as many ads as the budget permits. The broadcast media present similar problems and opportunities. Your news item or feature idea may or may not be used—or, if used, may be cut to a few words—but your advertisement *will* be used without alteration.

Control of Timing

If timing is an important factor, advertising can guarantee that your message will be timely. Prompt response to a public issue, a fixed sequence of messages, and continuity of communication—all can be maintained through advertising. To the gatekeeper, your message may be just as usable on Tuesday as on Wednesday; but for your purpose, Tuesday may be a day too early or a day too late. You can't be sure unless you pay for it. To a magazine editor, May can be as timely as June; but to you, May can be premature. If you want your message presented in June, you can guarantee the date by buying an advertisement.

Avoiding Media Restrictions

The broadcast media are supposed to give equal time to both sides of public controversies. Unfortunately this doesn't always work out to the satisfaction of all parties. When Mobil tried to broadcast its side of a controversy, the networks said that Mobil's message was too controversial. Mobil even offered to pay for opposing commercials, but this idea was rejected, so Mobil bought newspaper and magazine advertising to carry its story to the public.

Political Restrictions

The use of advertising to state the position of an organization has often been challenged by the organization's opponents. Consumer groups have attacked public utilities for using advertising to carry messages to the public. The AFL-CIO once attacked corporate sponsorship of television shows on PBS. Insurance companies have been sued by lawyers for running ads proclaiming that rising insurance costs are linked to rising awards for damages. You must check the political and legal climate carefully before you decide to run any advertisements on public issues. It is advisable to consult the organization's legal department or counsel.

PITFALLS IN PUBLIC RELATIONS ADVERTISING

Much public relations advertising is wasted because of errors in planning or execution. Most of the errors can be grouped into four categories: purpose, timing, media, and message.

Purpose

The purpose of advertising is, according to the Association of National Advertisers, "to impart information, affect attitudes and induce action favorable to the advertiser." This applies whether the action is focused on marketing or on public relations. Unfortunately some people forget this and try to use public relations advertising to brag about the organization. This always fails because it focuses on the organization rather than the public it serves.

Another misdirection of public relations advertising is to use it to gain sympathy—a sort of "They're picking on us" complaint. This doesn't work for several reasons. No one likes a crybaby, and this applies to organizations as well as people. Furthermore, this type of reaction focuses attention on the complaint and gives it added circulation. Positive statements disproving false charges are much more effective than denials.

Timing

"Let's run an ad in the paper" is a frequent reaction to a crisis. This approach has one overwhelming fault. It is usually too late. It's like trying to buy insurance when the building is blazing. By the time a crisis has become evident, one advertisement or several won't do much good. People's minds are made up and few are likely to change their attitudes after the fight has started.

Conversely, advertising as a part of a well-planned communications program can be most useful. Because you control the timing, you can be sure of delivering your message to the chosen public at the precise time that will be most effective.

Media

Much public relations advertising is wasted by using the wrong media. Remember the old saying about the uselessness of "preaching to the choir"—or trying to persuade people who are already convinced. Advertising money spent in talking to people who are on your side might do more good if it were spent on the opposition.

Even if this idea is too extreme, there *is* a marked difference between publications. Bethlehem Steel studied a dozen different magazines, including such diverse publications as *Harper's, Forbes, Sports Illustrated, Smithsonian, Saturday Review,* and *Newsweek.* The steel company wanted to reach opinion leaders and persuade them to support Bethlehem's position. They found big differences in the attitudes of readers of two newsweeklies as well as in those of readers of two cultural magazines.

Reader attitudes are only one of many criteria for choosing media. Costs, editorial climate, demographics of the audience, competitive advertising, competitive media, position in a publication (near the front or back or buried in the middle), program adjacencies (between soap operas or between highly rated nighttime programs), audience interest in the particular medium, and numerous other factors may be considered. Research like this is normally done by the advertising agency. Few, if any, advertisers have facilities for this kind of research.

Message

Because advertising enables you to deliver a message to a rather specific audience, it is essential to tailor your message to that audience. Often a campaign sends the same message to all publics. With some it may be highly effective, but with others it may not succeed at all. The same broad idea may apply to all the publics, but the words used for each should be carefully chosen to fit their attitudes and their manner of speaking and thinking.

OBJECTIVES

There may be a wide range of objectives in public relations advertising, but most can be grouped into the four categories of advocacy, public service, public information, and announcements.

Advocacy

Persuasion is the primary goal in advocacy advertising. This often means trying to get the readers or viewers to agree with the position of the advertiser on some issue. Kaiser Aluminum & Chemical Corporation tried to run TV commercials about the free-enterprise system. These advocacy ads were rejected by the networks as too controversial. So Kaiser published the scripts in newspaper advertisements in major cities. These were advocacy ads in two ways. They advocated free enterprise *and* suggested that the networks should carry such commercials.

Planned Parenthood has used advocacy ads in several ways. One advertisement focused on teenage pregnancy and urged readers to support educational efforts to combat this problem. The ad also urged readers to write to their congressional representatives, urging them to increase support for these efforts. Another advertisement harshly criticized television for its frequent depiction of sexual encounters without any reference to possible pregnancy. This advertisement urged readers to write the networks protesting their casual treatment of the subject and their refusal to broadcast advertisements for condoms.

Public Service

Public service advertisements carry information that is useful to the public. The benefit to the advertiser and the justification for the expenditure is the expected goodwill. When an oil company tells how to get better mileage from a car, the expectation is that the reader will be grateful to the company and buy his or her reduced quantity of gasoline from that company. When a public utility tells how to reduce home heating bills, it can't expect any new sales but it can reasonably expect fewer complaints about the monthly gas or electricity bills.

Public Information

The objective here is to create goodwill for the advertiser. Essentially such advertisements concentrate on telling what the organization is doing for the public and how that good deed benefits the public. It is here that danger of bragging or crying is most severe. Often called "corporate advertising," this is probably the most heavily budgeted category of public relations advertising.

Among acceptable subjects for such advertising are messages like "What we're doing for the community," "How we're protecting the environment," "How we're cleaning up pollution," "How we're protecting your health," "How we're making safer products," and so on.

Announcements

Sometimes these are simple statements of fact, such as that a meeting will be held, an organization is moving, or some change in personnel is taking place.

Cocaine lies.

After nearly a decade of being America's glamour drug, researchers are starting to uncover the truth about cocaine.

It's emerging as a very dangerous substance.

No one thinks the things described here will ever happen to them. But you can never be certain. Whenever and however you use cocaine, you're playing Russian roulette.

You can't get addicted to cocaine.

Cocaine was once thought to be non-addictive, because users don't have the severe *physical* withdrawal symptoms of heroin—delirium, muscle-cramps, and convulsions.

However, cocaine is intensely addicting *psychologically*.

In animal studies, monkeys with unlimited access to cocaine self-administer until they die. One monkey pressed a bar 12,800 times to obtain a single dose of cocaine. Rhesus monkeys won't smoke tobacco or marijuana, but 100% will smoke cocaine, preferring it to sex and to food—even when starving.

Like monkey, like man.

If you take cocaine, you run a 10% chance of addiction. The risk is higher the younger you are, and may be as high as 50% for those who smoke cocaine. (Some crack users say they felt addicted from the *first time* they smoked.)

When you're addicted, all you think about is getting and using cocaine. Family, friends, job, home, possessions, and health become unimportant.

Because cocaine is expensive, you end up doing what all addicts do. You steal, cheat, lie, deal, sell anything and everything, including yourself. All the while you risk imprisonment. Because, never forget, cocaine is illegal.

There's no way to tell who'll become addicted. But one thing is certain.

No one who is an addict, set out to become one.

C'mon, just once can't hurt you.

Cocaine hits your heart before it hits your head. Your pulse rate rockets and your blood pressure soars. Even if you're only 15, you become a prime candidate for a heart attack, a stroke, or an epileptic-type fit.

In the brain, cocaine mainly affects a primitive part where the emotions are seated. Unfortunately, this part of the brain also controls your heart and lungs.

A big hit or a cumulative overdose may interrupt the electrical signal to your heart and lungs. They simply stop.

That's how basketball player Len Bias died.

If you're unlucky the first time you do coke, your body will lack a chemical that breaks down the drug. In which case, you'll be a first time O.D. Two lines will kill you.

Sex with coke is amazing.

Cocaine's powers as a sexual stimulant have never been proved or disproved. However, the evidence seems to suggest that the drug's reputation alone serves to heighten sexual feelings. (The same thing happens in Africa, where natives swear by powdered rhinoceros horn as an aphrodisiac.)

What is certain is that continued use of cocaine leads to impotence and finally complete loss of interest in sex.

It'll make you feel great.

Cocaine makes you feel like a new man, the joke goes. The only trouble is, the first thing the new man wants is more cocaine.

It's true. After the high wears off, you may feel a little anxious, irritable, or depressed. You've got the coke blues. But fortunately, they're easy to fix, with a few more lines or another hit on the pipe.

Of course, sooner or later you have to stop. Then—for days at a time—you may feel lethargic, depressed, even suicidal.

Says Dr. Arnold Washton, one of the country's leading cocaine experts: "It's impossible for the nonuser to imagine the deep, vicious depression that a cocaine addict suffers from."

Partnership for a Drug-Free America

An advocacy advertisement. Government and private industry launched a campaign to inform people about the dangers of cocaine. This ad focuses on some popular myths. (Source: Partnership for a Drug-Free America.)

More important are announcements that must conform with the rules of the SEC or other government body. Releasing news to the media may be adequate, but many corporations also use advertisements to make sure that there can be no question about disclosure.

PLANNING ADVERTISING

Public relations advertising must fit into the overall public relations plan. Accordingly, the first step in planning is to review the situation, objectives, audience, strategy, and tactics. Next is a determination of how advertising fits into the plan—what it is to do. This involves a thorough study of the message to be conveyed and the media that are to carry it.

Questions that might be asked about media are: Which media can best tell the story? Which publications or stations can most effectively reach the audience? Should we concentrate our efforts or spread them out? Should we try to reach everyone or just the most critical audience?

Questions about the message could be: Should we modify the message for different ethnic or language groups? Should we alter the message for different demographic groups?

Because advertising costs money, often large amounts, you must be very sure that you know just who you are going to reach, how you are going to reach them, and what you are going to say. What you say in an advertisement is not limited to the neutral and impartial information contained in press releases or feature stories. In advertising, you can be partisan, you can persuade, you can concentrate, you can be emphatic, you can repeat, you can do as much as the budget permits.

Because advertising concentrates on persuading someone to do something, it is imperative, in creating advertising, to consider the principles of persuasion described in Chapter 2. The advertising message may be delivered bluntly and directly, as in used-car advertising, or it may be done subtly and indirectly, as in some of the very successful campaigns that build a favorable attitude in the mind of the reader but never seem to be selling.

Building a mood takes a long time and considerable repetition. If you don't have a lot of money to spend you will be forced to be direct. In fact, most public relations advertising is of the direct type, although it doesn't have to take the hammer-and-tongs approach of used-car advertising.

Perhaps the best way to describe middle-of-the-road public relations advertising is to say that it approaches the subject directly but with a light hand. Points are made but not belabored. Facts are given but not in an oppressive way.

Put yourself in the position of the reader, listener, or viewer. Think of that person's attitude, interests, opinions, and desires, and then look at or listen to your advertising. If you can say, "So what," "Baloney," "Unfair," or "That's the same old stuff," it is time to take a different approach. Remember, the purpose is to convince someone that your ideas are for his or her benefit.

A defense against cancer can be cooked up in your kitchen.

Fruits, vegetables, and whole-grain cereals such as oatmeal, bran and wheat may help lower the risk of colorectal cancer.

Foods high in fats, salt- or nitrite-cured foods like ham, and

There is evidence that diet and cancer are related. Some foods may promote cancer, while others may protect you from it.

Foods related to lowering the risk of cancer of the larynx and esophagus all have high amounts of carotene, a form of Vitamin A which is in cantaloupes, peaches, broccoli, spinach, all dark green leafy vegetables, sweet potatoes, carrots, pumpkin, winter squash and tomatoes, citrus fruits and brussels sprouts.

fish and types of sausages smoked by traditional methods should be eaten in moderation.

Be moderate in consumption of alcohol also.

A good rule of thumb is cut down on fat and don't be fat. Weight reduction may lower cancer risk. Our 12-year study of nearly a million Americans uncovered high cancer risks particularly among people 40% or more overweight.

Foods that may help reduce the risk of gastrointestinal and respiratory tract cancer are cabbage, broccoli, brussels sprouts, kohlrabi, cauliflower.

Now, more than ever, we know you can cook up your own defense against cancer. So eat healthy and be healthy.

No one faces cancer alone.

AMERICAN CANCER SOCIETY®

A public service advertisement. It lists the foods to eat and those to avoid in order to minimize risk of cancer. (*Source:* American Cancer Society.)

You can pretest advertising with group interviews or even test campaigns. After your ad has run, there are numerous ways to find out how well it did. You can measure "reach" by determining the size the audience for the medium that carried your ad, and you can gauge the effectivness of the message by testing audience reaction.

DO IT YOURSELF

If advertising is not a regular part of your public relations program and there is no agency available, you could someday be stuck with the job of creating an advertisement for the local newspaper all by yourself. Since there are scores of books on the subject, perhaps we should not even try to tell you, in only a few words, how to do this. Nevertheless, here are some suggestions:

Purpose

Be sure that you have a very definite objective. Is it to inform or to motivate? Do you want the public to know that your organization has been cleared of charges of environmental pollution? Do you want people to attend a meeting to protest a ruling by some government agency? You must have a goal and it must be specific.

Attention

Hundreds of advertisements are published every day. If yours is to be seen, it must stop the casual reader. Size will do it—a full page is hard to ignore, but that may be too costly. A headline can do it—but it must be interesting to the people you most want to reach. A "shocker" headline is often effective, but it should be relevant. "Clean Bill of Health" might work for the ad about environmental pollution. "Fed Up?" or "Had Enough?" might lead the ad about the protest meeting.

Illustrations can also stop the browser and lead him or her to read the ad. A picture of a wrecked automobile might fit into an ad about safe driving—or drunk driving. A picture of environmental damage could be used in opposing some project. A cartoon or even a very simple chart might be used. But whatever your choice, remember that if you don't stop the reader, your effort is futile.

Message

You must convey specific information to the reader. If you get too wordy, if you aren't clear, if you aren't informative, you'll lose your reader's interest. To write effective copy, you should make an outline of the key points and then express them in the fewest, most effective words possible. The message must tell the whole story. Unanswered questions or incomplete explanations won't do the job. Readers will not read long-winded, irrelevant copy. Keep it simple, keep it direct, keep it pertinent.

Payoff

A salesman always asks for the order. Your ad should do the same. Tell the reader what to do, how to do it, when and where to do it, why to do it. Give phone numbers, names, or addresses if they are needed. The name of the advertiser *must* be included.

THE ADVERTISING AGENCY

With rare exceptions, all public relations advertising is prepared and placed by advertising agencies. The agency has people who are experts in all phases of creating the ads and getting them published or broadcast in the chosen media.

If your organization has an advertising department, it is likely to be the prime contact with the agency. However, there are some organizations in which the public relations department is the contact. In either case, the public relations people are identified as the "client," the entity that approves or disapproves the agency's recommendations.

This relationship must be one of enthusiastic cooperation. Agency and client are not adversaries but partners. In general, the public relations role is to determine broad objectives (the "what to do") while the agency determines the means (the "how to do it").

Advertising agencies do not normally charge anything for their services. Their compensation comes from the "agency discount" that is granted by most media. Normally this discount is 15 percent of the cost of the space or time, and it is *not* granted to advertisers. It works this way: If the space or time costs $1000, the agency bills the advertiser for the sum but remits $850 to the medium. The $150 difference is retained by the agency as pay for preparing the ad.

PRINT ADVERTISING

There are several distinct steps in the preparation of print advertising: copy, layout, finished art, production, orders, and billing. Each step must be approved by the client.

Copy

Copy comprises the words used in an ad—the words that persuade the reader. There is headline and body copy. The headline may carry the key idea, or it may be used to attract attention and lead the reader into the body copy. A good example of a key-idea headline is "AT&T Cuts Long-Distance Rates Again."

This was followed by body copy explaining the rate cuts. An attention headline was used by Planned Parenthood: "Why One Million Teenage Girls Will Get Pregnant This Year." The body copy explained why the problem existed and asked the readers to support sex education.

Copy may be very brief, or it may go into great detail. There is no rule beyond the rather loose one that copy should be long enough to carry the message but not so long as to discourage the reader. Writing copy is a highly skilled occupation, and it is not learned quickly.

Layout

A layout is a drawing showing just how the finished advertisement will look. It depicts the headline, illustrations, and body copy as well as the placement of all these elements. The layout may be rough or comprehensive, depending on the client's wishes.

Finished Art

Finished art includes the actual photographs or artwork to be used. Usually it is accompanied by proofs of the type that will go with the art.

Production

Once they have approved art and type, the production people prepare the illustrations and "lockup" the materials to make possible the preparation of a final proof. When this is okayed, the printing plates (or equivalent) are made and sent to the media.

Orders and Billing

The plates are accompanied by an order telling where and when the ad is to run. After publication, the paper or magazine sends a "tear sheet" to prove that the ad was published. At the same time, a bill is sent to the agency for the cost of running the ad. The agency then bills the client for the space plus production costs.

RADIO ADVERTISING

The steps in preparing radio advertising are copy, production, orders, and billing. As with print advertising, each step must be approved by the advertiser.

Copy

Commercial radio advertising may take many forms and use many kinds of sound effects. Public relations radio advertising is ordinarily quite straightforward, although music and sound effects may be used. Messages may be 10, 20, or 30 seconds in length. The copy is written much like news copy, with short sentences, simple punctuation, limited detail, and careful use of words to be sure that they are understandable.

Production

When the copy is approved, an announcer records the message—together with music or sound effects, if desired. Selecting the right announcer is especially important because these people vary greatly in ability. The best may cost several times more than an ordinary announcer would, but they are probably worth every dollar.

Orders and Billing

The stations or networks receive orders stating just when the commercials are to run. When the commercials have been broadcast, the stations or networks send an affidavit of performance to the agency along with the bill. The agency then bills the advertiser.

TELEVISION ADVERTISING

Television, the most costly and probably most effective form of advertising, requires very careful management.

Copy

The words used follow the radio guidelines of clarity, but beyond that must tie in to the visual. If the action is live, the people on screen say the words; with off-screen narration, the announcer is not visible but the words are carefully timed into the visual action. "Talking heads" must be avoided and action is imperative.

Storyboard

The storyboard is the equivalent of a layout for a print ad. It usually looks like a cartoon strip, with each frame showing one piece of the action. The number of frames depends on the number of scenes. Each frame is accompanied by the words that are to be voiced with that specific visual action.

Production

As stated in Chapter 8, the production of television materials is a job for professionals only. With an approved storyboard, the agency arranges for production with a producing organization. The tape is then shot and edited. When it

New therapies are available which may stop a heart attack in progress.

Every year, 1.5 million Americans have a heart attack. Half a million die. Two thirds of those die before reaching a hospital. The incredible news is, many of them die unnecessarily—and for one simple reason.

Denial.

While they're in the midst of the attack, they deny it *is* a heart attack. "Not me," they say. *"Can't* be." "Must be indigestion." "I'm just a little winded … or tired … or nervous."

Most heart attack victims wait three or more hours before seeking medical help, according to the American Heart Association.

solve the clot, restoring blood flow—and saving the heart.

But time is critical, because the earlier the treatment is given, the greater the benefit to the endangered heart muscle.

According to a survey commissioned by Genentech in February, Americans are well aware of the symptoms of heart attack (see chart). But because of fear, they pretend it isn't really happening. They waste precious time denying symptoms, instead of seeking immediate medical attention.

If you or someone you're with experiences any of the symptoms of a heart attack, don't

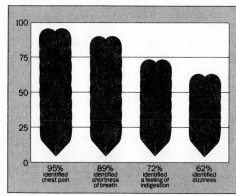

Do you know these symptoms of a heart attack? Most Americans do.

Eighty-one percent of Americans polled by Genentech said they could recognize the symptoms of a heart attack. But in reality, heart attack victims don't act on what they know.

Had they or their friends or relatives sought help immediately, many of them would still be alive.

Because today, *new therapies may actually stop a heart attack in progress.* They can also sharply curtail heart muscle damage if initiated early enough.

The reason: Most heart attacks are caused by a blood clot forming in an abnormally narrowed section of a coronary artery, blocking the flow of blood to the heart. Deprived of oxygen, the heart muscle begins to die. The new therapies can dis-

hope it's just indigestion. Don't be embarrassed. Don't wait to see if it goes away. Act.

Dial your local emergency number or 911.

Get an ambulance. Get to the hospital. Get medical help fast. Be one of the million Americans who lives through a heart attack.

♥ American Heart Association

Genentech, Inc.

A public service advertisement. It tells what causes heart attacks, gives the most common symptoms, and recommends action. (*Source:* American Heart Association and Genentech, Inc.)

has been approved, duplicate copies are made for the outlets that will broadcast the commercials.

Orders and Billing

These procedures are the same as for radio.

MISCELLANEOUS MEDIA

Other media that have uses in public relations are outdoor and transit advertising, posters, sponsored books, and "walking ads."

Outdoor Advertising

Most outdoor advertising employs paper sheets pasted on a wooden or metal background. The "24-sheet" poster is standard, but there are also "painted bulletins," which use no paper. Outdoor advertising reaches large audiences in brief exposures. Accordingly, advertising for this medium must be eye-catching and use few words. Ten words is a rule-of-thumb limit for outdoor copy. When design and copy are approved, the individual sheets of paper that will make up the whole advertisement are printed and then pasted to the background.

Location is vital in this medium—and prices are based on the traffic that is exposed to the showing. Occasionally, nonprofit organizations can obtain free or heavily discounted usage of outdoor space that is temporarily unsold. Showings are usually scheduled in monthly units, and there are times when there are gaps in the schedules. Therefore it may pay to keep in touch with local outdoor companies.

Transit Advertising

This category includes both the small posters placed in subway and commuter rail stations and the cards used in buses and rail cars. Both types of transit advertising require eye-catching graphics, but the copy can be longer than for outdoor posters. The person waiting for a train or hanging onto a strap on a bus or rail car has some time to absorb a message. Cards in transit vehicles often carry coupons or tear-off notes allowing readers to ask for more information or respond to some sort of offer.

Posters

Posters can be used in-house as reminders to employees to promote safety, courtesy, efficiency, economy, quality, and so on. They can also help to remind people on the outside of the organization's products or services. Museum ex-

A public information advertisement. Companies often use advertisements to tell the public about their social responsibility philosophy (*Source:* Chevron, Inc., San Francisco.)

hibits and art shows especially lend themselves to poster treatment. The poster can promote attendance and also serve as a souvenir of the show.

Posters can also be used as mailers to prospects. The American Management Association regularly sends posters to businesses. The posters promote the AMA's services and conferences; they are mailed in the hope that recipients will display them for some time.

Any poster must be highly visible. It should convey only one idea and use only a few words (eight or ten). Because the same person may see a poster many times, the message must be one that will stand repetition. That requires great care in the writing and pretesting of copy.

Posters can be printed by almost any printer. It is also possible to buy ready-to-use posters from printers and from such organizations as the National Safety Council.

Sponsored Books

Sponsored books may be written by anyone on your organization's staff. They may also be put together by freelance writers. If you should become involved in engaging such a writer, be sure that you read some of his or her work. One large national corporation once hired a famous writer to put together a biography of the founder. It was so bad that extensive rewriting had to be done by a member of the company's staff.

A sponsored book can be published by the organization. In fact, most such books are produced in this way. It is simply a matter of hiring a printer to print and bind the necessary number of copies.

If the book is of such importance that it should be produced by an established book publisher, the usual procedure is to guarantee the purchase of a sufficient number of books to give the publisher a profit. After the sponsor buys the guaranteed number, the publisher is free to market the book through its regular channels.

The New Arabians is a book that was underwritten by Bechtel Corporation. It is no coincidence that the company has extensive engineering contracts in the Middle East. *From Three Cents a Week* is the official history of the Prudential Life Insurance Company, while *The Truth About Energy* was written by the staff of Mobil Oil Corporation.

Books that directly relate to a company's product are also often underwritten by the company. General Mills has long been producing Betty Crocker cookbooks for Random House. *Creative Cooking with Aluminum Foil* was published for Reynolds Aluminum Co., while *Protect Yourself* is from Master Lock and Dell Publishing. Of course, one can also purchase Pan Am's travel guides or *How to Get Lost and Found in New Zealand* by Air New Zealand.

Corporate histories are often commissioned as part of an anniversary celebration. "How to" books can be published whenever there is a potential audience. Those we have cited may actually produce a net return for the publishers. In many cases, however, such books are planned for free distribution only; accordingly, the entire cost must be included in the budget as an item of expense.

Walking Ads

T-shirts have been described as "walking billboards," and some people, including sociologists, lament the fact that people are so materialistic that they willingly become walking ads for products, services, and social or political issues. The "why" is questionable, but the fact is that people do spend their own money to advertise something with which they may or may not have any direct connection.

Nevertheless, many people *are* willing to serve as billboards and you may find an opportunity to use this medium, which is particularly convenient for causes such as environmental protection. Often such groups make sizable incomes from the sale of T-shirts.

Corporations don't usually sell T-shirts, but they do distribute them to the troops at conferences, sales meetings, picnics, and other events. In these situations the T-shirts contribute to a feeling of belonging to the "team."

Almost every town and city in America has at least one shop where you can order T-shirts. You can specify just about anything your mind suggests—slogans, corporate logos, symbols, and so on. The process is simple and fast, and the costs are low. At some time, almost any organization may find T-shirt ads useful.

Akin to T-shirts are buttons. They are widely used in political campaigns and at special events. They are also useful in fund-raising, when they are distributed to those who make donations. In San Francisco one year, money was raised for the ballet by selling "SOB" buttons (Save Our Ballet) to pedestrians in the downtown area.

Buttons in general have a short life span. They are worn by convention delegates for a few days or by sales representatives during a trade show. Outside of these areas, people don't generally wear buttons unless they are highly committed to a particular cause.

Buttons call for some creative thinking in terms of expressing your message in one or two words. Advertising specialty firms can make buttons for you. The most expensive part is making the original plate or die; after that, buttons in bulk cost only pennies apiece to produce.

They don't walk but they do roll—bumper stickers. This once ubiquitous medium is still used to some extent. Most late-model cars have bumpers that are faced with rubber; neither this surface nor that of the car's body is a good place to attach a sticker. There are, however, a few places available on some cars, and there are some opportunities for the placement of stickers. As with posters the prescription is brevity. Five or six words is about right.

THE TELEPHONE

Whether the telephone should be classed as a medium of advertising is uncertain; but it is used for more than personal calls, so it deserves a place in the list of ways to reach the public.

Many organizations carry on extensive selling campaigns through phone calls. Political campaigns use the telephone to solicit support and to encourage people to vote. Charitable groups solicit funds. Special-interest groups activate their members, and public utilities use the phone to alert subscribers to interruptions in service.

Advantages

A ringing telephone is hard to ignore. Most people will answer if they are nearby. If the message is pertinent and politely delivered, it has a good chance of getting through to the "receiver." There are no delays, as happens with mail, and there are no unopened envelopes. Without question, the telephone is the fastest way to reach specific people, even if they are widely scattered through a city or country.

Disadvantages

Not all people can be reached by telephone, since some do not have phones and some numbers are unlisted. (In Los Angeles, for example, 38 percent of the numbers are not in the book.) Often the number called does not answer because no one is there. Sometimes the phone is answered by a child or by someone other than the person who is the target for the call. Many people resent calls from strangers, especially if the subject is not dear to the heart of the answerer or if it comes late at night. Some hang up the instant they discover the nature of the call.

Procedures

There are several ways to reach a large number of people by telephone. If they are members of an organization, such as a charitable or special-interest group, their numbers should be on file at the group's headquarters. Employee numbers should also be on file. All these can be reached readily. But if your target audience is not in an identifiable group, you will have to rely on the phone directory. In a very small town, it would be possible to phone every number. In a larger town or city, you can get a reverse phone directory that lists numbers by street numbers rather than name. With this you could phone every home on Cherry Street or every business on Third Street. Exchanges are usually concentrated in one area, so the prefix 342 may be suburban while 397 may be in the city's center.

If there are only a few numbers to call, it can be done by one person. If there are many numbers, it may be necessary to have several people call all the numbers on lists that are given to them. For very large numbers of calls, it is possible to use prerecorded messages and automatic dialing equipment. With this equipment, once the message is recorded and the numbers selected, the machines do the rest. The phone rings; when someone answers, the message is delivered; and when the connection is broken, the machine goes on to the next number. Telemarketing people even set their machines to dial every possible number whether listed or not.

Hot Lines

This use of the telephone is the reverse of those previously mentioned. Here, the call is initiated by someone outside the organization. Usually the purpose is to get information. For example:

1. The U.S. Weather Service has one or more numbers to call for the latest forecast. The message is prerecorded and updated as new information is received.
2. A state highway department may have one or more numbers to call for information about road conditions.
3. A disaster-control office may have a number to call for information about the extent of the damage and access to the area. Names and location of refugees may also be available.
4. A chamber of commerce can have a number to call for information about major events scheduled for the coming week.
5. The International Association of Business Communicators has a number to call for information about available jobs in the communications field.

To utilize a hot line, you must arrange with the local telephone company for this service. The number will be listed in the next published directory and can be obtained until that time by calling information. In addition to listing your number in the phone directory, it is a good idea to publicize it by using other communication tools.

SUMMARY

1. Advertising is an important communications tool of public relations.
2. Advertising enables you to deliver a message exactly as written to a chosen audience at the precise time you prefer and as emphatically as you choose.
3. In using advertising, you must be sure to avoid the errors made by some people who use the wrong message, for the wrong purpose, at the wrong time, or in the wrong media.
4. Public relations advertising may have a number of objectives. Most common are (a) advocacy, persuading people to believe or act; (b) public service, helping them with important guidance; (c) public information, explaining what you are doing for them; and (d) announcements, making certain that legal requirements for public information are satisfied.
5. When you plan advertising, you must make sure that it fits into the public relations plan. Within that plan, you must decide just who to reach, how to reach them, and what to say.
6. Public relations advertising is normally created and placed by an advertising agency. The relationship between the public relations people and the agency must be one of enthusiastic cooperation.

7. Print advertising—in newspapers and magazines—provides great flexibility in size, frequency, visual treatment, and audience specialization.

8. Radio advertising is especially adapted to ethnic and language audiences and to teaching people at specific hours or in special contexts.

9. Television advertising is the medium that can combine vision, voice, color, and motion to produce a powerful impact on the viewer. It is costly and in some cases not available for reasons of station or network policy.

10. In addition to the major mass media, you might consider the use of outdoor or transit ads, posters, sponsored books, and the highly personal "walking" ads such as T-shirts, buttons, and bumper stickers.

11. The telephone is a communications tool that should not be overlooked in considering ways to reach the public.

EXERCISES

1. Prism Industries, a manufacturer of precision engineering equipment headquartered in Dallas, has contributed $100,000 to help underwrite the cost of the city's symphony orchestra's upcoming season. In addition to issuing a news release, the company wants to place a full-page advertisement in the *Dallas Morning News* to tell the community about its support of the arts. Write the advertising copy and make a rough sketch of what the ad would look like in print.

2. An airline wants to emphasize its commitment to quality and safety. This ad will be used on television. Write the copy for the ad and prepare a storyboard, which would show the visual elements planned in the ad.

3. The local art museum will host a major traveling exhibition of French Impressionists during the month of March. This is the year's most elaborate exhibition, and only ten museums in the country were selected to present it. The local art museum wants large attendance and has decided to expend money on ads, billboards, posters, and buttons to promote the exhibit. Decide on a central theme for this promotion and plan how it could be carried out in the media mentioned. The finished assignment should contain copy and rough layout for a print ad, a billboard, a poster, and a button.

SUGGESTED READINGS

Bivens, Thomas. "Print Advertising." *Handbook for Public Relations Writing*. Lincolnwood, IL: NTC Business Books, 1988, chap. 3.

Brody, E. W. "Advertising Production." *Public Relations Programming and Production*. New York: Praeger Publishers, 1988, chap. 15.

Davids, Meryl. "Tough Stuff: 16th Annual Review of Corporate Advertising Expenditures." *Public Relations Journal*, September 1987, pp. 38–31.

Davids, Meryl, and Winkleman, Michael. "Blurred Vision." *Public Relations Journal*, September 1987, pp. 34–38.

Jeweler, A. Jerome. *Creative Strategy in Advertising,* ed. 3. Belmont, CA: Wadsworth Publishing, 1989.

Lewis, Jan. "Workshop: How to Write Corporate Ads." *Public Relations Journal,* September 1988, pp. 45–46.

Newsom, Doug, and Carrell, Bob. "Writing Advertising Copy." *Public Relations Writing: Form and Style.* Belmont, CA: Wadsworth Publishing, 1986, chap. 9.

Sethi, S. Prakash. *Handbook of Advocacy Advertising Concepts, Strategies & Applications.* Cambridge, MA: Ballinger Publishing, 1987.

Waltzer, Herbert. "Corporate Advocacy Advertising and Political Influence." *Public Relations Review,* Spring 1988, pp. 41–55.

Chapter
10

Working with the Media

T his subject was well summarized by a veteran San Francisco public relations counselor who said, "The name of the game, where the press is concerned, is service."

You must always provide accurate, timely, and comprehensive information. Only in this way can any medium adequately inform its readers, listeners, or viewers about matters affecting them. From your standpoint, you cannot effectively disseminate news about a client or an organization without the help of the media.

Today's reporters and editors spend most of their time processing information, not gathering it. No newspaper, magazine, or television station has enough reporters to cover every newsworthy event in a community. A former business editor of the *San Jose Mercury News* said it best when he described public relations people as the newspaper's "unpaid reporters."

The same thing was said in different words by Reg Murphy, former publisher of the *San Francisco Examiner*. He once told the San Francisco Public Relations Round Table that he could not publish his newspaper without the output from public relations personnel. And Jenkin Lloyd Jones, editor and publisher of the *Tulsa Tribune* for a number of years, once wrote, "Newspapermen often profess to despise PR people, yet I have found that those I can trust are often an immense help in the development of legitimate business news."

Jones made a succinct point in the use of the word "trust." He went on to say, "Things we cannot tolerate are loaded statistics and misstatements of fact. We do not cotton to people who mislead us, for they destroy our credibility too." The point is well taken. You must give honest, dependable service.

Gary Thompson, executive vice president of Ketchum Public Relations in San Francisco, says your relationship is neither as a partner nor as an adversary. You are not a partner because you have different objectives; you are an advocate by definition, seeking dissemination of a client's or organization's message to selected audiences.

You cannot attain that goal if you are an adversary of the press—that is, if your relationship involves hostility and tension. In reality, you and the reporter have a cooperative relationship, where each helps the other do his or her job. And the ultimate objective of this cooperation is to inform the public.

A good working relationship is based on mutual respect for each other's ability and professionalism. You can earn the respect of the media in any number of ways: preparing professional materials, being accessible, remembering deadlines, facilitating interviews with top organizational officers, being honest, and returning telephone calls—even when you know that the reporter wants to ask you about last quarter's dismal earnings report.

Dealing with the media is much simpler if you have the support and cooperation of the organization's chief executive officer. If the CEO is willing to be open with the media, to cooperate with them, and to let you work with the reporters on a team basis, it will be possible to have good relations with the media.

Thus, a very important part of your job is to "educate" the CEO about how the media operate and what they will need in order to give you a fair, objective story. This education may even include training the CEO to give a 30-second answer to a complex question so as to work within the tight time frame of television news. It also means that the CEO will understand why some stories, through no intentional malice, get garbled or even distorted as they move through several levels of personnel on a newspaper, magazine, or broadcasting station.

HELPING REPORTERS

There are many checklists for generating a good working relationship with personnel from the media. Most of them are well tested and proven, but you must also remember that there is no ironclad rule. Media people are also indi-

Helping reporters. Special events like the celebration of the U.S. Constitution's bicentennial in Philadelphia required the planners to build a platform for television crews and photographers. Giving some advance thought to the needs of the media generates goodwill and better coverage. (*Source:* Lewis, Gilman & Kynett, Philadelphia, PA.)

viduals to whom a particular suggestion may or may not be applicable. Here's a list of general guidelines:

1. *Be available.* You are the spokesperson for an organization. It is your responsibility to be accessible at all times, even in the middle of the night. Key reporters should have your office and home telephone numbers.
2. *Be truthful.* Give accurate and complete information even if it is not flattering to your organization.
3. *Provide requested information.* Get back to a reporter if you don't have the information at the time you are asked.
4. *Be accurate.* Your facts and figures must be clear and dependable.
5. *Answer questions.* There are only three acceptable answers: (a) "Here it is," (b) "I don't know but I'll find out for you," and (c) "I know but I can't tell you now because. . . ." A "no comment" is not one of the three alternatives.
6. *Protect exclusives.* If a reporter has found a story, don't give it to anyone else. If another reporter also discovers it, the matter is out of your hands.

7. *Protect sources.* If a reporter tips you off to something, you must conceal the source just as reporters protect their sources.
8. *Give all the news.* This means bad news as well as good news.
9. *Help photographers.* You may be able to suggest newsworthy ideas to the photographer and to offer help in setting up pictures.
10. *Balance your treatment of the media.* Competing media deserve equal opportunity to receive information.
11. *Explain.* Most reporters don't understand your organization or even the nature of your business. Give them background briefings and materials; tell them how decisions were made and why.
12. *Correct errors politely.* Ignore minor errors like misspellings of a name, an inaccurate age, or even a mistaken title. If it is a major factual error that skews the accuracy of the entire story, you should inform the reporter who wrote the story. If that doesn't work, go to his or her editor.
13. *Remember deadlines.* The reporter must have enough time to write a story. One good rule is to talk with him or her several days before you hope to see the story published.
14. *Praise good work.* If a reporter has written a good and accurate story, a note of thanks (with a copy to his or her editor) will be appreciated.

AVOIDING TROUBLE

Many news releases and story tips never see the light of day. There are any number of reasons for this, but the overriding reason is that the story doesn't fit the particular needs of the medium that received the material.

Several surveys have indicated that editors most commonly fail to use a news release because it has limited local interest. The other reason most often cited by editors is that the news release has no reader interest. Other reasons might be (1) poor writing, (2) reasons of policy, or (3) that the release is too commercial—it reads like an advertisement for a product.

You can avoid trouble if you are aware of why news releases get rejected. You can also avoid poor media relations by adhering to this basic list of don'ts.

1. *Don't evade.* Frankness is imperative.
2. *Don't mislead.* Reporters are expert at spotting this.
3. *Don't play favorites.* Everyone deserves an even break.
4. *Don't complain because your story wasn't used.* It won't do any good.
5. *Don't criticize.* It is the reporter's story—not yours.
6. *Don't try to use pressure from advertising.* The fact that your organization advertises in the medium has no bearing on the story.
7. *Don't go over the reporter's head.* Talking to his or her boss is certain to breed resentment.
8. *Don't ask reporters to kill stories.* They won't do it and will only resent your attempt to quash it.

9. *Don't be facetious.* The reporter might take you literally.
10. *Don't ask for clippings.* That is not the job of the media.
11. *Don't ask when or whether a story will run*—unless you do it tactfully. However, in the case of a feature, it is permissible to ask when it will run so that you can order reprints of a magazine story or watch a television story on the air.
12. *Don't ask to check a story before it runs.* However, if it deals with a complex or technical subject, you might possibly offer to check it for errors.
13. *Don't hinder reporters.* Any attempt to keep a reporter from getting a story will only increase his or her determination and suggest that you are covering something up.
14. *Don't "snowstorm" the media.* A blizzard of releases will not work.
15. *Don't send material that is not localized.* The most common complaint of gatekeepers is that they get material without local interest.
16. *Don't "color" the news.* Give facts, not hype.
17. *Don't get into a fight.* No matter how right you think you are and how wrong you think the reporter or editor is, you can't win a fight with either of them.

PROBLEMS WITH THE MEDIA

Nearly all politicians and many nonpolitical citizens have at some time accused the media of biased or inaccurate reporting. Business executives as well as administrators of nonprofit agencies also feel that the press has often not been thorough or objective in its coverage of news.

In many cases, those who complain about "biased" coverage are just saying that the story did not show their company in a favorable light. Indeed, a study of accuracy in news reporting by William Tillinghast, a professor at San Jose State University, found that news sources generally did not fault the facts of the story; they tended to be more critical of the story's slant or angle—a subjective perception at best.

It is wise to avoid the use of gimmicks in sending materials to the news media. For instance, don't send a teddy bear along with a news release on a new child-care facility or enclose a press kit for a sporting goods chain in a backpack. A press kit for Diet Rite Cola once included a pair of binoculars, a playback recorder, and a self-destruct tape because the theme of the campaign was a "Salt Assault" product promotion.

These gimmicks are meant simply to separate the news release or press kit from the stack on the recipient's desk. However, gatekeepers complain that such gimmicks constitute "gifts" or "freebies," which their organizations, on principle, do not accept. Some newspapers even return such minor gimmicks as keychains, T-shirts, and coffee mugs. In sum, if you're thinking about using a gimmick with a news release, carefully assess the recipient's potential reaction.

The possible bias of reporters against business and industry is probably based more on perception than on empirical evidence. After all, reporters also work for business organizations—as proved by the number of newspaper chains and broadcast empires that are now on the Fortune 500 list. Increasingly, reporters are finding that they are part of "big business," since their paychecks often come from media conglomerates.

In addition, no matter what the reporters' political leanings, they are taught throughout journalism school to be objective and fair, no matter how they personally may feel about a subject. To the overwhelming majority of reporters, objectivity and fairness—or the attempt to attain them—are much more important than the distortion of news stories for political advantage.

Faulty Reporting

A survey by the American Management Association found that 83 percent of the public relations directors who participated thought that sloppiness on the part of reporters was the major reason for inaccurate stories.

Another 82 percent of the public relations directors don't believe reporters do their homework or research before writing a story, and 65 percent of the reporters in the survey agree. Public relations directors (73 percent) also say that reporters don't understand the topics they are writing about.

Uninformed Reporters

Many reporters are generalists and have little or no background on subjects they are asked to cover. When you are dealing with a reporter who is not familiar with your business or industry, you must make it a point to explain the subject thoroughly. This is often called a background briefing. On a more informal basis, it means supplying the reporter with information that will enable him or her to get a grasp of the subject.

Increasingly, metropolitan daily reporters are learning to be specialists on certain topics: the environment, the computer industry, or energy. On the other hand, some editors routinely switch reporters around so they won't get too friendly with their sources.

The press was unprepared to cover the crisis of the Three Mile Island nuclear power reactor. Few reporters knew enough about nuclear reactors to assess the actual mechanics of a meltdown. As a consequence, the press got its share of blame for unnecessarily panicking the American public.

You, by providing background and assistance, can help the general assignment reporter do a better job. The payoff for you and your organization is better coverage of your project or business.

Inadequate Investigation

Even the most knowledgeable reporter often fails to gather all the facts. Pressed by deadlines and perhaps burdened with an inherent bias against the

On Being Quoted

In general, anything you say to a reporter may be quoted. In fact, one cynic has said, "If you don't want it published, don't say it." However, there are times when it is desirable to provide information while keeping its source confidential. Most reporters honor these expressions:

Off the record: The information may not be published.

For the record: The information may be published and the source given.

Not for attribution: The information may be published without revealing the source.

Spokesman (or Spokesperson): The source is officially empowered to release the information, but the name may be withheld in some cases.

Background: Information that may help the reporter understand an event or situation. It may be published if the reporter wants to use it.

If you use any of these terms, be sure that the reporter hears the statement and understands just what you intend.

topic, a reporter may find it all too easy to grab a handful of facts or pseudofacts and write a story that is misleading or inaccurate.

To prevent this, you should work with the reporter. By listening carefully to the questions he or she asks, you can often get an idea of where the story may be heading. Of course, you should answer the questions. But then, if necessary, you can go further, offering additional information that may put things in a different light. Assuming that your viewpoint is correct, your organization is much more likely to get fair treatment if the *whole* story is covered.

Broadcast Distortions

Television and radio use headline-type news stories with plenty of immediacy and human interest. As stations compete with each other for higher audience ratings, there is a tendency to seize upon the sensational, bizarre, or emotional; this can lead to the omission of key phrases or scenes that would make the report more accurate. The result is often to warp reality. Russell Baker, the *New York Times* humor columnist, says that after watching a night of crime and violence on television, any citizen would do well to take a walk around the block just to see that the entire city has not gone up in riot or disaster.

Television thrives on action and the ability to condense the most complex issue into a 30-second news clip. When a television crew is covering a story at your organization, try to put ideas into both words and actions that will be clear, active, and concise.

If at all possible, your story should focus on a key phrase and be illustrated by action. Television wants movement and brevity. Give it.

SOLVING MEDIA PROBLEMS

It is quite likely that you or your employer will have complaints about media coverage. If this happens, there are several steps you can take.

Ascertain the Facts

What exactly makes the story unfair or incomplete? It is not wise to tell a reporter that you didn't like the tone of an article because it implied (rightly or wrongly) that something was amiss. This kind of approach is very subjective, and you will probably be ignored unless you can actually show where a news item is wrong or misdirected.

Talk to the Reporter

Call the reporter and discuss the story with him or her. Point out where you think the story missed or distorted key information. Often, if the reporter agrees, he or she will ask the editor to make a correction.

Talk to the Editor

If you don't get satisfaction from the reporter (and the complaint is a major one), you may wish to write the editor a letter or ask for an interview. Another solution is a delegation. Hospital public relations directors in one large city finally went as a delegation to see a publisher about news coverage of health problems in the community. They felt that the reporter assigned to the hospitals was incapable of understanding the various health problems and also had a distinct bias against the hospitals. After the delegation met with the publisher, the newspaper sought to provide more balanced articles.

Record the Interview

Many companies are now demanding to videotape or record all press interviews. This trend may have been prompted by CBS's *Sixty Minutes*, where a two-hour interview can wind up as a two-minute segment on the air. Many people feel that much is bound to be lost by virtue of such compression. Although TV newspeople don't particularly like the idea of being recorded, they are finding that the practice is becoming standard. Organizations like the idea because it gives them good evidence for possible claims, later on, if the news report was skewed or distorted. (Some firms play back such interviews for employees, so as to give them an "inside" view.)

File a Lawsuit

This is the last resort, but it should be included in your list of options. If you feel that a media outlet has purposely and maliciously distorted the truth or broken an agreement, threat of legal action may prompt the offender either to write a correction or publish a retraction.

AIDS TO MEDIA COMMUNICATION

Several things will expedite communication between you and the media. Building up a stock of such aids will require a substantial amount of work, but once you have them available, it's a simple matter to keep them up to date.

Media Contact Cards

Make up a 3- by 5-inch card listing the name of your organization, its address, the name and phone number (office and home) of its principal media contact person (perhaps yourself), and a very brief thumbnail description of the organization. One of these should be given to every gatekeeper with whom you may be involved. It will enable the gatekeeper (reporter or editor) to reach you quickly and easily.

Media Files

For every gatekeeper on your list of possible publicity opportunities, there should be a card giving the name of the medium, its address, the name and phone number of the gatekeeper (there may be several within any given medium), and a notation of his or her specialty. The card should also indicate deadlines, publication hours, and dates—plus information about any special requirements. The file should be indexed and near at hand.

Fact Sheets

A fact sheet is an information summary planned to help reporters get the necessary facts and get them accurately. Fact sheets have three basic uses: (1) as background information about the organization, (2) as background material about an event, and (3) as a substitute for a news release. (A fact sheet may consist of one or several pieces of paper; it may even be a booklet.)

Organizational fact sheets should explain the organization—its nature and objectives, what it does, how it does it, who the key people are, what they do, and how the firm is organized. History and future trends and plans might well

```
HARDWARE AGE

        Chilton Way, Radnor, PA 19089
        (215) - 964-4000
    Ed. Ahn, Editor

        Lead time - 10 weeks
```

First Interstate *Bancorp*

Northern California **Public Relations**	345 California Street San Francisco, CA 94104

GENERAL INQUIRIES . . . . (415) 773-7500

SUSAN BANASHEK . . . . (415) 773-7505
  MANAGER
CHERYL MCDONALD . . . . (415) 773-7507
  OFFICER

Media contact cards. Public relations people often keep a file of key editors and their phone numbers. By the same token, company public relations personnel often send cards to media reporters for quick reference. (*Source:* First Interstate Bancorp, San Francisco, CA.)

adept
technology, inc.

150 Rose Orchard Way, San Jose, California 95134 • 408-432-0888 • TLX 171942 • FAX 408-432-8707

ADEPT TECHNOLOGY, INC.

CORPORATE FACTS SUMMARY

Company Profile:	Adept Technology, Inc. designs, manufactures, and markets flexible automation products for use on the factory floor. The company introduced the first commercial "direct drive" robot, the AdeptOne, in 1984. Since 1985 it has been the market leader in the small parts handling and assembly segment of the U.S. robotics industry, with a 34 percent market share in 1988. The company is also a leader in controls and system software and has a substantial machine vision business.
Founded:	In 1983 by Brian Carlisle and Bruce Shimano, who had pioneered many technical advances in the robot industry. Today Mr. Carlisle is chairman and chief executive officer; Mr. Shimano is vice president, research and development. Mr. Fredric Zucker is president and chief operating officer.
Sales:	Grew from $14 million in 1985 to $33 million in 1988. Became profitable in the first quarter of 1986.
Products:	Industrial robots, automation controllers and software, and machine vision systems. The AdeptOne, AdeptTwo, and AdeptThree robots provide excellent speed, precision, and maintainability. The Adept MC, Adept CC, and Adept IC controllers feature powerful multitasking capabilities using the proprietary V and V$^+$ operating systems. Four AdeptVision systems are available for both inspection and guidance tasks. Adept products have integrated sensory, control, and communication functions which make them easy to install and operate.
Customers:	AT&T, Northern Telecom, Digital Equipment, Apple, IBM, Hewlett Packard, Honeywell, Xerox, Olivetti, Kodak, Hughes, Boeing, General Motors, Ford, Electrolux, Thomson, Rockwell International. Half of Adept's sales go directly to end-users and half are sold through cooperative arrangements with experienced system integration firms located worldwide. Adept customers are supported by a direct sales force and an extensive customer service organization.
Manufacturing:	At Adept headquarters in San Jose, California. Approximately 1900 robots and 700 vision systems have been shippped.
Employees:	Adept employs 250 people. It has regional centers in Cincinnati, Ohio; Dortmund, West Germany; and Paris, France.

AdeptOne, AdeptTwo, AdeptThree, Adept MC, Adept CC, Adept IC, AdeptVision, V, and V$^+$ are trademarks of Adept Technology, Inc.

March 1989

Fact sheet. A brief company profile often is sent with a news release or becomes part of a press kit. It enables reporters to become familiar with a company and provides quick access to basic facts. (*Source:* Adept Technology, Inc., San Jose, CA.)

be included. It is a good idea to give one of these to each gatekeeper with whom you have frequent contact.

Fact sheets about events are almost always included in the press kits that are given to reporters. These fact sheets may include basic information about the organization, but they are generally edited especially for each particular event.

Fact sheets as substitutes for news releases are often acceptable to media that flatly refuse to use (without completely rewriting) the releases they receive. You can give them the facts easily with a news-story fact sheet that gives the who, what, where, when, why, and how.

Position Papers

A position paper is a statement of the organization's position on some public issue. An example might be the position of a public utility on nuclear power. Such a paper is an official document and is often prepared at the request of top management. However, an alert public relations person who keeps aware of public issues will suggest the preparation of a position paper when the need first arises. In either case, the paper must be approved by the head of the organization.

The first item in a position paper is an explanation of the issue. This must be presented clearly and honestly. It should be supported with enough background to let the reader understand exactly what is at issue.

The organization's position statement is next. It must be brief but complete, clearly written, and backed up with facts.

In many cases it is advisable to present and refute the position of the opposing side. Also, it may be a good idea to discuss alternative solutions and the reasons why they are not acceptable or workable.

Position papers may be distributed in response to media requests; they may be included in press kits; or they may be sent to all media that might want to know the organization's position.

Backgrounders

In contrast to the position paper, which states an organization's attitude, the backgrounder is only a recap of information and does not necessarily lead to any conclusion.

It is a summary of pertinent facts about some subject of public interest, such as strip-mining or use of chemical insecticides. It must be accurate and reasonably complete. Because new information often becomes available, backgrounders must be continually updated.

A good format for a backgrounder is to start with the history of the subject, follow that with a review of the situation at present, and end with a discussion of the implications of the facts presented. The tone is always neutral and factual.

PROMOTING NEWS AND FEATURES

The production of news releases, feature stories, illustrations, and broadcast materials is detailed in earlier chapters. You are likely to spend a large part of your time preparing such materials. All are essential for getting information published or broadcast, but these are not the only ways in which to do so. You can get the media to do it for you. This doesn't work all the time, but you can succeed occasionally, and it's always worth a try.

Success requires thorough knowledge of the media, a good idea which is thoroughly prepared, the right approach to the right gatekeeper; and complete support for the reporters who respond.

Knowing the Media

We have repeatedly emphasized the importance of knowing the media, but here we must do so again. You must be very familiar with what is wanted,

Specialized media. There are literally thousands of publications that reach every conceivable occupation, business, and special-interest group. Magazines serving a particular industry are commonly called "trade" publications, or the "trades." Much public relations writing is aimed at media like these. (*Source:* Photo by James McNay.)

what is published, and what is omitted. You should be able to say to yourself, "I'll bet the *Tribune* would like this," "This ought to appeal to XYZ-TV," or "This idea ought to be in the *Hypertechnology Quarterly.*"

Knowing the media also means monitoring what is being sent out from your mailroom. One company, for example, sent a letter to the business editor of a daily newspaper that started this way: "For years, your magazine has contended that a fundamental ingredient of improved productivity is the system that blends and balances techniques for material flow optimization and real-time visibility of operations status."

The letter, obviously geared to a very specialized high-tech magazine, should never have been sent to the business editor. What happened? Someone in the mailroom had simply used a standard mailing list without bothering to check the appropriateness of the letter. The result? At least one editor who is now predisposed to throw away all material from that particular company.

A Well-Prepared Idea

Your idea may be a news story or a feature. It may involve a photo session, a radio actuality, a TV tape, or simply a straightforward newspaper or magazine story. Regardless of what it is, it must be well thought out. If photos are involved, you must think of every possible one that might be used. Also, you must plan where and how the pictures are to be taken.

Timeliness

Standard Rate and Data Service publishes a monthly catalog giving the editorial calendars of many magazines and newspapers. With this information, it is possible to propose news or features at the times when they are most likely to be accepted.

Hewlett-Packard Media Guidelines

Hewlett-Packard (H-P) prepared a guide for its managers which contained a number of suggestions that are applicable to almost any organization. While these ideas are pointed at managers they can also help you when you must deal with the media. Following are some ideas adapted from H-P.

1. *Attitude toward the press.* Good relations with the media are vital. The media should be regarded as "customers" and their needs and requests (if reasonable) should be served.

2. *Aren't reporters hard to work with?* Some are. Some may be biased or antagonistic but most of them are courteous, fair, and reasonable.

3. *Don't reporters make mistakes?* Yes, but they can be minimized if we give them accurate information in clear and understandable words.

4. *Who initiates interviews?* Sometimes the organization arranges for a reporter to talk to a manager. This permits selection of the person to be interviewed—normally the one best qualified. It also allows time for preparation and gathering of needed data. Occasionally the reporter may call direct to some person. This may be tricky because the person called may not be the right one to answer, and certainly there is no time for preparation.

5. *What information may be asked for?* Almost anything. The reporter may want one specific piece of information. The reporter may want to do a story on the organization—products, services, technology, policies, techniques, or anything else. There may be an attempt to get the reaction to something which might affect the organization—actions of competitors, effects of laws and regulations, etc. The objective may be a "roundup" story in which the reporter may be gathering information from several competing organizations. This could range from new developments in electronic technology to product warranties, to employment prospects, to foreign imports.

6. *Do we ever refuse interviews?* Yes, but only when circumstances make it necessary. The reporter may want information which cannot be released. The right person to be interviewed may not be available. In general, reporters should be granted interviews if at all possible. If they don't get the story from you, they may get it from someone else. That source may be a competitor or an enemy. It's better to tell your own story than have some other person or organization tell it. Also, if you help the reporter get his or her story it improves the chances for getting the reporter to use our story some time in the future.

7. *What do I do when asked for an interview?* Don't panic. Keep cool. Ask for the name of the reporter, the publication, and when the reporter wants to do the interview. Ask for a list of questions he or she wants to ask. If you can't answer them tell the reporter that you will find someone who can answer. If you can answer, the list will give you some time to prepare. You may need some time to think. It's perfectly proper to tell the reporter that you are very busy at the moment but that you will call back. Then get the phone number—and do call back. If any questions are sticky or controversial don't hesitate to ask for guidance from someone who can help—higher officials, public relations, or even someone who has undergone the experience before.

8. *What information can be released?* Almost anything that isn't confidential or competitively important. For example.

   a. Anything that has been publicly announced by the organization.

   b. Information on products or services which have been placed on the market.

   c. Items of purely local interest, such as a plant closing because of a snowstorm.

   d. Group or division employment figures—in round numbers and not broken down by departments. Thus it might be O.K. to say there are about 500 employees in a plant, but not to say that thirty-eight are working in a specific laboratory.

   e. Policies and practices that are well-established and well-known. Normally, if they are in printed publications which are widely distributed the information can be released.

9. *What information cannot be released?* Generally anything that is confidential or which competitors should not know. Some examples:

    a. Financial projections. Anything about sales, orders, earnings, costs, shipments, or related internal figures must not be given out.

    b. Operating results for a specific division or a specific product or service.

    c. Market share. It's alright to say that the organization is a major factor or that it is growing but it is wrong to give details and figures.

    d. Marketing strategy. This includes plans, proposed expenditures, advertising plans and budgets, and anything else which would help competitors.

    e. Products under development. Until officially announced they should not be mentioned—directly or by implication.

    f. Legal matters. Don't say anything about patents, infringements, lawsuits, or labor negotiations.

    g. Upcoming changes. Shifts in personnel, acquisitions, construction plans, expansions, or contractions—all these are taboo.

These restrictions on release of information apply not only to press interviews but also to private conversations with any outsiders. Anything said outside the organization may wind up in the media.

Source: Hewlett-Packard, Palo Alto, CA.

Helping the Reporters

Your story idea may involve reporters, photographers, radio or television reporting teams, or any combination thereof. When they arrive, you must help them get the story in the shortest possible time. If any of your people are involved, you must be sure that they are available and prepared.

Your phone calls or letters have told the gatekeepers what you have to offer. Now your job is to give it to them—clearly, concisely, and quickly. You identify the people of your organization, you answer questions—you explain, amplify, and help in every way possible—but you *don't tell them how to do it.*

PROMOTING EDITORIALS

Jack Scott, president of Times Mirror Magazines, has said that an editor of a major publication who turns down good editorial ideas just because they come from outside his office may wind up on the list of endangered species.

To get an editor to run an editorial on a specific subject, you must be familiar with the medium. The proposal must agree with its editorial policy, and

Neale-May & Partners, Inc.

February 15, 1989 M A R K E T I N G & C O R P O R A T E S E R V I C E S

Ms. Kelly Richeul
Editorial Assistant
PENINSULA MAGAZINE
2317 Broadway, Suite 300
Redwood City, CA 94063

Dear Kelly:

Kapow! Zowie! Batman's back!

"Batmania" is sweeping the country during the Cape Crusader's 50th anniversary year. With licensing rights for the super hero and his cast of characters -- including Robin, The Joker and The Riddler -- DC Comics, Inc. cites Batman appearances on millions of t-shirts, watches, skateboards, jewelry and more. Market analysts around the world are predicting that, with his charm and unwavering commitment to defend law and order, Batman will be the hero of the 1990s.

Bringing Batman to millions of home computers will be the same marketing genius who brought Teddy Ruxpin to kids of all ages. Jim Whims, co-founder of Worlds of Wonder and now an executive vice president with Data East, a San Jose-based interactive entertainment company, will be bringing Batman to America by way of the personal computer. A $70 million manufacturer of coin-operated arcade, software and home video games, Data East is betting that Batman will take the PC game industry by storm.

With North America computer game licensing rights, Data East is gearing up to deliver its new title to the more than 20 million home computers by month's end. As a computer game, Batman will deliver the color and excitement of the comic strip and offer kids (of all ages) from California to Connecticut a chance to avenge justice and become the well-loved hero of Gotham City -- all from their desktop! It is expected that the new Batman computer game will fuel anticipation for the comic strip character's 50th anniversary in May, as well as the premier of the Hollywood motion picture this summer.

Jim Whims of Data East is available to discuss the company's plans for marketing the computer game version of Batman in the U.S., as well as to provide commentary on the coming Batman craze and merchandising opportunities. If you are interested in pulling together a "Batmania" feature and taking a closer look at the hero's new high tech image, I'd be happy to forward a copy of Data East's press materials and a copy of its new Batman, The Caped Crusader game title to you.

I'll follow-up with you shortly to determine your interest in the story angle and talking with Jim Whims. If you have any questions in the meantime, please call me at 415-967-4444.

Sincerely,

Maura Kendrick
Maura Kendrick
Associate

4920 EL CAMINO REAL, LOS ALTOS, CA 94022 (415) 967-4444

A *"pitch" letter.* An important part of helping the media do their job is to provide ideas and angles for stories that the publication may wish to develop on its own. This "pitch" to a regional magazine, about a Batman computer game, capitalized on the new popularity of Batman and offered editors an interview with the company's executive vice president. The result was a two-page feature in the magazine. (*Source:* Neale-May & Partners, Inc., Los Altos, CA.)

you must present the suggestion clearly and concisely. Usually this is done in a personal conference. There is no rule that applies in every situation, but the following example may be helpful.

A public relations man who felt strongly about a public issue arranged a meeting with the publisher of the *San Francisco Examiner.* He asked for five minutes, presented the reason why the *Examiner* should take a position on the issue, and wound up with a front-page editorial in every Hearst paper in the United States. He won this publicity because he had prepared a strong and well-organized case that agreed with the Hearst papers' basic editorial policies.

Guest Editorials

Some editors will use editorials written for them. *U.S. News & World Report* asked James A. Michener, the best-selling author, to contribute a guest editorial about the reporter who faked a feature story and won a Pulitzer prize. (The prize was later withdrawn.)

Some papers occasionally use contributed editorials; these are published as if they had been written by the publication's editors. Usually, they are sent out like news releases with no prior consultation. Such suggested editorials are sent only to media that are likely to agree with them. For example, an editorial about the regulations of the Occupational Safety & Health Administration (OSHA) would be sent only to publications that reach readers who are directly affected by OSHA. The format of the suggested editorial is much like a news release, but the headline should be "Suggested Editorial."

Letters

Many newspapers regularly publish letters to the editor, usually on the editorial page. Publication is determined by the editor. Often the letters selected are of little importance, but there are exceptions. A letter from a prominent person or from a recognized authority has a reasonable chance of seeing print.

When you notice an editorial or news item that is unfair or wrong you should write to the paper in hopes of getting your letter published (unless, of course, you decide that this might only make matters worse). The letter should be signed by a responsible spokesperson from you organization; preferably the chief executive officer. The letter must be clear, factual, and above all, temperate.

Sometimes it is useful to hand-deliver such a letter, thus ensuring its consideration. If the letter must be mailed, it is a good idea to telephone the editor and inform him or her that the letter is on the way. At large papers, one person is often specially assigned to handle letters to the editor.

Op-Ed Articles

A variation of the letter to the editor is an article, usually an analysis or commentary about news events or public concerns, on a page facing the daily newspaper's editorial page.

These articles, commonly written by someone who has special insight into a subject, may be a rebuttal to a previously published editorial or just a reaction to a series of news events reported by the newspaper. For example, a corporation executive may write an op-ed piece about the possible effect of the President's announced plans to levy new taxes on business. Or a professor of engineering may write an article about the innovative use of robots in Japanese industry and how this might affect technology in the United States.

The Hoover Institution, a think tank on the Stanford University campus, is an excellent example of how an organization can utilize op-ed articles for publicity purposes. This public affairs office regularly sends newspapers op-ed pieces written by prominent experts on the staff. In one year, it placed 240 such articles in publications like the *New York Times, Washington Post, Los Angeles Times,* and *Wall Street Journal.*

Op-ed Articles: An Excellent Outlet for Ideas

The following is an excerpt from an article by George Marotta, formerly public affairs director of the Hoover Institution in Palo Alto, California. It was originally published in *Thrust Magazine.*

Where can you get your ideas (a) circulated free to millions of readers, (b) written in your own words, and (c) even get paid for it? The answer is through articles on the op-ed pages of newspapers such as the *New York Times,* the *Washington Post,* the *Christian Science Monitor, USA Today,* and the *Los Angeles Times.*

"Op-ed" is journalese for the page opposite the editorial page in newspapers. It typically runs articles by syndicated columnists such as Jack Anderson, James Kilpatrick, and Art Buchwald. However, most newspapers also accept articles by outside writers from time to time.

These by-lined articles provide an excellent opportunity for the exposure of new ideas or the analysis of public policy issues facing our society. The op-ed page is the modern-day counterpart to the New England Town Hall meetings of yesteryear in providing a forum for the expression of diverse points of view.

Getting an article published as an "op-ed" is simple if you know how—and here are some tips on how to do it:

CONTENT

An op-ed article should concentrate on presenting one main idea. The style and complexity of the writing should match the readership of that particular newspaper. A good rule is to keep it simple and avoid the use of jargon.

Because national newspapers receive many more unsolicited articles than they can accept, the subject matter and the point of view should be somewhat unique.

A **must** for such articles is a good strong lead. The first few sentences have to accomplish two objectives: capture the reader's (and the editor's) attention and articles should be educational, but presented in a lively and interesting manner.

Daily newspapers generally prefer articles about 700–750 words in length—three typewritten, double-spaced pages. Sunday editorial page sections can use longer articles—about 1000 to 1500 words.

PROCEDURE

Op-ed articles should be submitted to the editorial editor of the newspaper in double-spaced, typewritten copy. Names of editors and addresses of newspapers can be obtained from *Editor and Publisher International Yearbook.* The writer should provide biographical data so that the editor will have some basis for judging the author's credentials.

The editor will usually take a couple of weeks to accept or reject the article. They will almost always give the article a catchier title when they publish it and may also perform light editing.

Many local newspapers accept essays by outside writers. Also, several magazines accept "opinion-type" articles. Examples are the "My Turn" page of *Newsweek* and the "Ideas and Trends" section of *Business Week* magazine.

OPPORTUNITIES

With a little thought, public relations and communication practitioners should be able to identify many opportunities to use op-ed articles. Here are some examples:

- whenever a member of your organization gives a speech on themes or ideas which might be of public interest

- upon the completion of an interesting study or research project

- summarizing testimony given at a public or legislative hearing

- correcting misconceptions about an organization's position

- educating the public on the basic workings of a free-market economy, etc.

A good way to stimulate the writing of articles is to encourage members of an organization to accept more speaking engagements. This will force officials to organize their ideas in a format suitable for popular consumption. Excerpts of the speech can then be used as the basis for an opinion article.

Another technique to promote the op-ed program is to circulate published articles among the various divisions of an organization. This will demonstrate to the staff that management encourages such writings.

The greatest value of this form of publicity is that it carries more prestige than just a letter to the editor. An op-ed item is, in effect, endorsed by the publication as an opinion that deserves attention because it shows insight into a matter of public concern. You should be familiar with the expertise of the people in your organization, so that you can submit an op-ed article when news events call for an informed viewpoint.

PRESS CONFERENCES

These should probably be called "news conferences," because they frequently include broadcast media, but the name "press conference" has been used for so long that it has stuck. Media people generally dislike these events because so many are called for no legitimate reason other than trying to stir up publicity. For this reason, a press conference should be scheduled only when truly necessary.

Reasons for a Press Conference

A press conference is justified when there is *important* news, when it is desirable to give it to all reporters at the same time, and when reporters may want to ask questions.

Legitimate subjects for press conferences are such things as political announcements, labor disputes, major policy decisions, major construction projects, major product developments, important meetings, celebrity appearances, and emergencies or catastrophes.

Scheduling a Press Conference

The conference should be scheduled at a time that is convenient for the reporters—that is, with an eye to the deadlines of the media represented. Weekends should be avoided; most media operate with skeleton staffs on Saturdays and Sundays. Evening cocktail parties and midday lunches preceded by drinks are undesirable. A morning (10 A.M.) conference will be suitable for afternoon papers and evening broadcasters.

With the decrease in the number of afternoon newspapers and the increased importance of local radio and television news, many media specialists suggest early afternoon as the best time to schedule a news conference. A 1 P.M. conference, for example, leaves plenty of time for morning-paper reporters but is still early enough for evening television news and for the 4 to 6 P.M. commuter radio news.

Separating the Media

Some people advocate separate conferences for print and broadcast media. This seems to give good results and to avoid overcrowding, since both print and broadcast reporters want to get their own microphones in front of the spokesperson.

Also, this system enables each broadcast reporter, in turn, to get a minute or two of exclusive film or tape.

Invitations

The invitation list should include all reporters who might be interested. It is better to invite too many than to omit some who may feel neglected. Invitations should be mailed seven to ten days in advance—though the telephone may be used when the conference is scheduled on short notice. The invitation, in any case, should state the time and place, the subject to be discussed, and the names of the principal spokespeople who will attend.

Press conference. A well-planned and well-run conference can generate media interest. This one was held in New York, the nation's media capital, and generated several hundred news stories. (*Source:* Ketchum Public Relations, New York, NY.)

Invitations should be marked RSVP, so you can make appropriate revisions for the size of the meeting room, the amount of food to be served, and the number of press kits or other materials you should have on hand. Reporters are notorious for not responding to RSVPs, so it is appropriate to phone them several days before the event to determine the projected attendance. If a key reporter cannot attend because of other assignments, make arrangements for him or her to receive all the press conference materials as soon as they are available.

Handling the Conference

The conference should be thoroughly planned and carefully controlled. Everyone involved must know the purpose of the meeting and who will do what. There must be a spokesperson for the organization—usually a senior executive. He or she must be thoroughly rehearsed, prepared with ready answers for anticipated questions, and told who to turn to for additional answers.

Arrangements should be made for photographers, for television and radio reporters, and for newspaper and magazine reporters. Your efforts to position these people so that they can get their stories easily and with a minimum of moving about will be appreciated. An elevated platform is always helpful.

Press Kits

It is general practice to provide a press kit to all reporters. This may be presented in a large folder or envelope and normally includes such things as a press release containing the full story that is presented at the conference, position papers, backgrounders, pictures, and anything else that will be of help in writing the story.

A press kit used by Commonwealth Edison Company at an environmental press conference contained the following:

Press Kit. An event, a press conference, or a new-product introduction often requires a press kit. This one contains general information, a schedule of events, and action photos about a rodeo. (*Source:* Photo by James McNay.)

1. News release
2. Statements by top officers
3. Technical papers on pollution of air and water
4. Paper on nuclear power
5. History of the company's efforts to protect the environment
6. Photographs of pollution-arresting facilities
7. Maps showing the location of Commonwealth Edison plants
8. Graphs showing trends in coal use and national sources of air pollution.

Get the Most out of a News Conference

Here are a few rules to follow in holding a news conference:

1. *Determine the appropriateness* of a news conference. News conferences, because they provide an active discussion between the press and the spokesperson, are best suited for controversial or complex announcements on financial and scientific matters that require extensive backgrounding.

2. *Pick a good location.* A central location, attractive facilities, and a knowledgeable staff are important. Remember that a television news director will not assign a crew to cover a press conference that requires considerable travel time.

3. *Choose the right day.* Early in the week is better than later. Monday generally is a slow news day, and media representatives are more readily available.

4. *Avoid the 10 A.M. "rush hour."* This is a popular time for news conferences, and media representatives are often confronted with too many going on at the same time. Early afternoon is a good alternative.

5. *Give proper advance notification.* Mail one-page invitations that include the basics: event, time, place, speakers, background. These should be mailed six to ten working days in advance. Call key outlets the day before the event as a reminder.

6. *Don't forget "daybooks."* AP and UPI, as well as some local news services, list upcoming events on a calendar for their subscribers. A listing of upcoming news conferences is included.

7. *Provide videotapes for television.* Television crews don't like "talking head" presentations. Handing out a background videotape—for example, one that shows the product in action or offers a tour of a facility—is preferable. Such footage can be handed out at the news conference or delivered to the station several days before the event.

8. *Use visuals.* Include large mounted blowups of printed documents such as photos, maps, charts, diagrams, and so on.

9. *Hire a photographer.* If the event involves a presentation, such as the giving of an award, a photographer can take pictures and rush copies to those media outlets who were not able to cover the event.

10. *Prepare the room.* Arrive one hour early to make sure everything is set up, including chairs, podium, microphones, coffee, and so on. Make sure the room is not too small or too large for the expected attendance. If it's in an old building, ask the electrician to stand by in case of blown fuses.

11. *Brief your spokesperson.* Develop a list of anticipated questions and have the spokesperson practice answering them.

12. *Keep the press kit simple.* A bulging, fancy press kit is not needed.

13. *Offer phone interviews to no-shows.* If key media don't show up, call them immediately after the news conference and offer a phone interview with the spokesperson.

Source: *Public Relations Journal,* September 1986.

MEDIA EVENTS

In addition to conferences there are other occasions for meeting with reporters; among the most common are previews, parties, and junkets.

Previews

Press previews are often scheduled in connection with some event to which the general public is invited. Usually the preview is held a day ahead of the event. Typical events are the opening of a new building, an important convention, an open house, a plant tour, a new-product announcement, and special occasions such as fairs, community events, and cooperative merchandising occasions (e.g., a fiesta in a shopping center).

By inviting the press early, the reporters are able to see the entire occasion minus the crowd—and they do so in time to get their stories and pictures published or aired on the day of the event. Normally a press kit is given to each reporter.

Parties

A press party is given as an expression of goodwill toward the media. The format may range from a cocktail party to a dinner. One large, nationally known company combined a press preview of its new headquarters building with a press party that included cocktails and a buffet dinner. Among the guests were reporters from all the media plus sales representatives of those media in which the company advertised. As the party ended, the media people asked company officials for the "handout." When told that there was no press kit or even a release, the reaction was one of delighted surprise. But the company received a large amount of favorable publicity.

Junkets

A variation on the press party is the junket. Although the use of junkets has declined in recent years, they are still part of the travel and entertainment industry. Junkets usually involve invitations to reporters for an expense-paid trip to witness an event or see a facility.

An example of a large-scale junket: Disney World in Florida invited 10,000 writers, publishers, and broadcasters to a three-day celebration of the park's fifteenth anniversary in late 1986. Although large numbers of media representatives took advantage of what columnist Mike Royko said was the largest "freebie" in U.S. journalistic history, a number of prominent newspapers blasted the event. The *New York Times* editorialized that the press was debasing itself by accepting Disney's hospitality and questioned whether reporters could be objective about Disney operations after accepting an all-expense-paid trip.

Junkets, particularly when there is little newsworthy information, raise considerable controversy among journalists and even public relations professionals. As a consequence, companies must carefully consider all aspects of sponsoring a junket and its possible negative effect on media relations.

Press parties or junkets, in order to be effective and garner media attendance, must be handled discreetly. It is against the code of ethics of the Society of Professional Journalists (SDX) and the Public Relations Society of American (PRSA) to have lavish banquets and expensive souvenirs simply for the sake of impressing the press. Journalists, although they may attend, generally "bad mouth" the affair if they think there is an overt attempt to "buy" favorable coverage.

EDITORIAL BOARDS

Most large newspapers, news magazines, and broadcasters determine editorial policy carefully, deliberately, and generally after careful consideration of both sides of a situation by the senior editorial personnel.

Getting a medium on your side involves a session with the editorial board of the medium whose support is sought—and here preparation is vital. Position papers and backgrounders are indispensable. In addition, the organization's representatives should learn as much as possible about the editors' attitudes and past policies. The problem of approaching a receptive group is different from that of approaching one that may be doubtful or antagonistic. Every individual medium is different, and the more you know about it and its key personnel, the more likely you are to have a successful meeting.

Media Tours Require Planning

STAGE 4: SEVEN DAYS AHEAD OF TOUR START

- Practice packing and unpacking products. Label each box with its contents or obtain carrying cases. They're easier to repack.

- Phone each journal to confirm appointment. Check names of attendees.

- Phone each hotel and confirm rooms, other arrangements. Be sure you have confirmation numbers.

- Publish complete agenda and summaries. Make enough copies for each tour-team member plus extras for secretaries of each member. Provide special comments about each journal as required (doesn't use color, wants technical article, etc.).

- For leader of tour, make special book with chapters on each publication: personal quirks of editors, editorial calendars for six months, clips of recent articles on HP, responses to generic questions about HP—financial, Spectrum, RISC, etc.

- Remind HP people to take badges for easy identification by editors. Wear business attire.

- Tour PR leader should have plenty of credit in credit-card account. Enough cash should be taken to handle quick transactions plus tips to move equipment from car to hotel or office of publication.

- If going to Canada, prepare all paperwork before leaving. Also allow time for clearing customs going in and out of Toronto. Photos and printed materials may not be admissible. Check in advance with our host office in Canada.

- Carry the following items for the tour: two or more rolls of packing tape; small pocket knife for opening boxes and cutting tape; two-to-three prong plug converter; heavy-duty power cords with three or four outlets.

Source: This is an excerpt from a checklist used by Hewlett-Packard public relations personnel in planning and operating media tours. Reprinted by permission of Hewlett-Packard.

MEDIA TOURS

A media tour is somewhat like a traveling news conference. An organization's officials make calls on those publications that reach important audiences. The spokespersons, preparations, and materials are almost identical to those you would need for a press conference. The main difference in this sort of activity is that instead of asking reporters or editors to come to a conference, the conference comes to them.

It would be very difficult, for example, to get representatives from *Forbes, Business Week, Fortune, Time, Newsweek,* and similar national magazines to come to the offices of a small company. Yet by taking the president, the marketing director, and perhaps the chief financial officer to the magazines, it is possible to arrange for a "one-on-one" press conference with the publication's principal editors.

A small electronics firm on its first media tour met with 24 editors of 13 publications in 3 1/2 days. Within a few weeks, stories appeared in *Forbes* and *Business Week,* and several other magazines planned to run feature stories.

In planning a media tour, be sure to consider every possible publication. The company mentioned above manufactures office products and called on, in addition to the general media mentioned above, such magazines as *The Office, Western Office Products, Office Products Dealer, Geyer's Dealer Topics, Word Processing and Information Systems, Modern Office Procedures, Today's Office,* and *Office World News.*

Media Tours Pay Off

The media tour can be a valuable means of publicizing a product, service, or idea.

The most common media tour involves appearances by a spokesperson on radio and TV as well as interviews with print journalists. Book publishers, for example, often arrange media tours for best-selling authors. One author, Prince Michael of Greece, visited 12 cities in 29 days and gave 61 interviews to promote *Sultana,* his first novel, published by Harper & Row.

Another kind of media tour comprises a series of background briefings for key journalists and security analysts. A good example is provided by Dataspeed, Inc., a high-tech firm that wanted to be known as a telecommunications company with innovative products such as a portable stock market quotation device.

Regis McKenna Inc. of Palo Alto, CA., recommended a media tour. The counseling firm not only prepared Dataspeed's chief executive for media interviews but also arranged appointments with key journalists and financial security analysts on the East Coast. In a five-day swing, a Regis McKenna account executive and the corporation's president visited 22 journalists and analysts in New York, Boston, and Washington. They were able to see editors at *Fortune, Business Week, Time, Newsweek, Venture, High Technology,* and the *Washington Post*—as well as a number of key security analysts specializing in the high-tech field.

ISSUES, CRISES, AND EMERGENCIES

An issue is a matter in dispute—such as offshore oil drilling or the use of pesticides. A crisis is a turning point that can lead to a drastic change in public opinion—such as Union Carbide's Bhopal accident in India, which became the world's worst industrial disaster. An emergency is a sudden occurrence that requires immediate response—such as a fire or an explosion.

Issues are normally handled as part of the continuing long-term program. Crises and emergencies are handled as described in Chapter 18.

Media Communications

In any situation where the public is concerned, it is imperative to give the media the truth, the whole truth, and nothing but the truth—and promptly.

The objective is to help the reporters get the facts quickly and accurately. If the media are not aware of the emergency, they should be notified in the fastest way—by phone.

Facilities should be provided—parking space, desk space, telephones, and access to the scene if it is safe. A temporary newsroom is helpful. Guards and doorkeepers should be instructed to admit properly identified reporters. The spokesperson should stay close to the news center if possible.

Reporters will want to know what happened, how it happened, when and where it happened. They will also want to know *why*, but on this point you should be careful. Because damage suits may result from statements blaming

Hot line helps reporters. Organizations often advertise a hot line number in publications for journalists. The publicizing of these phone numbers allows journalists to get quick answers to questions. (*Source:* Dow Chemical Company, Midland, MI.)

someone, it is imperative to withhold information on this. If reporters press this question, it is best to say that the cause is under investigation.

The Penalty of Silence

When Hooker Chemical Company sold the Love Canal property to the city of Niagara Falls, it warned the city of the chemical dump, told the city how to preserve the built-in protections, and received a statement from the city completely absolving Hooker from liability. When Hooker was accused of being the worst polluter in the country, its lawyers told the officers to say nothing because the company was legally in the clear. The result was that, although Hooker might have won in a court of law, it lost in the court of public opinion because they didn't tell their story promptly and completely.

"Truth Will Come to Light"

Shakespeare said it 400 years ago and he was right, as Chrysler discovered. Almost by accident, it was found that Chrysler dealers were routinely disconnecting the odometers of new cars, using the cars for business, and then reconnecting the odometers and selling the cars as "new." When this became widely known, Lee Iacocca, the president of Chrysler, had to make a public apology and pledge to stop the practice. Advertisements throughout the country said, "We Goofed."

Preaction Pays

The Insurance Information Institute got wind of a suspected attack by Jack Anderson, the columnist. Questions were being asked by Anderson's investigators about the settlement of insurance claims in the wake of a hurricane.

Anticipating what Anderson was likely to say, the institute prepared a tentative reply. When the column was published, the institute revised its reply and phoned it to the newspapers carrying Anderson's column. In some cases the reply was printed next to the column. The result was wide publicity for the institute's point of view and explanation, so that Anderson's column did not dominate the public discussion.

Here are a few guidelines to follow when you are reacting to attacks:

1. Take the initiative in commenting on issues; don't wait for the press to call you.
2. Correct inaccurate news reports immediately; respond while the issue is still in the news. If the attack is from a group, make sure the press has your reply the same day.
3. Make sure of your facts and data; wrong information is worse than no information at all.
4. Don't be lulled into a sense of security by a reporter's friendly attitude; he or she wants quotes and information.

SUMMARY

1. Cooperation is the key word in working with the media.
2. There are many ways in which you can help reporters, and if you help them, they will help you.
3. You can get into trouble with reporters in many different ways. Learn the things to avoid.
4. Most people in public relations have complaints about the way they are treated by the media.
5. Most problems with the media can be solved by the proper action.
6. Your communication with the media will be more effective if you know who they are, if they know who you are, and if you keep them supplied with facts.
7. It is often possible to suggest news stories, features, and editorials that the media will create.
8. Press conferences are often overdone. When needed, however, a conference that is well planned and conducted can materially help your efforts.
9. Editorial boards and media tours can accomplish the same things as press conferences—and can do so when a press conference is impossible.
10. In a crisis or emergency, the media can be of tremenduous help—*if* you communicate with them.

EXERCISES

1. The local newspaper has published a series of articles that criticize the quality of health care in the community. Your hospital, St. Vincent's, was the subject of an article in which a number of facts were misstated. For example, the article said that the hospital had the highest rate of patient deaths in the county. This is literally true, but the article didn't place this "fact" in perspective by saying that St. Vincent's Hospital operates the only hospice in the county—a facility where terminally ill patients are cared for until they die. What steps would you take to inform the newspaper of this and get a correction?

2. The owner of a local radio station has written an op-ed article for the weekly business tabloid about journalism as a major in college. He says that journalism courses are a waste of time and aspiring journalists or public relations personnel should get a broad-based education in the liberal arts. He says today's journalism majors can't write and would benefit from majoring in English or history. As a journalism or public relations major, draft a letter to the editor rebutting his ideas.

3. A company wants to hold a news conference announcing the acquisition of another large national company. Outline and describe the materials that should be placed in a press kit about this acquisition.

4. You are hired to organize a news conference for a company based in Norfolk, VA, that is announcing a major expansion of its department stores into the Florida and Georgia markets. Previously, the company had stores only in Virginia, Tennessee,

and South Carolina. Outline and describe the steps for organizing this news conference. The resulting plan should be a blueprint of the entire event, including selection of site, use of visual aids, and list of invitees.

5. The Arts Council of Northwest Florida is sponsoring the Great Gulf Coast Arts Festival October 31 through November 2 in Pensacola. About 2000 artists will exhibit their works, and there will be a series of jazz concerts. Write a fact sheet for the media about this event.

6. A national business magazine has decided to do a feature profile on your company because of its dynamic executive leadership and innovative manufacturing technologies. A reporter and photographer will be visiting the company next week. What would you, as director of public relations, do to plan for their visit?

SUGGESTED READINGS

Bernstein, Gail. "Meet the Press." *Public Relations Journal,* March 1988, pp. 28–32.

Blohowiak, Donald W. *No. Comment: An Executive's Essential Guide to the News Media.* New York: Praeger Publishers, 1987.

Brody, William. "Antipathy Exaggerated Between Journalists and Public Relations." *Public Relations Review,* Winter 1984, pp. 11–15.

Evans, Fred J. *Managing the Media: Proactive Strategy for Better Business-Press Relations.* Westport, C.T.: Quorum Books, 1987.

Evans, Fred J. "Business and the Press: Conflicts Over Roles, Fairness." *Public Relations Review,* Winter 1984, pp. 33–42.

Graham, James. "What to Do When a Reporter Calls." *Communication World,* April 1985, p. 15.

Guzzardi, Walter. "How Much Should Companies Talk?" *Fortune,* March 4, 1985, pp. 64–69.

Hannaford, P. *Talking Back to the Media.* New York: Facts on File, 1986.

Hattal, A. M. "Setting Up a News Conference." *Public Relations Journal,* May 1985, p. 34.

Howard, Carole M. "Managing Media Relations for Environmental Issues." *Public Relations Quarterly,* Summer 1988, pp. 24–26.

Howard, Carole M. "Managing Media Relations During Layoffs." *Communication World,* December 1985, pp. 17–19.

Howard, Carole M., and Mathews, Wilma. *On Deadline: Managing Media Relations.* New York: Longman, 1985.

Marken, G. A. "Thirteen Ways to Make Enemies in the Press." *Public Relations Quarterly,* Winter 1987–1988, pp. 30–31.

Peterson, Robert. "Perceptions of Media Bias Toward Business." *Journalism Quarterly,* Autumn 1982, pp. 461–463.

Pinsdorf, Marion. *Communicating When Your Company Is Under Siege.* Lexington, MA.: Lexington Books, 1987.

Ryan, Michael, and Martinson, David L. "Journalists and Public Relations Practitioners: Why the Antagonism." *Journalism Quarterly,* Spring 1988, pp. 131–140.

Sklarewitz, Norman. "Press Junkets: Sound Marketing Method or Boondoggle?" *Communication World*, February, 1988, pp. 32–35.

Taft, R. W. "How to Handle Negative Information.' *Public Relations Journal*, April 1984, pp. 26–29.

Wood, John H. "How to Arrange Successful Media Tours." *Public Relations Journal*, May 1985, p. 33.

Chapter
11

Message Dissemination

Delivering news to a local paper or station is simple. You give it to the appropriate gatekeeper. But what if you want to reach every fashion editor in the country, or every weekly newspaper in Montana, or all the trade magazines in the field of control systems? What if you want to reach every Spanish-language radio station or just those in Texas? Obviously you will need to know who the gatekeepers are and where they are.

You will also need to know how to deliver your material to them by way of the most efficient technology. You will need to know how to build and update a mailing list, how to produce quantities of releases and illustrations, how to handle the mailings. You should also know how and when to rely on release services as well as how to use the wire services and satellite distribution.

FINDING THE GATEKEEPERS

A country weekly newspaper is likely to have only one gatekeeper—the editor. A suburban weekly may have several, and a metropolitan daily may have scores. A trade or professional magazine may have only one—the editor. A special-interest magazine may have one or several gatekeepers. The same situation exists in radio and television. In every medium, there is some person to whom your information may be important—and there are numerous others who will ignore it.

To make sure that your news gets to the right gatekeeper, you must direct it to that one person—not just to the publication or station where someone in the mailroom will have to guess where to send it. Identifying the gatekeepers would be extremely difficult were it not for the existence of publicity directories, which make it a relatively simple matter.

Some of the largest directories attempt to list every possibility; others may confine their listings to one category, such as television or country weekly newspapers. All are as up to date as possible, but—because people change their jobs, features and programs change, and errors do occur—no directory is 100 percent accurate. In spite of these minor flaws, most directories are reasonably complete and usable.

Each directory has advantages and drawbacks. The only way to choose is to study several and decide which are most useful for your particular situation. (Many people use two or more.) The largest directories run to several volumes and cost several hundred dollars. Several of the directories issue corrections as the publishers learn of changes in personnel in the media or of changes in format or programming.

The better directories list not only the gatekeepers but also the kind of material wanted. Thus, it is possible to locate every radio or television talk show in the country and find out the name of the director, the preferred subject matter, whether live guests are used, whether film clips are used, and even the time the show is aired. Similar information is often available for publications.

You'll have to do some research to find the directories most suitable for your needs. Each publisher has descriptive literature that will be sent to you upon request. By reading this material, you can get a general idea of what kind of information is included. When you have made a preliminary selection, it is advisable to examine the directory in detail. This can be done by asking other people about the relative merits and demerits of each. Remember that they may have different needs, so make very sure that your needs will be filled by a directory before you buy it.

Following is a list of national directories. In addition to these, there are regional and local directories about which your colleagues can inform you.

Ayer Directory of Publications (newspapers, magazines)
Bacon's Newspaper Directory (newspapers)
Bacon's Publicity Checker (magazines)
Broadcasting Yearbook (radio, television)

Lodi

CA-D39 LODI NEWS-SENTINEL, 125 N. Church Street, P.O. Box 1360, Lodi, CA 95241; (m)17,200.   **(209) 369-2761**
Editors/Writers: 3,12—Traja Rosenthal; 4,CE—Bob Nishizaki; 5,17—Toni Mata; 7—Peter Melton; 8,9,16—Darlyne Kooyman; 14,19—Carl Underwood; ED—Fred Weybret; ME—Marty Weybret.

Lompoc

CA-D40 LOMPOC RECORD, 115 N. H Street, P.O. Box 578, Lompoc, CA 93436; (e)10,000;(S)10,500.   **(805) 736-2313**
Editors/Writers: 1,3,12,13,18,22—Steve Brown; 2,4,ED—Dan Bolton; 5—Chuck Bolcom; 6,7—David Wert; 8,9,10,15,16,20,24,27—Sherry Wittmann; 11,17—Lisa McKinnon; 14,19—Alan Hunt; 21—Al Thompson; 23—J. Samuel Cope; 25,CE—Rita Henning; 26—J.L. Sousa; PF—Jane Quinn.

Long Beach

CA-D42 LONG BEACH PRESS TELEGRAM, 604 Pine Ave., P.O. Box 230, Long Beach, CA 90844; (d)134,300;(S)133,800.   **(213) 435-1161**
Editors/Writers:

2. Tim Grobaty	12. Jim Robinson	24. Harold Glicken
3. Jim Robinson	14. Jim McCormack	25. John Futch
4. John Fried	15. Harold Glicken	26. Mark Damon
5. Robin Hinch	16. Carolyn Ruszkiewicz	27. Todd Cunningham
8. Carolyn Ruszkiewicz	17. Todd Cunningham	ED. Larry Allison
9. Joyce Christensen	20. Carolyn Ruszkiewicz	ME. Rich Archbold
10. Carolyn Ruszkiewicz	22. Jim Robinson	MT. Mike Schwartz

Columnists: GE—Tom Hennessy.

Los Angeles

CA-D43 LOS ANGELES HERALD EXAMINER, 1111 S. Broadway, Los Angeles, CA 90015; (m)240,000;(S)190,000.   **(213) 744-8000**
Editors/Writers:

1. David Barry	15. Jim Burns	24. Andrea Herman
2. Jeff Silverman	16. Chris Hodenfield	25. Paul Zieke
3. Kathleen Ingley	17. Jeff Silverman	26. Jim Roark
4. James Kinsella	18. Betsy Bates	27. Joe Eckdahl
5. Debbie Anderluh	20. Martha Tarbell	ED. Maxwell McCrohon
9. Russ Parsons	22. Sharon Bernstein	ME. Andrea Herman
11. David Gritten	23. Don Frederick	CE. Larry Burrough
14. Rick Arthur		

Columnists: GE—Jane Birnbaum, Gordon Dillow; SP—Melvin Durslag, Allan Malamud.

CA-D45 LOS ANGELES TIMES, Times Mirror Square, Los Angeles, CA 90053; (m)1,136,000;(S)1,421,000.   **(213) 237-5000**
Editors/Writers:

1. Jim Risen	11. Aleene MacMinn	20. John Brownell
2. Jack Miles	12. Dick Turpin	21. Robert Smaus
3. Martin Baron	13. Lee Dye	22. Dick O'Reilly
4. Anthony Day	14. Bill Dwyer	25. Norman C. Miller
5. Larry Gordon	15. Jerry Hulse	26. James Wilson
6. Larry Stammer	16. John Brownell	ED. William F. Thomas
7. Bruce Keppel	17. Kathryn Harris	ME. George Cotliar
8. Bettijane Levine	18. Robert Steinbrook	CE. Dick Barnes
9. Betsy Balsley	19. Earl Gutskey	MT. David Rosenzweig
10. Virginia Gray		

Columnists: GE—Jack Smith; SP—Jim Murray, Scott Ostler.

Madera

CA-D46 MADERA TRIBUNE, 100 E. Seventh Street, P.O. Box 269, Madera, CA 93639; (e)8,600.   **(209) 674-2424**
Editors/Writers: 1,2,4,9,10,11,17,23,ED—Greg Robertson; 3,7,12,CE—David Snelling; 5—Kyle Nicholas; 14—Paul Bittick; 15—Sarah Williams; 26—Rita Valdivia.

Manteca

CA-D460 MANTECA BULLETIN, 531 E. Yosemite Avenue, P.O. Box 912, Manteca, CA 95336; (mS)6,400.   **(209) 239-3531**
Editors/Writers: 1,6,CE—Dennis Fleming; 2,16,20—Rose Albano; 3,7—Marguerite Shrader; 4,9,10,12,15,17,21,23,ED—KarenHodges; 5—Leo Holzer; 11—Karen Kopecki; 14,19—Dan Loumena; 18—Robin Bergmann; 26—Mark Du Frene.

---

1. Automotive	8. Fashion	15. Travel	22. Computers/High Tech
2. Book Review	9. Food	16. Women's	23. Political
3. Business/Financial	10. Home Furnishings	17. Entertainment	24. Features
4. Editorial Page	11. Radio/Television	18. Medical/Health	25. National News Editor
5. Education	12. Real Estate	19. Outdoor	26. Photo Editor
6. Environmental	13. Science	20. Lifestyle	27. Weekend/Sunday Ed.
7. Farm	14. Sports	21. Garden	ED - Editor
			ME - Managing Editor

CE - City Editor
MT - Metro Editor
COLUMNISTS:
AM - Advertising/Marketing
PF - Personal Finance
GE - General
SP - Sports

Media directory. There are a number of media directories that list publications, addresses, and names of editors. Whether you're looking for a list of aviation publications or want to know who is the business editor of the *Washington Post,* a media directory is an essential reference tool. Some directories are now available on computer disk. (Source: *Bacon's Publicity Checker,* Chicago, IL.)

Editor and Publisher International Yearbook (dailies, weeklies, syndicates)

Gebbie Press All-in-one Directory (newspapers, magazines, radio, television)

Hathorn's Suburban Press Directory (suburban newspapers)

National Radio Publicity Directory (radio)

Oxbridge Directory of Newsletters (newsletters)

Standard Periodical Directory, (magazines, internal publications)

Standard Rate & Data Service Print Media Editorial Calendar (editorial schedules)

Television Publicity Outlets, (television)

U.S. Publicity Directory, (newspapers, magazines, radio, television)

Working Press of the Nation, (newspapers, magazines, radio and television, feature writers and syndicates, house magazines)

Larimi Communications sold eight of its directories to Billboard Publications in 1988. Included in the sale were *TV Contacts, Radio Contacts, TV News, Cable Contacts Yearbook, Investment Newsletters, Syndicated Columnists, News Bureaus in the U.S.,* and *College Alumni and Military Publications.* The prices of these directories range from $87 to $239.

COMMUNICATION TECHNIQUES

Earlier in this book, we described a release as a piece of paper delivered to some medium in the hope that the information it carried would be published or broadcast. In general this is true, but the revolution in communications that is now taking place may drastically change the means by which such releases reach the media.

Computer terminals are being installed in many places. Reporters are carrying portable word processors that enable them to transmit their stories directly to their newspapers. Office typewriters are being replaced by word processors. Mimeographing machines, photocopiers, and even offset printers are being displaced, at least to some degree, by the multiple copying abilities of the more complex word processors.

Photographs, drawings, charts, diagrams, and other visual materials are being transmitted electronically, either via telephone lines or direct to other computers. It is even possible to set up a conference and alter such visuals while they are being discussed.

This is not the place to make firm predictions, but you must be aware of these changes and keep abreast of the new communication techniques. The basic principles will not change, but the mechanical means of distributing materials to the media—and the means by which the media convey their information to the public—may be entirely different from those we have used for so long.

All these changes will take time, and they will occur step by step. Experiments are being conducted, trial facilities are being installed, and more innova-

25B-120 CIRCUITS MANUFACTURING (Continued)

MAY	Analysis of the developments in Low-Volume Assembly—Bare-Board AOI—Solder Masks Review.
JUNE	Surface Mount Technology Update—Small-Hole Plating Study— Update on the latest developments in New Reflow Techniques.
JULY	Surface Mount 1989 Preview Issue—SMT Inspection, Cleaning and Components Update.
AUGUST	SMT Solder Masks Developmental Update.
SEPTEMBER	Hi-Rel and ISHM Issue—CAM Stations Section—Laser Plotters Review—Reflow Soldering Study—Repair Report.
OCTOBER	1989 Buyer's Guide.
NOVEMBER	SMT Design for Manufacturability Review—Fine-Line Imaging Study—SMT Cleaning Update—Solder Paste Feature—SMT Components Issue.
DECEMBER	Hi-Rel and DOD 2000 Study—Fluxes Update.

25B-160 COMPUTER DESIGN, 119 Russell Street, Littleton, MA 01460; (617) 486-9501, Mr. John Miklosz, Editor; Mr. Dave Allen, Publisher ; Semi-Monthly, 100,000.

LEAD TIMES: Features and News - 2 months prior, Adv. - 1st, 1 month prior.

EDITORIAL PROFILE: Edited for engineers and engineering management personnel responsible for the design, integration and application of computer systems. Highlights include new technology equipment trends, new software listings and developments of components and related peripherals. **Ad Rate:** $5,645

ISSUE	EDITORIAL FOCUS/SPECIAL ISSUES
JANUARY 1	CASE Report—Hybrid Technology Update.
JANUARY 15	Gate Array Focus.
FEBRUARY 1	Review of Real Time Operating Systems—High Level Design Languages Report.
FEBRUARY 15	Flat Display Technology Feature.
MARCH	Unix Focus—Device Modeling Showcase.
MARCH 15	Special Report on 32 Bit Processors and Coprocessors.
APRIL	Graphics Technology Round-Up—Static RAMs Review.
APRIL 15	Fiber Optics Focus.
MAY	Digital Signal Processing Report.
MAY 15	Development Tools Update.
JUNE	Military Computers Overview.
JUNE 15	Focus on Simulation Accelerators.
JULY	Profile of Programmable Logic Devices.
JULY 15	Emphasis on Image Processing Systems.
AUGUST	Profile of ASIC Memories.
AUGUST 15	Static RAMs Update.
SEPTEMBER	Focus on PCB Layout Tools.
SEPTEMBER 15	Product Trends Report.
OCTOBER	PC Based CAD Tools Review.
OCTOBER 15	Optical Storage Report.
NOVEMBER	Feature on 32 Bit Buses.
NOVEMBER 15	Digital Signal Processing Report.
DECEMBER	Report on Logic Synthesis.
DECEMBER 15	Graphic Windows Update.

25B-200 CONNECTION TECHNOLOGY, 17730 W. Peterson Road, P.O. Box 159, Libertyville, IL 60048; (312) 362-8711, Ms. Jennifer Rose, Editor; Mr. Neil Olsen, Sales Mng.; Monthly, 35,000.

LEAD TIMES: Features, News and Adv. - 1st, 1 month prior.

EDITORIAL PROFILE: Written for buyers, designers and manufacturing engineers who use and specify connectors and connection products. Editorial content stresses developments by members of the international connection products market. **Ad Rate:** $3,307

ISSUE	EDITORIAL FOCUS/SPECIAL ISSUES
JANUARY	Spotlight on Molded 3-D Interconnect—Printed Circuit Board Connectors Buyer's Guide.
FEBRUARY	Soldering Process Review—Overview on Appliances and Consumers.
MARCH	Focus on Contact Materials—Spotlight on Continuity Testers— *Electro '89* Coverage.

(Continued on Next Page)

Editorial focus. Advance information about special issues enables the public relations writer to prepare material that will be timed to fit the needs of the editor. Trade publications, in particular, have editorial calendars that focus on a major topic each month. (*Source: Bacon's Media Alerts,* Chicago, IL.)

tions are to come. In several cities, newspapers are already being delivered electronically onto a computer screen in the home. The *Wall Street Journal* is edited at one location but printed in a number of different plants. This enables the *WSJ* to deliver throughout the country on the day of issue. There is also a general newspaper, *USA Today*, which is centrally edited (thanks to electronics) but regionally printed. This is a truly national newspaper available everywhere at the same time of day.

MAILING LISTS

The first step in making up a mailing list is to decide who you want to reach. Assume, for example, that your job is to publicize ocean cruises for a company operating several ships. By referring to your media directories, you can find the names of newspaper travel editors. Obviously these should be on your list. But what about general magazines, do any of them have travel editors? Are there any feature syndicates that might be interested? Are there freelance writers who specialize in travel? Are there any radio or TV programs that could be prospects? Of course you will think of travel magazines, but remember that there are two kinds. One is the special-interest magazine that goes to potential travelers. The other is the trade magazine that goes to travel agents and others who are in the business of selling transportation. You will probably find several editors in each category.

For any other kind of problem, the procedure is the same. You check the directories for every possible gatekeeper who might be interested in your particular subject. Their names and addresses are then placed on your mailing list. If the scope of your operation is nationwide, the list may be very long. If your activity is confined to a community or a limited area, the list may be quite short. As this point, it may be in order to emphasize that only a few people regularly deal with the media on a national basis. Most news is local or limited to a special field. There are thousands of capable public relations people who have never sent out a nationwide release or given anything to the wire services.

To be effective, you must send to the media only that which has a reasonable chance of consideration. To apply this principle, you should specialize your mailing list or, if you prefer, make up several different mailing lists. To show how this works, we will go back to the travel field. General releases about the kinds of cruises available could go to newspapers. For magazines, you might want to send individually written releases. If your shipping line is offering a special deal of a free cruise to any agent who sells 25 tickets, you would send your release only to the travel trade magazines.

Specializing by Territory

Mailing lists can be specialized by territory, so that releases can be sent to selected geographical areas. The accompanying table is part of a form used by

LARIMI CONTACTS

The Media Pipeline for Public Relations People   Bill McLoughlin, Editor

WALL STREET JOURNAL
NEW YORK TIMES
Mc CALL'S
"HOME"
ABC TELEVISION NETWORK
LOS ANGELES, CA

IN THIS ISSUE
February 15, 1988

BETWEEN THE LINES:
Placing An Obituary
(Part II)

WSYX-TV, COLUMBUS, OH
ELECTRONIC DESIGN
KTAR-AM, PHOENIX, AZ
FREEBIES

WALL STREET JOURNAL
2-18/88 Priscilla Smith, now writing a daily column titled "OTC Focus," wants background information on companies traded over the counter. Annual reports and quarterly earnings are wanted as is information on new projects, promotion campaigns or major personnel changes that will have an impact on company stock prices. Interviews, tied to movement of the company's stock, with CEOs, CFOs and others "who can speak for the company" are also wanted. The column, begun on a temporary basis in October, was recently made "official." Circulation: 1,985,550. CONTACT: WALL STREET JOURNAL, 200 Liberty Street, New York, NY 10281 (212) 416-2000

NEW YORK TIMES
2-19/88 Alex Scardino, now writing the "New Yorker & Co." column for the business section, wants information and profile suggestions on prominent, colorful business figures who are making an impact outside of their individual industries. "People in the news," in "all the industries that make New York what it

is, "ranging from fashion, food and banking to advertising, communications, radio and television are of interest. Suggested subjects should "be of significant interest to a large audience." Mail queries preferred when time permits. Information more than 2 months old is not considered appropriate. Circulation: 1,056,924. CONTACT: NEW YORK TIMES, 229 W 43rd Street, New York, NY 10036 (212) 556-1234

Mc CALL'S
2-20/88 Colette Rossant, appointed to the newly created position of entertaining and home design director, wants information on children's storage for the October issue. For the July issue she wants information on outdoor entertaining, from barbecues to lawn furniture to table decor. She's also interested in "anything used for entertaining" including linens, china, glassware or candles. Color transparencies can be used. Ms. Rossant works 4 months ahead for all issues. Circulation: 5,000,000. CONTACT: MC CALL'S, 230 Park Avenue, New York, NY 10169 (212) 551-9500

NEW CONTACTS
"HOME"
ABC TELEVISION NETWORK
LOS ANGELES, CA
2-21/88 ABC Television Network is producing a new service and information series titled "Home," featuring Robb Weller and Sandy Hill as hosts. Utilizing experts who aren't household names, the program will cover cleaning secrets, childproofing homes, dealing with parents growing old and preparing inexpensive gourmet meals. "Home," airing Monday-Friday 11:30 a.m. - 12 noon, is geared to women and offers fix-it information, ranging from drippy faucets to rainy-day kids' activities to personal problems. Guests on the show include authors, experts and entertainers, booked by Producers Noreen Friend and Dan Weaver, who work 1-2 weeks ahead. Interviews are taped at KTLA-TV, Los Angeles, CA. Information on behavior, lifestyles, books, authors, entertainment, food, fashion, medicine, health, personal finance, products, sports, travel and leisure are needed. CONTACT: "Home," KTLA-TV, 5842 Sunset Boulevard, Los Angeles, CA 90028 (213) 871-8292

CONTACTS is published weekly by LARIMI COMMUNICATIONS ASSOCIATES, LTD., 5 West 37th Street, New York, NY 10018. (212) 819-9310. Larimi also publishes TELEVISION CONTACTS, RADIO CONTACTS, TV NEWS, CABLE CONTACTS YEARBOOK, INVESTMENT NEWSLETTERS, SYNDICATED COLUMNISTS, NEWS BUREAUS IN THE U.S. and COLLEGE ALUMNI & MILITARY PUBLICATIONS directories; produces the IMPACT! PR VIDEO TRAINING SERIES, PR SPEAKERS BUREAU, and PR LIBRARY; and sponsors the annual NATIONAL MEDIA CONFERENCE and ANNUAL REPORT CONFERENCE.
Michael M. Smith, President and Publisher.

Tip sheets. Newsletters like this report what editors want and when they want it. Because of constant changes in the media, these "tip sheets" are published weekly. A public relations professional who pays close attention to this kind of information can place stories efficiently and effectively. (*Source: Contacts,* Larimi Communications, New York, NY.)

an airline to indicate where any given release should go. For example, when the 02 and the 3 are circled, the mail-room personnel know that the attached release goes to travel editors in territory 2.

With a list as specialized as this, there is ample opportunity to send releases to the exact targets and to be sure that a news item that is significant in Denver will not be sent to Dallas, where it would be meaningless.

MAILING LIST

Territory	Recipients	
01	1	CITY EDITORS
02	2	BUSINESS FINANCIAL EDITORS
03	3	TRAVEL EDITORS
04	4	AVIATION EDITORS
05	5	SYSTEM WEEKLIES
06	6	SYSTEM RADIO
07	7	SYSTEM TV
08	8	(OPEN)
09	9	(OPEN)
34		STATION MANAGERS
12	R	BUSINESS FINANCIAL MAGAZINES
13	S	GENERAL NEWS MAGAZINES
14	T	AVIATION TRADES

Specializing for Exclusives

Another thing you'll have to do is make sure that the same item is not sent to competing publications. If it is only a brief announcement—as of a change in personnel—the same release could go to all media concerned. If your material is detailed, you will have to give different versions to different publications. For example, if there are two food editors in the same market, you'll give each of them a different recipe release. To reassure the editor, your release will be marked "Exclusive to you in your market." Then she or he will know that there is no chance that the recipe will appear in the competing paper.

To make the exclusive release really mean something, it may be necessary to have several variations, not just two. Suburban newspapers often reach subscribers who also read a metropolitan daily. These, too, should be given their own releases. A reader in Arlington, Virginia, may read a Washington paper and a local evening paper but probably not a paper published in Silver Spring, Maryland.

Another way to specialize mailing lists is by zip code. This is primarily applicable in direct mail, but the armed forces have found that by sending releases to newspapers in certain zip code areas and avoiding others, they greatly increase both utilization of the releases and response to the items published. Some zip code areas (and not necessarily low-income areas) have been found to be much better recruiting sources than others. By "rifling" their publicity, the armed forces have greatly improved their results.

With a properly specialized mailing list, you will be able to aim your releases effectively and efficiently. They will get to the right gatekeepers and *only* the right ones.

Mailing-List Mechanics

Having determined who is to be on your mailing list and how it is to be specialized, your next step is to get the names out of the directories and into a form in which they can be used. Obviously you can't expect anyone to go through the directories, find the names and addresses, and address the envelopes one by one.

For a small list, it would be feasible to transcribe the names and addresses onto one or more sheets of paper, which would then be used by a typist to copy them onto envelopes. For a larger list, it is faster and more economical to use labels, which are then attached to the envelopes. You can have the list typed onto a form and then print the names and addresses onto pregummed labels by a thermofax process. If a computer is available, it can print the labels for you.

Because your list may be specialized, it is advisable to place a code number on each address so that, when a release is returned because of nondelivery, you will be able to find just which sublist it is on and delete that name without trouble.

If at all possible, every address should include the name of the gatekeeper, not just the title. This will, of course, create a continuing problem for you. The names on the list will change, and you must keep your list accurate. You may learn of a personnel change from almost any source: a phone conversation, a news item, or a chance meeting on the street. Whenever and however you learn of a change, you must correct your mailing list. Nothing annoys the gatekeeper more than irrelevant releases, but a close second is a release sent to someone who hasn't been around for six months—or six years.

In addition to the working mailing list described in the preceding paragraphs, you will need a reference list so that you can see who is receiving your releases—and show the list to your superiors if they want to see it. A copy direct from the working list will do, but the purpose can also be served by a list that is skeletonized. An entry on this might be as brief as: "Joe Smith, City Editor, Salem, OR Statesman"; the working address would include the street address and zip code.

PRODUCTION

With a properly specialized mailing list, the total number of items going out to the media will be much smaller than if you send everything to everyone. The rate of use will be higher and your costs will be lower. Nevertheless, you will need several or many copies of certain releases. In planning to produce the necessary quantities, you must consider both quality and costs. What you send to the media must be clear, clean, and—above all—usable. A sloppily reproduced illustration or news release will not be used because it will be viewed as shoddy work unworthy of consideration. When you write a release or plan an illustration, you give great attention to putting interest and news-worthiness into it. Don't let your efforts be destroyed by poor production.

Releases

In Chapter 5 it was emphasized that carbon copies of news releases should never be sent to any medium, because the recipient of the carbon copy would know that someone else was the first choice. That same criticism does not apply to releases produced in quantity. Gatekeepers are used to receiving such releases and know automatically that a number of others are receiving the same release. If the item is newsworthy, it has a chance of being used.

Quantity reproduction of news releases may be done in several different ways. If you have a word processor with a printer, you will be able to produce quantities of releases direct from your original copy. Another procedure is to reproduce the needed quantity by using a photocopying machine or even by offset printing.

Illustrations

In Chapter 7 you were given considerable guidance on getting pictures that would appeal to the gatekeepers. If you need only a few prints of these, you can order them from your photographer. But if you want to deliver them to a sizable number of people on your mailing list you will need a good many copies. These can be obtained from one of the copying services listed in the Yellow Pages under "Photo Copying." To use such a service you must be sure that you do, in fact, own your negative. Refer again to Chapter 7 on this point. You *can* own the negative, and if you do, you'll be able to obtain copies of it more cheaply from a copying service than you could from a photographer.

It is possible to send color transparencies to a number of different, non-competing publications. Duplicates can be purchased at relatively low cost from several firms that provide this service. These, plus many other sources of needed services, can be found in *The Creative Black Book* published by Friendly Publications, Inc.

When you send out a number of illustrations, you will have to attach a caption to each. Some people, especially those who send out hundreds of copies at a time, have the caption printed directly on the photo print. Others have the captions reproduced by one of the quantity production processes and then attach them to the prints individually.

You should make sure that the illustrations will not be damaged in the mail. A cardboard stiffener in the envelope is a must, and a note on the envelope that it contains a photograph is also necessary. You can use a rubber stamp that says "Photograph—Do Not Fold" to mark every envelope used in this way.

As you prepare and select illustrations for release to the media, you will, of course, try to send out only those that are really newsworthy. Occasionally you will have one that is outstanding. When that happens, pick up the phone and call the wire-photo editor of AP or UPI. Describe the picture and ask if it sounds interesting. If the wire-photo editor wants the picture, send it in and forget about mailing multiple copies.

MAILING

As a general practice, all news releases should go by first-class mail. If there are a considerable number directed to any zip code area, it is possible to save on postage by presorting the envelopes according to zip code. This situation is not likely to occur with any but the largest organizations.

Mailing—and this includes inserting the material in properly addressed envelopes, applying the postage, and getting it all to the post office—is an "in-house" activity. In a small organization it may be done by anyone who has time. In a larger organization, there may be a completely staffed mail department that will handle all the details.

If the volume is substantial and the organization's mailing facilities are not adequate, you can use one of the mailing services. These are listed in the Yellow Pages under "Advertising—Direct Mail," but some of them can handle almost any mailing problem.

Regardless of the system you use, you should be familiar with the procedures of the post office and alternative distribution services. For example, all domestic mail goes by air if the distance is great; nearby mail goes by truck. Most mail is sorted at regional centers; thus local mail may be trucked fifty or a hundred miles away, sorted, and then returned to the city of origin. By paying a sizable extra fee, you can get overnight delivery almost anywhere in the United States. This service is offered by the post office and as well as several private firms.

Any mail sent overseas should go by air. If you send it by surface transportation, it may take weeks to get to its destination.

Mail early. In some cities, your letters will be delivered the next day—if they get into the post office before 5 P.M. Delivery to the post office saves much time. Most mailboxes show the times when mail is picked up, but be especially wary on weekends. A letter mailed on the Friday before a national holiday will probably arrive on the following Wednesday. Your own name should be included in every mailing to provide a check on how fast your releases move through the mail.

RELEASE SERVICES

Any or all of the work described up to now in this chapter can be done by a release service. Many people have found that if they delegate the mechanical procedures, they can devote more time and attention to the creative side of their work. The scope and cost of these services vary widely, but the mere

MDS

MEDIAMATIC® SYSTEM

BUSINESS EDITORS OF NEW YORK CITY DAILIES AND WIRE SERVICES, WSJ, J of C

Qty. 60

1 (N.Y. Times, N.Y. Daily News, Post, Wall Street Journal, Journal of Commerce. AP, UPI, Reuters)   Qty. 9

- 12 BUSINESS & FINANCIAL editor
- 20 PERSONNEL CHANGES editor
- 8 FINANCIAL STATEMENTS editor
- 21 ADVERTISING & MARKETING COLUMNISTS (4)
- 57 ACCOUNTING editor
- 22 AIRCRAFT & MISSILE MANUFACTURE editor
- 10 AIR TRANSPORTATION editor
- 23 AUTO BUSINESS editor
- 11 BANKING editor
- 24 BUILDING MATERIALS editor
- 25 BUSINESS MANAGEMENT editor
- 37 BUSINESS NEWS HIGHLIGHTS (2)
- 26 CHEMICALS & CHEMICAL PRODUCTS editor
- 38 COMMODITIES editor
- 27 COMPUTERS/COMMUNICATIONS editor
- 39 DRUGS editor
- 28 ELECTRIC & ELECTRONICS editor
- 40 FARM editor
- 29 FOODS & BEVERAGES editor
- 41 FOOTWEAR editor
- 30 FOREIGN TRADE editor
- 42 HOME FURNISHINGS & HOUSEWARES editor
- 31 HOTELS editor
- 02 INDUSTRIAL SCIENCE & ENGINEERING editor
- 03 INSURANCE editor
- 04 INVESTMENT ADVICE COLUMNIST (2)
- 05 INVESTMENT BANKING editor
- 07 JEWELRY editor
- 60 MACHINERY editor
- 13 MARINE editor
- 62 MEDICAL & HEALTH BUSINESS editor
- 61 MINING editor
- 14 MEN'S CLOTHING editor
- 06 METALS IRON & STEEL editor
- 18 METALS NON-FERROUS editor
- 15 MUTUAL FUNDS editor
- 16 NEW PRODUCTS editor (3)
- 17 NEW FINANCING & BONDS editor
- 19 OFFICE EQUIPMENT editor
- 31 PACKAGING editor
- 32 PAINT editor
- 58 PERSONAL FINANCE editor
- 33 PETROLEUM editor
- 34 PLASTICS editor
- 35 PUBLISHING editor
- 36 PULP & PAPER editor
- 43 RAILROADS editor
- 44 REAL ESTATE & CONSTRUCTION editor
- 45 RETAILING editor
- 46 RUBBER PRODUCTS editor
- 47 STOCK-MARKET ROUNDUP editor
- 48 TAXES editor
- 59 TECHNOLOGY editor
- 49 TEXTILES editor
- 50 TOBACCO editor
- 51 TOYS editor
- 52 TRANSPORTATION editor (see Air Transp. above)
- 53 TV & RADIO BUSINESS editor
- 54 UTILITIES editor
- 55 WALL STREET GOSSIP COLUMNISTS (2)
- 56 WOMEN'S CLOTHING editor

ALL DAILY & WEEKLY NEWSPAPERS AND BUSINESS STAFFS OF THE WIRE SERVICES, WALL STREET JOURNAL, JOURNAL OF COMMERCE

NEWSPAPERS

1

SELECT EDITOR BELOW:

This Business ed. group will not apply to NYC dailies. (see listing on left)

1 BUSINESS & FINANCIAL EDITOR
- 8 ADVERTISING editor (if any)
- 48 COMPUTER/TECHNOLOGY (if any)
- 27 FARM editor
- 39 OIL editor (if any)
- 26 REAL ESTATE editor

2 CITY EDITOR
- 20 AMATEUR PHOTO editor
- 44 AUTO editor
- 26 AVIATION editor
- 38 CONSUMER AFFAIRS editor
- 45 EDUCATION editor
- 42 ENVIRONMENT editor
- 46 HEALTH editor
- 41 MEDICAL editor
- 40 RELIGION editor
- 37 SCIENCE editor
- 39 TRAVEL editor

3 WOMEN'S/LIFESTYLES EDITOR
- 21 BEAUTY editor
- 9 DO-IT-YOURSELF editor
- 39 FASHION editor
- 22 FOOD editor
- 11 GARDENING editor
- 23 HOME FURNISHINGS editor
- 42 SOCIETY editor
- 31 TEEN-AGE editor
- 41 WINE editor

4 ENTERTAINMENT EDITOR
- 28 ART editor   42 ____ critic
- 20 HOME VIDEO editor
- 40 MOTION PICTURE editor   31 ____ critic
- 27 MUSIC editor   43 ____ critic
- 38 NIGHT CLUB editor
- 33 RADIO-TV editor   32 ____ critic
- 34 TV SUPPLEMENT editor (if any)
- 36 TV LISTINGS editor (if any)
- 35 TV PBS editor (if any)
- 37 TV PHOTOS editor (if any)
- 39 TV SYNDICATIONS editor (if any)
- 30 RESTAURANT editor
- THEATRE editor   44 ____ critic

5 SPORTS EDITOR
- 24 AUTO RACING editor
- 42 BASEBALL columnist (if any)
- 5 BASKETBALL columnist (if any)
- 27 BOATING editor
- 10 BOWLING columnist (if any)
- 18 FOOTBALL columnist (if any)
- 6 GOLF columnist (if any)
- 6 HOCKEY columnist (if any)
- 40 OUTDOOR editor
- 1 SKI editor
- 2 SOCCER columnist (if any)
- 25 TENNIS columnist (if any)
- 25 TV SPORTS columnist (if any)

6 EDITORIAL PAGE WRITER
- 25 PUBLISHER
- 28 ENERGY (if any)
- 27 OP-ED (if any)
- 31 POLITICAL WRITER (if any)
- 30 TOBACCO POL. EDITOR (if any)
- ACTION LINE editor (if any)
- **7** 10 BOOK REVIEW editor (if any)
- 9 LABOR EDITOR (if any)
- 39 TV & RADIO BUSINESS editor
- 26 LIGHT GENERAL INTEREST COLUMNIST (if any)

SELECT DAILY NEWSPAPERS BELOW:

		Qty. U.S. & Can.
302	NYC DAILIES (Times, News, Post)	4
102	NATL. DAILIES (USA Today, Christian Sci. Mon.)	3

OTHER DAILY NEWSPAPERS BY CIRCULATION

4	02	OVER 300,000 (except NYC dailies)	46
	14	300,000 to 200,000	35
	03	200,000 to 100,000	81
	15	100,000 to 50,000	141
5	02	50,000 to 40,000	81
	14	40,000 to 30,000	127
	03	30,000 to 20,000	181
	15	20,000 to 10,000	421
6	02	10,000 to 7,000	233
	14	7,000 to 5,000	186
	03	5,000 to 3,000	177
	15	3,000 and UNDER	29

FOR EXCLUSIVE MAILINGS IN A CITY CHECK CIRCULATION OF DAILY NEWSPAPERS ABOVE AND MARK A,B,C in RANK DESIRED BELOW:
- 59 LARGEST CIRCULATION NEWSPAPER
- 58 SECOND CIRCULATION NEWSPAPER
- 57 THIRD CIRCULATION NEWSPAPER
- 60 SINGLE CITY DAILY NEWSPAPER

WEEKLY NEWSPAPERS

7	3	ABC Audited Tri & Semi-Weeklies	46
	15	Non-ABC Tri-Weeklies	467
	4	ABC Audited Weeklies Over 5,000 Circulation	191
	16	ABC Audited Weeklies Under 5,000 Circulation	199
8	5	Non-ABC Weeklies Over 7,000 Circulation	1570
	17	Non-ABC Weeklies 7,000-4,000 Circulation	1231
	6	Non-ABC Weeklies 4,000-3,000 Circulation	905
	18	Non-ABC Weeklies 3,000-2,500 Circulation	561
9	7	Non-ABC Weeklies 2,500-2,000 Circulation	570
	20	Non-ABC Weeklies 2,000-1,500 Circulation	675
	21	Non-ABC Weeklies 1,500-1,000 Circulation	758
	9	Non-ABC Weeklies 1,000-500 Circulation	489
		Non-ABC Weeklies below 500 Circulation	92

REGIONAL BUREAUS OF NATIONAL MEDIA

2	20	Associated Press Bureaus	125
	8	United Press International Bureaus	118
	23	Reuters	12
	30	Wall Street Journal Bureaus	20
	22	Journal of Commerce Bureaus	23
	29	New York Times Bureaus	5
	10	NYC Out of Town Newsp. Bureaus	5
	24	NYC Out of Town Newsp. Bus. Eds.	24
	25	McGraw-Hill Bureaus	11
	31	Time-Life Publication Bureaus	10
	27	Newsweek Bureaus	7
		U.S. News & World Report	7
		Fairchild Bureaus	7

Complete release service. This is an extract from the catalogue of a news release distribution service, which is capable of sending news releases to more than a hundred thousand editors, broadcasters, and syndicated columnists. All the public relations person has to do is send one release to the service and indicate which list of publications and editors should receive it. (*Source: MDS/PRA Group, New York.*)

fact that they exist and thrive is proof that a release service is economically justifiable.

Because the release services are constantly changing their operations, it is not feasible to give a detailed description of what each can do. Rather, we will list the tasks that the various services do and leave it to you to decide which service best fills your needs.

Media selection and the construction of mailing lists is a prime service. A large release service will have access to *all* media directories. It will employ several people whose sole responsibility is to keep the mailing lists up to date. This ensures accuracy. With computers, it is possible to produce almost any conceivable specialization. Thus, a release service can readily send your releases to all suburban weeklies in Illinois or all automobile editors of daily newspapers with circulations of more than 50,000.

A release service can handle all the work of producing and distributing your releases. It can print the needed number of copies of news releases or pictures. It can insert, address, and deliver to the post office. In the simplest terms, if you give a release service one copy of a release and specify who you want to reach, the service can do all the rest. If you want to send out illustrations, it is equally simple—one print with caption and a negative is all you need to provide. Everything else is done for you.

An additional service is available from some of these firms. This is called a "mat service." Actually, they deliver not "mats" but "slicks," pieces of paper that carry type or pictures or both. Most smaller newspapers and many magazines print by the offset process, in which no metal type is used. Instead, the printing can be done from slicks. The mat service sends the publication large pages of slicks and the editor may use one or more of the group offered.

Here are some of the most widely known release services:

- Associated Release Service
- Derus Media Service
- Family Features Editorial Services
- MDS/PRAids
- North American Precis Syndicate

Family Features Editorial Services, for example, specializes in the distribution of feature stories to general-circulation newspapers and magazines. Manufacturers of food products, for example, may prepare a standard recipe and photo layout that editors can order from a catalog mailed to 4000 newspaper editors nationwide.

You can use a release service to reach TV and radio stations as well as newspapers and magazines. Three services that work only with broadcast media are:

- J-Nex
- Modern Satellite Network
- Newslink, Inc.

All these services will, on request, send you complete information about what they can do and what it will cost.

The Active Consumer

How To Select A Home Computer

Choosing a personal computer can be a lot easier than you think if you actively arm yourself with a list of questions so you can make an informed decision.

It's important not to rush. Becoming knowledgeable enough about personal computers, such as those offered by IBM is not as difficult as it may seem. The following is a list of questions to help you select the personal computer that fits your needs:

• *What are the strengths and features of each particular vendor's products?* All you have to do is ask any sales representative at a retail store. The salesperson will be happy to point out the best features of a company's products.

• *How much growth capacity will a system have?* This question is far more important than most first-time users imagine. How much difficulty you may have transferring information to a larger system, when you need it, should be considered today rather than five or six years hence.

• *How reliable is a particular system?* Talk to users of a particular computer. Local user groups will be able to supply you with names of people who are using their systems in ways applicable to your requirements.

• *Is the product covered under a warranty?* Select a computer from a company and dealer that offer the best warranty protection and service available.

Selecting the right kind of personal computer is important and can save you time and money.

• *What education and support are available?* Many of today's computers have help screens that explain how to proceed. Do you find these computer-given instructions easy to follow? How readable are the manuals?

• *Is the system user-friendly?* Select a computer that's easy to operate. Once you know first hand how user-friendly a system is and how close the commands are to everyday English, you will know how quickly you can master it.

• *Is there a hardware/software package that will meet your needs?* Not all software programs run on the same computer. Be certain the software you buy is compatible with the hardware system you intend to use.

Remember, the job of your personal computer is to save you time and money. A computer system that has been carefully selected will do just that.

Caring For A Computer

Today's small personal computers are surprisingly easy to care for.

With the increased use of personal computers, setting up a business in your home can be easier than ever.

The new personal computers, such as the IBM Personal Computer or IBM PCjr, are light in weight and occupy about as much space as a standard office typewriter or breadbox.

Although they need no special air-conditioned environment, they should not be subjected to extremes of heat or cold.

You cannot damage your personal computer by pressing any key or combination of keys. You can, however, erase the information on a diskette.

There are also a few sensible rules for caring for your diskettes.

• Always place the diskettes back in the protective jackets after use.

• Never touch diskettes through the slots where the magnetic surface is exposed.

• Keep diskettes out of direct sunlight and away from other sources of heat. Diskettes should be stored at temperatures ranging from 40 to 125 degrees Fahrenheit.

• Use a felt tip pen when writing on diskette labels to avoid damaging the diskette inside the envelope.

WIRE SERVICES

There are several wire services which will, for a specified fee, deliver your releases directly to newspaper and magazine business editors throughout the country. These services use highly sophisticated equipment that transmit both words and photographs.

By using such a service, you can be sure that your materials will be delivered immediately. There is no chance that your release will be lost or delayed in the mail. Some of these services will even check your items for accuracy and for news style. Electronic delivery ensures that all papers get the news at the same time. This is especially important with financial news, because using such a delivery method can assure the Securities and Exchange Commission that there has been complete and prompt disclosure of any developments that could affect the value of a given company's stocks.

Releases can be sent to a wire service by telephone facsimile (FAX), messenger, TWX, Telex, or telephone dictation. You can tell the wire service exactly where to send the release, and you can arrange to have one wire service deliver the message to another service for distribution to its outlets.

Here is a list of the principal public relations wire services:

Business Wire
Canada Newswire Ltd.
Mediawire
Newswire
Ohio Newswire
PR News Service
PR Newswire
Press Relations Newswire
Southeastern Newswire
Southwest PR Newswire
Universal News Service
U.S. Newswire

In addition to reaching the individual media (newspapers, magazines, and broadcasters), some of the larger wire services—such as Business Wire and PR News wire—reach trade publications, investment firms, news services (such as AP, UPI, Copley, Gannett, Newhouse, Scripps-Howard), and news bureaus. Even media in other countries can be reached.

Camera-ready features. Several distribution companies specialize in providing camera-ready features to newspapers. All the editor has to do is paste the provided material into the page layout. Most of these feature materials are consumer-oriented and can be used almost any time. The examples shown are from IBM, but notice that the company name is mentioned only once. The noncommercial approach is the one that is most acceptable to editors. (*Source:* North American Precis Syndicate, Inc., New York.)

Say "thanks," this Secretaries Week

Secretaries are vital players in today's business world, and offices across America will take time during the week of April 23 to recognize the vital role these men and women play in business, industry, education, government and the professions.

The occasion is Professional Secretaries Week, established in 1952 by the U.S. Department of Commerce to acknowledge "...the American secretary upon whose skills, loyalty, and efficiency the functions of business and government offices depend."

As national pride in secretaries has grown, so has recognition of Secretaries Week. Some firms have company-wide programs, luncheons and special tributes for secretaries. Others leave it up to individual supervisors to decide how they wish to remember their own right-hand assistant.

Many choose to express their appreciation to secretaries with flowers. In response to this, Florists' Transworld Delivery Association (FTD®) has specially designed a thoughtful gift choice.

Available from FTD florists for local or out-of-town delivery, the FTD Secretaries Week Bouquet includes an assortment of colorful flowers arranged in a coffee mug, the handle of which holds a useful roller-ball pen.

Experts in helping people express their thoughts and feelings with flowers, FTD florists will also have a variety of other flowers and plants from which to choose.

To select the "right" floral gift for your secretary, you can conveniently place your order by calling or visiting a local FTD florist who can offer advice on floral gifts for every taste and budget.

Being away from the office during Secretaries Week need not deter you from making a floral expression for the holiday. You can place an order with any of the more than 24,000 FTD florists nationwide and have it delivered promptly to your secretary.

While a personal gesture like sending flowers is an appropriate way to extend your thanks for a job well done, it is also important to recognize your secretary's professional needs throughout the year.

You can help your secretary with his or her professional development by de-

PERSONNEL GESTURE: The specially-designed FTD Secretaries Week Bouquet is an appropriate expression of your year-long personal appreciation for your right-hand helper during Professional Secretaries Week (April 24-28). It can be sent both locally and out-of-town by visiting or calling a local FTD florist.

termining what his or her individual goals are. Some secretaries may see their positions as stepping-stones to "professional/managerial" assignments, while others may hope to grow within the "paraprofessional" framework.

Depending on the goal, you may want to investigate training workshops or educational programs, perhaps sponsored by your company, and tailor assignments accordingly.

Also, you can show your secretary you consider him or her a respected member of the management team by including him or her in appropriate meetings, memos and work-related activities.   *TF896191*

Timely placement. The distribution of camera-ready material tied to a special week can be effective in generating publicity. Shown here is a feature prepared on behalf of the Florists' Transworld Delivery Association (FTD) for Professional Secretaries Week. (*Source:* Metro Creative Graphics, Inc., New York.)

SATELLITE DISTRIBUTION

Both VNRs and program features can be distributed via satellite. Usage of this channel is increasing rapidly, and improvements in technique are encouraging further reliance on this method of conveying information to viewers.

Modern Talking Picture Service, for example, now has a division called

Modern Satellite Network (MSN), which transmits company-sponsored programs by satellite to about 500 cable television stations with a subscriber base of about four million homes. The service is free to cable stations and networks (which is a large plus, given the cost of regular programming like Showtime, HBO, or CNN), and the cable stations have found that MSN fulfills daytime programming needs.

Essentially, MSN packages programs through which corporations and organizations can obtain high visibility by providing informational material. A good example is a program called *Viewpoints*. In one segment, a show hostess interviewed Betty Papke, national sales manager for Intertherm, Inc., a manufacturer of hot-water heating products. Ms. Papke presented ideas on holding down heating costs and conserving energy in the home by, of course, using Intertherm's products. On another segment, an expert butcher talked about how a pressure cooker could make less expensive cuts of meat taste better. The segment was sponsored, naturally, by National Presto, manufacturer of pressure cookers.

Although MSN is expensive to companies that pay the tab for such exposure, many feel that the cost is worth it if they reach two or three million people in one program. In other words, the cost per viewer is just pennies.

MSN can also be utilized by companies who want to reach large numbers of people with special reports. For example, Emery Air Freight used the satellite services of MSN to broadcast its corporate annual report. The special videotaped presentations, incorporating highlights of Emery's annual meeting, was placed on closed-circuit TV via satellite for Emery stockholders throughout the nation.

SUMMARY

1. It is imperative to send your releases to the right gatekeeper. You find these gatekeepers by using media directories.
2. The technology of communication is changing so rapidly that what is new today may be obsolete next week. You should keep in touch with these developments.
3. Mailing lists are essential to the mass distribution of releases. They must be well organized and up to date.
4. Mass mailings require the mass production of releases and illustrations. The quality must be high if they are to be accepted and used.
5. Release services can do the entire job of production, list compilation, and mailing for you.
6. Wire services can deliver your releases and photos to the newspapers and magazines as well as radio and television stations throughout the country and even in some foreign countries.
7. Satellite distribution is a rapidly growing channel for the distribution of news material.

EXERCISES

1. A bank in Omaha, Nebraska, has announced plans to build a new 12-story headquarters building. Using press directories, compile a list of local print and broadcast outlets in Omaha and the surrounding area that should receive a copy of the news release. In addition, compile a list of business or trade publications that would be interested in this announcement.

2. A manufacturer of golf carts has developed a new, smaller cart for one person that requires fewer batteries to operate. Using media directories, compile a list of trade and specialized publications that would be interested in this new-product announcement.

3. The Wisconsin Cheese Board has prepared a packet or recipes and photos showing the use of cheese in various food dishes. These packets will be sent to every newspaper food editor in Wisconsin. Using press directories, compile the names and addresses of food editors who would receive the packet.

4. A manufacturer of sunscreen lotion has developed a feature article about the need for protection to avoid the dangers of overexposure and skin cancer. The target audience for this kind of information comprises women from 18 to 35. Using press directories, compile a list of general-circulation magazines that reach this specific audience.

5. Using the library, compare the contents of two or three press directories. What are the advantages and disadvantages of each?

SUGGESTED READINGS

Albert, Jack. "Going Global With Your News." *Communication World*, March 1986, pp. 33–34.

Albert, John J. "The World of Satellites: Your Global Voice." *Public Relations Quarterly*, Spring 1987, p. 23.

Caruba, Alan. "Media Musical Chairs: A Guide to Media Directories Worth Owning." *Communication World*, July/August 1988, pp. 49–51.

Chambers, Wicke, and Asher, Spring. "Workshop: How to Work with TV Producers." *Public Relations Journal*, August 1985, p. 25.

Clark, Marcia S. "Workshop: Getting Your News Releases Through." *Public Relations Journal*, November 1986, p. 57.

Cooper, M. "In the Stretch: Electronic Mail." *Public Relations Journal*, January 1985, pp. 35–36.

Glazer, George. "Beam It Over and Out—Via Satellite." *Communication World*, March 1988, pp. 14–15.

Greenfield, Ellen. "Demystifying the Birds in the Skies." *PR Week*, April 11–17, 1988, p. 11.

"Publicity Distribution: Getting the Message Across." *PR Week*, June 6–12, 1988, pp. 9–11.

Stark, Steven. "Revolutionizing Mail and Marketing." *New York Times*, July 18, 1988, p. F2.

Weiner, Richard. "High Tech News." *Public Relations Journal*, January 1985, pp. 26–27.

Chapter
12

Directed Media

*N*ewspapers, magazines, radio, and television reach large audiences in an impersonal way. Conversely, letters, memorandums, proposals, and reports are usually very personal. They are normally directed to specific people. Even when the message, as in a corporate annual report, is not personalized, it is still sent only to people who are directly concerned.

OBJECTIVES

All the mass media have gatekeepers who control what is delivered to their audiences. With the directed media, you are the gatekeeper. You must be sure that what you send to these individuals is clear, complete, concise, correct, courteous, communicative, and cautious.

Clarity

You must be certain that whatever you write for the directed media is clear. Your reader is probably much more interested in what you have to say than in what is published or broadcast. A fuzzily expressed statement in one of the mass media can be ignored; but in a message directed to a specific person, it is *you* who are responsible. You can be the nerd who didn't answer the question or the smart aleck who gave an unsatisfactory reply. Your objective must be not merely to be understood but also to be so clear as to make misunderstanding impossible.

Completeness

Whether you are writing a 10-line memo or a 32-page annual report, you must be certain that it contains the information needed to serve its purpose. Ask yourself why you are writing and what your reader wants to know or needs to know. Supply that information. If more information will aid the reader's understanding, provide it—but don't give your reader a mass of irrelevant material just because you have it on hand. Here, too, an outline will help—this time in making sure that your message is complete but not loaded with superfluities.

Conciseness

Conciseness means brevity in form but completeness in content. To say it all in a few words is the epitome of conciseness. Use enough words to make your meaning clear, but don't use more. However, in the interest of conciseness, don't cut out anything that is necessary. Remember that conciseness and completeness are not opposites. Your objective should be to write things that are both complete and brief—the most possible information in the fewest words—but not to the point of telegraphic phrasing or choppy sentences.

Correctness

You must be accurate in everything you write. An item in any of the mass media may contain an error, and the blame may be spread among many people; but an error in one of the directed media is likely to be traced back to you. It certainly will be if your name is on the letter or memo, or if you prepared the proposal or report. Beyond the matter of hanging blame around your neck for an error is that of pride in succesful accomplishment. Be sure that what you prepare is accurate, and you will get credit for doing things right.

Courtesy

These are *personal* media. Personal names are used extensively, and both senders and receivers have considerable interest in what is sent from one to another. You might suppose that it would be well to make the messages as personal as possible, but in fact this should not be overdone. The writing should be polite but not flowery, personal but not intimate.

Communication

If your use of the directed media is to result in effective two-way communication, you must be sure that it is based on knowledge of your receiver. Whether it is a letter, memo, proposal, or report, it must start with your knowing what the receiver knows about the subject. If that receiver knows nothing, you must supply everything needed. If the receiver knows a lot about the subject, your communication can be brief.

Caution

This warning is especially applicable to letters. The other directed media are largely internal, but most letters go outside the organization. A letter is a highly visible record of what you say, so be careful. You must know and understand organizational policies and attitudes. You must be aware of the FCC and SEC and how easily you can say something that will make trouble. A simple letter to a stockholder, a competitor, or a customer may not be nearly so simple in the hands of a lawyer in court. (See Chapter 3 for further guidance.)

LETTERS

A letter is a written communication mailed to an individual. It is usually composed for one person only; in some cases, however, where the same message may be pertinent to numerous readers, one may use a form letter (a standardized form that varies only in the name and address of the recipient).

Purpose

A letter may be used to give information, to ask for information, to motivate, to answer complaints, to soothe or arouse, to warn, to admit, or to deny. In short, a letter can carry almost any sort of message to any individual. It is a written substitute for personal conversation. As a substitute, it is not as friendly as face-to-face conversation, but it has the advantage of allowing the writer to get facts in order and to phrase the message better than is likely in conversation. If you were to listen to a recording of almost any conversation, you would be surprised by how much uncommunicative noise is made and how little real information is transmitted. A letter enables you to include all that is needed and avoid the unnecessary.

How to Be Efficient in Handling Correspondence

It is estimated that the average letter today costs about $6.50 by the time it is dictated, typed and mailed. Here are some ways to be more efficient and keep costs low:

1. Produce courteous and effective printed forms for repetitive correspondence, such as requests for printed material, acknowledgements of inquiries, and the like.

2. Develop standard replies for often-asked questions or often-solicited advice where this is a part of the organization's routine business.

3. Develop standard formats for certain kinds of common correspondence to enable inexperienced writers to handle them easily and effectively.

4. Develop model letters for all important communications for use by those responsible in key areas. These letters might serve only as guides, but they would embody the best and most effective tone, quality of content, organization, and writing that the talent of the organization can provide and act as a standard for the less experienced.

5. Prepare a correspondence guide with a few hints and suggestions on keeping down the wordage and the volume of correspondence to reasonable and effective levels.

6. Place a brief heading on the letter after the salutation, indicating the letter's subject. Such headings will give the reader an immediate grasp of the letter's substance and also greatly facilitate filing.

7. Use subheads where the letter is more than two pages long, thus giving the reader a quick grasp of how the subject is treated and where the major topics are discussed.

8. Set up a system for exchange of copies of important letters among key executives to keep them informed of current matters.

9. Use note pads with your name printed at the top for short messages where appropriate to avoid putting everything through the stenographic mill.

10. To personalize printed materials, attach your card with a brief, warm message.

11. If a letter requires a brief response, it is increasingly acceptable to merely pen a note on the original letter and mail it back to the sender. Make sure you retain a photocopy for your files.

Content

A letter must be a complete message. The reader should not have to wonder why the letter was sent, what it is about, and what the writer expects. Frequently, letters open with a brief introductory paragraph that gives the "why." This is followed by one or more paragraphs carrying the body of the message; the letter closes with a wrap-up paragraph.

For example, a letter asking for an appointment could open with a paragraph stating that the writer would like to meet the reader to discuss some subject. The body of the letter would give the reasons why the meeting was necessary, and the final paragraph could suggest a time and place.

In any letter that leaves something to be resolved, it is wise to say something like this. "I will phone you Wednesday morning to find out if the time and place are satisfactory to you." This telephone follow-up is a proven way to ensure that the letter gets serious consideration.

Format

As a general rule letters should be written on white $8\frac{1}{2}$- by 11-inch paper. The letterhead should be printed and should carry the name, address, and telephone number of the organization. If the name does not make the nature of the organization obvious, there should be an explanatory line. For example, everyone knows General Electric Company, but who would know a company named Universal Electric? Do they make light bulbs, install wiring, or generate electricity?

Letters should always be typewritten. Usually they are single-spaced. Paragraphs should be indicated by either indention or extra space between paragraphs. One page is the preferred length. Two pages are acceptable; but if the letter runs longer than that, you should consider putting the bulk of the material in a separate format that is introduced by a letter of transmittal.

The full name and address of the intended receiver are obvious inclusions, but how do you address the reader? If your reader is a man, you can say "Dear Mr.————," or "Dear Sir"; if it is a woman, you probably will be safe if you say "Dear Ms.————." If the letter is in response to one wherein the woman has indicated that she is "Miss" or "Mrs.", you should use the same designation in reply.

The salutation of a letter to an organization is often "Dear Sirs" or "Gentlemen," but this excludes women, who may hold important positions in the firm. A letter to the Girl Scouts or D.A.R. might begin with "Ladies," but there could be men in either organization. There is not yet a generally accepted solution for this problem; regardless of what you say, you may be criticized by some.

Closing a letter isn't quite so big a dilemma. You can say "Yours truly," "Truly yours," "Sincerely," "Sincerely yours," or "Yours sincerely." You can also add a "Very" to any of these, or make up your own. Some bold correspondents omit both the salutation and the close, since they aren't really necessary—especially in cases such as that of General U.S. Grant, who wrote a letter to his opponent at Ft. Donelson, demanded his immediate and unconditional surrender, and closed with the phrase "I am sir, your obedient servant."

DIRECT MAIL

Standardized letters sent to large groups of people are commonly called "direct mail." Computers enable the senders to mail personally addressed letters to thousands of people previously identified as probable respondents. People who have bought books by mail soon find themselves receiving mailings from other booksellers. Members of political parties get letters from officials or candidates. Activist organizations send many letters to their members. A large part of this country's mail is in this category. In 1987, it represented 38 percent of the total.

Purpose

All this mass of mail has one basic purpose: to get the recipient to do something. He or she may be asked to vote, to send money, to buy something, to write to a political figure, to arouse enthusiasm, to attend a meeting, or to take some other action. Whenever a number of people can be identified as potential supporters for any cause or action, it is logical to reach them with direct mail.

Content

A direct mail letter contains three basic elements: (1) an introduction which tells the recipient why the letter is being sent; (2) a body, which gives the facts—often with a strong emotional overtones; and (3) a summary or conclusion, which calls for some action. The letter may be long; some of them run to three or four pages. There are often enclosures, and there is always something to help the reader respond. This may be an order blank, a return card or letter, a telephone number to call, a suggested amount to contribute, or an outline for a letter to be written to some third party (such as the mayor, a congressman, or a senator).

There are two things to remember in this area. First, don't provide a standardized letter or card to be mailed to a politician. Give the facts to your would-be writers, but tell them to use their own words. A mass of individual letters will be much more impressive to the recipient than a stack of identical form letters or cards would be. Second, when you ask for money, it is advisable to suggest several different amounts—and to register the idea that even the smallest contribution will be appreciated. (Both these rules are followed by the most successful organizations.)

Format

Direct mail letters usually look like any other business letters, but sometimes a radically different format is used. A one-page letter may have three or four paragraphs, which makes it look rather normal; but a four-page letter with 48 paragraphs and a postscript is a bit off the usual track. It is always important

KAISER ALUMINUM
& CHEMICAL CORPORATION

May 8, 1986

Dear Fellow Employee:

We'll be putting out a press release, but wanted you to be the first to know: Our shareholders elected the company's slate of directors by a landslide margin of more than 4½ to 1 over the slate proposed by the Frates-Clore-Holmes group!

We just received the official word by phone from The Corporation Trust Company, the independent election judges who counted and verified the vote. The company's directors each received at least 27,732,347 votes, while those proposed by the Frates-Clore-Holmes group received only 6,004,435.

(That's right: the Frates-Clore-Holmes group, which has reported it owns or controls approximately 9.9 million shares, didn't even get out its own vote!)

We told you after the annual meeting that shareholders "voted overwhelmingly" for our slate of directors, but we did not expect that the margin would be so lopsided. This victory is a tribute to each and every one of you. It shows that our shareholders endorse the steps we're taking and that they are confident you'll work just as hard to make the company profitable as you did to defeat the Frates-Clore-Holmes group. You should all be very proud of the work you're doing and your efforts to make Kaiser Aluminum the best it can be.

Thanks ... and congratulations!

Warm Regards,

Cornell C. Maier   A. Stephens Hutchcraft, Jr.

P.S. Please join us for a reception at 4 p.m. next Tuesday, May 13, outside the cafeteria on the 2nd floor.

Employee letter. Letters can be a timely way to inform employees about a crucial matter without waiting for the next edition of the regular employee newsletter. This letter, for example, tells employees that management had just defeated an unfriendly takeover attempt by another company. (*Source:* Kaiser Aluminum & Chemical Corp., Oakland, CA.)

QUANTITY		PRICE
17,300	Delicatessens	$40/M
29,500	Decorators, Interior (Services)	$40/M
8,600	Delivery, Messenger Services	$40/M
500,000	Democratic Contributors	Inquire
4,100	Demolition Contractors	$40/M
11,000	Dental Laboratories	$40/M
65	Dental Schools	$75
19,500	Dental Students	Inquire
1,500	Dental Supplies	$75
10,300	Dental Technicians	$40/M
141,000	**DENTISTS**	$40/M
31,000	Dentists, Home Address	$40/M
4,400	Dentists, Oral Surgeons	$40/M
10,000	Dentists, Orthodontists	$40/M
2,200	Dentists, Pedodontists	$40/M
3,000	Dentists, Periodontists	$40/M
23,100	**DEPARTMENT STORES**	$40/M
986	Department Store Chains	$75
3,350	Department Stores, Largest	$40/M
38,000	Department Stores, Buyers & Executives (Can be Selected by DEPARTMENT or SPECIFIC ITEM)	Inquire
9,700	Department Stores, Self-Service & Discount	$40/M
5,900	Dermatologists	$40/M
19,400	Design Engineers	$40/M
1,750	Designers, Industrial	$75
810	Designers, Package	$75
11,000	Desks & Office Furniture Dealers	$40/M
4,300	Detective Agencies	$40/M
21,800	Developers, Land	$40/M
9,300	Dictating & Business Machine Dealers	$40/M
4,980	Diplomats, Foreign, in U.S.	$50/M
5,625	Direct Mail Advertising Services	$40/M
250,000	Directors of Corporations	$40/M
60,000	Directors of Corporations, Home Address	$40/M
11,800	Directors of 2 or more Corporations	$40/M
7,500	Directors of 3 or more Corporations	$40/M
11,300	Disc Jockeys	$40/M
6,500	Discount Stores	$40/M

Direct mail list. This is an extract from the catalogue of a firm offering names and addresses of people whom someone may want to reach by direct mail. By using such lists, public relations people can reach everyone from avocado growers to zoology professors. (*Source:* Alvin B. Zeller, Inc., New York, NY.)

to make the letter stand out from the mass of "junk mail" that so many people receive. That is why we see so many innovations.

If you plan to use direct mail, it will be well worth your while to consult a direct mail specialist. Such organizations are listed in the Yellow Pages under "Advertising—Direct Mail." There are often a number in any sizable community, and most of them are quite knowledgeable about both the mechanics of computerized mailings and the preparation of effective appeals.

Writing Direct Mail Letters

A large percentage of fund-raising for charitable institutions is conducted through the direct mail letter. The purpose of the letter, of course, is to produce a response—that is, a donation. Writers of fund-raising letters have learned to use these approaches:

1. Make use of an attention-getting headline.

2. Follow this with an inspirational lead-in on why and how a donation will be of benefit.

3. Give a clear definition of the charitable agency's purpose and objectives.

4. Humanize the cause by giving an example of a child or family that benefited.

5. Include testimonials and endorsements from credible individuals.

6. Ask for specific action and provide an easy method for the recipient to respond. Self-addressed, stamped envelopes and pledge cards are often included.

7. Close with a postscript that gives the strongest reason for the reader to respond.

MEMORANDUMS

A memorandum—memo for short—is a written message. Usually it is a half page or less, in length, but it can sometimes be longer. A memo is an internal message; that is, it is directed to one or more people inside the organization. Normally it is informal.

Purpose

A memo can serve almost any communication purpose. It can ask for information, supply information, confirm a verbal exchange, ask for a meeting, schedule or cancel a meeting, remind, report, praise, caution, correct a previous statement or memo, state a policy, or perform any other function that requires a written rather than oral message. There can be doubt about what was said orally; there can be no question about what was said in a memorandum.

Content

A memo should be brief—the very name suggests that it is a reminder, an aid to memory, a condensed message that eliminates every idea and word which can be avoided. In writing a memo, you must remember that while it is internal and informal, it is also a definite record of what you have said. Accordingly, when you write a memo, take a little time to look it over and think about its effect. Also, although the memo is internal and informal, it might be seen by

SIERRA CLUB   730 Polk Street   San Francisco, California 94109   415·776·2211

April 8, 1988

Dear Sierra Club Member:

I'm writing you today because ten minutes of your time -- the time it takes to write a letter to your representative, Ernest Konnyu -- may make the difference between saving or losing much of America's arctic wildlife. Forever.

Interior Secretary Donald Hodel and the oil industry are waging an all-out campaign to destroy a unique and extraordinary place, Alaska's Arctic National Wildlife Refuge, by opening a critical portion of it -- the 1.5-million-acre coastal plain -- to massive oil and gas development.

Rep. Konnyu is a member of the House Merchant Marine & Fisheries Committee, which will soon begin debate on legislation that could decide the fate of the coastal plain wilderness. Rep. Konnyu could play a very important role in stopping any development of the coastal plain, which is so essential to the integrity of the entire 18-million-acre wildlife refuge in northeastern Alaska.

BACKGROUND

Though Americans can no longer thrill to the sight of clouds of bison passing over the Great Plains, there is still one place in our country where wildlife continues to flourish on such a grand scale: the wilderness of the coastal plain of the Arctic Wildlife Refuge. It is here that the 180,000 animals of the Porcupine caribou herd travel hundreds of miles each spring to give birth to their young. It is here that millions of migratory birds, representing more than a hundred species, come to breed and feed on the lush vegetation. And it is this broad plain, home to polar bears, grizzlies, muskoxen, wolverines and wolves, that has been aptly compared with the wildlife riches of eastern Africa. Truly, this is "America's Serengeti Plain."

But this national treasure is gravely endangered, because the Reagan administration and the oil industry are waging an all-out campaign to open up the refuge to massive, destructive oil and gas development.

Rep. Morris Udall (D-AZ), chairman of the House Interior Committeee, realizes the importance of this refuge and introduced legislation, H.R. 39, that would designate as wilderness the 1.5-million-acre stretch of arctic coastline -- the only stretch not now available to the oil industry for leasing. More than 55 million acres is already available to the oil industry, both onshore and offshore, in arctic Alaska.

(over, please)

To explore, enjoy, and protect the wild places of the earth . . .

A "cause" letter. A large number of direct mail letters are written to secure public support for some cause. Standardized form letters are a cost-efficient way of reaching key publics and potential contributors. (*Source:* Sierra Club, San Francisco, CA.)

anyone inside the organization. So don't say that "Old Baggy Pants thinks we should have a meeting." "Old Baggy Pants" might see your memo.

Format

Every memo should have these elements: sender, recipient, subject, and message. Printed forms are often used. These may say "From the desk of ———," which has led at least one person to address her reply "To the desk of———." Seriously, a memo doesn't have to be printed or even identified as a memorandum. If it includes the essentials listed in the first sentence of this paragraph, it's a memo.

For example, a memo might look like this:

> From: John Jones
> To: Planning Committee
> Subject: Thursday meeting
> Mr. Green and Ms. Brown have gone to St. Louis to look at the damage done by Saturday's hurricane. Accordingly we will have to reschedule the meeting after they return.

PROPOSALS

A proposal is a written, formal suggestion or recommendation that something be done. In most situations, a proposal calls for a major decision by top management. Almost anything can be proposed, but to give you a starting point, here are some possible subjects of proposals: to move the office, to adopt a ten-hour day or four-day work week, to provide a child-care facility at the plant, or to modify the employee benefit plan. Proposals are very important in public relations; they may be used to suggest campaigns or to suggest that the firm be engaged by a client.

Purpose

The purpose of a proposal is, of course, to get something accomplished—to persuade management to approve and authorize some important action that will have a long-lasting effect on the organization or its people. By putting the proposal into writing, you enable management to know exactly what is proposed, what decisions are called for, and what the consequences may be. A verbal proposal may be tossed around, discussed briefly, and discarded; but when the idea is put into writing and formally presented, it forces management to make a decision.

Content

A proposal must state exactly what you propose, how it will be done, what good it will do, and what it will cost. It will also request approval. Preparing a proposal requires thorough research, consultation with people who might be affected, study of the results obtained by others in similar situations, and guidance from specialists in technical areas. You must think about who would be affected and why, when, where, and how they would be affected.

For example, the proposed change in workdays could involve employees, their families, state and federal labor laws, labor unions, customers, suppliers, competitors, local transportation systems, the police traffic department, suppliers of janitorial services, and so on.

Format

A proposal may be presented in a few typewritten pages or in a voluminous brochure, depending on the size of the organization and the scope of the proposal. A major proposal could embrace the following:

1. *Transmittal*—a memo, letter, or foreword in a booklet that tells why the proposal is being made and gives highlights.
2. *Table of contents*—a list of all items in the proposal.
3. *List of tables and exhibits* and where they are in the proposal.
4. *Summary*—a condensation of the proposal, which gives readers the basic information and enables them to appraise the idea before they go on to the details.
5. *Introduction*—giving the scope, the approach, how information was obtained and evaluated, limitations, and problems. This is to help the reader understand the idea and weigh its impact.
6. *Body*—a complete, detailed statement of what is proposed.
7. *Recommendation*—a clear, concise statement of just what is suggested and how it is to be implemented.
8. *Exhibits and bibliography*—items substantiating the statements in the proposal and assuring the readers that the proposal is based on thorough study of the problem or the opportunity.

A proposal like that outlined above might be in the form of a printed brochure or a carefully typed (or desk-top-published) assemblage of pages in a distinctive cover. Less elaborate proposals should still be neat, clean, well organized, and attractively presented.

SPECIAL REPORTS

A special report is usually prepared in response to a request from management; however, such a report can also be initiated at a lower level. A special report usually covers only one subject. It is normally a one-time production. Almost always, it covers a problem or an opportunity.

Purpose

The purpose of a report is to give management the information necessary to make an intelligent decision. A very simple report might give the results of an open house or plant tour. A more complicated report might tell what was accomplished during an election.

Major decisions require complete information. If the information is sound and accurate, the decision can be sound. This means that when you are asked to make a report on some subject or when you foresee a need and start a report

Annual reports. The "flagship" publication of most companies is the annual report. It is often the most expensive publication to produce, because high-quality paper, color photos, and computer graphics are extensively utilized. (*Source:* Photo by James McNay.)

on your own initiative, you should know how to turn out a product that is useful and usable.

Content

A report must be identified—who it is from, who it is to, and what it is about (this means the problem or opportunity). The reason for the report must be stated—that it is either a response to a request or an initiative from someone. The report must contain facts—what they are, where they were obtained, how they were analyzed, how valid they are. There should be a discussion of the information and a weighting of the facts. For example, supporters of an idea may be numerous but quiet, while the opponents may be few but noisy.

The report must contain your conclusions—what you think the evidence means. And your recommendations—what you think should be done.

There are two ways in which to present your recommendations. You can give the facts first and let them lead to the recommendations, or you can make the recommendation and support it with the facts. Either method is appropriate.

Format

A report must be long enough to do the job but not longer than necessary. Some reports can be made in a letter or even a memorandum, but others may require a large, many-paged document. Shorter reports can be modeled after the more formal kind described here. (Yes, it is much like the outline for a proposal.)

1. *Transmittal*—either a separate letter or a page in the brochure that tells why the report is made, who it is from, and for whom it is intended.
2. *Table of contents*—what's in the report and on what page.
3. *List of exhibits*—and their location.
4. *Summary*—a brief statement of the findings, the conclusions, and the recommendation.
5. *Introduction*—this tells why the report is made, how information was gathered and assessed, and what points are especially worthy of notice.
6. *Body*—the complete findings of the investigation.
7. *Conclusions*—what you think the facts prove.
8. *Recommendations*—what you think should be done or not done.

ANNUAL REPORTS

All corporations and many or most nonprofit organizations make annual reports to their owners or members. Some corporations also prepare social-responsibility reports and reports to employees. These reports are usually drafted by the public relations department, although in some firms it is done by a special stockholder relations division of the public relations department.

Purpose

The purpose of an annual report is to tell the readers what the organization has done in the past year and where it is going in the future. It should be readable and informative. It should be complete and interesting but not flashy or ornate. Above all, it must be accurate. Too many reports are overoptimistic. All reports seem to tell the good news, but too many omit or gloss over the bad news.

Content

The successes and failures of a profit-making organization can be measured largely in dollars and cents. Nonprofit organizations must use different methods of appraisal, but the more numbers and facts that can be included, the more informative will be the report. The reports of nonprofit organizations have no specified requirements. The writer includes whatever is believed necessary. With profit-making firms, there are some "musts."

Every corporation whose stock is publicly held must prepare and distribute an annual report to its shareholders. Basically this is a financial document, but management usually tries to give the shareholders something more than the figures required by the Securities and Exchange Commission (SEC). These figures are compiled by the financial staff of the company (nominally, the treasurer) and include assets and liabilities, earnings, financial condition of the company, dividends, stock prices, the nature of the business, trends of the business, names of directors, and so on. The goal is to supply all the information needed to appraise the value of the stock. The complete SEC regulations can be obtained from the SEC or from many public accounting firms.

If you do work on an annual report, you will be primarily involved with the nonfinancial part. A large part of the report may comprise tables of figures but it is more interesting if it contains items like a letter from the CEO or interesting details about the products or services and the people who make them. Other topics could be plans, problems, opportunities, and prospects. Predictions are dangerous, but calling attention to something that is likely to affect the organization in the future is certainly reasonable. For example, a lumber company might report a change in Forest Service policies, which could alter the lumbering operations; an oil company could discuss changes in rules for offshore drilling, which could modify the supply situation. Other subjects that could be included are construction plans and progress, supplies of raw material, labor and legal problems, manufacturing, personnel, taxes, tariffs, marketing, advertising, social responsibility and public relations.

Report Writing: A Checklist After Your First Draft

1. Does the title tell substantially the nature and value of the report or memorandum and make the recipient want to read it?

2. Is the report so organized that the reader can skim through it and get a good idea of its value and the nature of its contents?

3. If the report is long, is there a table of contents or an index enabling the reader quickly to locate desired material?

4. Is the length of the report or memorandum properly suited to the nature and value of tha material, that is, a short report for slight material and a longer report for more weighty matter? In any event, is the report as short as possible and yet wholly effective?

5. Is the prose suitably garnished with subheads, sideheads, or other display devices that quickly indicate the substance of the paragraphs they adorn?

6. Is the tone of the report authoritative and courteous and in tune with those who are to receive it?

7. Does the report possess a sense of completeness? Is it so organized that the reader immediately grasps its total structure and underlying theme? Is there a brief "wrap-up" summary and conclusion at the end?

8. Is the report concise? Does it give the reader the most meaning for his reading time? Are repetitions eliminated? Are main points briefly summarized and displayed?

9. Is the report concrete? Are there exhibits, graphs, charts? Is there a liberal use of illustrations, examples, etc., that illuminate and relieve long explanations? One good example is worth a thousand words.

10. Is the report readable? Are sentences generally short, with few-syllabled words preferred to many-syllabled words? Is the meaning as clear as possible to the target audiences?

Source: George deMare, *Communicating at the Top.* John Wiley & Sons, 1979.

Format

Most annual reports are prepared in booklet or brochure form. A few have been printed in a newspaper format and some have been taped and distributed by satellite. These innovations have merit, but few organizations go far from the tried and true publication that is so widely used.

The readers of annual reports are of two sorts: the nonexpert individual and the sophisticated financial analyst. The amateur is mainly interested in the quality of the management, earnings, dividends, stock appreciation, and the outlook for the industry. The experts—who advise investors or manage large holdings—want much more information, which they feed into their computers. This difference in information needs leaves the organization with a problem. A few hundred people want great masses of data, while thousands don't want the detail. Some people have proposed the preparation of two reports—one for each group. Another alternative is to prepare a basic report and supplement it with a voluminous "fact book."

Preparing an Annual Report

Preparing an annual report is a vital and prestigious job. It is also expensive, time-consuming, and highly exacting. There are people who do nothing but prepare annual reports, either for their own organizations or as outside suppliers, but most reports are prepared in the public relations department.

An annual report usually covers every department of the organization. Consequently, every department head may want to get into the act, and each may have very different and very emphatic ideas. The task of the public relations people involved is to coordinate, plan, consult, write, design and produce the report. It takes tact, perseverance, and determination to get the job done.

Work on the report may start six months before the date of issue. The first step is to try to anticipate the socioeconomic and political climate that will prevail when the report is issued. This requires continuous monitoring of public and owner attitudes, so you will know what is going on and coming up. It also necessitates frequent briefing of management on these trends.

With this program established, you can start planning the report. First, you should look at the last report; compare it with those of other organizations; criticize it; think of ways to make it better, more informative, more understandable, more useful.

There are many sources of information that should be tapped for possible use in writing the report. Among the most important are questions asked by stockholders (or members); questions asked by security analysts and the reports they issue; (S. &. P. Reports and Value Line and other research services.)

Especially critical are internal reports, planning documents, market research findings, and capital budgets. You should also review the 10-K (annual) and 10-Q (quarterly) reports filed with the SEC.

When you have thoroughly informed yourself about the situation, you can start consulting the key executives and establishing the theme of the report. Basically, the objective is to inform, but the theme makes the report more interesting. Usually it focuses on one phase of the business—people, products, public relations, the future, and so on. The theme will have to be approved by management.

When the theme is established, it is time to think of design—just how the report will look, what will be included, how the various elements will be treated. You can get some useful ideas by studying the reports that are cited each year by the Financial Analysts Federation. The *Public Relations Journal* also publishes examples of outstanding reports.

The appearance of the report may affect public perception of the organization. An elaborate report containing a dismal financial statement can backfire. A report that reeks of success may bring in new investors. Reports range from "bare bones" documents to elaborate and costly productions, and the styles seem to go in waves. Some stockholders complain about wasting money on appearances, and others like big, colorful reports. What is right for one firm may be wrong for another, even though both may be equally profitable.

Producing the report usually involves working with a printer (see Chapter 13), and requires careful checking of all materials, frequent struggles to get information from others, and a constant eye on deadlines. Six months can become six days before you realize it.

SUMMARY

1. Letters reach faraway people with clarity and, one hopes, brevity. They can prevent misunderstanding and provide a concrete record of an understanding or transaction.
2. Direct mail makes it possible to reach many people with a "personalized" message. It is especially useful in activating the recipients.
3. Memos convey brief messages clearly and accurately.
4. Proposals suggest action on major topics and require management to make a decision.
5. Special reports are usually prepared in response to a management request for complete information on one problem or opportunity. The report must enable management to make an intelligent decision.
6. Annual reports enable the owners or members to evaluate the performance of management. In the case of corporations, they also ensure compliance with regulations of the SEC and FASB.

EXERCISES

1. Delta Airlines, reacting to extensive unfavorable publicity about the safety of its service, wrote the following letter to people enrolled in its Frequent Flyer program. Attached to the letter was an internal memo sent to Delta employees. Both of these documents are reprinted below. After reading them, write a critique of their format and effectiveness. Are the principles of effective writing utilized? Why or why not?

DELTA AIR LINES, INC.
HARTSFIELD ATLANTA INTERNATIONAL AIRPORT
ATLANTA, GEORGIA 30320

W. WHITLEY HAWKINS
SENIOR VICE PRESIDENT
MARKETING

August 14, 1987

Dear Frequent Flyer:

You have selected Delta for a substantial amount of your travels and we sincerely appreciate it. By your making this selection, we have always thought of you as part of the Delta family - a matter we take very seriously.

We also take very seriously our responsibility to provide you with the finest and safest air transportation in the world. In keeping with this responsibility, we feel an obligation to share with you the attached memo written to all Delta personnel by Ron Allen on July 31, 1987, regarding the incidents involving Delta between June 18 and July 12 which have received so much media attention. (At the time the memo was written, Ron was our President and Chief Operating Officer. He has since become our Chairman and Chief Executive Officer.)

Your overwhelming support during this very trying period has been extremely gratifying to all of us here at Delta. The cards, letters, phone calls and comments many of you have made to the media have sustained us through these very difficult times. It is during times like these that people's true colors are shown and when real friends become highly visible.

We are proud to have you as friends and customers, and we renew our pledge to you to provide you the finest airline service possible. All of the slashing comments, jokes, political cartoons and questionable reporting cannot erase the fact that Delta has the finest service record of any airline in the world. We owe it to you to keep it that way, and we will.

Thank you for being so special.

Sincerely,

Whit Hawkins

Attachment

(FOR INTRACOMPANY CORRESPONDENCE ONLY)

DELTA
AIR LINES

Date: July 31, 1987

TO: All Members of the Delta Family

FROM: President and Chief Operating Officer

The events which have occurred over the past month have been puzzling and frustrating for you just as they have been of deep concern for all of us in the management of Delta. From June 18 through July 12, we had a series of five isolated but significant incidents. That is unusual in any airline but, to say the least, in Delta.

Rather than take the time in this memo to outline again the events of each one of those incidents which have been so well publicized, I simply wanted to let you know that each individual incident has been carefully investigated. While each had several contributing factors, human error or a breakdown in cockpit discipline appears to be the primary cause. As such, positive corrective action and firm individual disciplinary action have been taken where appropriate. While these individual incidents have been disappointing, I feel without a doubt that we have the finest and most professional pilot group in the industry and they have my complete support, admiration and trust. No one has felt any worse about the recent events than the members of our pilot staff.

As a result of this aberration in the operation of our company, the media (newspapers, radio and television) has singled us out to monitor almost every flight in our system, and we have such things as flat tires and loose monkeys in the cargo bin appear as front page or prime time news. In addition, we have become the focal point of many jokes. I know this hurts you as it hurts me. The safety and professionalism of our operation is something we take very seriously and never joke about.

How do we as individual members of the Delta family respond to this negative reflection on our company? How do we answer questions from the customers whom we are privileged to serve? How do we react to the media, our neighbors, our friends, etc., who wonder if something has changed at Delta? There is only one way we can respond—to be clear that Delta has not changed; that the best, safest, most caring service possible remains our over-riding objective; and that the incidents they have witnessed are truly an aberration in no way indicative of Delta Air Lines' operation.

We must respond with the same professional attitude toward service to our customers and dedication to our individual responsibilities that we have shown over our many years.

Each of you is well qualified and has been well trained for the position that you occupy. I ask you to rededicate yourself to doing your individual jobs to the absolute best of your ability, whether it be flight attendant, pilot, agent, mechanic or other position in the field or in the General Office. If at any time you have questions about the best way to perform your part of our operation, it is important that you seek answers so that the traveling public whom we are privileged to serve continues to see Delta as the airline run by professionals and as the world's premier air transport company.

When you are asked by others about Delta and what we stand for, you can remind them that over many years Delta has earned an outstanding reputation for the best in air transpor-tation; that we are still the first choice of most pilot applicants as they apply for positions in the airline industry; that Delta has more cities staffed with maintenance personnel than any other airline, thereby ensuring that our professionally-trained mechanics maintain our airplanes in the safest possible manner; and that Delta has had the fewest number of passen-ger complaints of any airline since 1974, a record for which all of you are responsible, and a record in which you take much pride. You can remind them also that Delta still has one of the best overall safety records in the industry.

It is important not to overreact and respond in a negative way to the overreporting and unusual scrutiny of the press. The media has a job to do, and it is news when an airline such as Delta has such an unusual series of events. It is important that we speak with one voice. This is why you have seen most of the interviews with Delta conducted by Bill Berry, our Director of Public Relations. As you can well imagine, Bill and his staff in Public Relations have been under a tremendous amount of pressure having calls coming to their offices and homes 24 hours a day. We have been very open and responsive to the media inquiries and have tried to react in a direct and factual way to every question while at the same time pointing out the positive aspects and the contributing factors of each situation. On the other hand, we do hope that we are near the end of the media's over-zealous publica-tion of events that occur in our day-to-day operation (which normally would never even be mentioned) while events on other airlines of a much more serious nature have occurred and either go unreported or are buried somewhere deep in the midst of other news.

Recently there have once again been several favorable news articles about Delta. Much of this is the result of interviews with individual members of our Delta Family. We welcome the media to come in and look at our operation. We only want them to provide objective and complete coverage without singling us out and trying to make news out of something which is not.

Thank you for your patience, your dedication and your understanding as we go through this difficult time. Remember that a true test of the strength and character of people is not measured so much during the good times when things are going well and everyone is saying nice things about you, but instead in those difficult times such as we have experienced in the past 30 days. These are the times in which we must redouble our efforts to pull together as a team to demonstrate to all concerned that Delta truly is a caring and highly professional family made up of individuals who are dedicated to serving the traveling and shipping public.

On a final note, all of you know that after some 41 years of service to Delta Air Lines, Dave Garrett will retire as Chairman and Chief Executive Officer on August 1, 1987. Dave, who attained the mandatory retirement age for senior management of 65 on July 6, has devoted much of his life to the leadership of Delta Air Lines. One of the greatest blessings Dave leaves us is a legacy of maintaining the highest ethical standards for our operation. Fortunately, he will remain very close to our operation as he continues on our Board of Directors and will serve as Chairman of the Board's Executive Committee. Dave will maintain an office and will be available for advice and counsel on a regular basis.

Please join me in thanking Dave for his leadership and his many contributions to Delta over his years of active service and in wishing him well in his retirement years.

I now ask you for your continued support for Hollis Harris, our new President and Chief Operating Officer, and for our entire management team. As we face the many challenges and opportunities that lie ahead, we will continue to lead Delta under the standards that have been established by the previous leaders of our company. It is a privilege to be a part of this outstanding team and I thank you for your past, present and future dedication to excellence in your particular place in the Delta family.

Ron Allen

2. A customer has written to your company complaining about the quality of service in one of your retail outlets. She claims the clerks were busy gossiping among themselves and totally oblivious to her requests for assistance. She further states that the company's advertisements about "friendly service" are dishonest and encloses her cut-up credit card, saying she will never shop at your store again. Draft a letter to this irate customer with the objective of winning back her confidence in the store.

3. As a director of public relations, you must write a memo to the company's executive vice president requesting approval for upgrading the company's quarterly publication to a monthly periodical. Although no increase in staff is necessary, another $20,000 will be needed to cover increased publication expenses for the next year. Write a persuasive one- or two-page memo that succinctly states your case.

4. Charitable organizations often use direct mail to solicit contributions. Such letters must be skillfully crafted and organized to grab the readers' attention and motivate them to give money. Write a direct mail letter on behalf of the local humane society.

SUGGESTED READINGS

Badaracco, Claire. "Smoke and Substance: Trends in Annual Reports." *Public Relations Quarterly*, Spring 1988, pp. 13–17.

Blicq, Ron S. *Guidelines for Report Writers: Complete Manual for On-The-Job Report Writing*. Englewood Cliffs, NJ: Prentice-Hall, 1982.

DeNeve, Rose. "Crash Landing." *Public Relations Journal*, October 1988, pp. 22–26.

Denmarsh, Robert, and Esteban, Francis. "Workshop: How to Produce a Credible Annual Report." *Public Relations Journal*, October 1988, pp. 35–36.

Hirasuna, Delphine. "Ten Tips to Creating An Award-Winning Annual Report." *Communication World*, December 1985, pp. 20–22.

Kulkosky, Edward. "Brave New World of Annual Reports." *Wall Street Journal*, Feb. 10, 1987.

Labaton, Stephen. "What's New in Annual Reports." *New York Times*, March 29, 1987, p. 21F.

Miller, Allen. "Workshop: How to Develop a Direct Mail Piece." *Public Relations Journal*, April 1988, pp. 31–32.

Newsom, Doug, and Carrell, Bob. "Memos and Letters, Reports and Proposals. *Public Relations Writing: Form and Style*. Belmont, Ca.: Wadsworth Publishing, 1986. chap. 15.

Purdum, Todd. "What's New in Annual Reports." *New York Times*, April 21, 1985, p. 17F.

Runyon, Robert. "Survival of the Fittest." *Communication World*, September 1987, pp. 24–27.

Chapter
13

Leaflets and Brochures

*T*he writing and production of printed materials is a major activity in most public relations programs. The various kinds of items produced go by many different names. To simplify the subject, we will eliminate all these and classify the printed materials into two groups, leaflets and brochures.

A leaflet is a single piece of printed paper. It may be folded into several pages or consist of only one page. It may be printed on one or both sides.

A brochure consists of several printed pages that are bound together. The pages are printed on both sides. Eight pages are the minimum, but it may run up to 48 pages or even more. Sometimes a brochure has a cover made of different paper from that used in the body.

LEAFLETS

Leaflets, because of their small size and relatively low cost, are used mainly to deliver simple messages that do not involve much explanation. Among the more typical kinds of leaflets are the following:

1. *Notification.* For example, announcing a rate increase by a public utility.
2. *Information.* Updating the public on new interest rates.

What Can I Do If I Have A Problem With My Lawyer?

Be an informed consumer.

Good communication is the key to a good lawyer-client relationship. When you hire a lawyer, make sure that you:

- Understand the kind of work the lawyer will do for you.
- Get an estimate of how long the case may take.
- Ask how and for what you will be charged. Various kinds of fee arrangements can be made, and some must be in writing. In addition to the lawyer's fee, you may have to pay certain expenses, such as court costs.
- Find out when and how the lawyer will keep you up-to-date on your case.
- Help your case along by promptly giving your lawyer all the information and papers you have. Continue to give your lawyer additional papers as you receive them.

Get in touch with your lawyer at the first sign of a problem.

No matter what the problem, phone your lawyer to express your concerns. Maybe the trouble is a misunderstanding that can be cleared up in a frank conversation.

If you do not get a response, write a letter and keep a copy. Tell the lawyer exactly what is bothering you and suggest getting together to talk about it.

If you still don't get results, the steps you can take depend on the kind of problem you have.

Solving Your Specific Problem:

You suspect that your "lawyer" isn't really a licensed lawyer.

Call the State Bar of California in San Francisco at (415) 561-8200 or in Los Angeles at (213) 482-8220. Ask the bar's Membership Records department whether the person is a licensed lawyer.

Then, if your suspicions are correct, call the State Bar's Unauthorized Practice of Law (UPL) program at (415) 561-8221. UPL staff will refer you to a local law enforcement agency that may investigate these problems.

If your "lawyer" isn't licensed, ask for all the papers in your file back so you can hire a licensed attorney to work on your original legal problem. (For tips on finding a lawyer, read the State Bar's pamphlet, *How Can I Find and Hire the Right Lawyer?*)

You have a personal, not professional, problem with a lawyer.

You may think your landlord, who happens to be a lawyer, hasn't given you enough warning of a rent increase. Or, a lawyer who charged some tools at your hardware store hasn't paid the bill. Although the lawyer is licensed by the State Bar, the bar is not allowed to become involved in such matters. To solve these problems, exercise your rights as a tenant or a creditor.

You think your lawyer's bill is too high.

If you can't resolve the problem by discussing it with your lawyer, you can request *fee arbitration.* This is an out-of-court hearing in which one or more persons not involved in the dispute

Typical leaflet copy. Here are two pages from an eight-page leaflet designed as a general information piece. (*Source:* State Bar of California, San Francisco.) CA

3. *Greeting.* Welcoming visitors to an organization.
4. *Apology.* Asking public forbearance during construction.
5. *Activation.* Requesting help.
6. *Progress.* Giving periodic reports.

BROCHURES

Brochures are used primarily to give a thorough explanation of one specific subject. Almost anything that requires considerable detail may be covered. Among the subjects that lend themselves to such treatment are the following:

1. *Orientation.* For example, an explanation of the nature and composition of an organization.
2. *Rules and regulations.* Things employees or constituents should know.
3. *Safety.* Special warnings and procedures applicable to work and to emergencies.
4. *Benefits.* Health and retirement benefits available.
5. *Promotion.* Opportunities and procedures.
6. *Policies.* What the organization will and will not do.
7. *Training.* Study guides telling people how to do specific jobs.
8. *Obligations.* Things expected of employees beyond conformance to rules (e.g. dress, conduct on the job, release of confidential information, etc.).
9. *Recreation.* Organizational facilities and group activities available to employees.
10. *Recruiting.* Persuading people to join the organization.
11. *How to use it.* Getting the most from a product. (This category includes everything from installation and operating manuals for appliances, through recipe booklets, to owners' manuals for automobiles, to guides for home insulation.)

Whenever an organization needs to explain something to a large number of people—whether they are employees, consituents, or customers—a brochure is the way to do it.

Comic Books

This art form is effective because it combines concise and easily understandable dialogue with a visual representation. (Technically, a comic book can be classed as a brochure.)

Comic books are often produced and distributed directly by the sponsoring organization. Utility companies, for years, have been distributing comic books in the schools. These tell children about things like the dangers of flying kites around power lines, or *Mickey Mouse and Goofy Explore Energy.* Other corporations have produced comic books for schoolchildren that tell about the manufacture of a particular product or how the free-enterprise system works.

But comic books are not only for schoolchildren; they also have a valid place in communicating information to adults. In this type of application, comic books must be carefully considered and pretested. Their use can backfire if the audience perceives them to be patronizing.

Comic books can be done in two ways. If the company wants to give a specific, tailored message about its services or products, it is often necessary to engage a cartoonist to execute the project. If however, you merely wish to provide generic information to a group of people, you can often buy the comic book and have your company name imprinted on it. A division of Walt Disney Productions, for example, specializes in producing comic books on generic subjects as well as for individual companies.

PLANNING

The first step in planning a leaflet or brochure is to establish a need. These items are always prepared to reach a specific audience and to accomplish a definite purpose, so these questions should be asked: Who needs to know

Comic books. Public information campaigns directed to children and even adults with limited reading skills often utilize comic books as an effective tool. This is an extract from a comic book about water conservation. (*Source:* East Bay Utility District, Oakland, CA.)

Leaflets and brochures. The preparation of these materials is a major activity in public relations. The range is from the simplest one-page leaflet to elaborate color brochures. (*Source:* Photo by James McNay.)

about this subject? What do they now know? What should they know? How much do we tell them? How many of them are there? As these questions are asked and answered, the size and format of the material should begin to take shape in your mind.

At this stage, planning can lead to a conclusion that you need to produce a simple leaflet, a large four-page leaflet, a large brochure, or even a very large brochure and about how many you will need. Before you go any further, get copies of leaflets or brochures produced by others for similar purposes. These will help you visualize your own task and show different ways used to accomplish various communications jobs. Borrowing ideas and trying to improve on what others have done will help you produce effective materials.

Basic Guidelines

- *Define purpose and audience.* What exactly is the purpose or objective? Are you producing a sales document? An instruction booklet? An overview of your organization's service capabilities? And what will be the target audience? It is important to define the audience in most precise terms so you can tailor the message to their needs.

- *Determine usage and life span.* The size and format is determined by answering several questions. Will your publication be carried in a pocket? Mailed in a #10 envelope? Placed in an information rack? Used as a self-mailer? Distributed widely or only to VIPs? Will the copy need frequent updating? How long will it be used?

- *Position your subject.* No company, product, service, or concept is exactly like any other. Each has its unique personality, capabilities, and strong points. Determine what makes your organization's services or products different from those of the competition. In other words, your brochure should dramatize and focus on unique aspects that make your organization outstanding.

- *Establish budget parameters.* There's no point in thinking about a fancy four-color brochure when your budget will allow only a simple one-color approach. An approximate budget should be established early. It should include the costs of planning, design, writing, finished artwork, printing, and mailing.

- *Set up a realistic schedule.* Don't decide to do a brochure one week and expect it to be printed the next week. Printed items take a lot more planning (and various skilled personnel) than a basic news release. A simple flyer may be produced in a matter of days, but a complicated brochure—writing, layout, approvals, artwork, proofs, printing, mailing—can take several months. Corporate annual reports, for example, are typically started six months in advance of final publication.

- *Research other materials.* A review of other printed materials will give you ideas about the size, look, or feel that you want in yours. This research can also give you ideas about size of type, paper stock, use of illustrations, and use of color. Showing these items to upper management will also give them an opportunity to envision what yours will look like when completed.

Source: Adapted from guidelines written by Robert Clay, president of Clay Publicom, Irvine, CA.

WRITING

Writing leaflets and brochures is a unique process. It is not like news writing, where the purpose is to tell what has happened or is going to happen. It is not like feature writing, which tries to produce a definite attitude on some subject. With booklets and leaflets, the objective is to inform, explain, instruct, or persuade.

In one sense these publications are much like advertising. They are paid for and controlled. Consequently there is considerable freedom in what you say and how you say it. Nevertheless, what is said must be true and exaggeration must be avoided. Because reader interest is assumed, there is no need for the kind of headline used in news stories; there is, however, room for headlines telling what the publication is about and for subheads that break up the whole into digestible parts.

Above all, the copy must be understandable. It should be pretested on several readers who are representative of the audience for which the publication is intended. If they don't understand, the material should be rewritten. It may be necessary in some cases to use technical language, but this should be explained in nontechnical words.

Gathering Information

Gathering information for use in a leaflet or brochure may involve anything from asking a few questions to conducting a major survey. In most cases, the needed information can be found within the organization.

Keeping in mind the subject and purpose of the proposed publication, start by talking to the people in the organization who know most about that subject. Tell them what you want to accomplish and ask for the information that will enable you to prepare a clear explanation of the subject. Often all the needed information can be obtained from one source.

If you need more information, look through organizational records, photograph files, and other publications of the organization. Check the reference books and trade publications available in the office. If these don't give the answers, you may find them in the public records of government agencies, in local libraries, or in the files of local newspapers. If your organization belongs to a trade association or similar group, the information may be available there.

A good way to decide what to include in a leaflet or brochure is to put yourself in the position of a member of the prospective audience. Ask every question that person might have about the subject. The answers can comprise sections of the publication. You can even use the questions as subheads. One very successful brochure was entitled *101 Questions About———*, and the entire brochure consisted of questions and answers.

Putting It Together

These publications vary so widely that no general guide is applicable. Each has a different audience, a different purpose, and a different format. It is imperative to use words that will be understandable to your readers. If you have to explain a technical topic, check with the experts once you have put it into everyday English to be sure you've got it right. For any but the briefest publications, you will need to prepare an outline. This should cover all the main points to be included, and it should list the illustrations to be used.

The writing itself should be simple and concise. With the objective in mind and a clear understanding of the audience to which the message is directed, you will give the readers the information they need. Keep the copy in short blocks; long, rambling statements are boring. Use subheads to break up the pages and to indicate what is in each block of copy under the subhead.

As you write and plan the layout of the publication, remember to put visual variety in your pages. Illustrations, blocks of copy, and headlines serve not only the direct purpose of communication but can also make the pages attractive and interesting. Some writers recommend preparing a complete layout before starting to write. Others prefer to develop the layout after the writing is finished. A practical compromise is to prepare a rough layout before writing and then to revise it as the writing progresses.

An excellent source of practical information about the design of brochures and newsletters is a regular column by Roy Paul Nelson in *Communication World*, the monthly magazine published by the International Association of Business Communicators. Each column, entitled *Look of the Book*, is a critique of a particular brochure or newsletter with many helpful hints about what works and what doesn't.

PRODUCTION

With the copy written, illustrations selected, and general format decided, it is time to think about production—getting the material printed. So far this chapter has been devoted to leaflets and booklets, but we can now include newsletters, posters, placards, and anything else that involves the use of typeset material and some kind of printing press. Here we give you only the highlights. For full information, see *Pocket Pal*, published by International Paper Company. Another helpful publication is *Fundamentals of Printing*, published by Kimberley-Clark Corporation.

Printing Processes

Four main processes can be used:

1. *Letterpress* uses metal type or metal plates made from metal type. The ink is placed on the surface of the type and transferred directly to the paper. Letterpress is very flexible; it can be used for short runs and odd sizes.

2. *Gravure* uses a metal cylinder. The type is etched into the cylinder, which revolves in the ink. Excess ink is wiped off, leaving only that which remains in the hollows. As the cylinder rotates, it deposits the ink on the paper. Gravure is expensive and best on very long runs where color is used.

3. *Offset lithography* is based on the fact that grease and water don't mix. It uses a thin metal plate on which the material to be printed is grease-receptive and water-repellent. Nonprinting areas are water-receptive and grease-repellent. The plate, which is mounted on a cylinder, rotates first through water, which dampens the nonprinting area and prevents the pickup of ink. Then

the plate rotates through the greasy ink, which is picked up on the material to be printed. The cylinder next rotates against a rubber blanket, which picks up the ink and then deposits it on the paper. This is called *offset.*

Offset is the most common and popular printing process. Very flexible and economical, it is available almost everywhere and is the process you are most likely to use.

4. *Screen printing* uses a fine screen of stainless steel, nylon, Dacron, or silk. A stencil made on the screen blocks out nonprinting areas and allows the ink to be forced through the screen by a sort of squeegee. Printing is done on a flat-bed press that holds the paper or cardboard under the screen. The whole process can be executed by hand, but there are automatic presses that work much faster. A wide range of color is available. Screen printing can be used on paper, cardboard, plastic, wood, or almost any flat surface. Any size is usable, and the applications range from menus through placards and posters to 24-sheet billboards.

A fifth method of production is desktop publishing, which uses computer techniques to write and design printed materials. Desktop publishing is discussed in Chapter 14.

Steps in Printing (Offset)

Type is set and a proof is pulled. The proof is carefully examined for errors. Any corrections are indicated by marks on the proof. When the typesetter has made the corrections, a revised proof is submitted for approval. The editor marks the revised proof with an "O.K." and his or her initials. If the errors are minor, the corrected proof may be marked "O.K. w.c." This means "O.K. with corrections."

When all the corrections are made, a printing plate is made. This is done by means of a photographic procedure that puts the printing copy on the thin plate previously described. This plate is made from "camera-ready art," which will be described later.

Finding a Printer

In large cities there are many printers and every printing process is available. In even the smallest town, however, there is likely to be at least one printer. Some small-towns may have only a photocopying service, but in most cases there will be an organization that can do offset printing.

In any case, you must find some firm that can print your material. The classified phone directory will list all of the possibilities. If there are only a few, it is possible to call on them and find out what they can do. In larger cities, the number may be so large that your task will be like hunting for a needle in a haystack. In such a situation, you can call on those nearby or talk to your colleagues and get their recommendations. In fact, this "word of mouth" may be the best way to choose a printer.

Having located some prospects, you should meet with them or their sales representatives. Tell them what you want to do and ask what they can do. Look at samples of their work. Find out what their services cost. Some firms can and will do everything—even the writing. Others may be specialized. There are firms that do typesetting alone. Some will prepare camera-ready art from your copy and layout. Some will print only from the camera-ready art. There are also firms that do only binding.

Working with the Printer

If you plan to produce a monthly newsletter, it may be advisable to ask several printers for their bids. The objective is to pick one who will do the job regularly without submitting bids on every issue. On the other hand, if you produce a variety of materials it may be in order to get a bid on each job. The lowest bid is not necessarily the best. Consider the quality of the work.

Another possibility is to work from estimates rather than bids. Here you tell the supplier what you want and ask for cost estimates and cost-cutting suggestions. Frequently the supplier will be able show you how to reduce costs by changing your tentative specifications. Even if you plan to work with several suppliers, the number should be limited. If suppliers expect to serve you on a continuing basis, you will get better service than if they feel that the only reason they got the job was that their price was the lowest.

Choosing the Format

Before deciding on the format of printed materials, get samples of items like those you want to produce. Note how they were done and be guided by them. The basic formats are (1) leaflet, one piece of paper that may be folded, and (2) booklet, two or more pieces of paper bound together. The binding may be "saddle-stitched," in which case the pieces of paper are folded in the middle, placed one upon the other like a saddle on a horse, and then, as they lie open, stapled together on the centerfold. If the booklet is large, it may be "side-stitched." Here, with the booklet closed, the pages are stapled about $\frac{1}{4}$ inch from the centerfold. A side-stitched booklet will not lie flat when it is open, while a saddle-stitched one will. If the booklet is side-stitched, it will require a separate cover. Booklets can be "self-covered" or have covers made of a different paper.

With either format, you must think about the number of pages. Leaflets may be folded in many different ways, from a simple fold into four pages to elaborate arrangements with numerous pages. Remember that booklets are done in four-page units. Your booklet should therefore be made up of four pages or a multiple of four. For example, if you have material for fourteen pages, you will either have two extra pages (which may be blank, for a total of sixteen), or you must cut two (for a total of twelve).

PAPER

The weight of the paper may range from very light (such as bond) to very heavy (such as cover stock). There is also a range of weights within these classes. Usually the heavier the paper within a class, the more it costs. Thus, a 100-lb cover is more expensive than a 50-lb cover. These weights are based on the actual weight of 500 sheets of that paper in the standard sheet size. For your purposes, you need only remember that heavier paper is bulkier, stronger, and more expensive.

The intended use will guide you in selecting the weight of paper. A simple one-page leaflet might be printed on 20- or 24-lb bond. If you want it to be more substantial, you could use a 65-lb text. Booklets or brochures are usually printed on fairly substantial paper. This makes them look more impressive, and it also ensures longer wear. Another thing to consider is the total bulk of the booklet. If you pick too heavy a paper for a booklet that is to be mailed, you may have to pay more for postage. Still another thing to bear in mind is folding; for example, heavy paper does not fold as readily as lighter paper.

Paper Grades and Sizes

The types of paper you are most likely to use are bond, coated, text, book, offset, and cover. Their characteristics and sheet sizes are as follows:

Paper Type	Paper Size	Description
Bond	17″ × 22″	Lightweight paper used mostly for stationery.
Coated	25″ × 38″	A smooth-surfaced paper that lends itself to high-quality reproduction, especially with color.
Text	25″ × 38″	A paper available in many textures and well suited for use in booklets, brochures, and announcements.
Book	25″ × 38″	Available in a wide range of weights—used in books, brochures, etc.
Offset	25″ × 38″	Especially made for offset printing and ideal for newsletters.
Cover	20″ × 26″	Cover stocks come in a wide range of colors, weights, and textures. Some are simply heavier versions of coated and text papers, thus permitting a close match of body and cover.

In selecting your paper, work closely with your supplier, who can guide you in finding the best one for your purpose at the most reasonable price. Also, if the press run is to be large, it may be necessary to place a special order with the paper mill. Thus advance planning is important.

TYPE

In thinking about type, you must be familiar with a few special words that apply to all type sizes and faces. "Uppercase" means capital letters, "lowercase" means small letters. "Ascender" means the part above the body of the letter, like the top of the letter "h," and "descender" means the part below the body of the letter, like the bottom of the letter "g." Capital letters do not have ascenders or descenders. "Serif" means the tiny line that projects from the main stroke of a letter, such as the foot on which the lowercase "r" rests. Type size is measured from the top of the ascender to the bottom of the descender.

Type Books

Every typesetter can provide you with a type book showing the kinds and sizes of type he can supply. Even the smallest firms can now provide a wide range of type because of the new computerized and photographic typesetting techniques. A type book is essential for the design and production of any printed material.

Type Classes

There are several ways in which to classify type, but the simplest is to group the various faces into three groups: "serif," "sans serif," and "decorative."

"Serif" types, such as the old style Caslon and the modern Caledonia, are very readable because the serifs help guide the eye along the lines of type.

"Sans serif" types, like Helvetica, are very popular at present. Some of the earlier types in this group were hard to read in body copy but quite satisfactory in headlines. The newer designs seem to work well for body copy also.

"Decorative" typefaces, like Script and Old English, should be used with great care. They work well on certificates and invitations but should not be used when a large amount of copy is involved.

Type Families

Any typeface may be available in numerous variations. Among the possibilities are light, regular, medium, bold, ultrabold, and demibold. These same faces may also be available as italic, and all the variations may be condensed or extended.

For each of these faces, the typesetter needs a "font"—a complete set of letters and figures enabling him or her to set copy in the face and size selected. The typesetter's type book will show the available fonts. Few typesetters are

BODONI BOOK
(with italic and small caps)   (Machine Set)

● **10 Point (leaded 2 points)**

Up in the composing room of the Tribune there was even greater electricity in the air. It reminded old-timers on the crew of the good old days when Horace Greeley used to come down and dictate a few scorching headlines. They missed old Horace and still chuckled over the time when a prankster had inked a rooster's claws. set him loose on a

● **10 Point (leaded 2 points)**

Up in the composing room of the Tribune there was even greater electricity in the air. It reminded old-timers on the crew of the good old days when Horace Greeley used to come down and dictate a few scorching headlines. They missed old Horace and still chuckled over the time when a prankster had inked a rooster's claws. set him loose on a

● **12 Point (leaded 4 points)**

Up in the composing room of the Tribune there was even greater electricity in the air. It reminded old-timers on the crew of the good old days when Horace Greeley used to come down and dictate a few scorching headlines. They missed old Horace and still chuckled over the time when a prankster had inked a roos

● **12 Point (leaded 4 points)**

Up in the composing room of the Tribune there was even greater electricity in the air. It reminded old-timers on the crew of the good old days when Horace Greeley used to come down and dictate a few scorching headlines. They missed old Horace and still chuckled over the time when a prankster had inked a roos

BODONI BOOK with italic & small caps

Typefaces. A large variety of type is available for the production of printed materials. This is a page from a type book showing a few of the variations. Computer software programs for desktop publishing also include various type fonts.

able to offer all possible faces, so rely on the type book rather than specifying a typeface he may not have.

Printers' Measurements

Type letters are measured in points. There are approximately 72 points to an inch, so a 72-point letter is about an inch high. Type lines are measured in picas. There are approximately 6 picas to an inch, so a 24-pica line is about 4 inches long. Picas are also used to measure the depth of a block of copy. Thus a page that is 42 picas deep will measure approximately 7 inches. Inch measurements are *not* used in typesetting. Always specify type by points and picas.

The normal range of type sizes is from 6 to 72 points. If larger sizes are needed but not available, they can be made by photo enlargement.

One size of type that you are not likely to use but which you should know about is "agate," a very small 5- or 6-point type that is seldom used but often referred to in relation to newspaper advertising. With agate type, it is possible to print 14 lines of type in one inch of depth. Advertising rates are usually quoted in agate "lines." This means 1/14 of an inch in one standard column of the publication. A 700-line advertisement uses 50 column-inches. It can be 5 columns wide and 10 inches deep.

Another term used in typesetting is "em," which is the square of the type size (or roughly the size of the letter "M"). A 12-point "em" is about 1/6 inch high and 1/6 inch wide. The use of ems is largely limited to indicating paragraph indentations. A very narrow indentation might be one em. A wide indentation could be four or five ems. The em is always related to the size of type being used in the body copy of the material being typeset.

Legibility and Readability

Legibility is affected by the typeface. Any Garamond letter is more legible than any Old English letter. Readability is affected by the legibility of the type and by letter spacing, line spacing, the length of the lines, the color of paper and ink, the kind of paper, and the total amount of reading matter involved. A leaflet could be effective with a few words printed in 36-point Times Roman, but using such big type in a 16-page booklet would waste paper and discourage reading.

The only purpose in printing anything is to get it read. Accordingly, any printed material should be planned with readability in mind. Select a legible type and, if necessary, use letter spacing to spread headlines that are set in capital letters. Use line spacing to improve the readability of lowercase body copy. Keep the length of lines short enough that each can be read as one unit. As a general rule, try to use type no smaller than 10-point for body copy. Its readability will be improved by line spacing—placing the lines farther apart. Line spacing is called "leading" and is specified in points; thus type may be 10 points high with 2 points of leading between the lines.

INK

Many colors of ink can be used, but black is the most common in leaflets and booklets. Other colors are generally used to add emphasis or variety. The use of a second color of ink adds to the cost. With any color of ink, you must consider the color of the paper on which it will be printed. No color of ink, even black, will read well against a dark background. Light-colored papers are always best. Printing on cover stock is especially tricky. Don't repeat the mistake of the man who designed a booklet with a dark-blue cover and tried to print the title in yellow. After three trips through the press and a sizable increase in costs, the title was still green. The desired effect could have been attained by using a yellow cover stock and printing a blue reverse plate. (A reverse plate is one in which the the background area is raised above the letters and only it prints.)

Full-color (or four-color) printing can be done for any kind of material, but it will not be explained here. (International Paper's *Pocket Pal* takes 18 pages to explain it.) If you need to produce anything of this sort, you must consult with a printer who does this special kind of work.

PREPARATION OF COPY

Preparing copy for printing is a meticulous job. The typesetter will set exactly what you give him, errors included; so be sure that you check for spelling, punctuation, paragraphs, capitals, abbreviations, and grammar. Errors can be corrected, but this adds to the cost. After the copy has gone to the typesetter, don't make changes unless absolutely necessary. Adding or deleting a paragraph or even a few words can force many other changes.

Your copy should be double spaced on $8\frac{1}{2}$-by 11-inch white bond paper. The lines should be of uniform length and on one side of the paper only. Each page should be identified and numbered. The title or job number make a good identification. The last sheet should be marked "end."

Be sure to keep a copy of your manuscript. The original might get lost— or you might want to discuss the material with the typesetter over the phone. Corrections should be made above the affected line, and in ink. If there are many corrections, the page should be retyped.

Copyfitting

This means determining how much typeset copy can be fitted into a given space or how much space will be needed for a given amount of typeset copy.

If there is too much copy for the allotted space, you will have to reduce the amount of copy, use a smaller typeface, or allot more space. If there is too little copy, you will have to add more, use a larger typeface, or reduce the amount of space allotted. To do this, you must understand how typewritten copy relates to typeset copy.

Copyfitting in Eight Easy Steps

By following these steps, you can determine how your typewritten copy will fit into printed materials.

1. Count the characters (letters and spaces) in an average line of typewritten copy. (Or measure the length, in inches, of an average line and multiply by 10 if it's pica type or by 12 if it's elite type. (e.g., $5\frac{1}{2}$ inches of elite type = 63 characters.)

2. Count the number of typewritten lines (e.g., 27 lines).

3. Multiply the number of lines by the number of characters per line (e.g., 63 × 27 = 1701 characters, total).

4. Decide how wide you want the lines of type (e.g., 24 picas).

5. From your typebook, select the type you want to use and count the number of characters in a line of 24 picas (e.g., 60 characters).

6. Divide this number into the total character count (e.g., 1701 ÷ 60 = 28.3 lines).

7. From your typebook, find out how many lines of the chosen type will go into an inch of depth (e.g., 7 lines per inch).

8. Divide the number of lines per inch into the total number of lines (e.g., 28.3 ÷ 7 = $4\frac{1}{4}$ inches = 26 picas).

Copy Markup

With clean, typewritten copy and an accurate calculation of the type, you can tell the typesetter what to do. This is done by writing in ink in the margin of the typescript. Specify the size, leading, typeface, and measure (line length) in order. Leading is indicated as a fraction: 10/11 means 10-point type with one point of leading; 10/10 means 10-point type with no leading. A sample type specification could be 10/12 Clarendon × 24. This means 10-point Clarendon type with 2-point leading, 24 picas wide.

Paragraphs may be flush or indented. Margins may be justified or set flush with a ragged left or right. Specify what you want.

Paragraph indentations should be marked in ems, and underlining should be used to indicate alterations in the typeface. One underline means italics, two underlines mean small capitals, three underlines mean large capitals, and a wavy underline means boldface.

PREPARATION OF ART

There are two steps in getting art and copy ready for printing: (1) preparing the layout and (2) assembling the copy and illustrations.

Layout

The layout is the plan for the finished piece. It may be rough or comprehensive, but it must be accurate enough for the person who assembles the parts to do exactly what you want. The first step in making a layout is to prepare a "dummy"—a blank-paper mockup of the finished product. It should be made of the paper to be used in the printed piece and it should be of the same size. If the piece is to be a booklet, the dummy should be stapled just as the finished booklet will be. If it is to be a leaflet, the dummy should be folded the same way.

With the dummy at hand, you can now plan where everything is to go. For a leaflet, the layout will be complete—it will indicate what is to go on each page. For a small booklet, the layout will also be complete, but if there are many pages, you will need to design only the cover and sample pages of the body.

Guidelines for Designing Brochures

The Document Design Center, based in Washington, D.C., offers the following guidelines for creating readable leaflets and booklets:

- *10-point type.* Research shows that 8- to 10-point type is most readable. Readers often skim over text that is too small.

- *White space.* Wide margins, indents, and occasional short pages are important elements of design. These features keep the document from looking crowded.

- *Ragged right margin.* This gives the document a relaxed, contemporary look.

- *Short lines.* A document is easier to read when the line of type doesn't go all the way across an 8½- by 11-inch page. Optimal line length for most text is 50 to 70 characters.

- *Use boldface.* This is good for headings or to emphasize a word or two. Using ALL CAPS for emphasis is not recommended because it is difficult to read.

Source: *PR Reporter,* April 27, 1987.

The layout indicates both type and illustrations. Thus, a page layout might show various blocks of copy, headlines, and the location of illustrations for that page. For very simple jobs, you may make the layout by yourself; however, most printers are able and willing to do this, especially on big jobs. Often it is possible to get several tentative layouts from the printer and select the one you prefer. In this area, the printer is the expert and should be relied upon.

Illustrations

The two types of illustrations most likely to be used are line (drawings, maps, diagrams, etc.) and continuous tone (photographs and paintings). Many variations and combinations are possible, but for the present we will discuss only the simplest applications.

If you plan to use illustrations, refer back to Chapter 7 for information on selection, retouching, and cropping.

Assembly and Printing

At the printer's place of business, your layout, copy, and illustrations will be put into production. Type will be set and the illustrative materials will be prepared. At various stages of putting things together, you will be shown proofs. When these are found to be satisfactory, the printer will assemble them into what is called "camera-ready art." This is photographically transferred to the printing plates that actually do the printing.

The printing itself may take relatively little time. One point to keep in mind is that it is often possible to combine press runs. If you have more than one piece to print, it may be possible to print them all at the same time. This is easiest if all your pieces are of the same size and specifications, but it is also possible to combine quite dissimilar pieces. Your printer will be able to help on this. In fact, your printer can help on all your problems. The printer is an expert and can save you much time and money.

SUMMARY

1. Leaflets are used primarily to announce or inform.
2. Booklets are used mostly for explaining things and for providing a semipermanent assemblage of information.
3. With printed items, planning precedes everything else. Each piece must be devised to carry specific information to a definite audience. There must be a need for the item.
4. Writing these materials is different from writing news releases and features. In some ways it is like writing advertising. Gathering information is a first step, and—in writing the copy—clarity of expression is extremely important.
5. Production involves printing, so you must understand the printing processes and know how to work with printers.
6. Paper and ink are the raw materials you work with. These come in many grades, sizes, and colors.
7. Type is available in numerous sizes and faces. Proper selection contributes to legibility and readability.
8. The copy you write must be properly prepared for the printer. It must be fitted to the space available and marked up so that the printer knows just what to do with it.

9. Art is an essential element in leaflets and booklets. You will need to determine the layout of the item and provide the needed illustrations.

10. Printing is the final step in production. It will pay off to work closely with the printer from the start of the project.

11. You should remember that comic books, while not regularly grouped with other booklets, can also serve a useful purpose.

EXERCISES

1. Get several leaflets and booklets produced by an organization—either a nonprofit charitable agency or a business. Based on the suggestions and guidelines offered in the chapter, write a critique of these sample materials from the standpoint of (a) purpose of printed piece, (b) intended audience, (c) writing style, (d) selection of type, (e) selection of artwork and other visual aids, and (f) selection of paper stock. At the end of your critique, provide an overall evaluation of the brochure's effectiveness.

2. The key to writing and designing an effective brochure is planning. Select a campus or community organization for the purpose of planning a brochure. Then, in outline form, provide information under the following headings: (a) name and brief background of the organization, (b) purpose or objective of the proposed brochure, (c) intended audience, (d) major theme and key copy points, (e) budget constraints, (f) estimated number of copies needed, (g) life span of proposed brochure, (h) method of distribution, and (i) time schedule for writing, designing, production, and distribution.

3. It often is necessary to calculate how much space typewritten copy will occupy once it's converted to the size of type used in a leaflet. Using the boxed insert in this chapter entitled "Guidelines for Designing Brochures" as the "original" copy, convert this material to an 18-pica line using 10/12-point type. We know from the type book that there are 45 characters in an 18-pica line of 10/12-point type and that it takes 5 lines of this type to equal one column inch.

SUGGESTED READINGS

Beach, Mark. *Getting It Printed: How to Work With Printers and Graphic Art Services.* Portland, OR: Coast to Coast Books, 1987.

Bivens, Thomas. "Collateral Information Pieces." *Handbook of Public Relations Writing,* Lincolnwood, IL: 1988, chap. 4.

Conover, T. *Graphic Communication Today.* St. Paul, MN: West, 1986.

Christ, William, and Pharr, Paula. "Readability of Brochures Produced by the State of Florida." *Journalism Quarterly,* Spring 1980, pp. 159–160.

Crow, W. *Communication Graphics.* Englewood Cliffs, NJ: Prentice Hall, 1986.

Davis, Bob. "Is In-House Publishing Putting Typography In the Outhouse? *Communication World,* November 1988, pp. 27–29.

Deegen, Mary K. "Choosing a Designer, for Better or for Worse." *Communication World,* February 1988, pp. 20–22.

DeNeve, Rose. "The Graphic Edge." *Public Relations Journal,* July 1985, pp. 19–25.

Marsh, P. *Messages That Work: Guide to Communication Design.* Englewood Cliffs, NJ: Prentice Hall, 1983.

McCullough, Mary Louise. "Working with the Human Resources Folks." *Communication World,* October 1987, pp. 28–29.

Morrison, Sean. *A Guide to Type Design.* Englewood Cliffs, NJ: Prentice-Hall, 1986.

Newsom, Doug, and Carell, Bob. "Newsletters and Brochures." *Public Relations Writing: Form and Style.* Belmont, CA: Wadsworth Publishing, 1986, chap. 13.

Producing Flyers, Folders, and Brochures. Chicago: Ragan Communications, 1984.

White, Jan. *Mastering Graphics: Design and Production Made Easy.* Ann Arbor, MI: Bowker, 1983.

Chapter
14

Newsletters

A newsletter is just what the name implies—a letter that carries news about an organization to its employees or constituents. The readers are usually interested; therefore, if the newsletter takes the right tone, it can be a valuable channel of communication.

A newsletter can promote organizational objectives, but it should not be used to mount harangues. If it is nothing more than the voice of management, it may be a failure; but if it provides genuine two-way communication, it can be a valuable part of a public relations program.

While primarily aimed at a limited audience, some newsletters do get quoted in the mass media. In this way they serve to supplement the news releases or features that may be sent out. Such publicity also boosts the status of the newsletter among its primary readers.

THE EDITOR

This is a position of great responsibility. The editor's basic task is to publish an interesting newsletter, usually with no help. More than that, a good editor will be a main factor in establishing and maintaining communication between management and the readers.

To do this effectively requires that the editor know and understand the policies and objectives of management. The editor must also know and understand the attitudes and opinions of the readers. To get this information requires frequent contact with both parties. Publishing a newsletter requires a lot of time at a typewriter or word processor, but even more important is the time spent away from the desk—asking questions, listening to what people say, testing ideas, thinking about the people at both ends of the communication process.

In some large organizations there may be several people working on the newsletter, but in most cases it is a one-person job. The editor gathers the news, writes the stories, decides what to publish, designs the newsletter, lays out each issue, selects illustrations, supervises production and mailing, and is responsible for the entire operation. With this responsibility should go the necessary authority. Unless the editor controls the newsletter, it will turn into a mere hodge-podge of items, each of which is considered worthy of publication by someone. Although the editor runs the newsletter, he or she does not function independently. The newsletter is an organization product, and the head of the organization must support the editor and approve his or her work.

In deciding what to publish, the editor must know what will interest the readers, what they should know, and how much to give them. The editor serves as both gatekeeper and reporter. Knowing the readers—their interests, attitudes, and problems—is imperative. The primary purpose of a newsletter is to serve the readers. It must not become the voice of management alone. Management may be given some space—as in a "president's page"—but it must not dominate the publication.

In general terms, most newsletters are aimed at either the employees of a profit-making organization or constituents of a nonprofit organization. There are, of course, exceptions to this, but dividing newsletters into these two types is a practical way to determine the kinds of news that should be used. Remember, however, that the lines are not rigid and that reader interest is the only true guide.

EMPLOYEE NEWSLETTERS

The content of employee publications depends very much on the type of organization and the number of its employees. In general, as organizations get larger, the employee newsletter becomes more formalized and professional; there are fewer articles written by a departmental secretary as the "correspondent from the tractor division."

Newsletters. A common vehicle of communication for most organizations is a newsletter. Shown here is a variety of newsletter mastheads. (*Source:* Photo by James McNay.)

Every newsletter is unique, but there are some guidelines that can be applied generally. The International Association of Business Communicators (IABC) and Towers, Perrin, Forster & Crosby, a consulting firm, surveyed 40 companies and 45,000 employees to determine what topics employees were most interested in. The topics, in descending order of interest, were:

1. Organization's future plans
2. Personnel policies and practices
3. Productivity improvement
4. Job-related information
5. Job advancement information
6. Effect of external events on my job
7. Organization's competitive position
8. News of other departments/divisions
9. How my job fits into the overall organization
10. How the organization uses its profits
11. Organization's stand on current issues
12. Organization's community involvement

13. Personnel changes/promotions
14. Financial results
15. Advertising/promotion plans
16. Stories about other employees
17. Personal news (birthdays, anniversaries, etc.)

It must be noted, however, that the range of interest was from 95 percent on the first item to 57 percent—still more than half—for the last. The study does indicate that today's employees are more concerned about the health and direction of their companies than they are about the fact that Joe in the metals division just celebrated his twenty-fifth wedding anniversary and went to Hawaii on a second honeymoon.

Most of the material in an employee newsletter can be grouped into three sections: employee questions, employee news, and organizational news.

Employee Questions

Answering employee questions can be a valuable service. Many employees have questions but often hesitate to ask them. One effective stimulant is to guarantee anonymity. Assurance that names will not be used will usually generate a steady flow of questions. A further stimulus is the assurance that management takes the questions seriously, that questions *will* be answered, and that management will *act*.

The best way to handle this service is to make the questions and answers a regular feature of the newsletter. It can take up a page, a column, or a box. It should have a regular title, such as *Questions & Answers, Letters to the Editor, Action Line, Hot Line,* or any other designation that seems appropriate.

Questions can be turned in through office mail, through regular mail (if the questioners are not regularly in the office), or by using a properly labeled box in a location available to all employees.

It may be necessary to shorten or even rewrite the questions submitted. In doing this, it is important to retain the core of the question. Editing the questions should not be a tooth-pulling operation. The more pointed the questions are, the more interesting they will be and the more valuable the answers.

Employee News

People like to read about people. People like to see their names in print if something favorable is said about them. In general, news about employees should be job-related. How a person performs at work is more pertinent than how he or she performs on the local softball team. Remember too that you must avoid invasion of privacy or defamation of character. This was mentioned in the chapter on the legal aspects of publicity, but it bears repeating here.

Almost anything an employee does may be worthy of mention in a newsletter. Among the things to look for are:

1. Job anniversaries
2. Sports

3. Promotion
4. Transfers
5. Awards and honors
6. Human interest
7. Work features
8. Employee organizations

Organizational News

What the organization is doing can be extremely interesting, but it should be presented in terms of what it means to the employees. Improved business may mean better dividends for stockholders, but this won't be of interest to employees unless that improved business also means greater job security, increased income, or better opportunities for promotion. News about the organization can cover such things as:

1. New or improved facilities
2. New or improved products
3. Changes in the organization
4. Sales results
5. Advertising campaigns
6. Organizational policies
7. Employee rules
8. Job openings
9. Opportunities for training
10. Organizational accomplishments
11. Employee benefits
12. Unfavorable news
13. Information about executives
14. History of organization
15. Awards to organization
16. General news affecting the organization
17. Sources of materials used
18. Use of products or services
19. Importance of organization to the public
20. Editorials
21. Chief executive's letter
22. Solicitations for charitable contributions
23. Sponsored activities and events

CONSTITUENT NEWSLETTERS

The principal categories of nonprofit organizations that publish newsletters are:

1. Trade and professional associations
2. Special-interest groups

3. Charitable organizations
4. Politicians and political parties
5. Governmental agencies

Each of these has different purposes and each sends a different kind of information to readers. Because the problems and interests of these groups are so diverse, there is likely to be very little similarity among their newsletters. Each must concentrate on a narrow field and each will probably have a different objective. There are, however, a few general guidelines as to content. Of course, many of the items mentioned in the section on employee letters may apply to constituent newsletters as well.

Associations

Associations are organized to achieve, through cooperative action, things that will benefit the members and which cannot be accomplished by individual effort. The association must maintain and increase membership and financial support. It must also get results that help the members.

Association newsletters may contain such items as problems confronting the trade (or industry or profession), accomplishments of the association, business trends, statistics about the trade, governmental actions, legal problems, membership growth, news about members, reports on meetings, general news affecting the trade, reports on research, suggestions that will help members, and appeals for individual action in support of association activities—such as asking members to communicate with their congressperson or state legislator.

Charitable Groups

This category includes everything from the American Red Cross to the local hospital auxiliary. These groups raise money and recruit volunteers to help people in need. Their newsletters are sent to the people who contribute time and money to the organization. The basic objective is to encourage continued contributions. This is done by telling the contributors where their efforts go and what they accomplish. The second general topic covers solicitation of support.

Raising money and getting people to work on various projects is a never-ending problem. Thus, a large amount of the space in a charitable newsletter may be devoted to requests for help; reports on financial conditions, fund-raising efforts, and volunteer activities; and to efforts to increase membership.

The other major classification of news deals with the accomplishments of the organization, responses of beneficiaries, and details of just how the organization has helped people individually or collectively. Anything that makes people feel that the results are worth the effort belongs in the newsletter. Meeting reports, calendars of events, schedules for workers, and messages from the head of the organization to the members are also in order.

Special-Interest Groups

The primary purpose of a special-interest group is to persuade people who are not members of the group. Typically the objective is to pass a law or prevent passage of a law. Opponents of offshore oil drilling, opponents of nuclear power, supporters of state and local zoning restrictions, proponents of tax exemptions for private schools, and hundreds of others fit into this category.

Newsletters for such groups may contain information similar to that which is included in association newsletters. Because the special-interest group has one purpose, however, most of what is published is concentrated on that topic. Reports on group activities, the results of the activities, and exhortations for the members to help in projected activities are likely to represent most of the material in the newsletter. Generally these newsletters go only to group members, but occasionally the distribution may be expanded to reach nonmembers who may be sympathetic.

Political Groups

Elected officials at all levels send newsletters to their constituents. Most of the content deals with legislation—bills introduced, bills passed, the official's voting record, comments on the effects of legislation, and requests for expressions of opinion. Frequently the newsletters contain questionnaires asking the consituents to indicate how they feel about pending legislation.

Government Agencies

This category ranges from the Social Security Administration to the local health department or school board. Any agency serving the public may use a newsletter to inform the public about its activities or services. A county agricultural extension agent may have a newsletter for farmers, a home economics extension agent may use a newsletter dealing with food and nutrition, and a social service agency may use one on child care.

In general, these newsletters are planned to help the readers. They contain information that readers can use in their daily activities. A large part of the material is of a "how to" nature—what to plant, when to spray, how to preserve fruits and vegetables, information about new products or services, and so on.

DESIGN

Most newsletters are exactly what the name implies—letters containing news of significance to the readers. Usually they consist of from one to four pages of $8\frac{1}{2}$- by 11-inch paper. When the amount of available news and the importance of that news to the readers exceeds the space limitations of the letter format, the newsletter generally grows into a newspaper or magazine. These are often called "house journals" or "house magazines."

Company magazines. In addition to newsletters that have frequent publication schedules, companies also produce slick magazines comparable to anything found at the newsstand. These publications are directed to internal and external audiences. High-quality magazines effectively communicate information and create a sophisticated image for an organization. (*Source:* Photo by James McNay.)

The editing and production of these larger publications can require the full-time efforts of one or many people. This area of communications is almost a profession in itself. The International Association of Business Communicators (IABC) grew from an association of internal magazine editors and—while it is still devoted very much to that field—it now deals with all areas of organizational communication.

To cover the subject of organizational publications adequately would justify an entire book, and there are several available. Here, however, we will deal only with the simplest of these publications—the newsletter. For additional readings on newsletters, see one or more of the following:

Arnold, E. C. *Editing the Organizational Publication.* New York: Ragan Communications, 1984.

Beach, Mark. *Editing Your Own Newsletter.* Portland, OR: Coast to Coast Books, 1988.

Carter, David E. *Ideas for Editors.* Ashland, KY: Decathlon Books, 1978.

Darrow, Richard W. *House Journal Editing.* Danville, IL: Interstate, 1975.

Hudson, William Penn. *Publishing Newsletters.* New York: Scribner's, 1982.

Reid, Gerene. *How to Write Company Newsletters.* Deming, WA: Rubicon, 1980.

Reuss, Carol, and Silva, Donn. *Inside Organizational Communication.* New York: Longman, 1981.

White, Jan. *Mastering Graphics: Design and Production Made Easy.* Ann Arbor, MI: Bowker, 1983.

Format

An $8\frac{1}{2}$- by 11-inch newsletter can consist of one page printed on one side—or that same page can be printed on both sides. It can be two pages stapled together. It can be one sheet of paper folded into four pages and printed on all sides. Other sizes and other folds can be used, but it is simpler and more economical to stick to this basic format. The actual printing may be done by photocopying, letterpress, offset, or computer. For each of these processes the design of the newsletter is the same.

Although the most common newsletters are $8\frac{1}{2}$ by 11 inches in size, many organizations now use a tabloid newspaper format for communications to employees, members, or the general public. The advantage is more space for graphics and layout plus the cost-effectiveness of using newsprint.

In fact, a new term, "magapaper," has now been coined. Essentially, this is a tabloid newspaper, but it is laid out like a magazine, with plenty of large headlines, white space, and large pictures.

For ideas on the content and design of newsletters plus other publications, you should subscribe to the publications of the International Association of Business Communicators (IABC), Suite 940, 870 Market Street, San Francisco, CA 94102.

Heading

A newsletter should be identifiable at a glance. For this reason a distinctive heading should be used at the top of the first page. Some editors have the basic heading printed on the paper to be used for the letter. The heading should carry the name of the newsletter and the name of the organization. The address should be included as well. The name may be anything that seems appropriate, but it should be short. It is desirable to use distinctive type or hand-lettered art for the name. The cost is a nonrecurring item and this small investment will make the newsletter more attractive. The heading should include the volume number, the number of the letter, and the date. These can be added to preprinted headings for each issue of the letter.

Layout

This means the arrangement of the material in the newsletter. Location and size of headlines, location and size of illustrations, columns (whether two or three or a combination), boxes, departments, and—if the letter is to be mailed without an envelope—the information required by the post office.

There is no exact rule for any of these items. The more important subjects should get the most space, and—as in a newspaper—the most important items should go on the front page, with a runover to a later page if space is needed or if several items should go on the front page, each to be continued elsewhere.

Most newsletters use a two- or three-column format. For those that are photocopied, a two-column layout is preferred because typewriter type isn't adapted to a three-column structure. For printing, a three-column format is common. This can, of course, be varied. Headlines can use the full width of the page. Some items go well when spread across the width of two columns. Two-column illustrations work well in a three-column page.

The basic layout of a newsletter should be the same from issue to issue, but each issue will have to vary depending on the kind, amount, and importance of the material available. One issue may have one major story, but the next may have two or three, which will dictate a modification in the arrangement and placement of the stories.

Design Suggestions

Keep these ideas in mind as you plan your newsletter.

1. Work with all the elements.
   a. White space
   b. Photos
   c. Line drawings
   d. Headline sizes
   e. Headline typefaces
   f. Subheads
   g. Boldface type
   h. Length of articles
2. Break up copy as much as possible.
   a. Keep articles relatively short for maximum interest.
   b. Break up longer articles with subheads and illustrations.
3. Be consistent.
   a. Use the same margins for each page.
   b. Use only one or two headline faces—don't combine too many different typefaces in a newsletter.
4. Keep the design simple—don't clutter your newsletter.
5. Work with two-page spreads.
   a. Try to have pages in balance with each other. Don't put illustration on one page and all type on the facing page.
   b. Offset one bold illustration with another on the other page.

    c. Remember that pictures must be balanced—a big black spot on one page must be balanced by something of similar weight on the other page, such as a bold headline.

6. Be careful with paper selection.
    a. Don't use flimsy paper. It may be cheap, but it looks cheap too.
    b. Colored paper may be used, but stick to pale pastels.

Mailing Requirements

There are three ways in which to mail a newsletter: by first-, second- or third-class. Each has advantages and disadvantages. First class is the fastest and most expensive. There are reduced rates if the mail is presorted by zip code. Second class is ordinarily for newspapers and magazines, but a newsletter can qualify if it is set in type and printed and if it is published at least four times a year on specified dates. Third class can be used for small mailings of identical pieces.

Because the rules and rates change from time to time, it is essential to consult with the post office. A mailing permit is necessary and certain information must be included in the newsletter, especially on the mailing panel or envelope. To determine the costs and applicable rules and regulations, you should prepare a sample copy of the proposed newsletter and tell the post office clerk how it will be produced, how many you plan to mail, how often it is to be published, if yours is a nonprofit organization (and is therefore entitled to special rates), and anything else needed to establish which information you must print on the letter or envelope and what else you must do. There are rules about presorting as well as about bundling, bagging, and boxing. All are critical, so don't hesitate to ask questions.

EDITING

The editor has four jobs: to gather the news, to write the stories, to get the illustrations, and to prepare the newsletter for reproduction.

News Gathering

To get news from the organization, the editor must become a reporter. This means finding out what is going on—watching, asking questions, and asking people to help. The editor must get out of the office and make contact with everyone in the organization who might have some information that should be passed on to the readers. Refer back to the chapter on what makes news and then look for things of that nature in the organization.

Another source of news is the outside media: radio, television, magazines (trade, general, and special-interest), newspapers, and the newletters and house magazines of other organizations. Any of these may publish something that should be brought to the attention of your readers. It is not possible to watch, listen to, or read all of the news and features that are published. However, it *is* possible to look out for items bearing upon your organization.

When such material is found, make a note and then use the item at the first opportunity. Generally it is safest to rewrite any items that have been published elsewhere. If an article or item seems worth using exactly as published, you must get written permission from the publisher.

Contributions from readers should be handled with great care. People can be highly offended if their ideas are rejected or altered, but it may be necessary to do just that. The person who submitted the material should be informed, tactfully, as to the reason for the rejection or alteration; but the editor should retain control of the content of the newsletter.

News Writing

News items and features in a newsletter should be written to the same standards as those used when sending news releases or features to a newspaper or magazine (see Chapters 5 and 6). Newsletters often contain a number of very short items, but even these should be clear and complete. It isn't always necessary to include the who, what, why, when, where, and how in every item, but they should be remembered and used if needed.

Headlines

Newspaper and magazine people write their own headlines and seldom use those on the press releases they receive. In a newsletter, the editor must write headlines for the articles or departments. Two criteria apply in this situation: the headline must invite reading and it must fit into the available space. A headline may be a title or label, such as *President's Column* or *What's New*. These are best for regular departments and continuing elements. For news items, a sentence headline should be used; for example, "Membership Increases 43%," "Governor Smith to Address Meeting," "EPA Hearing Set for June 5."

"Kickers" and subheads can be used to amplify headlines. These are set in smaller type and appear above or below the main headline. Thus

Another Delay—
EPA HEARING
SET FOR JUNE 5

or

GOVERNOR SMITH
TO ADDRESS MEETING
—fireworks expected

The type used for headlines should be consistent. That is, one size of type and one typeface should be used for major headlines, and smaller type can be used on secondary or tertiary headlines. Using the same typeface throughout is desirable.

In writing headlines that require two lines, be sure to avoid splitting ideas beteen lines. A Virginia newspaper once headlined a story about preparations for a veterans' convention thus:

RICHMOND DRESSES
UP FOR VETERANS

Writing Good Headlines

Sentence headlines are preferable to label heads because they can be more interesting and give your readers more information. Sentence headlines actually are just the skeleton of a sentence; short words such as "a" and "the" are usually deleted, while "and" is often replaced by a comma. Some verbs, especially the "to be" verb forms, can often be omitted from headlines as well. Here are examples of sentence headlines:

Members Seek Advice
from County Attorney

Brady, Jones file
for state offices

The first example is called a caps/lowercase headline because all words except prepositions and short verbs have initial caps. The second example is called downstyle because only the first word and proper nouns are capitalized, just as in a sentence. All-capital headlines are the least legible form because words appear as blocks and the letters lose their distinctive, identifiable characteristics.

If you have a story about an upcoming convention and you plan to announce the date, location, theme, and schedule, choose the most important item or items—perhaps the date and location—and include them in your headline. For example:

Regional convention set
for Oct. 5–7 in Chicago

The following headline has the same problem found in many sentences. It uses a *passive construction:*

Gift awarded
to 4-H Club

Try to use what is called the "historical present tense" (describing past actions with present-tense verbs) when you write your headline, and include a subject with the verb whenever possible. A rewritten headline, with a historical present-tense verb, might be:

Chapter awards gift
to local 4-H Club

Here the headline tells us who did what to whom. To indicate upcoming events, use "to" or "will"; for example, "Chapter to meet" or "Delegates will decide."

Avoid poor splits of words between lines of your headline:
Poor:

Pastor leaves for Good
Friday services at prison

Better:

Pastor to lead prison
Good Friday services

Avoid ending lines with a preposition:
Poor:

Fredericks plans to
take 6-month leave

Better:

Fredericks to take
6-month sabbatical

Abbreviate only those words you would normally abbreviate within your body copy. Don't use such forms as "Asst.," "Chrm.," "Assoc." Use only the accepted abbreviations listed in a style book (such as the AP's).

A headline must fit the space available. If it is to appear in typewriter type, the fit can be determined by trial and error. Start with the words you want to use and type them into the amount of space available. If it is too crowded, use shorter or fewer words. If there is too much space, add words or use longer words.

If you have a word processor available it may be able to set your headline in a special large type (display type). In this case you must find out what your particular word processor can do. Another way to use display type in a newsletter, which is basically typewritten, is with cut-out or rub-off letters. These can be placed on the page in the correct location and the page can then be replicated by photo-copying. These letters can be bought at stationers and at many copying and duplicating services. Instruction are on the package.

Many of the firms offering copying and duplicating service can also set display type on a word processor or a photo-typesetter or apply the cut-out or rub-off letters to your typewritten finished copy. They can also do the entire job by working from your layout and rough (but neat) copy.

Writing headlines requires that you know the width of the space allocated for the headline in the layout sheet. Although headlines written on a video display terminal connected to a computerized typesetting system can be enlarged or reduced to fit the available space, it is still a good idea to know something about character counts.

The simple way, used by most editors, is to count the number of characters and spaces in a previously printed headline of the size and in the typeface you want to use. Assuming that there are 20 letters and spaces in the sample head-line, you should allow 20 letters and spaces for your headline.

Illustrations

If possible, newsletters should be illustrated. Chapter 7 discusses the basic requirements for illustrations used in newspapers and magazines. The same criteria apply to newsletters. The illustrations must be clear and interesting. What can be used depends upon the type of equipment available for producing the newsletter.

REPRODUCTION

There are several ways to produce the number of copies needed to reach the newsletter's audience: printing, photocopying and desktop publishing. All are changing and improving rapidly, so what is appropriate today may be outdated tomorrow.

Printing

Printing can be done by either letterpress or offset. In either case, the copy is set in type, illustrations are prepared, and the various pieces are assembled in a form that can be printed. Chapter 13 describes the printing processes and procedures.

Photocopying

In its simplest form, photocopying is what can be done on any office photocop-ier. Typewritten copy is placed in the machine and copies are made by pushing the right button. Most machines will print sheets that are $8\frac{1}{2}$ by 11 or $8\frac{1}{2}$ by 14 inches in size. Some will handle sheets as large as 11 by 17 inches, and some can reproduce pictures.

Photocopying is not limited to typewritten copy. You can, of course, make up material with drawings, type proofs, or paste-on letters and print it on your office copier. For more elaborate material and a wide choice of type faces and illustrations, you can go to a copying and duplicating service. Some of these limit their work to photocopying; others also provide offset printing capacity. Many will take your rough copy and layout and prepare camera-ready art; they will then run the needed pages in their machines.

Desktop Publishing

Recent advances in computer techniques make it possible for you to create professional-looking newsletters and graphically illustrated material on a per-sonal computer right in the office.

Desktop publishing allows you to design and lay out reports, newsletters,

FMC Defense Systems Group
San Jose

June 3, 1988

Inside Track

Vol. VI, No. 22

'Welding' better customer relations

Some may think a purchasing agent's place is in the office. For buyers Dolly Replogle and Linda Linden, it is – for 30 hours a week.

For the other ten hours, it's a different story. Each morning, Monday through Friday, the two Ground Systems employees pull on their overalls, fire-resistent gloves and protective hoods for a 2-hour lesson in welding techniques.

Replogle and Linden, along with CEL Mechanical Engineer Elizabeth Downing, are enrolled in a specially-designed class at FMC's Technology Development lab to learn about the fundamentals of welding. Their aim is not to become welders. Instead, they simply want to learn enough about

Continued on page 6

Purchasing agents Linda Linden (left) and Dolly Replogle (center) and CEL Mechanical Engineer Elizabeth Downing are spending ten hours a week learning about welding so they can be better at their office jobs.

FAADS team meets delivery challenge

On Feb. 29 of this year, employees at Plant 7 began working on four modified Bradley chassis as part of an air defense subcontract from Martin-Marrietta. That was leap year day, and the employees involved in this project have been leaping ever since.

Ground Systems finalized the contract with Martin-Marrietta May 3 to modify and deliver the chassis, which will carry the missile system for the U.S. Army's Forward Area Air Defense Systems

(FAADS) program. But, in fact, FMC has been involved in the air defense program for more than a year.

In April 1987, FMC formed a joint-venture company with two other defense contractors – Norden Systems Inc. and British Aerospace Ltd. (BAe) – to pursue the FAADS program as the prime contractor. That joint venture, known as United Aerospace Defense Systems, pitted the Tracked Rapier armored vehicle (BAe's Rapier

missile system on an FMC M548 chassis) against three other competitors – Martin-Marrietta and its ADATS system, Hughes' Roland

Continued on page 4

> ### See inside for election information insert.

Desktop publishing. This newsletter was produced entirely by desktop publishing. The use of a computer to write copy, format it, and place it on a page layout is rapidly becoming the predominant production method. (*Source:* Defense Systems Group, FMC Corp., Santa Clara, CA.)

brochures, and presentations by manipulating copy and graphics on a computer screen instead of on a drawing board. The computer software enables a person to (1) draw an illustration and then crop it to size, (2) use different type fonts and sizes, (3) vary column widths, (4) shade or screen back graphics, (5) add borders around copy, and (6) print out camera-ready pages for offset printing in large quantities.

The primary advantages of desktop publishing are savings in time and money. For less than $10,000, you can purchase all the components necessary to produce high-quality newsletters and graphics: a personal computer, a word processing program, a graphics program, page-making software, and a laser printer. By producing camera-ready materials in-house, this system reduces the fuss and expense involved in using a commercial printer. Apple Computer, a leader in the field, claims that desktop publishing systems pay for themselves in six months.

In terms of time, Apple Computer sales literature claims that a 16-page newsletter would take only 8 hours with desktop publishing, as compared with 26 hours if you did it the old way—including typesetting, corrections, proofreading, camera work, and final pasteup.

Desktop publishing is gaining widespread acceptance in business and industry, thanks to new software packages and sophisticated laser printers that can produce newsletters in full color. For maximum quality, you can now take your computer disk to a commercial service that will print multiple copies of your newsletter on high-speed laser printers that provide extremely high resolution.

SUMMARY

1. A newsletter can be a valuable means for communication between an organization and its employees or constituents.
2. A newsletter must not become the tool of management; it should be a channel of two-way communication.
3. The editor is responsible for the newsletter: content, format, design, production, and effectiveness.
4. Employee newsletters must give the kind of information that the readers want. Especially important are answers to their questions, news about people, and news about the organization, especially future trends.
5. Constituent letters reach people who, while not dependent on the organization for income, do take great interest in what the organization is doing—its problems and its successes.
6. Designing a newsletter requires consideration of the format, size, shape, pages, layout, heading, typefaces, illustration and mailing requirements.
7. Editing includes news gathering, news writing, headline writing, and general supervision of the thrust of the newsletter.

8. Illustrations should be used if possible. They contribute greatly to the interest and effectiveness of the newsletter.
9. A newsletter can be printed, photocopied, or "desk-top published." All these processes are being steadily improved.

EXERCISES

1. Newsletters come in all sizes and styles. Call on some organization and ask for the past three or four issues of their newsletter. You should critique these newsletters from two perspectives. First, using the categories in the IABC study described in this chapter, do an analysis of the newsletters' content. After doing this, write a critique using the design guidelines listed in this chapter. What is your overall evaluation of the newsletter? What changes would you recommend?

2. Writing headlines that are active and informative takes practice. Write a one- and two-column headline based on the following information. For your purposes, assume that one column is 15-count and two columns are 30-count. The headlines are being prepared for an employee newsletter.

   a. Lion Industries has just received a major contract from Macy's Department Stores to produce 50,000 shirts with the Macy's label in them. The $750,000 contract assures full employment at the Connecticut plant and will even necessitate the recruitment of another 50 workers.

   b. Advanced Micro Devices (AMD), because of high earnings last year, has announced a 5 percent bonus for all of its 9,000 employees. According to David Sears, president of AMD, the bonus payment will be made in the July payroll.

   c. FMC Corporation will have an awards banquet on May 15 to honor 35 workers who have made significant contributions to improving the company's productivity and reducing unnecessary costs. The workers' suggestions and ideas saved the company about $1 million in operating costs last year.

3. You are editor of a four-page newsletter for Community Hospital. The newsletter has a basic 8½- by 11-inch format but measures 11 by 17 inches when opened up. The purpose of the newsletter is to inform community residents about hospital services and give tips on preventive health care. Prepare a dummy layout, showing the placement of possible stories in this newsletter. Indicate where headlines and photographs or other visual elements would be placed.

SUGGESTED READINGS

"An Update on Desktop Publishing Systems for Communicators." *Communication World*, November 1987, pp. 14–15.

Arnold, E. C. *Editing the Organizational Publication*. Chicago: Ragan Communications, 1984.

Beach, Mark. *Editing Your Newsletter*. Portland, OR: Coast to Coast Books, 1983.

Berkowitz, Dan. "A Quick Solution for a Good Looking Magazine." *Communication World*, February 1985, pp. 15–17.

Bivens, Thomas. "Newsletters and House Publications." *Handbook of Public Relations Writing.* Lincolnwood, IL: NTC Business Books, 1988. Chapter 5.

Day, Brian, and Fisher, Kimberly. "Making a Case for Desktop Creativity." *Communication World,* November 1987, pp. 16–19.

"Four Ways to Make Desktop Work." *Communication World,* November 1988, pp. 19–26.

Healy, David. "Publishing Comes of Age: Pagemaker 2.0." *Communication World,* November 1987, pp. 20–21.

Hudson, Howard Penn. *Publishing Newsletters.* New York: Scribner's, 1982.

Jeffers, Dennis, and Bateman, David. "Redefining the Role of the Company Magazine." *Public Relations Review,* Summer 1980, pp. 11–29.

MacGibbon, John. "Desktop Publishing: A Threat to Communication Standards." *Communication World,* November 1987, pp. 30–32.

Malerba, James F. "How to Be a Good Editor." *Communication World,* February 1986, pp. 31–33.

Maxwell, Linnea. "Taking Desktop Publishing One Step Further." *Communication World,* November 1988, pp. 30–32.

Pavlik, John. "Why Employees Read Company Newsletters." *Public Relations Review,* Fall 1982, pp. 22–23.

Rose, Douglas. "An Update on Desktop Software." *Communication World,* November 1988, pp. 14–18.

"Supplier's Directory." *Communication World,* November 1987, pp. 34–38.

Winer, Laurie. "Puff Pieces: The World According to Philip Morris." *Wall Street Journal,* Aug. 4, 1988, p. 15.

Winkleman, Michael. "Post-Modern Magazines." *Public Relations Journal,* March 1986, pp. 24–27.

Chapter
15

Speeches and Speakers

The United States is a society of speakers and audiences. An executive of Ruder, Finn & Rotman (a public relations firm) once estimated that companies and associations convene close to a million meetings annually, all of them focusing on speakers in endless succession.

Today, the public is demanding more open corporate disclosure, and this is stimulating many executives to mount the speaker's rostrum. As a consequence, more executives are taking courses designed to improve their public speaking skills. Cincinnati Gas & Electric, for example, holds seminars of this kind for both managers and line employees. Levi Strauss & Company teaches "effective presentation skills" to middle managers. Other companies have also rushed into speech training for executives, creating a major boom for consultants who train employees at all levels to represent their firms in public forums or television interviews.

THE NATURE OF A SPEECH

It is important to know the basic structure of an effective speech and imperative to incorporate these concepts into every speech you prepare.

A Speech Is Heard Not Read

The average speech has only one brief exposure—the few minutes during which the speaker is presenting it. There is no chance to go back, no time to let it slowly digest, no opportunity for clarification. The message must get across *now* or never.

You may be an accomplished writer, but you must realize that speaking is something else again. As Louis Nizer once said, "The words may be the same, but the grammar, rhetoric, and phrasing are different. It is a different mode of expression—a different language."

One major difference is that you have to build up to a major point and prepare the audience for what is coming. The lead of a written story attempts to say everything in about fifteen to twenty-five words right at the beginning. If a speaker used the same form, most of the audience probably wouldn't hear it. When a speaker begins to talk, the audience is still settling down—so the first one or two minutes are devoted to giving unimportant information: a humorous comment, remarks on how nice it is to be there, and so on.

You should also be aware that people's minds wander. As your speech progresses, you must restate basic points and also summarize your general message.

One platitude of the speaking circuit, but still a valid one, is to "Tell them what you are going to tell them, tell it to them, and then tell them what you have told them." In this way, an audience is given a series of guideposts as they listen to the talk.

Some concepts used by writers are of course, transferable to speaking. The words you use should be clear, concise, short, and definite. Use words that specify, explain, and paint pictures for the audience.

A Speech Must Fit the Audience

Because every speech is aimed at a specific audience, you must know as much as possible about yours. Who are they? Such factors as age, occupation, sex, religion, race, education, intelligence, vocabulary, residence, interests, attitudes, group memberships, knowledge, politics, income, and others may bear on what they will find interesting.

Perhaps this point is best illustrated with some examples. If you were preparing a speech for a Rotary Club, a bit of research would tell you that the audience will probably be made up mainly of Caucasian men, mostly in their forties and fifties, who are lawyers, medical doctors, dentists, clergymen, civic officials, and business executives. They will be upper middle class, well educated, and on the conservative side politically.

A talk before a professional group can also end up being more relevant if you prepare for it by doing some audience analysis and basic research. Talk to members of the profession. Get an idea of the issues or problems that face them. If you don't know anyone in the profession, at least go to the local library and read five or six issues of the group's professional journal. This will give you some insight and perhaps even provide you with some quotations from leaders in the field.

In sum, most audiences have a core of common interests; this should help you to prepare a speech that will appeal to them. A talk to the stockholders of a corporation should be considerably different from one to employees or to a consumer group.

You should find out how much your listeners are likely to know about the subject you plan to address. Don't give them a speech they have heard before. Consult superiors, program chairpersons, and group members to find out about the group's interests and about past speakers and their subjects.

A Speech Must Be Specific

People remember only a small part of what they hear. You must therefore make sure that they hear things they can remember. A vague generality has little or no chance of being understood, let alone remembered. The speech must be built around specific ideas phrased in clear and memorable language.

A vague statement—for example, "We ought to do something about illegal immigration"—has no chance of being effective. If it were more specific—say, "We should stop illegal immigration by requiring everyone to carry a tamper-proof identification card"—it would offer the audience an idea that is definite and understandable.

A Speech Must Get a Reaction

If a speech gets no response from the listeners, it is a waste of the speaker's breath and the audience's time. Regardless of the subject, a speech must convey ideas and arouse some emotion in the audience. At least the listeners must feel that they have received new information and insight on a topic that concerns them.

In most cases, a person is asked to speak because the audience perceives him or her to be an expert on a given subject. Consequently, the audience wants the benefit of that persons's thinking and analysis. They don't want a bunch of platitudes or statements that are already self-evident. An economist should offer more than the flat statement that the economy is in trouble; he should at least say *why* it is in trouble and what he thinks the solution might be.

A Speech Must Have an Objective

This is probably the most important requirement of all. There is no point in making speeches unless they accomplish something. In preparing a speech, the first step is to determine what you want the audience to know or do. In other words, what attitude do you want the audience to have after listening to the speech?

A speech may inform, persuade, activate, or celebrate. It may also amuse or entertain. That particular kind of speech will not be considered here, but this does not rule out the use of *some* humor in the other kinds of speeches.

An informative speech is one that tells the audience something it does not know or that it does not understand. An informative speech might tell the audience about how their new sewage system works, the results of the latest United Way campaign, the expansion plans of a major local corporation, or even budget problems facing the state's system of higher education.

A persuasive speech is designed to convince the audience about the merits of some idea. Such a speech, for example, could try to convince people that the tamperproof I.D. card previously mentioned could easily be adopted and implemented. A similar speech could convince people of the need for a higher sales tax or better funding for the police force's crime-fighting efforts.

A persuasive speech appeals to the audience's self-interest. You might mention that more money for police protection will make the listeners' families safer; on the other hand, you would *not* want to point out that better funding would make the city's police force the best paid in the United States.

An activating speech is designed to get the listener to do something. Direct and specific action is suggested and urged. It is a basic principle of persuasion that a speaker should provide an audience with a specific course of action that they can take: to write to a congressman, vote for a candidate, purchase a product, take steps to conserve energy.

A celebrative speech is one designed to recognize some person or event. Such speeches are often trite and boring, but they don't *have* to be. If a person is being honored for lifetime professional achievement, why not start out with an anecdote that best exemplifies the feats being honored? This is much better than a chronological account of the person's life as if it were being read from an obituary.

Events like grand openings, anniversaries, and retirements usually have friendly, receptive audiences. In such cases, you can be more emotional and get away with some platitudes, which probably will be warmly received. When you prepare such a speech, however, keep it brief. Five minutes should be ample.

A Speech Must Be Timely

Regardless of the nature and objective of a speech, it must be interesting *now*. It must include up-to-date facts and information; it does no good to talk about a situation that is no longer current or which has no present interest for the audience. If the topic is an old one, it is imperative that the speaker talk about it in a new way. For example, everyone knows that dinosaurs are extinct, but their demise still retains current interest as scientists argue over the reasons for it.

If the speech is one of several in a general program, it is wise to learn what

Speeches can inspire. Here, James Earl Jones opens "We The People," the celebration of the bicentennial of the U.S. Constitution. His speech was heard by thousands at the ceremony and by millions who heard it on radio or television. (*Source:* Lewis, Gilman & Kynett, Philadelphia, PA.)

others will be talking about. This will provide a context for the talk—and add interest by reference to the other topics and speakers. It will also help you to avoid saying the same thing as other speakers.

Another dimension of timeliness is the length of the speech. In general, shorter is better. For a meeting that has no other business, or housekeeping chores, the talk should be about twenty minutes long.

It is a typical practice in many organizations to put the speaker on after a half hour of organizational announcements and committee reports. In such a situation, since the audience will already be getting tired, the talk should last no more than ten to fifteen minutes. If it is one of several speeches, the limit should be ten minutes.

The time of day is very important. A morning speech generally finds the audience most alert and receptive. On the other hand, at the end of the day with the cocktail hour only minutes away, a speaker is at an extreme disadvantage. The latter situation calls for more skills on the part of the speaker; he or she must be more enthusiastic, more forceful, and more attention-getting than his or her morning counterpart.

SEMISPEECHES

A speech is controlled by the speaker. He or she knows what is going to be said. The subject matter is complete and well organized. At the end, he or she may be asked a few questions—and if the talk runs too long, the chairperson may try to speed the closing. Still, the speaker is the boss.

Control passes to others when the speaker participates in semispeech activities such as panels, debates, talk shows, and interviews. Here someone else is directing the action, and other people may be talking to the same audience. These semispeech opportunities are valuable aids to public communication and should be used whenever possible.

Panels

A panel usually consists of a moderator and several people, each of whom makes an opening statement on the subject and then answers questions from the audience.

Opening statements should not last longer than five minutes. The number of questions that are answered depends on the time available. Often the moderator of the panel will prepare a sizable list of questions, which are distributed to the audience. The questions are numbered. When someone wants an answer to a question, he or she merely says, "I'd like an answer to question sixteen," whereupon the moderator asks a member of the panel to give the answer. Usually there are more questions than can be answered, but this procedure does permit answering those that are most interesting to the audience. In preparing for this situation, it is necessary to decide in advance who will answer which questions. It is your job to give your speaker the answers to the assigned questions, unless the answers are already known.

Debates

In high schools and colleges, a debate is generally conducted by teams of several speakers. Most debates in the world of public relations are not team efforts. They pit two opponents against each other and each carries the burden of making the case of his or her side and rebutting the statements of the opponent. The so-called debates of our presidential campaigns are not really debates; they are merely presentations during which the rivals offer their answers to the same questions.

In a true debate, each speaker prepares and presents his or her own case. The only questions are those of the opponent, and each tries to prove that the opponent is wrong. Each is allowed a short time to rebut the statements made by the other.

Debates are frequently staged in political campaigns. They may involve one candidate versus another or both sides of an issue. Two people running for the U.S. Senate may schedule one or more debates. On issues, such as proposed laws on taxation or changes in environmental protection, there may be numerous debates in which several different people may participate. Thus in one state, during one campaign, there could be several debates between the two senatorial candidates as well as a series of local debates on the issues in which local people are the speakers.

The management of political debates is not within the purview of this book. That is best left to the political specialists. But any reader of this volume may at some time have to handle a debate on some public issue. Aside from the need to know something about debating, in general there is one special warning worth heeding. This involves the situation in which a moderator may try to split the debate into two parts, with each speaker being allowed a brief period for rebuttal. A toss of the coin determines who will be first and who will be last.

It is very advantageous to be last in such a situation, since the last speaker may have ten or more minutes in which to try to demolish the statements of his or her opponent. The rebuttal period may be only a minute or two, and this is hardly adequate to overcome the effect of a long windup statement. The audience is left with a much stronger impression of what the last speaker said. To avoid being caught at such a disadvantage, you should insist that the debate be broken into short segments—five minutes would be a good length. Then the debate would consist of several five-minute statements by each speaker and a short summary rebuttal.

Debates may be conducted at a meeting hall or a broadcasting station. In either case, they are arranged with the program director of the organization which is holding the meeting or the director of the radio or television station.

Interviews at the Organization

Interviews on your own ground have several advantages. There is the psychological benefit of being "at home" under familiar circumstances. There is also the benefit of ready access to information and other people who may be needed to answer some question that is not anticipated.

If a reporter calls you on the phone or comes to your office and asks for information, you should give it provided that there is no policy reason for refusing. When there *is* such a reason, you should explain just why you cannot release the information. If the reporter should ask to speak to some other person, you should find out just what information is wanted or why the reporter wants to talk to that person. The reporter may ask for someone whose name he or she knows, but that person may not be the right source. Your job is to get the reporter to the person best qualified to talk on the subject at hand.

In some cases the reporter may call some person in the organization directly. For these situations, all personnel who might be approached should be informed as to what to do and what to say.

If several reporters call and ask for the same person or for the same information, there must be broad interest; therefore all concerned media should, if possible, be given what they ask for. The solution here is to arrange a press conference. It may have to be done in a hurry, but it must be done (see Chapter 10).

There are numerous occasions when an interview with some key person can generate valuable publicity. For example, a researcher may make an important discovery or patent a significant invention. Or perhaps a particular

How to Answer News Media Questions

- Be relaxed, confident and honest.

- In using your voice, changes in pitch and rate will make for variety.

- Build a "cutoff" into your answer if you wish to drop a given subject.

- Discuss only those activities and policies that lie within your area of responsibility.

- Admit you don't know the answer if that's the case. If you promise to provide more information, deliver.

- If the situation permits, tape the interview yourself.

- Don't use jargon, acronyms, or technical terminology.

- Don't use speech mannerisms such as "er-ah."

- Don't be curt, even with the dumbest question.

- Don't answer more than one question at a time.

- Don't restate the question.

- Don't begin with such trite phrases as "I'm glad you asked that."

- Don't give a "no comment" response; if you're unsure of the answer or can't discuss it, say so.

- Don't get into a verbal fencing match if it's proprietary information; say so and move on.

- Don't volunteer information unless it supports a positive point you want to make.

- Don't be defensive—make all your responses positive.

- Don't ever assume anything is "off the record"; there is no such thing unless you're certain the reporter will honor the agreement.

- Don't let anyone put words in your mouth; agree only if the facts and figures are correct.

Source: Gary Beals Advertising & Public Relations, San Diego, CA.

feature writer expresses interest in doing a profile of the new president of a university or the new chairman of a charitable organization. A representative of an environmental protection group might wish to register opposition to some law or regulation. The chief executive officer of some corporation might want to convey important information to the public by way of an interview.

You should hunt for opportunities to arrange such interviews. To set one up, you first get a commitment from the person to be interviewed and then ask a reporter, editor, or program director if an interview would interest him or her.

When you have a favorable reply, you then arrange for the time and place. You also prepare the speaker for the interview. This will be detailed later. One important point in arranging an interview is to have an agreement on the amount of time to be devoted to it. If the reporter has only a limited amount of time or if a deadline must be met, it is your responsibility to inform your principal of this requirement. The reverse is also important. If your principal must be in a meeting at 3 P.M. or must catch a plane at noon, the reporter must know that there will be a definite stopping point.

Interviews can make news. Whether it is a quiet "one on one," as shown here, or an organizational spokesperson facing a shouting crowd of reporters, an interview with the media is always important. (*Source:* Ryder Truck Rental, Miami, FL.)

Interviews at the Media

In these interviews the speaker is on foreign (and in some cases hostile) ground. There is the psychological disadvantage of being in unfamiliar surroundings and the physical disadvantage of being unable to get additional information or help from the office. In spite of these drawbacks, such interviews should be arranged when possible.

There are three basic situations that call for an interview at some medium: a meeting with the editors of a publication, an appearance on a panel at a broadcasting station, and participation in a radio or television program where only one person is interviewed but may be questioned by several reporters.

Broadcasting stations usually want only one representative from the organization. If there are several participants and one moderator, the program may be devoted to one topic, such as the environment or consumer interests, and the discussion will be limited to that area.

Advice for TV Talk Shows

Ketchum Public Relations gives the following advice to potential spokespersons:

1. Say it in 60 seconds.
2. Deliver your message convincingly.
3. Know your facts.
4. Rehearse your message.
5. Dress conservatively.
6. Stay alert.
7. Participate in discussion.
8. Get your message across.
9. Don't get mad.
10. Don't look at the camera.

In programs where only one person is interviewed, there are two procedures. The simplest is typified by the type of talk show where the interviewer introduces the speaker, tells why that person is there, allows an opening statement, and then questions the speaker. Often there will be an arrangement for members of the listening audience to phone questions to the studio. These shows are commonest on radio, but there are some TV shows that follow the same procedures.

Last and most critical are the shows, usually on TV, in which several reporters or editors interview one person. These are typified by *Meet the Press* and *Face the Nation.* The area covered in programs of this nature may be very wide, and the speaker may be asked questions about anything within his or her range of responsibility. The questions may also roam far afield and get onto topics bearing little relation to the anticipated nature of the interview. In these programs the speaker must expect to be challenged, to be given touchy questions, and to be grilled by people who are experts in prying information out of their interviewees.

SPEAKERS

Justin Dart of Dart & Kraft has said that any chief executive officer who does not devote a third of his or her time to public relations should be fired. Peter Drucker, the management consultant, once said that chief executive officers used to spend three-fourths of their time running the organization and now spend almost the same amount of time on public affairs, including a lot of personal appearances.

PR Reporter, a weekly newsletter, does an annual survey of how much time top management spends on public affairs, and the percentage goes up every year. For example, in one recent survey, it was found that (1) over half the surveyed executives spent ten or more hours each month meeting with outside groups, (2) the majority average twenty speeches a year, and (3) about two-thirds of CEOs spend time on press conferences while another third appear on radio and TV.

One TV talk show host, noting the increase in the number of top executives who are willing to represent their companies on talk shows, notes, "Businessmen have come to realize they must tell their side of the story and take a stand."

Finding Speakers

In most organizations there are people who are able and willing to make speeches. Some of the would-be speakers will be known, others may need to be found. This can be done by recruiting volunteers or by asking people to suggest the names of individuals who might be willing to serve. A Toastmasters Club is a good source. If the organization is some sort of nonprofit group, the membership at large may contain a number of potential speakers. In any organization, the employees may be a good source of speakers.

Selecting Speakers

It is imperative to select speakers who can convey ideas and information effectively. In some cases the chief executive officer is the only possibility. If reporters demand a statement from the president, their request must be granted; but if circumstances permit, it may be better to choose someone else.

J. L. Kraft was the founder of Kraft Cheese Co. (now a part of Dart & Kraft). He was a very able man but had a voice like a rock crusher. He was a very poor speaker. Both he and his people knew this, so Mr. Kraft made very few public speeches. This is not to say that speakers should be selected because of their dulcet voices or attractive faces, but the possible public reaction to any speaker should be considered.

Another factor in choosing a speaker is expertise. The speaker will be expected to have considerable knowledge of the subject to be discussed. If there is only one person in the organization who is familiar with the subject, that person is the logical candidate; but if there are several who are knowledgeable, it may be advisable to choose the one who will make the best impression.

The ideal speaker is one who knows much about the subject, whose voice and appearance will help him or her to make a good impression, and who is a polished public speaker. You won't always find ideal speakers; but if you consider the desirable characteristics and make reasoned selections, your speakers should be effective.

When speakers are identified, their names go into a speakers' file. This may be a card index or a notebook listing each speaker by name, title, and subject or subjects on which he or she can talk. Biographical data should be included, and there should be a running record of speeches given and the responses received.

Preparing Speakers

No one should ever make a public appearance without preparation. Even if a hostile reporter is sitting in the reception room and demanding an immediate hearing, the spokesperson must take time to prepare for the session. On most occasions, there will be enough time to do the job thoroughly; but even when time is at a premium, a few minutes must be set aside for at least a minimum of preparation. Preparation includes providing information, determinating the key points to be made, coaching or training, and giving suggestions on grooming and personal mannerisms.

Informing Speakers

The speaker must know the nature of the session. If it is a panel, a debate, or an interview, the speaker must know what procedures will be followed. Most of these are similar, but there may be slight differences and you should warn the speaker of any deviations from the norm. If there is to be an interview at a radio station, the speaker should listen to at least one program. If a TV appearance is to be made, the speaker should first watch at least one show.

A session on home ground will be in familiar surroundings, but if the appearance is to occur at a station, the speaker must know where to sit, where to look, and to whom to talk. Placement of cameras, microphones, and lights is important; your speaker should be familiarized with the setup well before the program is to start. This means early arrival.

If the appearance is a panel, your speaker must know who the other people are and what they are likely to say. This will enable him or her to avoid echoing others and to supplement their remarks rather than repeating them.

If the appearance is a debate, it is imperative to know the arguments of the opposition. If the speaker knows what the other side is going to claim, it may be possible to demolish its erroneous statements and to present more effective arguments. Debating coaches often start their teams by having them present the opposition's arguments. A team that is to argue in favor of the value-added tax might start by preparing a strong case against it. In this way the debaters will be prepared for the arguments they are likely to face.

The value of knowing the answers to opposing points was proved in a series of debates conducted during an election campaign to pass a law affecting farm labor. One side repeatedly charged that the opposition was largely financed by the oil companies. The public relations director for the opposition tried repeatedly to get the facts but didn't succeed until the campaign was almost over. The facts showed that the oil companies had given about 0.5 percent, but the information came almost too late to use.

It is particularly important to know who is going to ask questions. If it is a moderator, the speaker should know something about the way in which that moderator conducts a session. If it is a reporter, the speaker needs to know as much as possible about the kind of person he or she is. A friendly reporter may only be after facts, but a hostile reporter may be hunting for something to confirm previously established convictions.

A hostile reporter might open an interview by asking, "Does your product contain a substance that can cause cancer?" Faced with such a question, the respondent might truthfully answer yes and never get a chance to explain that the quantity of the carcinogen is so low as to be insignificant. (Many natural foods—containing no additives whatever—do contain minute quantities of substances that have, when given in enormous quantities, caused cancer in laboratory animals. Even peanut butter comes under this cloud.)

In short, the person being interviewed should always remember that a reporter may be looking for a headline—something that will be sensational.

By studying the reporter or interviewer and the publication or program that he or she represents, you may be able to make some informed guesses as to the kind of questions that are likely to be asked. Anticipating questions and preparing answers is a vital part of an interview. Fortunately for the person to be interviewed, many such sessions are devoted purely to fact-gathering. In such instances, the speaker merely needs to know what information is wanted and to have it ready. Your responsibility here is, insofar as possible, to find out before the interview just what the reporter wants.

Coaching Speakers

The great increase in investigative reporting and the bad impressions made by some people in responding to questions has led to the creation of special training courses for people who may have to face these reporters.

In these courses, the students (who in some cases are the chief executives of major corporations) are grilled by reporters. Frequently the interviews are taped and then played back to the students. When one of the students sees and hears himself or herself blushing, floundering, stumbling, and generally displaying incompetence and incoherence, there is a powerful stimulus to do better the next time. Results of these sessions have been excellent, and they are attracting an ever-growing number of executives.

Since the costs of such training sessions often run into thousands of dollars, organizations with limited budgets may not be able to afford them. If you find yourself in such a situation, it is still possible to train the spokespeople of your organization.

First, you must get a commitment from the interviewee to spend some time learning how to give effective interviews. You can teach him or her many of the basics that have been discussed here. You can also play the role of the reporter and ask questions. Expected questions should be supplemented by others, such as "trick and trap" questions. You should heckle, storm, charge the respondent with ducking the questions, and try in every way possible to make your student lose his or her temper.

Although your student may become somewhat irritated with you, such a session will enable him or her to feel much more confident in a real question-and-answer situation. Another thing you can do is to hire a local reporter or editor as a consultant to spend an hour or two in a simulated interview with your spokesperson. This will give your student a chance to meet a real live reporter in a controlled situation. Mistakes here will be much easier to bear than those that might occur on a live show being broadcast to thousands.

Key Points

People remember only a small part of what they see and even less of what they hear. Out of a possible several thousand words in a speech, the listeners may remember only a few. If the entire speech is published, most readers still won't remember much of what they read. Therefore every speech should contain at least one memorable key point. In a debate or on a panel, the same rule applies. Be sure that the most important ideas are stated in a clear and memorable way. With interviews this is doubly important, because if the interviewer is from a publication, he or she will rely on notes and may take down only the highlights. If the interview is for a radio or television program, a large part of what is recorded may not be used. People frequently complain that after they have given an hour-long interview, only one or two minutes is actually broadcast.

Determining the key points requires a thorough study of the subject to be covered. Among all the ideas that might be pertinent, there are always a few that are vitally important. A good way to find them is to try to boil everything down into a few brief sentences. Each of these sentences should be a clear and positive statement covering one of the main ideas.

For example, in the election campaign previously mentioned, the proponents of the proposed law constantly claimed that farm laborers needed protection from the big growers. The opponents based their campaign on the fact that

Project Category: Speech

Project: Address by Thomas A. Cooper
            President & Chief Operating Officer
            Bank of America, San Francisco
            President – BankAmerica Corporation

Venue: 5th Annual International Retail Banking Conference
            London – November 10-12, 1986

Title: "Retail Banking Strategies –– Where Are They Leading The Industry?"

Public Relations Objectives:

o In an appropriate forum, publicly announce Bank of America's strategic
   decision to disengage from international retail banking activities and
   explain the business and marketplace realities behind this decision;
o Establish understanding for the company's overall strategy to focus
   its retail activities on the West Coast of the United States and the
   company's wholesale strategy of focusing its activities on top-tier
   corporate and institutional customers in the U.S. and
   international markets;
o Communicate the benefits of this focused strategy for Bank of America
   including increased capital and expanded wholesale banking
   business relationships with international financial companies;
o Minimize press perception and reportage that this action is a
   retrenchment forced by the company's financial difficulties.

Public Relations Tools and Techniques:

      A major policy speech, a subsequent question and answer session with
reporters, and a targeted mailing of the speech to key media were the major
communications vehicles used to achieve these objectives. Key to the public
announcement of changes in Bank of America's international retail banking
strategy was the identification of an appropriate forum.

      The desired characteristics of a forum for the announcement included (a)
broad industry, business, and financial press coverage, (b) sufficient
prestige to warrant an address by the president of Bank of America; (c) a
target audience which included participants and knowledgeable observers of the
financial services industry; and (d) a non-U.S. site.

Target Audiences:

      Key target audiences for this communication were financial services
industry participants worldwide and the international business, financial, and
banking industry press. Through media coverage, the communication was
expected to reach extended target audiences including financial analysts,
current and potential corporate customers worldwide, BankAmerica shareholders,
and the general public.

Budget:

      The speech was conceptualized, researched, and developed by on-staff
public relations professionals. Travel and lodging expenses were paid by the
conference. Related expenses were insignificant.

Speeches must be planned. This is the plan for a speech announcing a major change in
operations of one of the world's largest banks. (*Source:* Bank of America—Corporate
Communications, San Francisco, CA.)

Results:

The International Retail Banking Conference held annually in London was identified as the most appropriate forum in terms of media coverage, prestige, industry participants, timing, and location. Through contact with the sponsoring organization, it was arranged for the president of Bank of America, Thomas A. Cooper, to give the keynote address of the conference.

The address was well received by the approximately 500 retail bankers from around the world attending the conference, and both the immediate and subsequent media coverage of the bank's disengagement from international retail activities reflected a clear understanding the bank's strategy.

Measurements:

A key measurement was the tone and content of press coverage immediately following the address. A clear understanding of the bank's strategy was crucial, both in the near-term as well as setting the foundation for subsequent press coverage related to specific implementation of the strategy.

> "The task of restructuring will involve substantial asset sales. Mr. Cooper said that Bank of America would probably sell most of its retail businesses in Europe and concentrate its consumer activities in California, the world's seventh largest economy." (<u>Financial Times</u> - Tuesday, November 11, 1986.)

> "The bank expects to leave most of the non-domestic markets where it has conducted consumer banking operations, focusing more on top-tier corporate, institutional, and sovereign customers in its global wholesale banking business." (<u>The Times</u> of London - Tuesday, November 11, 1986.)

> "Worldwide, BankAmerica will sell retail and other banking businesses that do not fit its current strategy. That strategy is to remain an international wholesale bank with a large retail banking business mostly on the West Coast of the U.S." (<u>Wall Street Journal</u> - Tuesday, November 11.)

> "With the sale of CC Bank, BankAmerica will will have effectively moved out of consumer banking in Europe following its announcement last year that it intended to drop retail banking internationally." (<u>American Banker</u> - Thursday, March 5, 1987.)

> "BankAmerica, continuing to shed assets in an effort to focus its businesses and strengthen its capital base, said Thursday that it will sell two West German units -- its consumer banking subsidiary and credit card operations." (<u>Los Angeles Times</u> - Friday, March 6, 1987.)

> "The proposed sale is in line with BankAmerica's previously announced plans to shed a number of foreign subsidiaries to raise cash and concentrate on its institutional markets abroad." (<u>Wall Street Journal</u> - Friday, March 6, 1987.)

In sum, the media understanding of the strategic foundation for the company's actions and resulting editorial coverage positioning these actions appropriately validate the success of the speech in reaching its objectives.

Speeches can create publicity. Mr. Cooper's speech was widely and favorably reported in major media throughout the business world. This is a report of the success of the speech. (*Source:* Bank of America—Corporate Communications, San Francisco, CA.)

there was an adequate law in existence and that the new law would involve a dangerous invasion of privacy.

Speakers must constantly be advised to stress the key points in whatever they say. Individual statements may vary. Some people may give twenty-minute speeches and some may be interviewed for only a minute or two, but all must know the key points to be included.

Grooming

If the person to make an appearance is a celebrity or performer, the choice of what to wear won't be a problem. On any of the shows originating in Las Vegas or Hollywood, men commonly wear boots, big hats or very casual clothing. Women may wear flamboyant outfits that freely expose legs or bosoms. This is part of the image they are trying to project, but—as said before—these are "personality" shows whose sole purpose is publicity.

For those who want to get a serious message across to an audience, there is a difference set of rules. Here the speaker must be dressed conservatively and show or do nothing that might distract attention.

Men should wear conservative suits. A sports jacket might be permissible in some cases, but it must not be loud. Wild plaids or violent colors won't do. Suits should be dark; if there is a pattern, it should be so subdued as to be almost invisible. White reflects light, so it should be avoided. Colonel Sanders of Kentucky Fried Chicken fame defied this rule because his white suit was part of his image, and he was selling his personality as much as his chicken. Your speakers should even avoid white shirts. A pale blue, gray, or tan with no noticeable pattern is best.

Men should wear knee-length socks. A few inches of bare skin between sock top and trouser bottom is ugly and distracting. Flashy rings, large cufflinks, and big belt buckles are unacceptable. If a man has a dark beard, a shave just before the appearance is a good idea. For any television appearance, the producer may suggest some makeup. This should not be resisted; even the nation's Presidents have used it.

Women should dress conservatively in dresses or suits. A businesswoman should be sure that when she is seated, her legs are not exposed above the knees. Makeup should be the kind that is normally worn for business. Any jewelry that dangles, jingles, or flashes is taboo.

Another important point is that the speaker is "on stage" at all times. A surreptitious scratch or adjustment of clothing may be seen by some members of the audience or picked up by a TV camera. No speaker should take a chance that any gesture he or she might make will not be seen.

Interview Tips

Speeches, panels, and even debates are usually definite in structure. Interviews, on the other hand, may go far off the expected track. To get the best results from an interview, a speaker should remember these tips:

1. Most reporters may merely want information, but some will be looking for headlines. To appreciate this, just watch a presidential press conference. Note the kinds of questions asked and visualize the headlines that might result from an injudicious reply.

2. Conversely, it may be desirable to make headlines. If you do want to see special attention paid to something, say it in a way that can be quoted—or even headlined.

3. Watch for loaded questions. Take time to think. Don't repeat a derogatory remark; shift to another subject. When Carl Gernstacker of Dow Chemical was asked if pressure from environmentalists had caused Dow to stop making Napalm, Gernstacker said "No, we don't make Napalm now, but I'd like to talk about some things we do make." Then he described a new medical discovery made by Dow.

4. Prepare for the worst. Think of every question that might possibly be asked, reasonable or unreasonable. Then prepare an answer for each.

5. Be sure to state your key points early in the interview. Use examples and anecdotes. Don't tell half-truths. Don't exaggerate. Don't brag about your organization or its products or services.

6. Watch your attitude. Don't be arrogant, evasive, or uncooperative. Don't argue. Admit mistakes—and tell how you have corrected them. Don't use jargon. Don't lose your temper.

7. Don't memorize your statements, but do use notes for reference. Speak from the public viewpoint; it's their interest that is important. Look at the interviewer when he or she is asking a question, but face the audience or the television camera when you are answering.

8. Be cooperative, but don't surrender. Watch for presumptive questions: "Why are you resisting the efforts to control pollution?" "Why do you charge such outrageous prices?" Deny the statement and shift to another topic.

9. If a question is unfair or too personal, say so and refuse to answer. You don't *have* to answer any question. Decline with a smile, but don't say "no comment."

10. Never say "off the record." Anything you say is on some sort of record—videotape or the reporter's notes.

11. Don't challenge figures unless you *know* they are wrong. Remember that there are many ways to cite statistics.

12. Be as relaxed and informal as possible. A humorous remark may be used if it is appropriate, but don't be facetious; you might be taken seriously.

To Speak or Not to Speak

You may be the person who sets up interviews, gathers the material needed, helps select the appropriate spokesperson, coaches and trains, and even sits in on the interview.

This is not to say that a public relations person doesn't give interviews or make personal appearances—he or she often will when the press inquiry is fairly routine and the reporter only needs some basic information.

On the other hand, your role is primarily that of facilitator—not of key spokesperson. Surveys consistently point out that reporters prefer to interview those who are the experts or have the most influence. This means that the chief executive officer, a chief engineer, or a marketing vice president is more important than you are. These people are, in a reporter's eyes, more credible and more newsworthy.

It is important that you communicate this to the top management. A company or organization that thinks a public relations person on the staff makes it unnecessary for top executives to make personal appearances is making a serious mistake. You can make it easier, but you cannot take the place of the CEO or the chief scientist as the only available spokesperson of the organization.

Finding Audiences

There are, in every community, a sizable number of organizations that meet periodically and need speakers. Generally there is a program chairperson whose primary job is to arrange for speeches. In some cases, this individual may solicit speakers; in other cases, it may be necessary to write or phone him or her and offer a speaker.

Your job is to determine which organizations will provide the most valuable audiences—the audiences which, by their response, can benefit your organization. The key is to know exactly what your organization is trying to accomplish and which people can help or who will be helped. If you are trying to raise money, the audience should be people who can give money. If you want people to know how your organization can help them, the audience must be people who need that help or who can and will convey that information to those who do.

Getting to the Audience

When an audience has been scheduled, you should prepare a booking sheet. This lists the name and title of the speaker, the name of the organization to be addressed, an explanation of the nature of that organization (if it is not obvious), the date of the speech, the time, the location (including room name or number), the name of the program chairperson or other contact, the size of the audience expected, and any properties needed by the speaker (such as easels, charts, etc.).

A copy of this sheet should be given to the speaker and to the program chairperson, but don't depend on this to complete the job. Your responsibility is to make sure that the speaker gets to the meeting at the right time and meets the program chairperson. He or she must also know where to sit, when to speak, and where the needed properties are.

Publicity

The number of people reached by a speech or semispeech can be materially increased by thinking of them as news events. This was mentioned in Chapter 4, and it is mentioned again here. Whenever anyone from your organization speaks in public, you should be sure that the media are informed. Advance copies of the speech may be released, reporters should be accommodated, or—if none show up—there may be an opportunity for a news release containing all or part of the speech.

If a speech is really important, it can be printed in some attractive format and mailed to selected opinion leaders with an accompanying buck slip from someone other than the speaker. Be aware of *Vital Speeches*, which reprints selected speeches. Some newspapers, the *Washington Post* for one, carry excerpts of speeches and statements on an editorial or Op-Ed page.

SPEECH WRITING

The good speech writer has the ability to place himself or herself in the shoes of the person who must give the speech. Sociologists call this "empathic ability"—meaning the ability to think and feel much the same way as the person who will give the speech. In a sense, you become your client's alter ego.

Such understanding and empathic ability, of course, do not arise in a vacuum. They can develop only after a great deal of research and thorough discussion with the person for whom you are writing.

Know the Audience

If you are given a speech-writing assignment, the first step is to find out everything possible about the audience. Who? Where? When? How many people? Time of day? Purpose of meeting? How long a talk? Purpose of talk? Other speakers and their topics?

To find the answers to these questions, it might be necessary to talk with a number of individuals. Don't necessarily trust the information you get if it appears to be only a guesstimate. Too many speakers have innocently blundered because they received bad information about the nature of their audience.

Know the Speaker

The second step is to learn everything you can about the speaker. Listen to the speaker talk—either to other groups, to subordinates, or even to yourself. Get a chance to see how his or her mind works; what word phrases are constantly used and what kinds of opinions are expressed. In addition to listening, it is also a good idea to go over material that the client has written or, if written by others, that the client really likes in terms of style and method of presentation.

Ideally, a writer should have lengthy conversations with the speaker before beginning to write a rough draft of the talk. In a conversational setting, you and the speaker should talk about the speech in terms of the objective, the approach, the strategy, what things should be emphasized, the scope of the talk, and what facts or anecdotes the speaker would like to include.

The Objective

The first step is to determine the objective. Just what is the speech supposed to accomplish? What attitude should the audience have when the speech is concluded?

Everything that goes into the speech should be pertinent to that objective. Material that does not help to attain the objective should not be used. Whether the objective is to inform, persuade, activate, or commemorate, that particular objective must be uppermost in the mind of the speech writer.

The Approach

The approach might be described as the tone of the speech. A friendly audience may appreciate a one-sided talk, with no attempt to give both sides of an issue. For example, a politician at a fund-raising dinner of supporters does not bother to give the opposition's views. And, of course, an executive talking to the company's sales force does not need to praise the competitor's product.

Most speaking engagements, however, take place before neutral audiences (Rotary, Lions, Kiwanis, and any number of other civic or professional organizations) where the audience may have mixed views or even a lack of knowledge about the topic.

In such a case, it is wise to take a more objective approach and give an overview of the various viewpoints. The speech can still advocate a particular position, but the audience will appreciate the fact that you have included other points of view. From the standpoint of persuasion, you also have more control over how the opposition view is expressed if you say it instead of waiting for an audience member to bring it up. You lose control when someone stands up and says: "What you say is fine, but you didn't consider the problem of. . . ."

If you have included the "problem" in your talk—and perhaps have even admitted that this is a valid point—it takes the wind out of audience opposition.

Mentioning several aspects of the problem—and giving the opposition's views—also makes the speech more credible. It establishes objectivity, and it treats people as mature, level-headed citizens who are intelligent enough to understand the pros and cons. In addition, when you acknowledge the opposition, your advocacy of one viewpoint over another appears to be based on a systematic, logical analysis of all sides of the issue.

Hostile or unfriendly audiences present the greatest challenge. They are already predisposed against what you say and they tend to reject anything that does not square with their opinions. It is somewhat like the old saw, "Don't confuse me with the facts, my mind is already made up." The best approach is to find some common ground with the audience. This technique lets the audience know that the speaker shares or at least understands some of their concerns.

For example, a nuclear power advocate talking to environmentalists can say that the utility is working on solar energy, but the current state of the technology is such that it is not feasible to light an entire metropolitan area with it. The advocate might also mention coal as a source of power, but point out that it creates major problems of air pollution. All this may not produce a rousing ovation at the end of the talk, but many in the audience may somewhat modify the intensity of their opposition.

The Strategy

This is the *how* of speech writing. Once you've determined the objective and the approach, your next step is to decide what ideas and information will be needed to convince the audience.

Alex Osborn, the famous advertising man, was once asked how he got so many brilliant ideas. He replied, "By constantly thinking about the problem." This prescription applies well to speech writing. By constantly thinking about the problem of convincing the audience, you will come upon many ideas that will help you to reach this goal.

At this stage, it is advisable to start making notes. As you think of ideas or examples you want to use, jot them down somewhere, perhaps on a pocket-sized note card. Don't rely on your memory; often, many of our best ideas are no more than fleeting mental flashes that are quickly crowded out by more immediate problems.

The idea of thinking about the problem also applies to the material—newspapers, reports, magazines—that you read. Many successful speech writers are great clippers of articles. When they see an article on some topic of interest, they clip it and put the story in an appropriate file. It may be a broad topic like "higher education" or something more specialized like "residential applications of solar energy."

By clipping articles on a regular basis and keeping them in a well-organized idea file, you can easily find new and usable information. This can ensure that the talk will contain current facts and figures as well as contemporary examples.

The Outline

Having gathered the necessary material, you must now prepare an outline. This contains three main parts: the opening, the body, and the closing.

The opening is the part of the speech that must get the attention of the audience, establish empathy, and point toward the conclusion. It is wise, in the opening, to tell the audience what the topic is about, its importance to them, and the direction you plan to take in addressing the topic.

The body of the speech represents the evidence that leads to the conclusion. The outline should list all the key points. In this section, you will use quotes from acknowledged experts in the field, facts and figures, and examples that drive home your point of view.

The conclusion summarizes the evidence, pointing out what it means to the audience.

The outline should be submitted to the speaker, and if it is approved, you can go on to the next step.

Drafts

The next step is to write a rough draft for the speaker. The speaker should use this draft to add new thoughts, cross out copy that doesn't seem to fit his or her views, and even rewrite sentences that better reflect his or her vocabulary and favorite expressions.

Don't feel rejected if the first, second, or even third draft comes back in tatters. It is only through this process that the speech becomes a natural expression of the speaker's personality.

The process just described delineates the ideal. The most successful speakers are those who take the time to work with their speech writers. Unfortunately, however, far too many executives don't seem to understand this simple concept.

A report prepared by Burson Marsteller (a public relations firm) discussed several reasons why businesspeople have trouble explaining themselves to the public. The report noted,

> All too often the chief executive expects a speech to appear magically on his desk without any contribution on his part. He feels too busy to give the speech the attention it deserves. In the end, he becomes the victim of his own neglect. He stumbles through a speech which, from start to finish, sounds contrived. And then he wonders why nobody listened to what he said.

Raymond K. Price, a staff writer on the *Wall Street Journal*, has added to this thought in an article about executive speeches. He says, "It wasn't the writer's stamp of personality that was missing. It was the speaker's."

The Words

A speech talks *to*, not *at*, the listeners. Your choice of words can either electrify an audience or put it to sleep. As someone once said, "The best idea in the world isn't worth a damn if it cannot be expressed well." Here are some tips about wording:

1. Use personal pronouns like "you" and "we." This makes the talk more conversational and lets the audience know you are talking to them.
2. Avoid jargon. Do not talk about the "acquisition range" of an F-14 jet fighter—talk about an F-14 jet that can shoot down another plane 10 miles away.

3. Don't use long figures. Don't say "243,629,384 Americans." Say "More than 240 million Americans. . . ."

4. Use simple words to communicate. Don't say "print media" when you mean "newspaper." Don't say "perish" when "die" says the same thing. Don't say "possess" when "have" is what you mean.

5. Use active verbs. Say "I think," not "It is my conviction that. . . ."

6. Avoid modifers such as "very" or "most"—these are crutches.

7. Avoid empty words such as "of the nature of." Instead, say "like." Don't say "in the event of"—say "if." Don't say "at that point in time"—say "then."

8. Use short sentences. Don't use clauses between the subject and the predicate of a sentence. Don't put a clause at the end of a sentence. Start a new sentence.

9. Use direct quotes. You could say: "Here is what my friend Allan said," and then quote him.

10. Use questions. (For example, "Does anyone know how many refugees there are in the world today?")

11. Use comparisons or contrasts. Compare exotic locales with others that are familiar. ("New Zealand has about the same land area as California, but it has only 3 million people as compared to California's 30 million.")

Speaker Help

In addition to writing the speech to suit the speaker, there may be a need for coaching. Whether the speech is memorized, partially read, or read entirely, it should be voiced enough times for the speaker to become familiar with it and to permit improvements in the way it is delivered. The tone of voice, the emphasis given to certain words or phrases, the pauses, the gestures, the speed—all are important.

Some speakers prefer to have certain phrases underlined and to have detailed cues in the script such as "pause," "look at audience," "pound on lectern," and so on. Others don't want such cues. It is a matter of individual preference.

Typing format is also a matter of personal preference. Some people prefer double spacing, others want triple spacing. A few like to have the speech typed entirely in capital letters, but most prefer the normal upper- and lowercase format that is used to present most material which is to be read. There are also speakers who like to have capital letters used in the words that are to be stressed. Any of these formats is acceptable if the speaker likes it that way.

The speaker should be sufficiently familiar with the note cards or prepared text to enable him or her to shorten it on brief notice. Such advance thinking is particularly important for a speaker at a luncheon meeting. All too often, the meal is served late or the group takes an excessive amount of time discussing housekeeping chores and making general announcements. And often, because of all this, the speaker may finally be introduced only ten minutes before the meeting is to end.

The same thing can happen at an evening banquet. The awards ceremony takes longer than expected and the speaker is introduced at 9:15 P.M., about three hours after everyone has sat down to dinner. In this instance, the most applause is for the person who realizes the hour and makes a five-minute speech.

SUMMARY

1. A speech can be a powerful tool of communication. It must be prepared for listeners—not for readers. It must fit the audience, be specific, get a reaction, have a definite objective, and be timely.
2. Semispeeches—panels, debates, interviews, and talk shows—follow the same basic principles as speeches; however, they also involve special preparation for dealing with opposition, interruptions, and possibly hostile questions.
3. Public speaking by representatives of the organization is a vital part of the public relations program. Speakers must be found, prepared, informed, provided with key points, properly groomed, and coached. Audiences for the speakers to address must also be located.
4. Speech writing is a difficult, prestigious, and important job for public relations people. To write a good speech, you must know the audience and the speaker. Jointly you and the speaker must establish a clear objective, an effective approach, and sound strategy. You must get the facts, organize the speech, and prepare as many drafts as are needed to get a speech that will please the speaker—and be effective. When the speech has been written, you must help the speaker rehearse the speech and get to the audience.

EXERCISES

1. This chapter gives a number of guidelines about giving an effective speech. Attend the meeting of a campus or community organization where someone is scheduled to give a speech. Write a critique of the speaker and assess the overall effectiveness of his or her speech.
2. It is important for speakers to know the composition and background of an audience if they are to tailor their remarks to the occasion. Select an organization that regularly has a speaker for its monthly meeting. Compile a short memo that would help the president of the university prepare for a talk before this group. You should include (a) some brief background on the organization, (b) a profile of the membership, (c) the time and place of the meeting, and (d) the format of the entire meeting, and (5) the requested length of the talk.
3. Speech writing is a highly refined skill. Say that the president of a local company hires you to write a ten-minute speech for him, which he plans to present at the monthly meeting of the American Marketing Association. This group, consisting of

people who work in marketing, wants to hear the president's views on protective legislation that would restrict the importation of Japanese goods to this country. The president is a busy man, but he does tell you that he thinks protective legislation is a bad idea. Taking the audience into consideration, do some research and draft a speech for the president.

4. The president of your company has been asked to appear on a television public-affairs show to discuss the company's plans to initiate mandatory drug testing of all potential and present employees. This is a controversial subject. You are expected to coach the president on how to answer specific questions from the show's host or members of the live audience. Compile a list of possible questions that he may have to deal with.

SUGGESTED READINGS

Ailes, Roger. *You Are the Message: Secrets of the Master Communicators.* New York: Dow Jones-Irwin, 1987.

Beckham, James. "How to Make Speeches Work." *Public Relations Journal,* August 1985, pp. 29–30.

Bivens, Thomas. "Speeches and Presentations." *Handbook for Public Relations Writing.* Lincolnwood, IL: NTC Business Books, 1988; chap. 6.

Cone, Russ. "Reporter Interviews Media Trainers." *Communication World,* January 1987, pp. 32–35.

Detz, Joan. "Speechmakers: Learn Podium Math." *Communication World,* February 1987, pp. 26–27.

DeVito, Joseph A. *The Elements of Public Speaking,* 4th ed. New York: Harper & Row, 1990.

Fletcher, Leon. *How to Design and Deliver a Speech.* New York: Harper & Row, 1985.

Gilda, Robert L. "Speaker, Writer—Let the Twain Meet." *Public Relations Quarterly,* Summer 1988, pp. 21–22.

Graham, James. "What to Do When a Reporter Calls." *Communication World,* April 1985, p. 15.

Hess, Ron. "Are We Misdirecting Our Priorities?" *Communication World,* May 1987, pp. 20–22.

Jeffrey, Robert C., and Peterson, Owen. *Speech: A Basic Text,* 3rd ed. New York: Harper & Row, 1989.

Newman, Joyce. "Speaker Training: 25 Experts on Substance and Style." *Public Relations Quarterly,* Summer 1988, pp. 15–20.

Reibstein, Larry. "For Corporate Speech Writers, Life Is Seldom a Simple Matter of ABCs." *Wall Street Journal,* June 30, 1987, sec. 2, p. 1.

Rosenberger, Brent. "Workshop: How to Recognize and Work With a Speechwriter." *Public Relations Journal,* January 1988, pp. 31–32.

Tarver, Jerry. *Corporate Speechwriter's Handbook.* New York: Quorum Books, 1987.

Tarver, Jerry, and Geigel, Sara. "It Is With Great Pleasure That I Introduce. . . ." *Communication World,* June 1988, pp. 30–32.

Tarver, Jerry. "Making a Speech in a Different Culture." *Communication World*, February 1984, pp. 2–22.

Wann, Al. "Want to Be a Great Corporate Spokesperson?" *Communication World*, May 1987, pp. 16–19.

Wilcox, Dennis L., Ault, Phillip and Agee, Warren. "Spoken Tactics." *Public Relations Strategies and Tactics*. New York: Harper & Row, 1989, chap. 23.

Chapter
16

Audiovisual Presentations

*T*he tremendous impact of television is ample proof that a combination of sight and sound is the strongest means of communication. That is why so much effort is devoted to audiovisual communication in public relations programs.

It has been said that people remember 10 percent of what they hear and 50 percent of what they see. The figures may not be provable, yet they are probably close to correct. At any rate, when we combine sight and sound, our message gains in impact. People get the idea more clearly and more memorably.

Generally, when we speak of *audiovisual communication*, the term is assumed to mean things like motion pictures, but the field is much wider. It includes charts, overhead projectors, slides, filmstrips, motion pictures, and videotape—and each of these calls for both visual and aural components. Charts and slides can be shown without sound; even the overhead projector could be used in silence, but without an accompanying verbal explanation, they will have little impact. Accordingly, any use of a visual aid must be tied to words that may be either spoken or recorded but always closely keyed to the visual. In the simplest terms, you must "Tell them what you show them; show them what you tell them."

PLANNING

Large amounts of money have been wasted on audiovisual materials because someone leaped into production without considering the purpose to be served, the audience to be reached, and the aid that would be most effective. Motion pictures have been produced when a slide presentation would have done the job. Slides have been prepared when charts or an overhead projector would be better. Costs have been overlooked and budgets wrecked because decisions were made with no thought to the need and the values of the various aids.

The Purpose

Is the purpose to explain, to teach, to persuade, to arouse, to inform—or is it to flatter the head of the organization who would like to see his or her face on the silver screen? If it is the last of these, the result may be an expensive and worthless film.

Whenever you consider audiovisual aids, your first question should be: What are we trying to accomplish? The purpose may be as simple as making a speech more understandable or as complex as showing and telling how a proposed construction project will affect the environment.

The Audience

Audiovisual aids are always planned to serve a specific audience. In addition to the general questions about who they are and what they know, there are other specific questions to be asked and answered. Is this to be one small audience? Will it be a number of small audiences? Is it an audience comprising thousands of people? Is it an audience comprising thousands of people scattered across the country?

The size of the audience, the chance that the aid may be used repeatedly, and the circumstances under which the aid will be presented must also be kept in mind, as well as the person or persons who will do the presenting.

Choosing the Aid

For a meeting of less than about fifty people, charts are probably most efficient. If the meeting is larger, it may be necessary to use an overhead projector. If pictures are important, it may be advisable to use slides. If the presentation is to be given many times and in scattered locations, a filmstrip is probably the best choice. If movement and emotional reaction are important, a motion picture may be indicated.

CHARTS

In the chapter on illustrations, the word "charts" was used to describe drawings used to make figures more understandable. They were described as pie charts, bar charts, and graphs. In this chapter, the word "chart" means a large piece of paper or cardboard used to help a speaker explain something to an audience. The content of these charts may be diagrams, pictures, or words.

Slides vs. Video vs. Film vs. Print

	Slides single/multiple	Video	Film	Print
Cost	low/wide range	in-house productions can be "free" -- out of house wide range	expensive	wide range
Production Time	days/weeks	one day up to weeks	months	wide range
Projection Equipment	common/complicated	various formats	commonly available	none required
Revisability	easy/easy	usually inexpensive	difficult and costly	varies
Advantages	can be tailored to specifications/ can have big audience impact	immediacy, can stop, review, closely study	maximum emotional impact, easily presented to large audiences, all elements under maximum control	self-pacing, can be retained for reference, passed along, large information content
Disadvantages	little impact - no impressiveness of presentation/ cumbersome or expensive equipment package, need technicians to run program	often poor production values, "video look"	rigid, linear presentation can't communicate a lot of specific information	not a "captive" audience, not as much emotional impact
SUMMARY	inexpensive, easily "tailor made"/ most useful for special one-time events	immediacy, fast turn around, disposable information	most emotional impact, long-term, wide spread use, permanent information	most useful, required basic information

Sunset Films, 625 Market Street, San Francisco, California 94105, Phone: (415) 495-4555
Lane Publishing Co., Menlo Park, California 94025

Pros and cons. Various kinds of audiovisual materials have advantages and disadvantages. This chart summarizes the differences and can help you select the appropriate medium for your message. (*Source:* Sunset Films, San Francisco, CA.)

Advantages

Charts are the simplest, most economical of the visual aids. They can be made quickly and—if the budget is limited—they can be prepared by anyone who can do simple lettering with a felt-tipped pen.

Charts can be used to show key points in a talk or to display an outline of the talk. When the speaker shows the audience what is being discussed and tells them what they are seeing, the presentation is much more effective.

Preparation

Charts may take two basic forms:

1. Soft sheets of paper that are fastened together across the top and turned over the back of an easel one by one.
2. Stiff cards that are all placed on an easel and removed as they are used, one by one.

Every chart must be readable by everyone in the audience, so the size of the audience determines the size of the chart. For a group around a conference table, a small chart may be adequate. For a big meeting, it may be necessary to go to the largest practical size. It is a good idea to pretest readability.

Most charts are done in black ink on a white background, although a yellow background gives the highest possible visibility. Other colors can be used, but they should provide good contrast. Never use a dark color for a background.

For a small meeting around a conference table, the letters should be at least an inch in height. If the distance from the chart to the most distant member of the audience is 25 or 30 feet, you should use letters at least 3 inches high. For a larger audience, it will be necessary to test letter size for legibility from the rearmost seat. Remember that not all people have 20/20 vision. Too big is never a problem, but too small *is*.

Use Roman capitals—they are easier to read than uppercase and lowercase. Never use script or italic lettering. The individual letters must be strong. For a 3-inch letter, the components should be not less than $\frac{3}{8}$ inch thick. Keep the letters *bold*.

Any charts should be reduced to the barest essentials, but the lines or bars must be heavy enough that they can be seen from the most distant seat. Photographs or drawings must be sharp and have lots of contrast.

In preparing a chart presentation, the first step is to print all charts by hand on ordinary $8\frac{1}{2}$- by 11-inch paper. If the finished charts are to be vertical, the layout should be vertical. (Charts made up of soft sheets should be vertical.) If they are to be horizontal, the layouts should also be horizontal. The size of the finished charts may be as small as 11 by 17 inches or as large as 34 by 44, depending on audience size. Other possible sizes are 17 by 22 and 22 by 34. All these sizes are proportional to the $8\frac{1}{2}$- by 11-inch layout, so if your layout looks good on the small sheet, it will work on a large one. Each chart should be a complete unit.

When the layouts are complete and the proper sizes have been determined, the finished charts can be made. If a commercial artist is to make them, he or she should be asked for suggestions that may improve impact or readability. Discussion of the purpose to be served and estimation of the costs involved will yield a better set of charts at a more reasonable price.

Presentation

Soft sheets must be fastened securely to a stiff board backing in such a way that the sheets can be turned over easily and will stay in position. When too many sheets are used, the roll at the top may get so thick that previously used sheets keep slipping back into view. It is also essential that the back of the easel be low enough to permit the sheets to hang properly behind it after their use.

With cards, you may use a double-faced easel that lets you stack the used cards on the back. If such an easel is not available, the used cards can be stacked on a nearby table. Because the cards are not fastened together, they may become disarranged. To avoid this, each must be numbered. Then, if the easel collapses or someone inadvertently drops the cards, they can easily be put back in order. With either sheets or cards, the easel must be big and stable enough to hold the charts securely.

A pointer is very helpful in chart presentations. The easel should be placed to the right of the speaker if he or she is right-handed or on the left if he or she is left-handed. This permits the speaker to use the pointer without turning his or her back to the audience. The listeners' attention will be held better if the speaker can always look at them—except for a brief glance at the chart now and then in order to place the pointer.

Two presentation techniques will help to make charts more effective. The first involves using plain cards to cover parts of a large card, so as to focus attention on the part that is exposed. When that part has been discussed, the blank card can be removed, revealing the remainder of the chart. This keeps the audience from getting ahead of the speaker.

A second technique is to use overlays. Either transparent or opaque sheets can be hinged to the base chart and swung into position when needed. This allows the speaker to build up a chart as it is discussed with the audience.

Any presentation, whether with charts or other aids, will be smoother if the presenter has help. If he or she has to do everything—moving charts, changing slides, operating equipment, or doing anything not directly connected to the presentation—the audience may become confused and the speaker distracted.

THE OVERHEAD PROJECTOR

This device uses typewritten material or charts which are reproduced on transparent sheets; these are then placed on a ground-glass plate. Light passes through both this and the sheet, is reflected by a mirror, and is then projected through lenses onto a large screen. The transparencies are usually 8 ½ by 11 inches in size, but the projected image can be as large as the screen permits.

Advantages

The advantages of the overhead projector are as follows:

1. Low cost—the equipment and materials are relatively inexpensive.
2. Portability—the projector is small and light in weight.
3. Ease of production—the materials can be produced without professional help.
4. The equipment can be used in a semidark room.
5. Any size of audience can be served by moving the projector closer to

This is an untouched reproduction of a plot created with HP's Drawing
Gallery software and an HP 7550A plotter.

Headline service. A few words and simple graphics are effective for a slide or overhead transparency. This one was quickly formatted by using a computer software graphics package. (*Source:* Hewlett-Packard Company, Palo Alto, CA.)

or further away from the screen, thus reducing or enlarging the size of the image.

Production

Acetate (or plastic) transparencies are easy to produce. If you have typewritten or lettered sheets, you simply load them into a photocopier stocked with acetates and run off the transparencies. Photocopy shops can also give you a variety of colors—blue, green, or yellow—so that your black-lettered transparency will have a more interesting background.

Don't make your charts too detailed. Many people use long tables of figures or complicated diagrams. Remember that what you are showing is a chart—not a piece of paper that will be held at normal reading distance.

Presentation

Generally, the speaker using an overhead projector stands by the projector, facing the audience. The transparencies are placed on the ground glass as needed. There are four techniques that will add to the effectiveness of such a presentation:

1. Use of a pointer to draw attention to some item on the chart.
2. Use of a felt-tipped pen to underline or circle key points or to add a word or two for emphasis. Be sure to pretest the pen to make sure that it will write on the acetate sheet. Some inks are oil-based and merely bubble up on the sheet. If you use a pen with water-soluble ink, it will work satisfactorily—and the marks can be removed after the presentation by running water over the sheet.
3. Use of a blank sheet to conceal a part of the chart. This enables you to uncover points as you discuss them and keeps the audience from reading the entire list while you are still talking about the first item.
4. Use of overlays by (a) placing a colored strip on your chart to emphasize major points or (b) implementing a "building-block" approach to expand a basic diagram. Thus you can add fenders, doors, and bumpers to the skeleton of a car, or you can start with the president of the company and, with successive overlays, build an entire organization chart. These overlays are usually fastened to the transparency with hinges made of masking tape.

SLIDES

Slides are especially adapted to reporting or explaining something. A charitable organization might show how its activities affect its beneficiaries. A manufacturer might show how a product should be used. A director of training could use slides to show new employees how to do their jobs.

Usually a slide presentation is planned and used for a one-time showing to one audience. The slides are always described and explained, either by the speaker or by using an audio cassette or record. The purpose of the slides is to clarify and amplify a voiced message.

Advantages

Slides have several advantageous characteristics. Portability is one—since a single person can carry the reel, projector, and screen. Thus a slide presentation makes a much more usable package than a stack of large charts and an easel.

Flexibility is another advantage. Slides can be arranged and rearranged. It is possible to use a few or many. Slides can be used in one presentation and then reused in another. Slides can be omitted or additional slides inserted. A slide can be held on screen as long as necessary and, conversely, it is possible to show a number of slides in rapid succession. It is also feasible to go backward and reshow one or more slides or an entire sequence.

Slides can show words, photographs, charts or diagrams, or any combination of visual materials. Remember however, that slides are aids. They can't tell the story alone. They are used to illustrate and explain what someone is saying. As a general rule, a slide presentation should not be shipped off to a stranger. The person who makes the presentation should accompany the slides, should have seen all the slides, and should have rehearsed the presentation thoroughly.

Production

The first step in producing a slide presentation is planning. It is possible that slides will be available before a presentation is planned, and it is often possible to use slides in more than one presentation. Regardless of the availability of slides, their use must be based on the purpose to be accomplished.

Every important point in the message should be illustrated. This requires that the speech be written before the slides are prepared or selected from an already existing stock. When the speech or talk is complete, it is time to review the points to be illustrated and determined how to do this. In planning a slide presentation, you should remember these points:

1. Limit the number of words on any slide—ten should be the maximum.
2. Avoid empty space on a slide—use closeups rather than long shots.
3. Avoid monotony—intersperse pictures with charts or words.
4. Don't be repetitious—each slide should show something different.
5. Coordinate the script with the slides—the same words should be in both.
6. Don't get "arty"—your purpose is to convey ideas, not to be clever.
7. Get human interest into your slides—show people doing something.

The length of a slide presentation depends on the purpose to be served. It is possible to make a good presentation with only a few slides—provided that

Five Slide Mistakes to Avoid

1. *The unrehearsed slide show.* Don't wait until you're up there at the podium to find the kinks in your slide presentation. Go through the entire presentation—with your slides—beforehand. Rehearse every move you're going to make. You don't want any surprises.

2. *Relying on a slide operator.* Always check your slides yourself. Be sure you have given consideration to the projection format. Rear-screen projection requires that the slides be trayed differently from front-screen projection.

3. *The slide surprise.* A slide upside down or backwards does very little to help you look professional. Always check your slides yourself to make sure they're correctly positioned.

4. *The awkward anecdote.* Keep your remarks concise and reflective of key points. Avoid unrelated remarks so as to keep your presentation moving along. If you feel that a particular part of your presentation will stimulate unrelated remarks, put in a blank slide so that the screen goes black.

5. *Treating your slide like a script.* Don't read your slides verbatim off the screen. Try to use the same terminology, but speak in complete sentences and in a conversational tone.

Source: Genigraphics Corporation, Liverpool, NY.

the story can be told briefly. Conversely, a presentation can use a hundred slides if they are pertinent. One example was a presentaion on the potential market for American food products in Japan. The presentation showed scores of scenes in food stores. The presentation was not too long because no one in the audience had ever been in Japan and all were unfamiliar with the marketing procedures there.

Authorities differ radically on the rate of projection. Some say it should be about four slides per minute; others say it should be ten or twelve. Your guide should be to use enough time for each slide to permit the audience to see and understand it.

Some slides may stay on the screen for ten or twenty seconds; others, especially in a related sequence, may be shown only briefly. The pictures of the Japanese food stores were shown at the rate of about ten per minute.

In preparing or selecting slides for use in a presentation, it is necessary to make sure that they are all visually clear and uniform. All slides should be 35 mm, and all should be horizontal. They should be in color. If charts or diagrams are to be used, it is desirable to have the basic charts or diagrams prepared on colored board. Black and white can be used, but the slides will be more attractive if the background is colored. If the slides are likely to be reused, they should be placed in metal frames. This protects the slides and ensures better feeding through the projector.

Photographs taken by amateurs can be used for slides, but if the presentation is important, a professional photographer should be engaged. This is especially true if charts or diagrams are to be used.

Projection

For projecting, the slides must be in a tray or reel that fits the projector. With some machines, the reel is vertical, while other projectors use a horizontal reel. The slides are loaded differently in each of the two types. Essentially, all slides are upside down when projected. If you are not familiar with the projector you plan to use, test the first slide for correct placement by actually projecting it. Once you are sure of the right placement, the other slides can be placed into the reel in the same position. Most slide processors suggest that the shiny side of the slide be toward the light bulb. When all slides are loaded, the entire reel or tray should be projected to be sure that all slides are properly placed.

If the slide presentation must be used in the field without the help of a qualified spokesperson, it is often best to place the narration on an audiocassette. By using a sound/slide synchronizer (available for rental through camera stores), you can insert electronic signals into the tape so that it automatically trips the projector to the appropriate picture.

A dissolve unit is another piece of equipment that can make the slide presentation look more professional. Instead of the normal split-second change from one slide to the next, this device makes the slide dissolve off the screen while another takes its place. At this stage, you are getting very close to multiple projection, which will be discussed shortly.

Another device that can improve a slide presentation is the electric pointer, which projects a luminous arrow onto the screen. This enables the presenter to indicate items of importance. Such equipment can be rented from the same sources as those providing other audiovisual rental equipment.

Before the presentation, the projector should be placed in the correct position in relation to the screen. The focus should be checked and a spare bulb should be at hand. The projector's power lines should be secured so they will not become unplugged. In some cases, the speaker will operate the projector. If someone else does this, cues for changing the slides must be established. "Next slide please" is distracting, so try to device some signal, such as the use of a "cricket" or a low-pitched electric signal. Even better is a system whereby the projector operator has the full script of the speech, with notes as to when to change the slide. With careful rehearsal, this can result in a very smooth presentation, free from any distracting sounds.

Multiple Projection

By using a number of slide projectors, it is possible to to make a multiple-screen presentation. The results can be anything from a fiasco to a spectacular and moving display. The best results will depend on careful planning, accurate projection, and tight control. Presentations of this sort may use anywhere from two or three projectors to as many as eight or ten. Generally, there is one sound track, which must be synchronized with the projectors.

Productions of this sort are relatively costly; they require several projector operators and a room large enough to accommodate the necessary screens. Obviously such a presentation would be mounted only for a sizable audience. Because the objectives of such productions vary so widely, there are few guidelines.

In general, the objective is to present an idea in so spectacular a manner that the audience will be moved more strongly than than they could be with a simple one-projector presentation. If there does seem to be a justification for a multiscreen presentation, the planning can start. At the same time there must be a continuing estimation of the costs and personnel needed to do the job. Another essential is repeated rehearsals. Difficulties multiply in a geometric ratio. Five projectors are not five times as hard to coordinate as one. They may be twenty-five times as hard to synchronize.

FILMSTRIPS

These aids are sometimes called slide films or strip films, but all are the same—strips of 35 mm motion picture film that contain a series of still pictures. In one sense they can be considered slide presentations on strips of film.

Filmstrips are particularly useful when it is necessary to distribute a presentation to a large number of audiences. They are extensively used by commercial organizations such as food manufacturers and other suppliers of consumer goods. Many of these strips are used to provide instruction in a wide variety of skills.

Advantages

While a slide presentation can be cumbersome and is subject to possible disarrangement, a filmstrip avoids these drawbacks. It is small, easy to mail, inexpensive, and easy for anyone to present. Usually a filmstrip is accompanied by a script that is meant to be read by the presenter; otherwise there may be a record or cassette that tells the story. If a script is used, it carries cues for changing frames. If a record or a tape is used, there is normally a sound signal, such as a faint chime, to tell the projector operator when to change frames. (Some projectors operate automatically, advancing the frames on a pulse from the tape.)

Production

Because filmstrips are normally produced in quantities that may run into the hundreds or thousands, they should be produced by professionals. Before consulting a professional producer, you should have a clear idea of the purpose to be served by the filmstrip.

Usually a filmstrip is used to show, step by step, how to do something. This requires a thorough understanding of the entire process that is to be explained. As you study the process, it will become evident that there are certain key steps, each of which must be shown in the proper sequence. In some cases there will be only a few steps, while in others there may be a considerable number. There is no general guide as to the number of steps to be shown. It depends entirely upon the points to be explained.

Once you have a definite idea of the steps that are to be shown, your next move is to prepare a list of the pictures to be taken and to write the explanation that is to accompany each picture. In form, this is much like a motion-picture script. When it is finished, you will have to consult with the photographer who will take the pictures, asking him or her to submit a cost estimate.

Once the photographer has been selected, the next step is to schedule a time and place for the shooting and to arrange for such technical help as may be needed.

With a finished script and a complete set of photographs plus the needed titles and captions in hand, the next procedure is to arrange with a film production organization (often a motion-picture producer) to make as many strips as are needed. Usually these firms work from the negatives of the pictures selected, making a master negative of each and using this to prepare the required positive prints.

Some users of filmstrips may handle the entire production; others may use an outside producer to do everything. Regardless of the method selected, the steps in the process of production are the same.

Projection

Filmstrips are shown with a projector that is different from the type used to show slides. Both operate on the same principles, but the filmstrip projector must be fed through a special device that moves the film through the machine one frame at a time. Generally, it is operated by a lever or button that the operator activates on cue. Some have a remote control that can be used from some distance away.

As with a slide presentation, the screen must be set up and the projector placed at an appropriate distance. Focusing the image and testing the filmstrip before the actual presentation is a must. A spare bulb must be available and the wires must be secured.

MOTION PICTURES

Motion pictures are the most effective—and most expensive—kind of audiovisual aid. Production of a motion picture should therefore be approached with caution. It is possible to produce one for $100,000, but it is also easy to spend

$1,000,000. Obviously, then, no one should casually decide to produce a movie without thinking about the life of the film and the audience potential. If a motion picture costs $100,000 and is seen by 1,000,000 people, the cost is only 10 cents per viewer; but if the picture is seen by only 100,000 people, the cost per viewer rises to is $1. Analogously, for an audience of 10,000, the cost would be $10 per head. Be sure that you will have a large enough audience before you start production.

Advantages

Motion pictures have great emotional impact, attracting audiences that would not be drawn to a filmstrip or slide presentation. Because it combines movement, color, sound, and the persuasive power of the human voice, a motion picture can be a powerful channel of communication.

Audience demand for motion pictures is strong. Modern Talking Picture Service reports that they never have enough film subjects to fill the potential demand. For example, a movie called *Refinery*, produced for Chevron USA and starring McLean Stevenson as narrator, was getting 300 showings a month at the time this was written. If your budget is big enough, you should seriously consider the use of motion pictures in your program.

Film Versus Videotape

The usage of videotape is growing rapidly. There is still some production of films, but their eventual disappearance is predicted by many experts in the field. With videotape, it is possible to produce a motion picture in far less time than with film. Instant playbacks allow the director to see a "take" immediately after it is shot. Corrections can be made at once, and editing can be done without the long delays required to develop film. The ability to erase unwanted material is another advantage. A bad shot can be eliminated by pushing a button. Thus the tape is cleared of the unwanted scene and a new one can be inserted.

With film, the negative must be developed and positive prints must be made. These are then viewed on a Movieola or projected on a screen and evaluated. Then there is the laborious process of editing the positive, cutting and splicing the negative, and making new positives. The process is tedious and costly in contrast to the speed and simplicity of tape. The picture quality of tape is questioned by some producers, but tape is being continually improved, so the trend is likely to continue.

When it comes to prints for distribution, the videocassette has almost entirely displaced the reel film. One producer reports having produced one reel of film and 300 videocassettes of one subject.

Production

Any motion picture produced for public relations should be in color. Most of these films use "off-screen narration." This means that the sound track carries the voice of an announcer who tells the viewers what is going on. If "live" sound is used, with actors doing the talking, the cost becomes vastly greater.

Animation is attractive and sometimes may be essential, but it is very expensive. In some cases, "stop-motion" photography will serve. In this procedure, the motion picture camera is set to take one or two frames at a time. The subject matter is moved slightly for each exposure, and the resulting film, projected at normal speed, creates the illusion that the things shown on the screen are moving by themselves. (The California raisins are an example.)

Motion pictures can be used for several years. In fact, many users plan for five years of use before replacement. If a film is keyed to a current situation, it may be obsolete in a short time; this should be considered in planning. If the cost of the film must be charged into one year, that should be known at the outset.

Assuming that a film is approved for production, the first step is to write a script that describes every scene and every word or sound that is to be in the finished film. This job should be done by an expert, and since most scriptwriters are employed by motion picture producers, you will face a dilemma. That is, you may be obliged to use a writer who is already on the staff of a production firm.

It is not possible to obtain bids on a film without a complete script; but if a production firm submits a script that is then approved, such approval carries an obligation to let this same firm produce the film. This rules out competitive bidding.

One way to get around this problem is to write a very detailed treatment of the proposed film, specifying length, kind of narration, location for filming, special effects, the kind of scenes to be shown, (whether interior or exterior), and possibly a rough outline for the script. With this information, it is possible to consult with several producers and negotiate for bids.

An alternative to this is to use an independent scriptwriter. There are a few who are not associated with production firms, and if one of these is used, the procedure is to secure a finished script and then ask for bids.

In either case, consultation with producers should yield suggestions that will improve the film or reduce the costs. These people are experts and their advice can be invaluable.

An important prelude to negotiation with either an independent scriptwriter or a production firm is to consult with others who have used their services and to see some of their finished works. Satisfied customers and high-quality films are the best possible guarantee that your film, too, will be good.

The lowest price is not necessarily the best one. Selection of the producer must also consider quality. Another intangible but important factor is understanding. If you don't understand the producer, or if he or she doesn't understand you, there is little chance that you will make a good film together. Rapport is hard to measure, but a detailed discussion of the project will soon show whether the two parties are really reading each other's minds. If so—go ahead. If there is not complete understanding, it is time to call a halt.

Having finalized a script and signed a contract with a producer, your re-

IMPROVED COAL-FIRED POWER PLANT VIDEOTAPE

FOURTH DRAFT SCRIPT

DATE: 1/19/88

_____

1) COAL shots: coal piles at power plants, on conveyors, etc. Then scenes of large coal-fired power plants.

        NARRATOR (V/O):

                Coal: the most abundant fossil fuel. For generations, it has played a major role in the production of electric power.

                In the past, large coal-fired units have supplied base-load power, supplemented by other plants more suited to cycling with the daily peaks and valleys of demand. Today, though, coal's role is changing.

2) Research Scenes

        NARRATOR (V/O):

                Now, technologies are becoming available that will make coal-fired power plants flexible enough to change load quickly, economically, reliably.

                These innovations are coming from utilties, researchers and manufacturers around the world. They have arisen in response to local challenges, policies and economics. For, while the laws of thermodynamics are universal, local factors heavily influence power plant design.

                Yet there is much each utility can learn from how others have solved their problems.

                For America's electric utilities, improving the design of coal-fired power plants is becoming an urgent priority.

3) Kurt Yeager at conference Superimpose name and title

        KURT YEAGER (12:11:24:00) (SYNC):

                "There is going to be, in the mid 1990's, a sudden re-cognition that capacity is going to be needed in this country.

        NARRATOR (V/O):

                New advances in coal plant technology will help util-ities -- in the United States and elsewhere -- meet the need for new production capacity.

The script is the beginning. Scripts for videotapes and films can be written like this, with narration following the description of the visual element. (_Source:_ Electric Power Research Institute, Palo Alto, CA) sponsibility now becomes that of production expediter. If the film is to be shot at your place of business, you must arrange for the film crew's access. If organization people are to be filmed, they must be informed and told what is expected of them. Releases should be checked and new ones signed if they are not already on file.

If anyone or anything from your organization is needed for a location shot at a place away from your place of business, you must arrange for them to be at the right place at the right time. A general guide for this is to ask the producer what he or she wants—and to provide it.

The Many Uses of Videotape

Increasingly organizations are finding videotape to be a highly useful medium for a variety of tasks. Here are some examples:

• Emhart Corporation prepares a videotape summarizing its annual stockholder meeting and makes it available to any stockholder who requests it. It is also sent to financial analysts.

• Hewlett-Packard produces a videotaped corporate magazine that employees may watch in the cafeteria or take home in cassette form for family viewing.

• Genentech of San Francisco, a genetic engineering firm, showed a 26-minute video about itself to potential investors as part of a financing program.

• Louisiana State University raised money for its athletic program with a video, sold commercially, in which a quartet (consisting of the governor and former governor of Louisiana as well as two LSU coaches) sang four LSU songs about football and basketball.

• Fashion designers send videos of their creations, often in a fantasy setting, to cable TV stations, talk shows, and marketing outlets. They are also sent to nightclubs, which use them as backdrops.

• A Massachusetts congressional candidate distributed a 15-minute videotape of himself for campaign workers to show in voters' homes.

• Many corporations utilize videotapes at orientation meetings for new employees or to upgrade the job skills of current employees.

Projection

Videotape is usually shown on monitors, although large-screen projection equipment is becoming more widely available. The ease with which a videotape can be shown is undoubtedly one of the factors in this rapid increase in usage. It is much easier to slip a VCR casette into a slot and push a button than to go through the laborious process of threading film into a projector, putting up a screen, focusing the lens, and so on. If you do have to project film, you should get acquainted with the projector you will use.

You must be sure that the film is properly threaded. Always run off a few feet of film before it is shown to an audience. Then back up the film to the starting point. Be sure that you have the projector set to run forward after this test. It is embarassing to press the start button and have the film back out of the projector and leave a glaring, empty screen.

When the showing is ended, be sure to rewind the film onto the original reel. Never leave it on the take-up reel. The next user will thank you for leaving the film in condition for immediate use.

Instructors' Guides

While motion pictures always have sound tracks and filmstrips have scripts or records that tie in to the visual material, there is something else that can greatly increase the effectiveness of these audiovisual aids: namely, a guide for the instructor.

Such a guide tells how to use the material, what it means, what to note especially, points to emphasize, the significance of what is on the screen, and so on. The guide may also suggest class assignments, additional reading, preparation of the group for the showing, questions to be asked after the showing, and many other suggestions designed to help the instructor.

These materials should always be planned with a specific objective in view. The planner presumably knows more about the subject than the user and therefore should be able to prepare a guide that will help the user achieve the intended aim. Modern Talking Picture Service enthusiastically recommends the preparation and distribution of these guides.

DISTRIBUTION

Filmstrips and motion pictures are produced primarily for distribution to outside organizations. This can be done by the sponsor or by a commercial distributor.

Sponsor Distribution

This procedure is usable by a small organization that may have only a few films to distribute and a limited number of potential users. The operation is handled by whoever is available, and ordinarily the procedures are informal.

Some large organizations that produce and distribute a considerable number of films have a special department comprising facilities and personnel for receiving orders, repairing, reconditioning, and shipping. This requires record keeping, plus equipment and storage space.

Commercial Distribution

There are a number of firms that will handle the entire activity. (The largest is Modern Talking Picture Service.) All the sponsor has to do is supply the necessary number of films and establish the audiences to be reached. The distributor sends out the films and recovers them from the users. Repairs and reconditioning are done as needed. These distributors can be found through film producers or from their advertisements in the visual aids trade magazines. They can also be located in the classified section of the telephone directory. The listing is "Motion Picture Film Distributors."

PROMOTING USE

An unused film is a wasted film. If potential users know about the availability of films, they may order them. There are several ways to inform people that these materials can be obtained. Among the most frequently used channels are direct mail, catalogs, advertising, and film distributors.

In using any of these channels, it is important to make the ordering as easy as possible. An order form that states the items wanted, the dates involved, and the name and address of the user should be provided.

Direct Mail

Booklets or leaflets listing and describing the available materials can be mailed to prospective users. The mailing list can include instructors, specialists in audiovisual education, program chairpersons, and any individuals associated with groups that might want to see the films. The mailing list should be kept up to date.

Film Catalogs

Several organizations publish and distribute catalogs of available materials. Among them are the U.S. government, Modern Talking Picture Service, and Educators Progress Service.

Advertising

Advertisements describing filmstrips and films can be published in the visual-aids trade journals (*Audio Visual Communications* and *Business Screen*). Ads can also be inserted in the trade journals of those industries or occupations most likely to be interested.

Distributors

Most of the firms that distribute films will also promote use. Their income comes from use, and the more use they promote, the more money they make.

Theater and Television

There is some opportunity for the use of sponsor-produced motion pictures in theaters and on television. The first are reached through the film distribution houses, which handle the output of the studios. The commercial film distributors previously mentioned will handle circulation to television stations. Both of these outlets will tolerate little if any identification of the sponsor.

SUMMARY

1. Each audiovisual aid has its advantages and disadvantages. Each is best for certain uses. You must know the audience and the purpose to be served in order to decide which aid to use.
2. Charts are simplest and cheapest. They are best suited to a small audience. They must be highly visible and must tie into the speech that is to be illustrated.
3. The overhead projector is especially useful when large amounts of data and great detail must be presented. But don't make the transparencies too detailed.
4. Slides are portable, flexible, and particularly useful in explaining and reporting. Slides should be simple and colorful. A written script or sound cassette should accompany a slide presentation.
5. Filmstrips are best adapted to distributing a presentation to multiple audiences. In effect, they are slide presentations on film. They should always be accompanied by a record or tape explaining and amplifying the visual.
6. Motion pictures are highly effective—and quite costly. Videotape is rapidly displacing the older type film in both production and later projection.
7. An instructor's guide is a desirable adjunct to any filmstrip or motion picture. The guide elaborates on the aid and can greatly increase its impact.
8. Distribution can be handled by the organization or by an independent distributor, who can handle all details of the work.
9. Promoting use is important. Many people who might use the strip or tape can be found through film catalogs, through distributors, and through advertising.

EXERCISES

1. Select a topic on which you would like to give a ten-minute talk to the class. Prepare three 8½-by 11-inch roughs for 17- by 22-inch charts to use with the talk.
2. The local YMCA needs a simple slide presentation to introduce parents to its summer camp. The camp, offering one-week stays, exposes grade school girls and boys to a variety of outdoor activities. You are commissioned to script the slide presentation,

which will last about five to seven minutes. The script should include brief descriptions of the slides to be coordinated with the script.

SUGGESTED READINGS

Alsop, Ronald. "Selling by Satellite: Stage More Videoconferences." *Wall Street Journal*, Sept. 25, 1986, p. 37.

Berger, Warren. "What's New in Corporate Video." *New York Times*, Aug. 21, 1988, business section.

Curran, John. "How Computer Graphics Can Change Your Workstyle." *Public Relations Journal*, July 1985, pp. 35–36.

"Dead Men Don't Use Flip Charts." *Communication World*, August 1984, pp. 20–22.

Degan, Clara, *Understanding and Using Video—A Guide for the Organizational Communicator.* New York: Longman Publishers, 1985.

Gordon, Gloria. "Desktop Video: New Toy or Effective Communication Tool?" *Communication World*, March 1988, pp. 20–21.

Horne, Grant N. "Making Video a Full Partner in PR." *Public Relations Quarterly*, Summer 1986, pp. 23–26.

Johnson, Marti. "Thanks for the Memory." *Communication World*, July/August, 1988, pp. 44–45.

Kieckhafer, S. "Successful Slide Presentations." *Public Relations Journal*, September 1983, pp. 17–18.

Laibe, Constance. "What's New in Industrial Films." *New York Times*, July 20, 1986, p. 19F.

Lefferts, Robert. *Elements of Graphics: How to Prepare Charts/Graphics for Effective Reports.* New York: Harper & Row, 1981.

Lewis, Kevin J. "Safety Videos Pay Off at Chevron." *Communication World*, November 1986, pp. 33–35.

Mathis, Georgia. "Workshop: How to Plan a Satellite Videoconference." *Public Relations Journal*, February 1986, p. 33.

Miller, John. "Video Teleconferences on a Small Budget." *Communication World*, September 1985, pp. 26–27.

Neustadt, David. "Action! Camera! It's Time for a Video Meeting." *New York Times*, Nov. 10, 1985, p. 6F.

Pollack, Andrew. "The High-Tech Blackboards." *New York Times*, Oct. 24, 1985, p. 30.

Stecki, Ed, and Corrado Frank. "Workshop: How to make a Video, Part I." *Public Relations Journal*, February 1988, pp. 33–34.

Stecki, Ed, and Corrado Frank. "Workshop: How to Make a Video, Part II." *Public Relations Journal*, March 1988, pp. 35–36.

Sutherland, Don. "Designing Audiovisuals? Just Think Backward." *Communication World*, January 1985, pp. 33–34.

Sutherland, Don. "Dueling Concepts: AV Soul vs. Glitz." *Communication World*, January 1986, pp. 2–25.

Chapter
17

Events

*A*n event may be anything from a small meeting to a large convention, from a grand opening to a charity benefit. The variety is limitless and each event is different from every other. However, some general guidelines apply.

GENERAL PRINCIPLES

Every event must have a purpose. It must also be planned. It must be budgeted. It must be controlled. Someone must be responsible.

Planning

Every event must be planned to the last detail. If anything *can* go wrong, it probably *will*. To avoid this, you must check and double check everything.

Become the devil's advocate and go over the plan step by step and item by item. Rehearse everything that can be rehearsed. Start planning early. Set up a timetable for all preparations. Be sure everyone knows what he or she is to do. Involve the people in your organization. Publicize the event to all who should know about it. If it is an internal affair, use internal communication tools. If the general public is interested, use the mass media. For every step or item, ask what can fail and what you will do if failure occurs. Then arrange things so that they cannot go wrong or that they can be corrected immediately.

Budget

Events cost time and money. All too frequently, people make arrangements for some event without making a thorough analysis of the costs. To set up a budget, you must know what everything will cost and precisely what is to be included. Every budget should include some money for unexpected charges, but be careful in relying on this safety net. A casual approval of some extra item without knowing the price may send the budget far into the red and you into the doghouse.

Purpose

Every event must have a purpose. Something must be accomplished, and this must be clearly defined. If the goal is precisely known, it will later be possible to evaluate the results—to determine if the event was worth the time and money.

Control

Every event must be controlled. Someone must be the center of the operation. That person may not do all the work, but he or she must be familiar with the objective, the plan, and the budget. Often committees are involved, but a committee cannot manage an event. Frequently the chief executive officer has much to say about it, but he or she usually has other duties that take priority, so the actual management of the event is delegated, usually to the public relations director.

Responsibility

When you are in charge of an event, be sure to work out a clear understanding of your authority and responsibility. Don't accept responsibility for things you cannot control. Find out what decisions you can make and which questions must be referred to higher authority. With these lines established, go ahead and concentrate on making the event a success.

IF YOU WORRY ENOUGH BEFORE AN EVENT,
YOU WILL NOT HAVE TO WORRY AFTERWARD.

Welcome to 444 Market's Safari Party
P R O G R A M

SEVENTH FLOOR

Camp Buffet and Exotic Refreshments

Music by Tropical Nights

Enter our special drawing for a Banana Republic gift certificate. Deposit your business card in the pith helmet as you sign in.

NINTH FLOOR

Safari Bar

Visit our new Model Office with its central conference room, now available for use by building tenants.

View the design boards for 444 Market's "architectural enhancement program" now underway.

Pick up your own 444 Market "Executive Survival Kit."

THANK YOU FOR VISITING WITH US TODAY.

Owner: MLH Income Realty Partnerships IV & V
Building Management: PMS, Inc.
Exclusive Leasing Agent: The Rubicon Group
Tenant Architect: Brown/Matarazzi Associates
Advertising/Public Relations: Claire Harrison Associates, Inc.

"In a City of Great Office Buildings, One Stands Apart."

Events can have many objectives. This is the program for an event designed to promote rentals in a new office building. In this case, getting prospective tenants was more important than getting news coverage. (*Source:* Claire Harrison Associates, Inc., San Francisco, CA.)

389

MEETINGS

Meetings may be small or large, but most of them, regardless of size, fall into two basic types: participation and listening. A participation meeting is one where those present discuss things. A listening meeting is one where the audience listens to one or more speakers. The differences are not rigid. A participation meeting may start with a talk and a listening meeting may include questions from the audience and general discussion of what a speaker has said.

Participation meetings are best suited to discussion and the solution of problems. Committee meetings are typical. Usually they are relatively small and informal. It is hard to visualize a meeting of a thousand people discussing and solving a problem, but twenty or thirty or even a handful can get results.

Listening meetings are appropriate for imparting information. The conduct of the meeting is formal. The speech or speeches constitute the main content of the program, and the audience is generally large. (Formal speeches to a group of twenty or thirty people are obviously ridiculous, but they are quite acceptable to an audience of a hundred or more.)

The Plan

The size and purpose of the meeting dictate the plan. Every plan must consider these questions: How many will attend? Who will attend? When and where will it be held? How long will it last? Who will speak? What topics will be covered? What facilities will be needed? Who will run it? What is its purpose? How do we get people to attend?

A small, informal meeting may require only the preparation of an agenda for the chair, selection of a meeting place, and notification of those who are expected. For a large and more formal meeting, the preparations must be extensive and detailed.

Timing

The meeting must be scheduled at a day and hour that is convenient for the people who are to attend. To find an appropriate day and hour, you must know the proposed audience, their schedules, and their commitments. Weekends, Monday mornings, Friday afternoons, holiday eves, and busy seasons should be avoided. Another factor is the availability of a meeting place. Advance reservations are imperative. The perfect site may not be available at the time selected, so a change in time or place may be necessary.

The length of the meeting is another factor. People who may be willing to attend a one-hour meeting might resist one that would last a half day or more. The subject and importance of the meeting will have a major effect on the potential audience's reaction. A long meeting can get good attendance if it offers a worthwhile program.

UPDATE - May 19, 1987

Opening Ceremony
WE THE PEOPLE - 200
Monday, May 25
2:00 - 3:00 P.M.
Independence Hall, Philadelphia

CONTACT: Marjorie Segal, (215) 351-0400

PROGRAM TIMELINE

Description:

   This event commemorates the 200th anniversary of the
convening of the Constitutional Convention. It is also the
official opening cermony for We the People - 200, a four month
celebration of the Constitution which will culminate on
September 17.

   Our goal is to touch people with words, music and pageantry
so that they can personally identify with the Constitution, and
the We the People celebration.

Location:

   The stage will be built on the north side of Independence
Hall. A statue of George Washington, in the center, will appear
to preside over the ceremony. The audience will be situated on
a block-long grass mall, bounded by Chestnut and Market, Fifth
and Sixth Streets. The stage is a modified T-shape with
official speakers seated in the center, in front of the
Washington Statue, and the delegates seated on the two side
"wings." (see diagram attached)

Participants:

   Vice President George Bush; Chief Justice Warren E. Burger;
Governor Robert P. Casey; Mayor W. Wilson Goode; We the People
Chairman, Willard G. Rouse, III; Independence National
Historical Park Superintendent, Hobart G. Cawood; Reverend
William Pindar; Iman Kenneth Nurid-Din; Brother Patrick Ellis;
Rabbi Patrice Heller; Opening Speaker, James Earl Jones; Guest
Soloist, Andrea McArdle; Delegates from the thirteen original
states (teachers, students, historians, business people); The
Old Guard Fife and Drum Corps; The First Troop City Calvary;
The Philadelphia Singers, conducted by Michael Korn; A 20-piece
orchestra; Edd Kalehoff - composer/conductor "We the People";
Napoleon Williams, Philadelphia High School Student introducing
Vice President Bush.

Events require meticulous planning. This is the first page of the plan for "We The
People," the celebration of the bicentennial of the U.S. Constitution. This page dealt
with generalities. Later pages gave specific details. (*Source:* Lewis, Gilman & Kynett,
Philadelphia, PA.)

OFFICIAL OPENING CEREMONY...WE THE PEOPLE 200

Monday, May 25, 1987 (2 to 3 p.m.)
Independence Mall
(Chestnut St. between 5th and 6th Sts.)

TIMELINE

2:00 p.m.   The bell in Independence Hall Tower rings 13 times.
Members of the Commander-in-Chief's Guard and the First
City Troop, Philadelphia City Cavalry take their posts on
the stage by the 13 flagpoles.

2:02 p.m.   A 200-piece all-star marching band, drawn from the high
school bands of 35 states, performs "God Bless America"
in front of the stage.

2:04 p.m.   Entrance of speakers, clergy and delegates from
Independence Hall, in procession to musical fanfare.

2:05 p.m.   Lt. General Robert Arter of the U. S. Army reads a
proclamation honoring the thousands of Americans who have
given their lives defending our Constitution. Arter then
introduces the Old Guard.

2:07 p.m. - The Old Guard Fife and Drum Corps of the U.S. Army,
dressed in authentic 18th century military garb, plays
fifes, drums, and bugles, in a traditional ceremonial
performance.

2:12 p.m. - A joint invocation is delivered by:
Reverend William Pindar, Old Pine Presbyterian Church
Rabbi Patrice Heller
Brother Patrick Ellis, S.S.C., Ph.D., of LaSalle
University
Iman Kenneth Nurid-Din of the Philadelphia Masjid

2:14 p.m. - Hobart G. Cawood, Superintendent of Independence National
Historical Park, welcomes the audience and introduces
James Earl Jones.

2:15 p.m.   James Earl Jones opens the program, and takes us back to
the historical setting in which the Constitution was
drafted, points to the changes which have occurred over
the past 200 years, and to the continuing importance of
the Constitution to present and future Americans.

Events require exact timing. This is the time schedule for the first quarter hour of "We
The People." Note the exact timing and the way in which one part of the event leads
to another. (*Source:* Lewis, Gilman & Kynett, Philadelphia, PA.)

Another thing to consider is possible conflicts. You must be sure that
your proposed time has not been preempted by some other person or organization. For internal meetings, you can check within the organization. For
external meetings, it may be necessary to check community calendars and
other organizations that might want to reach the same audience you have
selected.

Location

If the meeting is to be held on the premises of the organization, the room can be reserved by contacting the chief executive officer, office manager, or building superintendent, depending on who is responsible for such arrangements.

If the meeting is to be held at some outside location, you will have to talk to the person in charge. In a hotel or motel, that person is the catering manager. In a school, it may be the superintendent or custodian; in a church, it may be the minister or priest. Many business firms have rooms that are made available to nonprofit groups, so this possibility should be considered if your organization is eligible.

The meeting room must be the right size for the expected audience. If it is too large, the audience will feel that the meeting has failed to draw the expected attendance. If it is too small, the audience will be uncomfortable. Most hotels and motels have a number of meeting rooms ranging in size from small through medium to large or very large. If a meal is to be served, there may be no charge for the use of the the room.

Having selected a room, you must make sure that the audience can find it. The name of the meeting and the name of the room should be posted on the calendar of events. If directional arrows are needed, they should be posted in conspicuous spots.

In choosing a room, you must consider the nature of the meeting and the facilities that will be needed. Be sure that there is enough room for the speakers as well as any properties or equipment to be used.

Meeting Checklist

Every meeting requires its own specialized checklist, but here is a generalized "to do" list for a local dinner meeting of a service club or a professional association:

ADVANCE PLANNING

- What is the purpose of the meeting? Strictly social? Continuing education? Combination?

- What date and time is best for maximum attendance?

- What size audience do you realistically expect?

- Select restaurant facility at least four to six weeks in advance.

- Confirm in writing the following: date, time, menu, cocktails, seating plan, number of guaranteed reservations, and projected costs.

- Enlist speaker four to six weeks in advance. If speaker is in high demand, make arrangements several months in advance. Discuss nature of talk, projected length, and whether audiovisual aids will be used that require screens, projectors, etc.

- Publicize the meeting to the membership and other interested parties. This should be done a minimum of three weeks in advance. Provide complete information on speaker, date, time, location, meal costs, and how to make reservations.

- Phone committee should be organized to call membership 72 hours before the event if reservations are lagging. A reminder phone call often is helpful in gaining last-minute reservations.

THE MEETING DAY

- Get a final count on reservations, and make an educated guess as to how many might arrive at the door without a reservation.

- Check with speaker about travel plans and whether he or she has any last-minute questions, requirements.

- Give catering manager revised final count for meal service. In many instances, this might have to be done 24 to 72 hours in advance of the meeting day.

- Check room arrangements one to two hours in advance of the meeting. Have enough tables been set up? Are tables arranged correctly for the meeting? Does the microphone system work?

- Prepare a timetable for the evening's events. For example, cocktails may be scheduled from 6:15 to 7 P.M. with registration going on at the same time. Dinner from 7 to 8 P.M., followed by ten minutes of announcements. At 8:10 P.M., the speaker will have 20 minutes to talk followed by an additional 10 minutes for questions. Your organizational leadership, as well as the headwaiter, should be aware of this schedule.

- Set up a registration table just inside or outside the door. A typed list of reservations should be available as well as name tags, meal tickets, and a cash box for making change. Personnel at the registration table should be briefed and in place at least 30 minutes before the announced time.

- Decide on a seating plan for the head table, organize place names, and tell VIPs as they arrive where they will be sitting.

- Make sure three or four members of the organization are designated as a hospitality committee to meet and greet any newcomers and guests.

AFTER THE MEETING

- Settle accounts with the restaurant, or indicate where an itemized bill should be mailed.

- Check the room to make sure no one forgot briefcases, handbags, glasses, etc.

- Send thank-you notes to the speaker and any committee members who helped plan or host the meeting.

Seating

For a small group such as a committee, the best arrangement is to seat the participants around a table where everyone can see and be seen.

For a meeting where the audience may wish to take notes, where materials may be handed out, or where they may wish to ask questions, the seating should be of the "schoolroom" type. This uses long tables with chairs on one side, facing the speakers.

Large meetings primarily designed for listening are best served by "theater" seating. Here there are no tables and the row of seats are fairly close together, all facing the speakers. Sometimes such meetings are actually held in theaters, hence the name for this seating arrangement.

Occasionally large meetings are broken into discussion groups. Typically, the audience meets in one room, where the speaker states the problem. The audience then moves into another room, where tables seating eight or ten people are available. A discussion leader is designated for each table. After the problem is discussed, the leaders gather the opinions and the audience returns to the first room, where the table leaders report the conclusions of the participants.

Facilities

A small meeting may not need very much along this line, while a large and formal one may require a considerable number of things. Following are things that should be considered—and supplied if needed. You should check everything at least two hours before the meeting.

1. *Meeting identification.* Is it posted on the bulletin board near the building entrance? Are direction signs needed?
2. *Lighting.* Is it adequate? Can it be controlled? Where are the controls? Who will handle them?
3. *Blackboard.* Is it visible? Are chalk and erasers available?
4. *Charts.* Are they readable? Is the easel adequate? Who will handle the charts?
5. *Screen.* Is it visible to entire audience? If some seats are badly located, how do you prevent people from using them? Who will refer people to better locations?
6. *Projectors.* Are they hooked up? Focused? Is there a spare bulb? Are materials to be projected in the right order and properly loaded? Who will operate the projectors? What are the cues and signals?
7. *Monitors.* Are they in right position? Hooked up? Are VCRs available? Who will operate them? What are the signals and cues?
8. *Seating and tables.* Are they arranged properly?
9. *Tape recorder.* Is it loaded? Set for right speed? Hooked up? In right position? Who will run it?
10. *Telephone.* Where is it? If in meeting room, who will answer?

11. *Wiring.* For all electrical equipment, can wires be kicked loose or trip someone? What about switches?
12. *Speaker's position.* Is it on stage? On dais? Can it be seen? Is there a lectern? What about a reading light? Is there a PA system? Is it working? How many people will there be on the speakers' platform? Are there name signs for the speakers?
13. *Water and glasses.* For speakers? For audience?
14. *Audience and speaker helps.* Are there programs or agendas? Will there be notepaper, pencils, handout materials?
15. *Name cards.* For speakers?

Invitations

For internal groups, an announcement of the meeting—time, place purpose, and who is to attend—should be adequate. For external groups—people who are not required to attend but whose presence is desired—invitations are necessary. They should go out early enough for people to fit the meeting into their schedules—three or four weeks is a common lead time. The invitation should tell the time, date, place (including the name of the room), purpose, highlights of the program (including names of speakers), and anything else that makes the meeting sound worthwhile. A map showing the location and parking facilities is advisable. A return card for acceptance of the invitation is sometimes used if it is particularly important to have certain people attend. In such cases, it is necessary to check acceptances and possibly phone those who have not replied.

Meeting and Greeting

A representative of the sponsoring organization should be at the entrance of the room. If the number attending is not too large, a personal welcome is in order. Where hundreds of people are expected, this isn't possible; but the chairperson should greet the audience in his or her opening remarks.

Registration

If everyone knows everyone else, registration and identification are highly informal; but if the group is large, it is customary to have a registration desk (or table) at the entrance. Here the names of arrivals are checked against the invitation lists. If there is no invitation list and the presence or absence of any of the people who were invited is not important (as at a regular meeting of a club or association), the arrivals generally sign in on a plain sheet of paper and no one checks the membership roster.

Identification

Identification tags are desirable at almost any large meeting. Names should be printed in large block capitals with a felt-tipped pen. Longhand and typewritten name tags should never be used. They are hard to read and many people who wear reading glasses are annoyed at having to put them on just to read a name tag. The tags should be of the adhesive type—don't rely on straight pins or cards that slip into a man's breast pocket—few women have them.

Program

At any meeting, the word "program" has two meanings. It is what goes on at the meeting, and it is the typewritten or printed listing of what goes on. For large meetings, the program should be printed.

The meeting must have a purpose. To attain that purpose, it is necessary to have a chairperson who controls and directs the meeting, introduces the speakers, and keeps discussions from wandering. It is necessary to have speakers who will inform, persuade, or activate the listeners. If the meeting is a celebrative or commemorative occasion, the speakers must avoid the trite or boring.

The printed program that is handed out to the audience tells them what is going to happen, when, and where. It lists all the speakers, the time they will speak, coffee breaks, lunch breaks, and any other facts they should know about the meeting. Because speakers may have last-minute changes in their plans the programs should not be printed until the last possible moment.

Speakers

Speakers should be selected early—several months in advance if possible. They should be chosen because of their expertise, their crowd-drawing capacity, and their speaking ability. It is a good idea to listen to any prospective speaker before inviting him or her to speak. At the least this point should be checked with someone who has already been in the prospect's audience. Many prominent people are simply not effective speakers.

When a speaker has agreed to give a talk, it is essential to make sure that he or she gets to the meeting on time. Written confirmation of the commitment and the specifics of time and location is desirable. This should be followed up with a reminder a day or two before the meeting. Some public relations people go a step further and phone the speaker a few hours before the meeting, just to make sure.

If the speaker is coming from out of town, it is necessary to make hotel reservations, meet the speaker on arrival, and make sure that he or she does have the reserved room. At the meeting, the speaker must be met at the door and introduced to the chair, other speakers, and other important people.

For especially important speakers, you might consider a suite instead of a room. Flowers, fruit, and a stocked bar add to the cordiality of the occasion. Preregistration and a personal escort from the sleeping quarters to the dais are also appropriate.

CONVENTIONS

A convention is a series of meetings usually lasting for two or more days. The purpose is to gather and exchange information, meet others of similar interests, discuss and act on common problems, and enjoy recreation and social interchange.

Most conventions are held by associations and fraternal or social groups. Because the membership is widespread, a convention is nearly always "out of town" to many attendees, so convention arrangements must give consideration to this.

Planning

It is necessary to begin planning far in advance of the actual event. Planning for even the smallest convention should start months before the scheduled date; for large national conventions, it may begin several years ahead and require hundreds or thousands of person-hours. The principal things involved in planning a convention are timing, location, facilities, exhibits, program, recreation, attendance, and administration.

Timing

This must be convenient for those who are expected to attend. It should avoid peak work periods. Summer vacation is appropriate for educators, after harvest is suitable for farmers, preholiday periods are bad for retailers, midwinter is probably a poor time in the northern states, but it may be very good in the South. Here, as in every area dealing with the public, it is imperative to know the people who are to attend and to plan for their convenience.

Location

The location must be convenient. For a national convention, it can be anywhere in the country. A statewide convention should obviously be in that state, and a regional convention should be in the region. But these are not the only factors. You must think about transportation and distance. A national convention in Fairbanks, Alaska, is unlikely; yet one in Honolulu could be a great success, because the glamour of the location would outweigh the cost and time of travel. Many organizations rotate their conventions from one part of the state, region, or country to another in order to equalize travel burdens.

Another factor in choosing a location is the accommodations available. There must be enough rooms to house the attendees and enough meeting rooms of the right size. Timing enters into this, because many such accommodations are often booked months or even years in advance. Large cities usually have large convention facilities and numerous hotels, but early reservations are necessary. Even smaller towns are likely to require a long lead time for some accommodations.

When a tentative location is selected, you must find out if the convention can be handled at the time chosen. Early action on this can forestall later changes. Be sure to get a definite price on guest rooms as well as meeting rooms.

Small conventions are often held in resorts, but their accessibility is a factor. If the visitors have to change airlines several times or if the location is hard to get to by automobile, the glamour may fail to compensate for the inconvenience.

Your search for a good location can be expedited by referring to any of the trade magazines devoted to meetings. There are several that publish annual directories of meeting and convention locations, attractions, and facilities. Three good ones are:

Successful Meetings, published by Bill Communications
World Convention Dates, published by Hendrickson Publishing Co., Inc.
Meeting News, published by Gralla Publications

Facilities

For every meeting of the convention it is necessary to have a room of the right size and with the equipment needed for whatever is to go on in that room. The convention might start with a general meeting in a very large room where seating is theater fashion and the equipment consists of a public address system and a speakers' platform with the necessary accessories. After opening remarks, the convention might break into smaller groups that meet in different rooms with widely varied facilities.

One room may require a film projector, another may need a blackboard or an easel for charts, still another may have to have a tape recorder. In one room the seating may be around the conference tables; another may have schoolroom seating. To get everything right, you must know exactly what is to happen, who is going to participate, and when.

Exhibits

The people who make and sell supplies that are used by those attending the convention frequently want to show their wares. This calls upon the convention manager to provide space suitable for that purpose. Most large convention centers have display rooms that can accommodate anything from books to bulldozers. There is a charge for the use of these rooms, and the exhibitors pay for the space they use.

The exhibit hall may be in a hotel or in a separate building. In Chicago, for example, there is McCormick Place, an enormous building on the lakefront. It is an easy taxi trip from the Loop, where conventions usually have their headquarters and where the visitors sleep. Eating facilities ranging from hot-dog stands to elaborate dining rooms are to be found in almost any such building.

In some situations, the exhibit space is out of doors—in a parking lot, a vacant field, or a side track near convention headquarters. Here the manufacturers of farm machinery, trucks, and even railroad equipment may show their newest offerings.

Program

A convention program usually has a basic theme. Aside from transacting the necessary organizational business, most of the speeches and other sessions will be devoted to various aspects of the theme. Themes can range from "The Effects of Automation" to "New Developments in the Treatment of Cancer." The theme, of course, must fit the organization. A farm group might concentrate on "Insecticides," a business group might feature "Government Relations," and a teachers' group could devote a convention to "Discipline in the Classroom."

With a theme chosen, the developer of the program then looks for prominent speakers who have something significant to say on the subject. In addi-

Events need a theme. This the opening ceremony of "We The People"—a salute to the flag by principal participants, including representatives of the "Old Guard" of the 3rd U.S. Infantry—a unit that predates the Constitution. (*Source:* Lewis, Gilman & Kynett, Philadelphia, PA.)

tion, there may be a need for discussions, workshops, and other sessions focusing on particular aspects of the general theme.

The printed program for the convention is a schedule. It tells exactly when every session will be, what room it will be in, what the subject is, who will speak, and on what. Large conventions often schedule different sessions at the same time. The attendees then choose which session they prefer.

The program should be small enough to go in a man's pocket or in a woman's handbag. Large programs may look impressive, but they are nuisances that are cumbersome to carry and easy to misplace. Printing of the program should be delayed until the last possible moment. Last-minute changes and speaker defaults are common; therefore, to keep the program accurate, hold off the actual press run as long as possible. Type changes can be made with even a few hours of warning, but it is usually impossible to reprint the entire program.

Recreation

Recreation is a feature of practically all conventions. This may range from informal get-togethers to formal dances. Cocktail parties, golf tournaments, sightseeing tours, and even free time with nothing specifically scheduled are among the possibilities. Sometimes recreational events are planned to coincide with regular program sessions. These are patronized by spouses and by delegates who would rather relax than listen to some speaker.

Attendance

Getting people to attend a convention requires two things: an appealing program and a concerted effort to persuade the members to attend. Announcements and invitations should go out early enough to allow attendees to make their individual arrangements. (Several months should be allowed.) A follow-up just before the convention is in order. Reply cards should be provided, accompanied by hotel reservation forms. (Remember that hotels generally offer special lower rates for conventions.)

Administration

Running a convention is a strenuous job. The organization staff is likely to see very little of the program and a great many delegates with problems. Among the things which must be done are arranging for buses to convey delegates from the airport to the convention (if it is in a remote location) and to carry them on tours. Meeting speakers and getting them to the right place at the right time is another task.

People arriving at the convention headquarters must be met, registered, and provided with all the essentials (name tags, programs, and any other needed materials. A message center should be set up so people can be informed about phone calls or other messages. (This can be as simple as a blackboard near the registration desk.) Special arrangements should be made for the media. A small convention may interest only a few people from trade publications, but larger conventions may draw attention from the major media. In this case, a newsroom should be set up with telephones, typewriters, tables, and so forth.

EATING AND DRINKING

The "three-martini lunch" has been widely and probably justifiably criticized. Even if the cost is disregarded, the effects may be negative. On the other hand, events in which groups of people eat and drink together are valuable aids to communication.

Arrangements for these events must be made well in advance. The contact is the catering manager or, in some cases, the maitre d'hotel. All details must be in writing. The agreement must specify exactly what will be served and how much it will cost. This includes food, beverages, taxes, tips, corkage (if the customer provides beverages), and bartender charges if they are not included in the beverage charge. Sometimes the host pays for the beverages by the bottle. Sometimes beverages are bought by individuals and paid for as served. This is called a "no host" bar.

In planning an event of this sort, you should think about religious, dietary, or even regional restrictions and preferences. Some ethnic groups are highly sensitive to the least violation of their rules.

Generally any meal will require a guarantee. This means that you contract for a specific number of meals. If they are not eaten, you must pay for them anyway. If a few more are eaten, they are charged for at the per meal price of the guarantee. If many more guests than expected show up, they may have to eat whatever the kitchen can produce at the last minute. To avoid these situations it is imperative to demand and enforce reservations—even charging meals to people who say they are coming and then fail to arrive.

Guarantees can be adjusted up or down provided that this is done before the meal—and with enough time to allow the chef to increase or decrease the order without wasting food or coming up short. There is always a deadline for this, usually 24 to 72 hours. Be sure you know the deadline.

If any special or unusual food is to be served, it is incumbent on the host to make sure that the chef knows precisely how to cook and serve it. There are a large number of horror stories about what can happen when this simple precaution is overlooked.

Breakfasts

Breakfasts are frequently used to assemble people who cannot or will not attend a meeting later in the day. Usually some business is transacted. At conventions, the prime purpose is to get the delegates up in time to attend the morning sessions.

Because people will not arrive at a uniform time and because breakfast appetites are so varied, it is not practical to provide a uniform breakfast for all unless it is limited to juice, rolls, and coffee. Getting individual orders processed through a kitchen is slow and often unsatisfactory, so this should be avoided. Instead, the breakfast should be served as a buffet with a choice of fruits, juices, eggs, breakfast meats, rolls, and toast. This, plus self-service coffee urns and teapots, will satisfy any normal breakfast appetite and get the meal finished on time. Such a breakfast should be listed on the program with a time range—for example, "Breakfast, 7:30 to 8:30."

Luncheons

With rare exceptions, luncheons feature at least one speaker. The meal starts at a specific time and should end in the same way. A nonconvention luncheon should end early enough for people to get back to their offices and accomplish something during the afternoon. At a convention, there will probably be a scheduled session after the luncheon. At many luncheons, a cocktail period precedes. This should be short and should stop when the luncheon starts. A good schedule for a typical luncheon is cocktails, 11:30; luncheon, 12:00; adjournment, 1:30. In rare instances the adjournment can be as late as 2 P.M., but it should never be later than that.

If there are fewer than twenty people, they can be seated at one table; but if there are more, there should be several tables, each seating eight or ten. In this case there should be a head table where the chairman and speaker or speakers are seated. This should be visible from any point in the room. Frequently it is elevated on a platform and equipped with a lectern and public address system.

You'll need to have an accurate count of the number of people who will attend; there should not be a large number of empty seats. It is always possible to bring in another table and accompanying chairs. Strangely, this slight bit of disorder can make all present feel that the event has turned out to be better than the planners expected.

With a very small luncheon, it is possible to serve individual orders; but if there are more than about fifteen or twenty guests, a fixed menu is necessary. Most people who work in offices prefer a luncheon that is light, so keep this in mind when choosing the food—but also keep the prospective eaters in mind. There are some outdoor types who think that steak and french fries are just right.

Dinners and Banquets

A dinner is a fairly formal occasion, and a banquet is even more so. With either, there is generally a head table and one or more speakers. Guests are seated at small tables of eight to ten each, but there are exceptions when long tables are used. In many situations, tables are reserved for groups who have asked to sit together or where some person or organization has bought a number of tickets for employees, clients, or friends.

When tables are reserved, they must be marked with an easily visible sign showing a number or the name of the group to be seated at the table. Tables should be numbered in some logical sequence; if there are many, a chart at the entrance of the room should show the location of each.

Color-coding the tables can be a great help. At a banquet with 150 tables, the person in charge divided the tables into five groups of thirty. Each group of thirty tables was identified by differently colored balloons. The first group was red, the second blue, and so on. Thus the tables were easy to find even though 1500 guests had to be seated.

A dinner or banquet has a fixed menu. Sometimes it is feasible to offer a choice of two entrees, but this is strictly up to the catering manager. Rely on his or her judgment, because catering managers are experts in their field. And don't hesitate to ask questions.

Cocktail Parties

A cocktail party may precede a meal or be a complete event in itself. Before a luncheon, it should last half an hour. Before a dinner or banquet, it can go on for an hour or more. If there is no meal to follow and hors d'oeuvres or a buffet are offered, the party may last for several hours. If you do put on a cocktail party, you should monitor it closely. If some guests drink too much, there may be a problem with drunken driving or resulting lawsuits against the sponsoring organization.

In planning a cocktail party, there are several points to keep in mind. How many people will there be? What room will be used? Where will the bar be located? (It is better to have several small bars than one large one, which creates congestion). What beverages will be offered? More and more people are asking for wine—usually white. (Local preferences are important. In Wisconsin, you must provide brandy, because it is widely consumed in that state. However, it is seldom called for elsewhere.) Will food be served? (If so, what?) Will the hotel charge by the drink? By the bottle? What kinds of glasses will be used (real glass or plastic)? What about taxes, corkage, tips, service charges, room rental? Ask questions; be sure that you know exactly what you will get and what it will cost. Get it in writing.

Starting a cocktail party is easy—just open the bar at the announced time. Closing a party is not quite so easy. The only practical way is to close the bar. The invitation or program may indicate a definite time for closing, but don't rely on this. A vocal announcement will do the job. The smoothest way is to say "the bar will close in ten minutes." This gives the thirsty a chance to get one more drink if they want it. But close the bar when the time is up.

OPEN HOUSES AND PLANT TOURS

These events are conducted primarily to develop favorable public opinion about an organization. Generally they are planned to show the facilities where the organization does its work and, in plant tours, how the work is done. A hotel might hold an open house and show its registration activities, public rooms, guest rooms, meeting rooms, and kitchens. A factory might have a plant tour to show how it turns raw materials into finished products. A hospital open house could show its emergency facilities, diagnostic equipment, operating rooms, and patient rooms. A business firm's open house could be held at its offices and guests would be able to see the various departments and learn what is done in each.

Open houses are customarily one-day affairs. However, if very large numbers of people are to attend, the event may be extended to more than one day. Attendance is usually by invitation, but there are exceptions where the event is announced in the general media and anyone who chooses to may attend. In such cases, planning and control become almost impossible and the results are often unsatisfactory.

Plant tours may be one-day events, especially if a tour is in connection with a plant opening. There are, however, many plants that offer tours daily and regularly while the plant is in operation. These tours are most common among producers of consumer goods such as beer, wine, food products, clothing, and small appliances. These daily tours are geared to handle only a few people at any one time, while the other tours generally have a large number of guests and normal operations are not feasible.

Since the purpose of an open house or plant tour is to create favorable opinion about the organization, it must be carefully planned, thoroughly explained, and smoothly conducted. The visitors must understand what they are seeing. This requires careful routing, control to prevent congestion, signs, and guides. All employees who will be present should understand the purpose of the event and be thoroughly coached in their duties. Rehearsal plus much checking and rechecking is imperative.

Among the principal things to include in the plans for an open house or plant tour are:

1. *Day and hour.* This must be convenient for both the organization and the guests.
2. *Guests.* These may be families of employees, customers, representatives of the community, suppliers and competitors, reporters, or others whose goodwill is desirable.
3. *Invitations.* These should be sent out well in advance. A month is common.

If a plant tour is a continuing daily event, the availability of the tour should be announced by signs near the plant and possibly by advertising or publicity. For any open house or plant tour, think of these points:

Schedule of Queen Elizabeth's Visit to HP/Cupertino

Time of Day	Activity	Time
2:40–2:45	Arrive circular driveway Introduction of David Packard and Mayor of Cupertino Photo opportunity outside plant Party walks to DSD auditorium	5 min.
2:45–2:55	Briefing by general managers Doug Chance and Ed McCracken in DSD auditorium; introduction of David Baldwin, UK managing dir.	10 min.
2:55–2:59	Walk thru marketing/administration	4 min.
2:59–3:04	Stop at integrated circuit clean room: Paul Greene explains IC technology	5 min.
3:04–3:07	Walk to DSD printed circuit assembly area	3 min.
3:07–3:12	Franz Nawratil explains production and assembly Photo opportunity	5 min.
3:12–3:17	Walk past lead dip and automatic insertion room	5 min.
3:17–3:21	Walk past systems integration and test; Franz concludes	4 min.
3:21–3:24	Pass technical training rooms; Packard explains importance of training at HP	3 min.
3:24–3:28	Walk thru employee recreation area Photo opportunity	4 min.
3:28–3:31	Walk to demonstration room	3 min.
3:31–3:40	Demonstration of HP products; Packard concludes tour	9 min.
3:40	Depart circular driveway Photo opportunity	

Timing fit for a queen. The above timetable, courtesy of Hewlett Packard, shows the minute-by-minute breakdown for a tour of a manufacturing facility by Queen Elizabeth during a California visit. The exact time was important from the standpoint of (1) the Queen's schedule, (2) security by the Secret Service, (3) photo opportunities for journalists, and (4) briefing HP executives involved in the visit.

1. *Vehicles.* Parking must be available, and a map on the invitation showing how to get there and where to park is desirable.
2. *Reception.* A representative of the organization should meet and greet all arriving guests. If guests are important people, they should meet the top officials of the organization.
3. *Rest rooms and cloakrooms.* Should be provided and identified with large signs.

4. *Safety.* Hazards should be conspicuously marked and well lighted. Dangerous equipment should be barricaded. First aid must be at hand.

5. *Routing.* This should be well marked and logical (e.g., in a factory it should go from raw material through production steps to finished product). A route map should be given to each visitor if the routing is long or complicated.

6. *Guides.* Visitors must be led through the tour by guides who know the route and what the visitors are to see. Guides may lead groups of visitors or they may stay at specified positions and send each group on to the next guide when they have explained the operation at their position.

7. *Explanation.* Signs, charts, and diagrams may be necessary at any point to supplement the words of the guides. The guides must be coached to say exactly what the public should be told. Many experts can't explain what they do, so a prepared explanation is necessary.

8. *Housekeeping and attire.* The premises should be as clean as possible. The attire of those present should be clean and appropriate. A punch-press operator doesn't wear a necktie, but his overalls need not be greasy.

9. *Emergencies.* Accidents or illness may occur. All employees should know what to do and how to reach the first-aid personnel, who should be readily available.

GRAND OPENINGS

For some reason, all openings of new facilities are called "grand." Grand or not, these events are really open houses or plant tours embellished with crowd attractions and ceremony. Invariably they are firsts: the *first* open house or the *first* plant tour.

While open houses and plant tours are normally sponsored by one firm, a grand opening may be sponsored by a shopping center, a mall, or a newly refurbished street or shopping area.

Usually there are speeches, participation by civic dignitaries, possibly parades, and often special attractions to draw crowds. These special attractions can include appearances by entertainers, contests, drawings for prizes, and carnival attractions (such as carousels, ferris wheels, and stunts).

Invariably there is a symbolic act of opening. Ribbon cutting, turning on the lights, or starting the machinery are typical. This is customarily done by the most impressive personage available—the mayor or governor is a likely person.

Managing a grand opening is much like managing an open house or tour. The same preparations are made and the same checklist should be followed.

PROMOTIONAL EVENTS

These events are planned primarily to promote sales. They may center on a consumer product or service or on a retailing area. If the focus is on a product or service, the event is likely to be held in one building, such as an auditorium or exhibit hall. The event's focus may range from a cheese festival to a home-repair exposition or stereo show. If the focus is a retailing area, it may be a mall, a downtown area, or a shopping center. In this case the event will occur throughout the specified area and all retailers in the area will benefit.

Running a promotional event requires complete arrangements for traffic control, parking, safety, and the many other details listed in the section on open houses and plant tours. In addition, there may be special decorations, lighting, entertainment features, and ceremonies.

If anyone may attend, the promotion is announced through any news medium available, and this may be supplemented by advertising. If attendance is restricted to any particular group—such as dealers, distributors, or any other

Events can reach many people. This crowd of more than 40,000 people attended the celebration of the bicentennial of the Constitution. Millions more read about it in print, heard it on radio, and saw it on television. (*Source:* Lewis, Gilman & Kynett, Philadelphia, PA.)

limited class of people—the announcement is made by mail, usually as an invitation. In either case, the announcement specifies the location, purpose, and day or days of the promotion.

Charitable organizations frequently run events to raise money. These can range from rummage sales to fashion shows, from barbecues to athletic events. Regardless of the nature of the specific event, they all involve getting people to attend the event and handling a crowd. Because the ways to raise money are so varied, we cannot attempt here to give specifics on how to run them. Rather, you will do best to rely on the guidelines for other events previously stated and adapt them to the particular money-making activity decided upon.

DISPLAYS AND EXHIBITS

Displays and exhibits are often very economical ways to reach key audiences. These may be as simple as several posters in a bank lobby or a sampling of products in a shopping-center mall. On the other hand, they may be as complex as a full-fledged world's-fair exhibit.

Displays and exhibits are found almost anywhere crowds of people congregate. No national convention is complete without an exhibit area, and any county or state fair is likely to have several buildings of exhibits. Trade shows, for the most part, are just exhibit booths and displays manned by various companies. For example, a recent computer trade show in New York had more than a thousand display booths and attracted fifty thousand people.

Such displays and exhibits are highly effective because they enable a company to zero in on the potential market for its wares. A manufacturer of pet food finds dog shows an ideal place to display wares, just as a book publisher finds the ideal audience at a meeting of the American Library Association.

Design Suggestions

Any display or exhibit should be designed for maximum visibility. Here are some points to keep in mind:

1. Make the display or booth visually attractive. Use bright colors, large signs, and working models if possible.
2. Think about putting action in your display. Have a movie or slide presentation running all the time.
3. Use involvement techniques. Have a contest or raffle where visitors can win a prize.
4. Give people an opportunity to actually operate equipment or do something.
5. Have knowledgeable, personable representatives on duty to answer questions and get a visitor's address for follow-up.
6. Offer useful souvenirs. A keychain, a shopping bag, a luggage tag, or even a copy of a popular newspaper or magazine will attract traffic.

You will notice that the above list omits the idea of having shapely models as drawing cards at a display or exhibit booth. Although a female model will attract a lot of attention at a trade show dominated by men, many companies have now concluded that the model—not the company's products—gets all the attention. The use of scantily clad women also makes the company vulnerable to charges of sexism from an ever-increasing number of female executives who have the power to make decisions about purchasing a company's services or equipment.

Hospitality Suites

"Our research shows that hospitality suites can be more effective than booths," says one Monsanto Co. advertising executive. At a recent convention of picture framers, Monsanto built a mock theater at its hospitality suite and showed a thirty-minute film about one of its framing products. The company attributed an increase of more than 20 percent in the product's sales to the presentation.

The idea is that potential customers will stay in a hospitality suite long enough to hear an entire presentation, whereas they are likely to stop at an exhibit-hall booth for only a few minutes. But in using a hospitality suite, invitees must be carefully screened to make sure that they are prepared to place orders and authorized to do so. Along this line, the *Wall Street Journal* recently reported that hospitality suites no longer offer unlimited supplies of liquor and attractive female companionship. Companies, the article concluded, want more than goodwill from a hospitality suite—they want product orders and sales leads.

SECURITY

There are two dangers which should be considered in planning any event: accidents and disruptions. Both can be avoided or minimized if you keep them in mind from the beginning.

Accidents

In this era of litigation, any accident can lead to a lawsuit. Mishaps that were once brushed off as "acts of God" are now considered the fault of someone other than the victim. Accordingly, you should go over the site of your event with an eagle eye. Anything that could, by the wildest stretch of the imagination, contribute to an injury should be eliminated. The grounds for charging negligence are often ridiculous, but the charges are made and juries often make enormous awards for injuries, physical or mental, that the uninvolved might see as the fault of the victim. You cannot be too careful. (see Chapter 3.)

Liability insurance is a necessity for any organization conducting a public event. Consultation with the carrier should begin when the idea for the event is first crystallized. If your organization has a blanket liability policy, the insurance company should be informed of your plans. If there is no liability policy, you should obtain one. If no company will insure the event, you should drop the plans.

Disruptions

Disruption may range from the mere presence of a few uninvited gate-crashers to organized attempts to break up a meeting or run wild through the premises, damaging property and injuring people.

Gate-crashers can be kept out by placing guards at the entrances. Minor disruptions, such as heckling of a speaker by a person who is legitimately there, may be handled by an usher or a guard. The big threats are invasions by groups who are opposed to the organization or hoodlums who are bent on a little hell-raising.

For these risks, you should consult a security firm. You will find such firms listed in the Yellow Pages under "Security Guard & Patrol Services." Jointly, you should identify the risks, assess their severity, eliminate those that can be eliminated (e.g., locking back doors and rear gates), and set up a plan to handle the people who will be at the event.

A heavy-handed security force can cause more problems than it prevents. Be sure that the firm you choose understands the consequences of extreme actions. Rough treatment of demonstrators or would-be intruders can look very bad on television or on the front page.

SUMMARY

1. Events don't just happen. They must be planned and controlled. Nothing must be left to chance. If anything *can* go wrong, it probably *will*.
2. Meetings may be large or small, long or short, but for all meetings you must consider the following: time, location, seating, facilities needed, invitations (or notice), greeting, registration (or attendance check if needed), program or agenda, and speakers.
3. Conventions are normally a series of meetings. In addition to the items involved in shorter meetings, you will need to think about hotel accommodations, recreation, stimulation of attendance, and administration.
4. Eating and drinking activities may range from coffee and doughnuts to large banquets, from open bars to impressive cocktail parties with elaborate hors d'ouevres. All take planning and control.
5. Open houses and plant tours require meticulous planning and routing, careful handling of visitors, and thorough preparation of all personnel who will have contact with the visitors.
6. Grand openings feature the facilities being opened, plus speeches, decorations, and often entertainment. The visitors are not invited person-

ally—they are the public at large. Those who come are attracted by general publicity about the event.

7. Promotional events are basically sales promotions. Some product or service is the subject, and the objective is to attract people who may buy. Entertainment and spectacle are usually included.

8. Displays and exhibits are common at conventions. They enable the sponsors to show their ideas or products to many prospective purchasers. Competition for attention is stiff so your display must be well designed and pertinent.

9. Security must be considered for almost any event. The things to be considered are accidents which can lead to lawsuits and disruptions which can ruin the event.

EXERCISES

1. Successful events require extensive planning and attention to every detail. Select a campus organization or a community group that has just completed an annual awards banquet or convention. You should make arrangements to interview the person in charge of the event in order to write a case-study analysis. This should detail the steps taken to plan and organize the event. It should include (a) budget, (b) time elements, (c) arrangements with hotels or restaurants, (d) speaker arrangements, (e) registration packets or invitations sent to potential attendees, (f) publicity vehicles utilized, and (g) in retrospect, what unexpected problems occurred that should be considered in next year's planning.

2. The School of Business at your university has scheduled its annual awards banquet for about six months from today. This banquet, held at a local hotel, usually draws about 500 guests, who are alumni, students, faculty, and members of the local business community. The usual pattern is to have a nationally known business executive give the major speech. You are charged with coordinating this event. Prepare a detailed outline of what must be done to plan the banquet, including a time line or calendar of what must be done by certain dates.

SUGGESTED READINGS

Bray, Nicholas. "Spain to Celebrate Columbus's Voyage at an $800 Million Coming-Out Party." *Wall Street Journal*, Oct. 27, 1988.

Brody, E. W. "Special Events." *Public Relations Programming and Production.* New York: Praeger Publishers, 1988, chap. 14.

Cooper, M. "The Big Media Event." *Public Relations Journal*, July 1983, pp. 12–15.

Coupland, Ken. "Father Knows Best." *Public Relations Journal*, December 1987, pp. 31–34.

Goldblatt, J. "How to Produce Special Events." *Public Relations Journal*, June 1985, pp. 35–36.

Gould, Mark. "Dr. J Puts New Spin on Basketball Awards Dinner." *Communication World*, December 1987, pp. 16–17.

Green, David, and Wall, Don. "Group Meetings: In-Person vs. Satellite TV." *Communication World*, March 1988, pp. 22–25.

Lehrman, Celia K. "Celebrating Champagne." *Public Relations Journal*, December 1985, pp. 18–21.

Peck, David. "Tips for Exceptional Exhibits." *Communication World*, March 1985, pp. 10–11.

Perilla, Bob. "Workshop: How to Work With Celebrities." *Public Relations Journal*, April 1988, pp. 33–34.

Sidley, John D. "When Nothing Can Go Wrong . . . Go Wrong . . . Go Wrong . . ." *Communication World*, June 1988, pp. 28–29.

Stevens, Art. "What's Ahead for the Future of Special Events." *Public Relations Journal*, June 1984, pp. 16–18.

Teague, Walter F. "Video Extravaganza: Pulling Out All the Stops." *Communication World*, February 1988, pp. 16–19.

Thomas, Vicki. "We've Got to Stop Meeting Like This." *Communication World*, May 1985, pp. 18–20.

Towns, Stuart. "How to Get Results from Meetings." *Communication World*, August 1986, pp. 20–22.

Ukman, L. "The Special Event Finds Its Niche." *Public Relations Journal*, June 1984, pp. 21–22.

Chapter
18

Planning

*P*lanning is imperative for any public relations campaign. It improves effectiveness; by gearing all activities together you will ensure a greater overall impact. Planning avoids waste of time and money on nonessentials and allows you to concentrate effort where it will do the most good.

A plan must explain why the action is necessary. It tells who to reach, how to reach them, and what to say. It also tells when things are to be done, how much the plan will cost, and how it will be evaluated.

ELEMENTS OF A PLAN

There is no standard description of the elements that go into a campaign. Different organizations designate these elements in different ways, combining or dividing them as seems appropriate. Nevertheless, and without regard to how its elements are described or organized, any good plan will include the Situation, Objectives, Audience, Strategy, Tactics, Costs, and Evaluation.

Situation

This is a summary of the relations of the organization with its public or publics. It tells why the program is needed and points out problems and opportunities. This may be the most important part of the plan. Unless management is convinced that a campaign is necessary, it is not likely to approve spending money on it.

Problem situations, which require remedial programming, include things like these:

- British Airways, due to the weakness of the American dollar abroad and airport attacks by terrorists, experienced a major reduction in the number of American passengers flying across the Atlantic.
- A. H. Robins Company, manufacturer of the Dalkon shield contraceptive device, was hit by numerous lawsuits after reports of an infection-related death and other health-related problems associated with the device. The courts ordered a 90-country information campaign to inform women about the dangers of the product and to tell them how to file claims for compensation.
- French cognac makers, faced with a proposed 200 percent tariff on imports into the United States, needed to convince Congress that such a proposal would cause major economic problems in the cognac industry.

Most public relations situations, however, are not problems that must be solved in a hurry but rather long-term, continuing interactions with one or more publics. Here are some examples:

- Savings and loan associations in numerous areas have had to be saved from bankruptcy by government action. This has led to worries about the solvency of the entire industry.
- Public utilities have a continuing problem of balancing the requirements of stockholders, employees, customers, and regulatory agencies.
- McDonald's Corporation found that it had few Hispanic customers, even in areas where there were many Hispanics.
- Miller Brewing Company had little recognition among women, yet women buy a lot of beer for home consumption.

In describing a situation, it is important to state the cause (if known) or to tell how the cause will be discovered (this is usually done with surveys).

Objectives

A good many years ago, one of the authors of this book returned from a disastrous meeting with a client who had roundly rejected every recommendation.

With the door shut and his feet on top of the desk, he pondered the problem. Why had he failed to secure approval? Finally the answer came. Neither he nor the client had a clear idea of the campaign's objectives.

The next step was to ask the question: What are we trying to accomplish? This led to considerable research and ultimately to a determination of the objectives. With the client in agreement on the objectives and the campaign revised to fit them, it was approved and carried out to the satisfaction of both parties.

The lesson from this case is that neither managements nor clients are likely to approve a campaign without clear objectives. Furthermore, even if a campaign is approved, it will surely fail without objectives.

Within any campaign, there may be multiple objectives. Smaller campaigns may have only one target and one objective, but in any planning you must be sure that you thoroughly understand what you are trying to accomplish. There are basically two kinds of objectives, informational and motivational.

Informational Objectives   A large percentage of public relations plans are designed primarily to increase awareness of an issue, event, or product. Here are some possible informational objectives:

- To inform people about the kinds of food needed for good nutrition.
- To tell people that cigarette smoking is a major cause of cancer.
- To proclaim the virtues of raisins.
- To alert people to the fact that aerosol sprays damage the ozone layer.

Although informational objectives are legitimate and used by virtually every public relations firm and department, it is extremely difficult to measure how much "awareness" was attained unless "before" and "after" surveys are done; these are expensive and time-consuming. In addition, awareness doesn't equal action. Consumers may have been made aware of your new product, but that doesn't necessarily mean they will buy it. Knowing is great, but buying is what counts.

Motivational Objectives   These objectives are more ambitious and also more difficult to achieve. Basically, you want to change attitudes and opinions with the idea of modifying behavior.

Some motivational objectives might be:

- To get people to eat healthier foods.
- To greatly reduce cigarette smoking.
- To increase the consumption of raisins.
- To prevent the sale of aerosol sprays.

Notice that motivational objectives are more "bottom-line-oriented." The effectiveness of the public relations plan is based on making something happen, whether it be increasing sales or changing public support for some issue.

Informational objectives, on the other hand, merely "inform" or "educate" people. Take, for example, the informational objective of making people aware of cigarette smoking as a major cause of cancer. This might be achieved successfully enough, but people who are "informed" and "aware" often continue to smoke. A better gauge of the American Cancer Society's success in its efforts would be an actual increase in the number of people who stopped smoking.

In setting objectives, you must be sure that they are realistic and achievable. Furthermore, they must be within the power of the campaign alone to attain. Sometimes the unwary set objectives such as "to increase sales" without realizing that sales may be affected by such things as product quality, packaging, pricing, merchandising, advertising, sales promotion, display, and competitive activity.

Objectives Fit for a Queen

It is important to make sure spokespeople are briefed to mention key informational points. This outline, courtesy of Hewlett Packard, was used by David Packard when he hosted Queen Elizabeth on a one-hour tour of a manufacturing facility. Note how the informational points support the stated objective.

Objective: Explain social context of Silicon Valley growth and electronics industry development in general, using HP as representative example.

SILICON VALLEY DEVELOPMENT

Evolution of Silicon Valley companies

Frederick Terman's vision

Continuing influence of Stanford University

Development of IC technology: Benefits of smallness, tube, transistor, integrated circuit, microprocessor

HEWLETT-PACKARD'S BUSINESS STYLE

Divisions structured for entrepreneurship

Stress on new products versus "me-too" commodities

Working conditions: Informality, teamwork, trust

MBO

Interrelation of self-financing, growth, job security

Promotion from within; internal training

Solution-oriented selling: Service/support commitment

ELECTRONICS INDUSTRY CHARACTERISTICS

Campuslike industrial/research developments

Education as most needed resource: Continuing education as important as under-graduate

Japanese competition: Emulation versus innovation

Quality of manufacturing as vital as quality of design

HEWLETT-PACKARD IN THE UNITED KINGDOM

British expertise in software: Pinewood's HP Mail

HP-UK "turnover" or sales grew faster than HP worldwide: 42 percent increase versus 19 percent corporate

HP-UK enhances UK trade balance: Queensferry exports 80 percent of products; overall HP-UK exports rose 34 percent

HP's investment: 2000 people, four major facilities

In establishing objectives, you must state exactly what you want the audience to know (e.g., a new product is now on the market), to believe (e.g., it will cut utility bills), to do (e.g., ask for a demonstration). Objectives must be measurable. At some point the people who pay for the campaign are likely to ask: What did you accomplish? Many practitioners rely on general feedback—random comments and isolated examples that indicate public reaction. The real professionals give facts and figures.

Later on this question of evaluation will be covered in detail; at this point, however, you must start thinking about setting goals that can be measured with figures. In an informational campaign, it is easy to state an objective like this: To increase to 75 percent the number of people who believe that carpooling is a good way to save energy.

A motivational objective in this situation could be: To increase the number of people who use carpooling. However, it would be far better to put it this way: To increase utilization of carpooling by 50 percent.

As you think about these numerical goals, you should realize that there must be a base point for such measurements. To know how many people have been convinced by your campaign, you must know how many people believed in carpooling before you began your campaign. With this figure in hand, you can prove that your efforts have increased awareness. When you then get figures on current carpooling, you will be able to prove that the campaign *has* increased utilization, and by how much. Finding these base points requires research, which will be discussed later on.

Public Relations Planning and Marketing Strategy

Product publicity makes a substantial contribution to fulfilling the marketing objectives of a business organization. It can:

- Develop new prospects for new markets, such as inquiries from people who saw or heard a product release in the news media.

- Provide third-party endorsements—via newspapers, magazines, radio, and television—through news releases about a company's products or services, community involvement, inventions, and new plans.

- Generate sales leads, usually through articles in the trade press about new products and services.

- Pave the way for sales calls.

- Stretch the organization's advertising and promotional dollars through timely and supportive releases about it and its products.

- Provide inexpensive sales literature for the company because articles about it and its products can be reprinted as informative pieces for prospective clients.

- Establish the corporation as an authoritative source of information on a given subject.

- Help sell minor products. Some products are too minor for large advertising expenditures, so exposure to the market is more cost-effective if product publicity is utilized.

Audience

The target audience for a campaign is the "receiver" portion of the communication process. These are the people you must reach in order to attain your objectives. In defining the audience, you must be very specific. In any situation, some people are more important or influential than others. There are individuals and groups whose support or opposition can be critical. The beliefs and attitudes of all the publics should be known and described.

In this portion of the plan, you list every important segment of the audience, stating who they are, where they are, how they think, what they know, and what they believe. This listing may include individuals, organizations, occupational groups, geographical groups, political groups, and possibly many others.

This approach can be applied to the identification of any audience. You should learn all you can about the target and then determine priorities. Some targets may be more important than others. They should be reached first and most forcefully. In some situations, there may be one or a few individuals who wield great power. They should be named. There may be activist groups that should be considered. There may be key occupations or organizations that sway many others. If your audience description is complete, it will list all those who can help and all who can hinder the successful attainment of the objectives.

Strategy

"Strategy" means the broad principles on which the campaign will be conducted. There are three general kinds of strategy:

1. *Communication.* This stresses information and is widely used in product publicity.
2. *Combat.* This concentrates on attacking opposing views. It is often used in political campaigns and when public issues are involved. The emphasis is on winning.
3. *Cooperation.* This emphasizes mutual understanding. It implies a dialogue between the parties. The goal is to win consent, not grudging acceptance.

There are advantages and drawbacks to using only one of these strategies. An intelligent combination of all three may be the most effective.

Strategy must be keyed directly to the objective. For example, when several environmental groups wanted to block construction of a coal-burning power plant in Utah, their strategy was to concentrate all their efforts on one point. They did not say much about coal-burning plants in general. The focus was on that particular plant at that particular place. The strategy was expressed in the statement "We must not build that plant there because it will pollute the air of Zion and Bryce Canyon National Parks." The campaign succeeded because the right strategy was used.

As you plan campaign strategy, you may borrow an idea from advertising professionals. They have proved that success depends on concentrating on what is called a "key selling proposition." If your campaign is a marketing campaign, the advertising people may have already settled upon that proposition, in which case you use the same idea. If no one else has done it, you should seek for and find the key idea that will be most persuasive and most convincing to your audience.

The idea should focus on the self-interest of the audience. What will the product do for them? How will they lose if a proposed law passes? How will they gain if another law is passed? How will they profit from taking a night-school course? The idea must be simply expressed. There may be several possible advantages or disadvantages in a given situation, but you should try to boil everything down into one clear statement. This *idea* should be included in *every* message that reaches the public.

The key statement is the "message" of the communication process. It must be aimed directly at the objective or objectives and it must be reiterated throughout the campaign. In some situations, it may be necessary to include more than one key point, but this should not lead to a long listing of virtues or faults. For example, in a campaign to defeat a proposed law, the opposition had two vital points. The key statement thus became: "This proposed law is a dangerous invasion of privacy—and we already have a law that guarantees all the rights the proposed law would grant." The campaign succeeded because it was aimed at the self-interest of the voters and because it concentrated all efforts on a definite idea.

In the campaign, the key statement does not always have to be expressed in exactly the same words, but it must be kept clear and simple. This is the idea you must communicate to the audience, and there must be no possibility of confusion or misunderstanding. Also, you must know the audience or audiences so that you can express the idea in terms they will understand and believe. Your message must be credible.

Tactics

This is the "how to do it" portion of the plan. In the communication process, it is described as involving the "channels" through which the "message" is conveyed to the "receivers."

Here you tell just how you propose to reach every individual, organization, group, or public whose support will help or whose opposition will hinder the success of the plan. Who is going to talk personally to whom? What groups will be reached with speeches? Who will give the speeches? What publications will receive news releases? What feature stories will be written? Where will they be offered? What radio or television programs will be approached? What will they be offered? What audiovisual materials will be needed? Where will they be shown? What printed items will be required? How will they be distributed? What events will be staged?

Not all of these proposals have to be worked out in great detail. For example, it will be reasonable to say that feature articles will be offered to the trade press or that you recommend a media tour to talk to the editors of certain media. You can't be sure that a certain publication will publish a feature story or that you will be able to get on a specific television program, but you can show what you intend to try to do. Be as specific as possible, but don't promise anything that you can't deliver.

Timing

There are two aspects of time that must be considered: (1) the time when the campaign is to run and (2) the sequence of the various elements of the campaign. Both are very important.

A campaign must be timely; that is, it must run when it can get public attention. Some subjects are seasonal, thus publicists release information on strawberries in May and June. They talk about insulation and roofing in the summer, when these things can be dealt with, not in the winter, when no one can install them.

Another factor to consider is external competition. Don't try to get the public's attention when all eyes and ears are focused on some other topic.

On public issues, the timing of a public relations plan must be keyed to its environmental context. That is, the situation or project must be relevant to public awareness and concern. A campaign to generate public support for feeding and caring for the homeless will be more effective after there has been a series of articles in the local newspapers about the human dimensions of the problem. By the same token, if the public is now focused on housing for the poor as an issue, this is not the time to run an information campaign for a new city arena that will be built by removing four square blocks of lower-income housing.

Other kinds of issue-related information campaigns are less dependent on environmental context. Anything about cancer, the high costs of health care, or pollution can get attention, because these issues are always on the public agenda. By constantly monitoring local, state, and national news coverage, you can plan effective public relations campaigns that coincide with the current focuses of public interest.

With a basic decision as to when the campaign will run, the next step is to plan a schedule for all the elements of the campaign. When will Mr. Blank talk to the Rotary Club? When and how often will you send out news releases? When will the media tour be conducted? When is the time for the open house? And so on.

Also, you should determine when certain printed items will be needed, when audiovisual materials must be available and when they will be shown, when certain speeches must be ready for delivery, and when the speakers will be coached and rehearsed.

A very important part of the time schedule is the sequence of the various elements of the communication mix. If the public must understand a problem before it can accept a solution, it is imperative to explain the nature of the problem before you present the solution. Thus, in the early stages, it may be necessary to concentrate on information. The best time to try to motivate the audience may be later, when people have had time to absorb the facts.

Thus, in a city with a desperate garbage problem, the campaign might start by stressing the fact that the city dump is nearly full and that some solution must be found. Later, several possible solutions could be suggested for consideration. Finally, one of these solutions would be pushed for acceptance as the most efficient.

To keep track of every element in the campaign, you must have a schedule. One of the best ways to set up the schedule is to prepare a large sheet or board in calendar form. Each action in the plan is shown on this "calendar" at the date when it is to be executed. For example: "Jones speech to Rotary Club on June 16." "Mailing to educators on September 1." "Booklet on casserole recipes on August 2." "Media tour starts October 6." The dates are shown in the corners of the rectangles and only the item is written into the space.

Timing is critical. Every public relations plan includes numerous elements that must be completed at specific times. This is an example of a timetable for a product publicity campaign. (*Source:* Ketchum Public Relations, San Francisco.)

TIMETABLE
DOLE FRUIT 'N CREAM

Week of	Aug. 5	Aug. 12	Aug. 19	Aug. 26	Sept. 2	Sept. 9	Sept. 16	Sept. 23	Sept. 10	Oct. 7
A C C O U N T / **A C T I V I T Y**	•Initial client/agency meeting •Research/write/present program •Program approved by client	•Research/develop press kit materials •Submit first draft of fact sheet and new product release	•Research/develop trend story •Submit final copy of: •fact sheet •new product release •trend story •Research Florida radio/newspaper markets	•Write D.J. press advisory •Contact radio stations •Set up D.J. deliveries •Finalize press kit •Set-up editor meetings	•Confirm editor meetings •Confirm D.J. deliveries •Research/purchase editor gifts •Finalize schedule/press kit availability with client		•Conduct D.J. deliveries •Conduct editor deskside meetings		•Follow-up media requests •Client/agency recap meeting	•Evaluation/Program review

(Arrows span from Sept. 9 through Sept. 23 indicating the duration of "Conduct D.J. deliveries" and "Conduct editor deskside meetings.")

Costs

There must be a budget for any campaign. It may be for a specific event, such as a cocktail party for a certain group, or it may be for a year-long program comprising many items, each of which should be described clearly. In any case, the people who are paying will need to know exactly what is going to be done and how much it will cost. Within a large program, it is necessary to itemize the cost of each element. No one is likely to approve a blanket appropriation without knowing the details. Also, at some point there may be a money shortage that forces a cut in the budget. If all items have a cost figure, it will be possible to decide which should be sacrificed.

Evaluation

In your plan, you must tell just how the results will be evaluated. With the method of evaluation clearly in mind, you should state the objectives in a form that can be measured. Having done this, you describe the evaluation procedure in this last part of the plan.

MAKING A PLAN

The first step in developing a plan is to consult with the client or with management. There are two purposes in this. First, it gets them involved; if they are interested they are likely to support the effort. Second, it is likely to give you the basic information needed to start making a plan.

In talking with the people who will pay for the campaign, you strive to identify the problems and opportunities confronting the organization. In some cases these will be apparent to all. At other times one party will have ideas that have not occurred to the other. Out of this discussion should come an agreement as to the general nature of the problems or opportunities and a preliminary establishment of objectives. All of this, of course, is subject to change when more information is gathered.

A good example is the California Avocado Commission. It faced the problem of selling Haas avocados on the East Coast. Sales were not good, and with a bumper crop of 600 million avocados, the California growers realized they had a problem. Some informal research found that New Yorkers were not acquainted with avocados that turned jet black when ripe; they thought the fruit was rotten. The objective, then, was to inform consumers that the Haas avocados were *supposed* to have black skins and that they had excellent flavor. The campaign succeeded because it was based on information and analysis of the information.

Gathering Information

You cannot know too much about the subject you intend to write about. Don't be satisfied with cursory investigation—dig and keep on digging until you have the whole story. There are several sources from which you can get the facts and figures that will enable you to plan an effective campaign.

1. *Organization.* There should be much basic information within the organization. Ask for marketing plans, public relations plans, and the research on which they are based. Talk to the people who deal with the public. Get an overall picture of the organization's successes and failures. Find out why things have happened or why they have been done.

2. *References.* Go through all the information in your files. Consult other files. Use libraries—either internal or public. Read Chapter 1; a long list of sources of information is given there.

3. *Questions.* Ask colleagues for their ideas. Review the experiences of others in similar situations. Read any case histories you can find. The trade press is a good source of these.

4. *Analysis of communications.* Field reports from representatives of the organization, inquiries on telephone hot-lines, and consumer complaints should be checked and studied.

5. *Brainstorming.* Get a group of six to ten people together and ask for suggestions. Remember that no idea is to be criticized; a freewheeling discussion encourages the presentation of more ideas. Many of the suggestions will be irrelevant, but some may contain the beginning of a good idea or point out the areas where more information is needed.

6. *Focus-group interviews.* Assemble a group of people who are representative of the audience you will want to reach. A moderator leads the discussion of the apparent problem or opportunity. The entire interview is tape-recorded and later transcribed. These interviews are not quantitative research, but they may point to a need for detailed research in a specific area. Also, such an interview may produce many helpful ideas and possibly point toward a possible strategy.

7. *Delphi studies.* In a Delphi study, a number of people representative of your anticipated audience are asked to name one important problem or opportunity. When all suggestions are received, they are listed on a form that is sent back to the respondents, who are then asked to rate the relative importance of each point. This is done on a rating scale ranging from "very important" to "not at all important." In this way, you can rank-order the issues that concern your audience most. This helps both campaign planning and the writing of materials geared to the interests of the target audience. An important aspect of the Delphi study is that that no one can know who suggested any given idea. This encourages frankness from the respondents and impartiality from the appraisers of the study.

8. *Readership studies.* These show what articles and items in a publication are read by the recipients. They are a good guide to relative reader interest in different subjects.

9. *Environmental monitoring.* This involves studies of public trends, actions, and events that may have an effect on your organization.

10. *Public relations audits.* These identify the groups that are active on public issues—their attitudes, tactics, and power.

11. *Surveys.* In many situations, it will be necessary to conduct a formal survey in order to ascertain the attitudes and perceptions of target audiences. Doing a survey takes a large amount of time and money. If the organization does not have the relevant data already on hand, you must either do the survey yourself or hire someone to do it for you. Before you start, you should know something about surveys.

In all surveys, it is important to know just what is to be found out and to be sure that answers are checked. Authorities may differ, and even the most carefully conducted survey may contain errors. If a survey comes up with an answer that defies reasoned judgment, it is imperative to go over the findings with a skeptical and critical eye. Even the most prestigious research organizations make mistakes.

12. *Media studies.* In order to plan your tactics, you need to know which channels of communication will be most efficient. Sales representatives of the media can provide very complete information about the audiences they reach. Your marketing or advertising department (if there is one) will probably have this information; if not, you can get it by asking the sales representatives for it. Be sure to get complete information. For example, the food editor of one magazine for women once said: "Don't send me gourmet recipes—my readers are the kind who buy mustard in gallon jars."

13. *Geodemographics.* This means that people of similar cultural backgrounds, circumstances, and perspectives tend to group together in geographic subareas, which can be readily identified by postal zip codes. In other words, the population of any individual zip code area will consist largely of the same kind of people, with similar incomes, life-styles, and purchasing habits. Using zip codes, it is possible to aim publicity at the most likely targets and even to choose the media that are most effective in reaching these people. Claritas Corporation (1911 North Fort Myer Drive, Arlington, VA 22209) has pioneered in this new approach to market pinpointing. They call it PRIZM. If your marketing department is not familiar with this concept, it might be a good idea to write for the booklet explaining it.

Analyzing the Information

Having gathered all pertinent information and conducted one or more surveys (if they are needed), your job is then to analyze all the facts and ideas. You must consider the reliability of what you have found out. If there are contradictions, you must eliminate the erroneous and confirm the credibility of what remains. Don't guess. If you are not sure about something, don't use it.

Now, with reliable information, you can start to draw conclusions. The situation, with its problems and opportunities, and the reason for the situation should be apparent. The objectives should be obvious and the strategy, after careful thought, should start to take form.

At this point you should prepare an outline of your findings and then discuss them with management or the client. You can say, "These are the facts that I have, this is the situation as I see it, these are the objectives I think we should select, and this is the strategy I suggest."

This discussion may result in an approval in principle. If it does, you can start preparing the plan. If the general idea is not approved, you must find out what is wrong and make the needed corrections or gather additional information and try again.

The procedures described here are applicable in many cases; but in large public relations organizations, there may be some differences. The preliminary discussion may be purely internal and the plan may not be presented to a client until it is in final form. Also, there may be other people working on parts of the plan.

Developing the Plan

Any plan must be practical. It must not be more costly than is reasonable. You may think of many things that would be desirable. Don't recommend them unless the organization can afford the money and personnel they would require.

A plan must be palatable to the people who will pay for it. This requires a thorough understanding of the organization and the people who will have to approve the plan. Personal tastes and even whims may be important.

With a clear understanding of the situation, the audience, the objectives, and the strategy, the next step is to work on the tactics. With due consideration for practicality, palatability, and appropriateness, you must decide just how and when you will convey the message to the audience. Here you think of all the channels that are available and decide which ones to use.

You determine priorities. What segments of the audience are most important? What is the best way to reach them? When will things be done? In what order will things be done? Be as specific as possible, but remember that problems may arise and changes may be necessary at some stage.

Costs must be specific. In general there will be three kinds of costs: purchases of materials, expenses such as travel, and time charges for the people who do the work. If it is an internal activity, personnel costs are already on the payroll and an estimate of the time used by various people in the organization will be needed. If the work is done for a client, it will be necessary to explain how costs are determined and how much will be charged for the work to be done. In some cases this is a flat fee, in others there is a charge per hour for the various kinds of people who will be involved. (Senior executives cost more than junior writers.)

On purchases, it will be possible to make estimates based on past experience. Thus if a 16-page self-cover booklet actually cost $1,600, it is likely that a 32-page booklet will cost about twice that much, provided that the quantities are the same and the price of paper and printing has not changed. Before submitting estimated costs for purchased materials, it is advisable to talk with suppliers and get good estimates.

Look over every element of the plan and be sure that you have a valid figure on what it will cost. At this stage you may discover that there isn't enough money or human power to do all the things that are desirable. This will require a revision in the plan or a request for additional money or personnel.

Pretesting the Plan

Before you submit a plan for approval, you should pretest it. Ask some knowledgeable person whose opinion you respect to read the plan and then discuss it with you. Check these points:

1. Spontaneous reaction—is he or she enthusiastic about it? If not, why not?
2. Is the situation clearly stated?
3. Is the audience the right audience—is it clearly defined?
4. Are the objectives attainable and measurable?
5. Is the strategy logical and effective?
6. Is the message persuasive—and memorable?
7. Are the tactics sound and effective?
8. Is the timing right?
9. Are the costs reasonable—and justified?
10. Will the proposed evaluation really measure the results?
11. Is the plan practical, palatable, and appropriate?
12. Is the plan logical, strong, and clearly written?
13. Are there any additions or deletions that should be made?

Ask yourself the same questions. Be sure to allow enough time for deliberate and unhurried review—and for making changes if they are needed. Do this several days before the actual presentation.

EXECUTING THE PLAN

With an approved plan, your work really starts. Now you must do all the things that you have recommended. You must write the releases and features, prepare the radio and television materials, produce the printed items, plan and conduct the events, and perform the many other tasks that are included in the plan.

To do all these things at the right time, you must have a very precise schedule. In the plan, you have told when things will be done; but many of these items require a long time for preparation.

A booklet may be needed on March 29, but you must start the booklet long before that date. To determine the starting date, you must know every step in the production of the booklet and how long it will take.

For example, you might need one week to prepare the outline and rough layout, one week to write the copy, one week to get the copy and layout approved, two weeks for photographs and charts, two weeks for typesetting and engraving, one week for approval of proofs, two weeks for printing and binding, and a safety allowance of two weeks.

This totals twelve weeks, so you must start your outline and layout on January 4. Then you must have the completed outline and layout by January 11, copy by January 18, approval by January 25, photographs and charts by February 8, typesetting and engravings by February 22, approval by March 1, printing and binding by March 15. This gives you two weeks before the deadline of March 29. You may need it, because there may be delays at any point in the process.

Use the same system for scheduling every activity in the campaign. Don't trust to memory or rely on notes or jottings on your desk calendar. The easiest way to keep everything on schedule is to prepare a working calendar-style chart similar to the one in the plan. In this case, however, you show every step of every job on your schedule. There may be numerous entries on any given day, so make the squares for each day big enough to include all of them.

One day alone could include such notes as "Start copy on orientation leaflet," "Ask M. G. if pix of meeting have come in," "Call Joe at Tribune re interview with boss," "Make airline reservations for media tour," and so on.

Another important part of managing a campaign is monitoring the progress. Keep track of everything that is going on and try to appraise the results. If problems arise, it may be advisable to make changes in the tactics. If anything goes exceptionally well, it may pay to intensify efforts in that area. Always try to find out why your ideas work or fail. Part of your answers will come from the formal evaluation, but don't wait for final figures; keep your eye on the campaign at all times.

THE HOT POTATO

An excellent example of a simple and well-conducted campaign is that of the common potato. The following was provided by Ketchum Public Relations.

Situation

Statistics compiled by the Potato Board, a national organization of 16,000 potato growers and processors, showed a year-to-year drop in the consumption of fresh potatoes. Ketchum surveyed consumers and groups who influence consumer eating habits and opinions (doctors and dietitians). The research indicated that the decline in consumption was due to misinformation and erroneous beliefs that potatoes were both fattening and nonnutritious. The truth is that potatoes have relatively low caloric value and high nutritional value.

Objectives

The objective was to stop the decline in consumption.

Audience

The major target audiences were consumers, teachers, doctors, dietitians, and food-service operators (restaurants for example).

Strategy

There were three basic strategies:

1. To correct the misconception that potatoes are high in calories
2. To convince consumers that potatoes are a good source of important nutrients, particularly vitamin C
3. To attack the "fad diets" that spread misinformation about carbohydrate foods like potatoes

The key message was that potatoes are low in calories, high in nutritional value, and a valuable part of the diet.

Tactics

A wide range of activities carried the key message to the audience. Among the tools used were:

1. Personal contacts with medical and dietetic groups.
2. Placement of speakers at nutritional meetings and seminars.
3. Development and promotion of university studies.
4. Placement of feature stories in professional and consumer magazines.
5. Spokesperson interviews with print and broadcast media.
6. Newspaper features on low-calorie potato recipes.
7. Newspaper features on the nutritional value of potatoes.
8. A consumer booklet on potatoes offered through both broadcast appearances and newspaper and magazine articles.
9. A three-day seminar for more than thirty consumer food, nutrition, and news writers. It featured Dr. Frederick Stare, chairman of Harvard University's department of nutrition.
10. A nutrition communications workshop sponsored at the annual conference of the Society of Nutritional Education.
11. A classroom home economics program that informed teachers and their students about the nutritional value of potatoes.
12. An elementary school program in which potatoes were promoted for use in lunch menus and potato nutrition was taught in the classrooms.

Timing

Since potatoes are not seasonal, the campaign was conducted on a year-round basis.

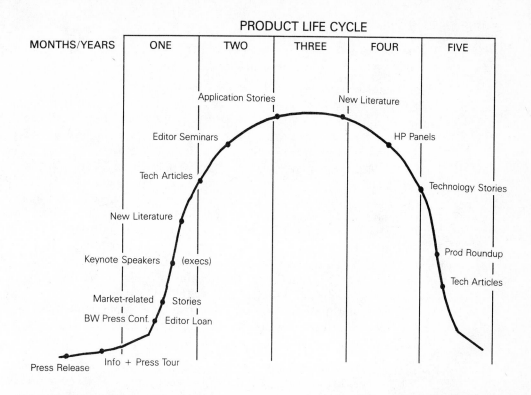

PRODUCT LIFE CYCLE

| MONTHS/YEARS | ONE | TWO | THREE | FOUR | FIVE |

Application Stories

New Literature

Editor Seminars

HP Panels

Tech Articles

Technology Stories

New Literature

Keynote Speakers

(execs)

Prod Roundup

Tech Articles

Market-related

Stories

BW Press Conf.

Editor Loan

Press Release

Info + Press Tour

Corporate Press Relations
Cycle

 **HEWLETT PACKARD**

A variety of tools is needed. This bell curve shows a product's life cycle and what kinds of public relations activities are needed at each stage. Note that multiple tools are used at the beginning in order to launch the product. (*Source:* Hewlett-Packard Company, Palo Alto, CA.)

Budget

This was planned to range from $300,000 to $500,000 annually.

Evaluation

A compilation of all measurable media coverage since the beginning of the campaign has shown an annual reach of over 800 million. Nearly 1,200 articles appeared in 900 newspapers. More than 100,000 nutritional fact sheets were distributed in response to offers through the media.

Most important, the campaign attained its objective. At the end of the first year the sales decline had stopped, in spite of higher prices. Since the first year, the campaign has continued with a slightly different objective—to *increase* sales. Strategy and tactics have been slightly modified from time to time, but the general thrust has been to tell consumers the truth about potatoes. It works because consumption of potatoes is increasing.

CRISIS PLANS

Every organization should have plans for dealing with crises. For many years, such plans were primarily devoted to handling accidents or fires; but in today's society, there may be other kinds of crises. Good management tries to anticipate problems and settle them before they become critical. Preaction is far better than reaction. Nevertheless some unanticipated crisis may occur, or the preactive effort may fail.

To limit the damage it is necessary to plan ahead. In addition to accidents, there may be strikes, product recalls instigated by a government agency (as with automobiles), product recalls instigated by the manufacturer (as with the tampon recall sparked by the outbreak of toxic shock syndrome), bomb threats or bombings, lawsuits, charges by activist groups or individuals, poisonings (as in drug tampering—e.g., with Tylenol) or poison threats, malicious rumors (like the Satanist charges against Procter & Gamble), takeover threats, demonstrations, boycotts, sabotage, and actions by goverment regulatory agencies such as the FTC, SEC, OSHA, USDA, FCC, FDA, and so on.

This is not necessarily a complete list. Remember Murphy's law: "If anything *can* go wrong, it probably *will*." Accordingly, there should be a plan for every possible crisis. These plans may not be lengthy, but each should include these major elements:

1. *Who is to be informed.* The general rule is that all concerned management plus the public relations department should be informed.

The Basic Elements of a Plan

A basic communication plan is essentially nothing more than a blueprint of what you want to do and how you will accomplish your task. Such a plan, either as a brief outline or as an extensive document, will enable you and the client or employer to make sure that all elements have been properly considered, evaluated, and coordinated for maximum publicity.

STEP 1: DEFINING THE PROBLEM

You cannot set valid objectives without understanding the problem. To understand the problem: (a) discuss it with the client to find out what he or she expects the publicity to accomplish, (b) do your own research, and (c) evaluate your ideas in the broader perspective of the client's long-term goals.

STEP 2: IDENTIFYING OBJECTIVES

Once you understand the problem, it should be easy to define the objectives. To determine if your stated objectives are the right ones, ask yourself: (a) Does it really solve or help solve the problem? (b) Is it realistic and achievable, and (c) Can the success be measured in terms meaningful to the client?

STEP 3: IDENTIFYING THE AUDIENCE

Identify, as precisely as possible, the group of people to whom you are going to direct your communications. Is this the right group to approach in order to solve the problem? If there are several groups, prioritize them according to which are most important for your particular objectives.

STEP 4: DEVELOPING STRATEGIES

The strategy describes how, in concept, the objective is to be achieved. Strategy is a plan of action that provides guidelines for selecting the communications activity you will employ. There are usually one or more strategies for each target audience. Strategies may be broad or narrow, depending on the objective and the audience.

STEP 5: TACTICS

This is the body of the plan, which describes, in sequence, the specific communications activities proposed to achieve each objective. Discuss each activity as a separate thought, yet relate each to the unifying strategy and theme. In selecting communication tools—news releases, brochures, radio announcements, etc.—ask yourself if the use of each will really reach your priority audiences and help you accomplish your stated objectives.

STEP 6: CALENDAR

It is important to have a timetable, usually outlined in chart form, that shows the start and completion of each project within the framework of the total program. A calendar makes sure that you begin projects—such as brochures, slide presentations, newsletters, special events—early enough that they are ready when they are needed. A program brochure that reaches its target two days after the event is not an effective publicity tool.

STEP 7: BUDGET

How much will implementation of the publicity plan cost? Outline in sequence the exact costs of all activities. Make sure that you include such things as postage costs, car mileage, labor to stuff envelopes, etc. In addition, about 10 percent of the total budget should be allocated for contingencies.

STEP 8: EVALUATING YOUR SUCCESS

Before you begin, both you and the client must agree on the criteria you will use to evaluate your success in achieving the objective. Evaluation criteria should be (a) realistic, (b) credible, (c) specific, and (d) in line with the client's expectations. Don't show stacks of press clippings if the client wants to see only sales results.

Adapted from a professional development seminar given to staff at Ketchum Public Relations, San Francisco.

2. *Who speaks for the organization.* All inquiries, and especially all reporters, should be directed to one person. Usually this should be the director of public relations; but if a very large organization is involved or if the crisis is of great importance (as with product poisonings), there will be demands for a statement by the chief executive.
3. *What information is released.* There should be a definitive statement in the plan as to what will be released—and something *must* be released. The "no comment" response or the refusal of executives to answer questions simply increases the probing. If legal action is involved, it may be necessary to explain that comments might be inadvisable. In other cases, however, some facts can be given. (If people have been killed or injured in an accident, their names must not be released until their families have been notified.)
4. *How to deal with the media.* The rule should be: Help the reporters get the truth. All interested media should be notified and their access to the spokesperson and to the premises should be facilitated. (See Chapter 10 for more on this.)

SUMMARY

1. Every public relations campaign should be planned—and in great detail.
2. A plan explains the situation, states the objectives, defines the audience, establishes the strategy, details the tactics, schedules the timing, estimates the costs, and tells how the evaluation will be done.
3. The preparation of a plan starts with extensive information gathering—perhaps even full-scale surveys.
4. Development of the plan starts with an analysis of the information and progresses to pretesting.
5. When approved, the plan must be executed—with constant attention to every item. Nothing may be taken for granted.
6. Every organization should have plans for crises.

EXERCISES

1. A new computer software company has started to manufacture sophisticated educational programs for children and adults. Officers of the firm believe their products represent the next generation of software programming in terms of graphics, ease of use, and versatility. From a public relations perspective, how would you write the objectives of a consumer publicity program? After doing this, write a list of strategies to accomplish objectives.
2. The Almond Advisory Board (a trade group of almond growers) is gearing up for a

major marketing effort to increase almond consumption among the American public. Write three informational and three motivational objectives for this campaign.

3. The University Theater opens its season on September 15. Before that date, however, a number of public relations materials must be prepared—including a direct mail brochure outlining the season and soliciting purchase of season tickets, a press kit about the theater and its personnel, posters for bulletin boards, a variety of news releases to the news media (including community calendars), and an opening-night reception for university and civic officials. Prepare a time line for these activities.

4. A large developer has decided to build a 40-story office building in a key downtown area. This is a major event for the downtown, which, over the years, has suffered a decline due to the rising numbers of suburban shopping malls and office complexes. Because of this, a gala ground-breaking ceremony is planned in three months. Prepare a public relations plan for this ground-breaking ceremony. The plan should include (a) background of the situation; (b) objectives; (c) publics to be reached; (d) strategies; (e) the action plan, often called tactics; (f) time line; (g) budget; and (h) how success will be evaluated.

SUGGESTED READINGS

Crowley, Claude. "How to Plan Your Communications Program." *Communication World*, November 1986, pp. 39–41.

Dardenne, Peg. "Warming Up to the Market for Cognac." *Public Relations Journal*, April 1984, p. 39.

Davids, Meryl. "Workshop: How to Handle a Crisis." *Public Relations Journal*, November 1987, pp. 43–47.

Donolon, Sally O. "PR Turns Media Spotlight on Historic City." *Communications World*, November 1988, pp. 33–35.

Dozier, David. "Planning and Evaluation in Public Relations Practice." *Public Relations Review*, Summer 1985, pp. 17–25.

Finn, P. "In-House Research Catches On." *Public Relations Journal*, July 1984, pp. 18–20.

Gorney, Carole. "Workshop: How to Use Public Participation Groups Successfully." *Public Relations Journal*, June 1987, p. 29.

Hamilton, Seymour. "Selling the CEO on A Communication Audit." *Communication World*, May 1988, pp. 33–35.

Hamilton, Seymour. *A Communication Audit Handbook: Helping Organizations Communicate.* New York: Longman, 1987.

Lindenmann, Walter, "Content Analysis." *Public Relations Journal*, July 1983, pp. 24–27.

Lindenmann, Walter. "Use of Community Case Studies in Opinion Research." *Public Relations Review*, Spring 1980, pp. 40–50.

Lomax, Linda. "Workshop: How to Survive the Risky Communication Audit." *Public Relations Journal*, November 1986, p. 51.

Mariampolski, H. "The Resurgence of Qualitative Research." *Public Relations Journal,* July 1984, pp. 21–23.

McNabb, D. "Future-Based Budgeting." *Public Relations Journal,* October 1982, p. 24.

Nager, Norman R., and Allen, T. Harrell. *Public Relations Management by Objectives.* New York: Longman, 1984.

Nassar, David. "Workshop: How to Run a Focus Group." *Public Relations Journal,* March 1988, pp. 33–34.

Pollock, John. "Getting the Most from Your Research." *Public Relations Journal,* July 1983, pp. 16–17.

Reid, Sheryll. "Workshop: How to Develop a Strategic Plan." *Public Relations Journal,* August 1987, p. 31.

Roach, William. "Taming the Planning Monster." *Communication World,* October 1984, pp. 12–15.

Ryan, Michael. "Guidelines for Proper Polling." *Public Relations Journal,* July 1983, pp. 18–19.

Shaffer, James C. "Mission Statements: Do We Have Them?" *Communication World,* June 1987, pp. 14–15.

Strenski, James. "Public Relations Budgeting." *Public Relations Journal,* October 1982, pp. 20–23.

Walker, Albert. "Anatomy of the Communications Audit." *Communication World,* September 1988, pp. 19–22.

Winkleman, Michael. "Their Aim Is True." *Public Relations Journal,* August 1987, pp. 18–19, 22–23, 39.

Zotti, Ed. "Thinking Psychologically." *Public Relations Journal,* May 1985, pp. 26–30.

Chapter
19

Evaluation

T he final step in any campaign or program is evaluation of the results. In other words, how well did we do? It is important to ask this question for two reasons.

First, you must show a client or an employer that the money, time, and effort devoted to the program were well spent and actually contributed to the realization of organizational objectives—whether it be attendance at an event, product sales, or even increased public awareness of a particular organization. This, like any other activity, must be evaluated from a cost-benefit perspective. If it costs more than the realized results, the approach should be drastically altered or even discontinued.

Second, you need to know what worked and what didn't work so you can do a better job next time. Such evaluations give you the benefit of fine-tuning your knowledge base so that things can be done more efficiently and perhaps with less turmoil next time. You, for example, may find that you need to distribute advance publicity on an event at least three weeks before the event—instead of the two weeks you allowed this time. Or you may find out that news releases sent to the local newspapers didn't generate the kind of ticket sales you anticipated, so next year you should supplement the news release with direct mail and paid advertising.

The evaluation should cover these major elements: (1) news releases and features sent to the mass media; (2) the organization's publications, such as advertising, newsletters, or house magazines, and printed materials—leaflets, and booklets; (3) events such as speeches, meetings, tours, openings and so on; and (4) attainment of organizational objectives.

NEWS RELEASES AND FEATURES

In reporting to management what you have done, you may use a number of measurement techniques to evaluate effectiveness.

Production

One elementary form of evaluation is simply to give a numerical account of how many news releases, feature stories, photos, or whatever were produced in a given period of time.

This kind of evaluation is supposed to give management an idea of your productivity. Professionals, however, don't think this kind of evaluation is very meaningful, because it emphasizes quantity instead of quality. It may be more cost-effective to write fewer news releases and spend more time on those that are really newsworthy.

Distribution

Closely aligned to the production of materials is their dissemination. Thus, we often find reports that a total of 438 news releases were sent to 657 daily newspapers, 207 weekly newspapers, and 111 trade publications in a year's time or that 57,000 copies of the annual report were distributed to stockholders, security analysts, and business editors.

Although such figures may be useful in terms of evaluating how widely a particular item is distributed, they still don't tell us anything about interest or readership.

Coverage

The most common way of evaluating coverage is to collect press clippings, either through your own efforts or by subscribing to a clipping service. There are regional and national clippings services that can be hired to review vast arrays of publications and to clip all articles about your client or employer. They are found in the Yellow Pages of most metropolitan phone directories and in advertisements in *Public Relations Journal, Communication World,* and *Editor and Publisher.* Large organizations frequently use two clipping services, because one service may find items that are missed by the other.

The purpose of systematically gathering press clippings is to find out if your news releases have been used by the media. By doing this, a company may be able to say, for example, that "the potential circulation of all publicity releases was 130 million readers" (that is, each published story multiplied by the circulation of the periodical that utilized it).

Analysis of coverage can also be done for radio and television, but less reliably. Given the fleeting nature of the radio or TV signal, the coverage must be monitored at the time it occurs. It is easier to do when you have a spokesperson on a national media tour and he or she appears on a number of talk

Counting by the inch and pound. One traditional way of evaluating the effectiveness of publicity is to count the number of press clippings that result from a news release. People still count clippings, but they should also analyze the clippings to determine if key copy points about the product or service were mentioned. (*Source:* Photo by Joe Swan.)

Reasons for Using a Clipping Service

- To check on response to your publicity releases.

- To find out what is said about your company or clients.

- To research any subject reference.

- To analyze competitor's publicity and advertising.

- To obtain sales leads.

- To measure business trends.

- To monitor labor developments and union activities.

- To obtain information on accidents, crimes, births, deaths, personnel changes, etc.

- To monitor coverage of special events.

Courtesy of Burrelle's Press Clipping Service, Livingston, N.J.

shows. In this way, you can easily compile statistics that the spokesperson's message reached, say, an audience of 96 million people (simply add up the average potential audience for each of the talk shows in which the person appeared). Audience surveys by independent research firms usually provide an estimated audience for broadcast shows. Thus, it can reasonably be said that a 30-second exposure on the Johnny Carson show reached an audience of 20 million people.

Dollar Value

The numbers game is also played by converting stories in the regular news columns or on the air into the equivalent of advertising costs. For example, the public relations department of a major corporation gave top management the following report: "When print inches are calculated as advertising space, the company received exposure worth $158,644 this year—a 27.5 percent increase over last year. If we make allowance for an 11 percent increase in advertising space rates, we have a real increase of over $33,000."

Many broadcasting stations send "bills" marked "No charge" to nonprofit organizations to tell the number of times a public service announcement was aired and the value if billed at commercial rates. Stations often take this information off their stations logs as a matter of routine.

Converting space received in the news columns or in broadcast time to the cost of that space or time at advertising rates, many say, shows management that the time and effort have paid off. After all, the coverage received

GROSS IMPRESSIONS:

RADIO	PLACEMENTS		IMPRESSIONS		TOTAL
KGO-AM	6	x	109,000	=	654,000
KCBS-AM	1	x	60,000	=	60,000
KYA	2	x	30,000	=	60,000
KMEL-FM	10	x	35,000	=	350,000

TOTAL GROSS IMPRESSIONS	1,124,000

Counting listeners. A simple method of estimating radio or television exposure is to multiply the number of messages by the estimated audience for the station.

has given the company $158,000 of "free advertising." Some also claim that such calculations clearly show the marketing department that product publicity is well worth the investment.

This may be true, but there is considerable distortion in the numbers game as a form of evaluation. First, reaching vast numbers of people is not the same thing as accomplishment; we still don't know exactly who actually saw or read the message or even if the message had any effect on them. Second, most studies show that an article in a magazine or newspaper is more credible than a comparable paid advertisement with the same information. Thus, it might be said that a news item is worth more than the comparable advertising space. Third, the equating of publicity with advertising rates reinforces the media gatekeepers' attitude that news releases are just attempts to get free advertising. Gatekeepers resent this kind of evaluation, and it does nothing to enhance mutual cooperation.

Analysis of Clippings

While press clippings are often weighed and measured by sheer bulk, a more systematic analysis can pay extra dividends in terms of (1) determining exactly what news releases are most utilized by which periodicals, (2) whether the key copy points are mentioned, and (3) whether the news media in key market areas are using the news releases.

In the first area, for example, a content analysis may show that 45 percent of your company's news releases are management and personnel stories, but that these releases account for only 5 percent of the stories published about the company. In contrast, stories about new-product developments may constitute only 10 percent of the news releases but account for 90 percent of the press coverage. Given these data, a logical step might be to send out fewer personnel stories and more product-development articles.

A systematic tracking system also shows what publications receiving the news releases are utilizing them. Your mailing list may include 500 different periodicals, but, by the end of a 12- month period, you may find that only half of these had any pattern of using your news releases. The others were not using the news releases. Given this information, you would be wise to call your mailing list and avoid the high costs of mailing. Ampex Corporation did such systematic tracking and found that it could reduce its mailing list from 447 publications to 358.

Computer analysis of press clippings, now done routinely by many large organizations, is a valuable way to make sure that key copy points are being included in the published stories. For example, a company may wish to emphasize in all its press coverage that is is a manufacturer of high-quality professional audio and video recording systems or that it is a well-managed company. Analysis may show that 87 percent of the stories mention the high-quality products but that only 35 percent mention or give the impression that the company is well managed. Such feedback can help you structure your news releases so that the more important points receive greater emphasis.

PR Data Systems of Wilton, Connecticut pioneered in the computer analysis of press clippings and can even tell a company if the media in key urban markets are being reached effectively. Other systems are also now available, but the fundamental purpose is the same. A computer profile shows whether your news releases are being published by the media in prime market areas. If they are not, it means that you will have to revamp your publicity strategy for greater penetration of the market.

A systematic tracking mechanism like the one just described is invaluable for making specific changes in publicity activities so that they are more cost-effective. The public relations staff of Ampex Corporation, for example, made the following recommendations to management after a year-long analysis of its press clippings:

1. Divisions should be discouraged from sending out releases on relatively small contracts because the media don't show much interest.
2. Press conferences do not generate as much publicity for new products as pre-trade-show publicity of new products.
3. There is slight media interest in stories about personnel promotions at the group-manager or regional-sales-manager levels. Such stories should be discouraged in the interest of economy and effectiveness.
4. The company's second largest division is not getting its share of product publicity (only 17.5 percent), so more news releases should be distributed about this division.
5. Media interviews with Ampex executives are given good coverage, so it would be in the company interest to make executives accessible for additional interviews.

Gatekeeper Surveys

An alternative to the systematic analysis of press clippings is the survey of periodical editors and broadcast news and program personnel to ascertain exactly what kinds of information they find most usable.

A questionnaire can be prepared and, if a token gift like a pen or a dollar bill is enclosed, a sizable number of gatekeepers (up to 50 percent) will fill out the questionnaire. It is important, however, that the questionnaire not be too long (25 questions maximum) and be written in such a way that respondents can answer with check marks. Here is an example:

Check the three major types of information sources that would help you to cover the microprocessor industry and Millennium Systems in particular:

- Interviews with top officers
- Mailed releases and product photos
- Press kits
- Feature articles
- Story-line synopses
- Brochures, data sheets
- Other _____

You can also assess what kinds of information an editor would most likely publish about a company. For example, a checklist might include the following categories:

- New products
- Technology breakthroughs
- Annual earnings of parent company
- Corporate personnel changes
- Profiles of top executives

ORGANIZATIONAL PUBLICATIONS

With communication materials produced by your organization, there is complete control of what is said and what is shown. While the word "publication" is usually applied to periodicals like newsletters, it can also be used for other items that are written and distributed—even advertisements. The key is your control; you are the gatekeeper.

Advertising

There are numerous organizations that evaluate both printed and broadcast advertising. Since advertising is normally placed through an advertising agency, usually in collaboration with the organization's advertising department, you should consult them regarding the procedure that will be used to measure the effectiveness of the advertisements. By using the right methods, it is possible to find out who was reached and how effectively.

Newsletters and Printed Materials

If you are an editor of a newsletter or employee magazine, it is wise to evaluate its readership on an annual basis. This can do a great deal to ascertain (1) reader perceptions of layout and design, (2) the balance of stories, (3) what kinds of stories have high reader interest, (4) additional topics that could be covered, (5) the publication's credibility, and (6) whether the publication is actually meeting organizational objectives.

Systematic evaluation, it should be emphasized, is not based on whether all the copies are distributed or picked up. This is much like saying that the news release was published in the newspaper. Neither information actually tells us anything about what the audience actually read, retained, or acted upon. If all newsletters or printed materials disappear from the racks in a few days, it may simply mean that the janitorial staff is very efficient.

The following discussion focuses on periodical publications, but the same methods can be used to evaluate leaflets, booklets, and brochures. Since many of these may be used externally, it will be necessary to study the reactions and opinions of people who are not employees. Informal questioning of readers, monitoring of mail, and requests for additional information all can show whether the material is being read and whether it is doing its job or needs improvement.

There are a number of ways that a newsletter, newspaper, or magazine can be audited. These include (1) content analysis, (2) readership interest surveys, (3) readership recall of articles actually read, (4) application of readability formulas, and (5) use of advisory boards or focus interview groups. An informal appraisal can be made by simply walking around the office or plant and learning if employees are talking about items in the publication.

Content Analysis Select a representative sample of past issues and categorize the stories under general headings. You may wish to cover subjects such as (1) management announcements, (2) new-product developments, (3) new personnel and retirements, (4) employee hobbies and interests, (5) corporate finances, (6) news of departments and divisions, (7) job-related information, and so on.

A systematic analysis will quickly tell you if you are devoting too much space, perhaps unintentionally, to management or even to news of a particular division at the expense of other organizational aspects. For example, you may think that you have a lot of articles about employee personnel policies and job advancement opportunities only to find, on analysis, that less than 10 percent of the publication is devoted to such information.

By analyzing organizational objectives and coupling the results of a content analysis with a survey of reader interests, you may come to the conclusion that the publication's contents require some revision.

Readership-Interest Surveys   The purpose of such a survey is to have employees give you feedback on the types of stories that they are most interested in reading.

This is a relatively simple survey. Merely provide a long list of generic story topics and have employees rate each one as "very important," "somewhat important," or "not important." In such a survey, you may be surprised to find employees expressing limited interest in personals (anniversaries and birthdays) but great interest in the organization's future plans. At least this was the case in a survey of 45,000 employees in 40 companies conducted by the International Association of Business Communicators (IABC).

A readership-interest survey becomes even more valuable if you can compare it to the content analysis of what your publication has been covering. If there are substantial differences, it is a signal to change the editorial content of your publication.

Article Recall   The best kind of readership survey is done when you or other interviewers sit down with a sampling of employees to find out what they have actually read in the latest issue of the publication.

Employees are shown the publication page by page and asked to indicate the articles they have read. As a check on the tendency for employees to tell you that they have read the publication from cover to cover (often called a "courtesy bias"), you also ask them (1) how much of the article they read and (2) what the article was about. The resulting marked copies of the publication are then content-analyzed to determine what kinds of articles have the most readership.

The method just described is much more accurate than a questionnaire to employees asking them to tell you how much of the publication they read. You do not get accurate data when you ask such questions as: "What percentage of the newsletters do you read? All of it? Most of it? Some of it?" In this case, employees know that the company expects them to read the publication, so you have a large percentage of answers at the high end of the scale. Very few people will want to admit that they don't read it at all.

It is also somewhat fruitless to ask the rank-and-file employee how he or she evaluates the graphic design and the quality of the photographs. Most employees don't have the expertise to make such judgments. It would be much wiser to ask these questions of individuals who are versed in graphic design and printing quality.

A variation of the readership recall technique is individual evaluation of selected articles for accuracy and writing quality. For example, an article on a new manufacturing technique might be sent (before or after publication) to the head of plant engineering for evaluation.

On a form with a rating scale (e.g., excellent, good, fair, and deficient), the person may be asked to evaluate the article on the basis of such factors as:

Technical data provided
Organization of the article
Article length
Clarity of technical points
Quality of illustrations

Such a systematic evaluation enables you, as an editor, to make sure that the articles are accurate and informative.

Readability Every publication should be evaluated for readability at least once a year. This can be done in several ways. An informal method is to ask people during a reader recall survey if they think the articles are clear and understandable. Comments like "I don't know what they're talking about" and "I don't get anything out of some articles" might indicate that there is a readability problem.

Also available are various readability formulas that quantify reading level. Rudolf Flesch was one of the first educational researchers to develop a formula, now commonly called the Flesch formula. There also is the Gunning formula, the Dale-Chall formula, the Fry formula, and even the Cloze procedure.

Basically, all these formulas allow you to determine how difficult a given piece of writing might be to read. They depend on measuring mean sentence length and counting the average number of multisyllable words. Some also include the number of personal pronouns used. In general, writing is easier to read (is accessible to readers at a lower educational level) if the sentences are simple and short and there are many one- or two-syllable words.

If a randomly selected sample of 100 words contains 4.2 sentences and 142 syllables, it is ranked at about the ninth-grade level. This is the level that most daily newspapers strive for.

If you are writing for an employee publication, ninth-grade level is usually a good starting point. However, if a large percentage of the employees are recent immigrants, you might want to strive for six or seven sentences and 120 syllables per 100 words.

For news releases to the general media and publications geared to all employees, you should write at a ninth-grade level. News releases to trade publications with a primary audience of scientists and engineers as well as publications geared to managers can be written at a higher level. For example, readability formulas show that a college-educated audience can readily cope with 3.8 sentences and 166 syllables per 100 words.

For more information on readability and charts showing educational levels, you may wish to look up Rudolf Flesch's *How to Test Readability* and Robert Gunning's *The Technique of Clear Writing*.

Advisory Boards and Focus Groups Periodic feedback and evaluation can be provided by organizing an employee advisory board that meets several times a year to discuss the direction and content of your publication. Between meetings, members of the advisory board would also be able to relay employee comments and concerns to the editor. This is a useful technique, since it expands the editor's network of feedback and solicits comments that employees may be hesitant to offer the editor face to face.

A variation of the advisory board is to periodically invite a sampling of employees to participate in a general discussion of the publication and its contents. It is important that all segments of the organization's employees be represented and that these sessions not become forums of charges and counter-charges. The purpose is to share information, generate new ideas, and mutually work to make the publication more valuable as an instrument of organizational objectives. This kind of session is often referred to as a focus group. It is a much better method of getting in-depth comments than just wandering around the hallways and asking employees what they think.

EVENTS

Speeches, meetings, presentations, tours, grand openings, and numerous other such activities have one important thing in common: They all involve group audiences to all of whom the same message is given at the same time. All events can be evaluated in the same way.

A first step in evaluating these activities is to count the number of such activities and the number of people who are exposed to the message. This can indicate the amount of work done and the size of the audience reached. Poor attendance at any of these activities may show that people were not interested or that there was not enough advance information. Good attendance proves that people were informed and that they were interested in attending.

The numbers are not conclusive. You must do more than count noses; you must find out whether anything was accomplished. A standing ovation at the end of a speech, spontaneous applause, complimentary remarks as people leave, even the "feel" of the audience as expressed in smiles and the intangible air of satisfaction that can permeate a group of people will give you an idea as to the success of the session.

On the other hand, if people are not responsive, if they ask questions about subjects that were supposedly explained, or if they express doubts or antagonism, the effort has not succeeded.

Some people stop here and think that they have evaluated a given activity, but this is not enough. Your management or client may accept your report that the meeting or presentation was a great success, but they will be much happier if you can give them some proof.

A good way to do this is to ask each person attending the event to fill out an evaluation form and turn it in at the door when leaving. A simple form might look like this:

YOUR EVALUATION OF THIS MEETING (Please check each item)

	Excellent	Good	Average	Could Be Better
1. Location	___	___	___	___
2. Costs	___	___	___	___
3. Facilities	___	___	___	___
4. Program	___	___	___	___
5. Speakers	(These should be listed by name.)			

Why did you attend? _____

_____

How did you learn about it? _____

Suggestions for future events: _____

_____

ATTAINMENT OF OBJECTIVES

It is imperative to report how the program has helped to reach organizational objectives. For example, Ketchum Public Relations won a Silver Anvil Award from the Public Relations Society of America (PRSA) by showing that its extensive campaign for the California Prune Board resulted in a sales gain of 4 percent for the year (with no advertising involved) following more than five years of declining sales.

Ketchum's simple objective was to increase prune sales. The strategy was to generate positive awareness among women aged 25 to 49 through a campaign on the theme "Prunes . . . Just Plum Good." By using a credible spokesperson and introducing prunes as a snack food for people interested in health and fitness, Ketchum attained the objective. They also tabulated the numerical counts to show dissemination and coverage.

- 1,189 consumer magazine and newspaper articles generating 143 million total impressions
- 7,000 *Feeling Energetic* booklets distributed as a result of TV and radio publicity
- 22,000 copies of basic fact booklet distributed

But the bottom line was the fact that the agency met its objective—it was able to increase prune sales. You must never forget that publicity in itself is not the objective. Publicity is only a communications tool utilized to achieve objectives.

Knowing the ultimate objective of the organization also does a great deal to help evaluate a campaign. For example, a shipping salvage company may have the objective of getting greater recognition and visibility among potential customers—shipping lines, insurance companies, governmental agencies, harbor facilities, and even naval authorities.

Publicity Tracking Report

Local Television

PLACEMENT	DATE (FREQ.)	TOTAL ADULTS	AVERAGE SIZE LENGTH	MEDIA UNITS	PUBLICITY EXPOSURE UNITS	IMPACT FACTOR	PUBLICITY VALUE UNITS
New York WNBC—News	9/17	566,400	5:00	3.3	1,869,100	1.4	2,616,800
New York WNEW—News	5/28	468,800	3:00	2.9	1,359,520	1.3	1,767,400
New York WNBC—News	5/21	566,400	4:00	3.1	1,755,840	1.0	1,755,840
New York WNBC—News	5/21	860,000	2:00	2.5	2,150,000	1.0	2,150,000
New York WPIX Action News	9/14	365,600	:30	1.0	365,600	0.8	292,500
New York WABC Eyewitness News	9/14	448,800	:19	0.7	314,200	0.8	251,300
New York WNBC—News	5/7	708,000	:23	0.6	424,800	0.5	212,400
New York WNBC—News	5/7	860,000	:32	1.0	860,000	1.1	946,000
New York WCBS—News	5/7	426,400	:52	1.7	724,880	0.5	362,400
New York WPIX—News	5/7	365,600	:25	0.6	219,360	0.6	131,600
Chicago WMAQ—News	12/30	273,800	:45	2.2	602,360	0.2	120,470
Chicago WMAQ—News	9/13	273,800	4:00	3.1	848,780	1.6	1,358,100
Denver KMGH—News	3/9	44,600	2:00	2.5	111,500	0.8	89,200
Baltimore People are Talking	3/11	36,100	15:00	2.8	101,100	1.4	141,500
Baltimore People are Talking	12/17	36,100	2:00	1.0	36,100	1.0	36,100
Boston WCVB—Good Day	3/1	31,200	:30	0.4	12,480	0.4	4,990
Boston WNEV—News	2/14	97,200	:30	1.0	97,200	0.4	38,880
Boston WNEV—News	2/28	97,200	:60	1.7	165,240	0.9	148,700
Boston WCVB—News	10/18	240,000	:15	0.6	144,000	0.4	57,600

More than just numbers. A sophisticated method of measuring the effectiveness of publicity is to assign various values for market penetration, copy points mentioned, and whether the tone of the article was positive or negative. (*Source:* Ketchum Public Relations, Pittsburgh.)

Given the objective and the target publics, the effective program would concentrate on specialized magazines, newsletters, and conferences that cater to the prospective customers. Sending news releases to daily newspapers in the Midwest or having a spokesperson for the salvage company on a daytime TV talk show wouldn't be logical or effective. It might generate a number of press clippings or exposure to thousands of viewers, but it would not help to meet the company's objective.

In sum, your work is best evaluated by analyzing its impact: its ability to motivate people, change their behavior or beliefs, or inspire them to utilize your service or product.

Attendance is probably the easiest thing to measure. A highly effective advance publicity program often takes the bow for generating a sellout crowd at a special event. On the other hand, a faulty effort may mean that three-fourths of the seats are empty. Effective product publicity can make the difference between a 10 percent increase in sales and no increase at all. In the political area, an effective campaign is often measured by who gets elected to office. Of course, there are always a number of intervening variables that exert some influence, but enough correlation studies have been done to show that major amounts of publicity and promotion do contribute to increased attendance, sales, or votes.

Benchmark Studies

Changing a person's perceptions about something is difficult to evaluate, but it can be done. One way is to sample the opinions of the target audience before and after the campaign. This means making "benchmark studies"—studies that graphically show percentage differences in attitudes as a result of increased information and persuasion. There are, of course, a number of possible intervening variables that may also account for changes in attitudes, but statistical analysis of variance can help pinpoint to what degree the attitude change is attributable to your efforts.

U.S. Steel, some years ago, did a benchmark study of its image among American business leaders and major educators. The company then sent a number of speech reprints and other publications to a selected sample of these opinion leaders while, at the same time, making sure that a control group did not receive the materials. At the end of the year, it was found that the group receiving company publications was considerably more positive about U.S. Steel as a progressive and well-managed company that spoke on behalf of the entire steel industry. On the other hand, the control group still retained its original low-level image of the company.

Mobil Oil Company, General Electric, and AT&T regularly utilize benchmark surveys to measure the effectiveness of publicity promotion campaigns. Surveys made after particular campaigns go a long way toward documenting their impact on the public. Continuing surveys, for example, do show that Mobil's sponsorship of *Masterpiece Theater* on the Public Broadcasting System (PBS) has gained the company a reputation among "opinion leaders" for corporate leadership and social responsibility.

Feedback

Benchmark surveys are only one way to measure results. You can also do evaluations on a less sophisticated level by simply keeping complete and thorough tabs on telephone calls logged and letters received—and even by conducting focus-group interviews with cross-sections of the publics being reached. The analysis of telephone calls and letters is very important in the area of consumer affairs. If a pattern can be ascertained, it often tells the company that a particular product or service is not up to standard.

The readership of product-publicity features is often monitored by offering readers an opportunity to write for a brochure or for more information. In this way, for example, Air New Zealand has measured the value of sending travel features to daily newspapers throughout the United States. Inquiries from toll-free "800" numbers are also monitored to find out where a person first heard about a particular product. Such monitoring often points out to top management that product publicity generates more sales leads than straight advertising.

Pretesting

Evaluation is important even before a campaign is launched. The concept is called pretesting. Check your message with a sample group from your targeted audience. Do they understand the message easily? Does it cause them to change or modify their opinions? Does it motivate them to try a new product?

A variation of pretesting is the experimental campaign. Before going nationwide with a program, companies often test the promotion in several key cities to see how the media accept the message and how the public reacts. This approach is quite common in product marketing because it limits the costs and enables the company to revamp or fine-tune the campaign before a full-scale commitment is made on a national level. On more than one occasion, a market test in a key city has failed so miserably that the company did not pursue the matter any further.

The split approach is most common in direct mail publicity campaigns. Two or three different appeals may be prepared by a charitable organization and sent to different audiences. The response rate is then monitored (amount of donations) to see what appeal seemed to be the most effective in motivating people to make a donation. On that basis, the most successful appeal is used for a widespread mailing.

Monitoring the Competition

There is an old saying that there are two sides to every question. This often applies when public relations is involved. If you are trying to promote a product or service, there may be competitors trying to promote *their* products or services. There may be noncompetitors who believe that what you are promoting is of little or no value. For example, egg producers may be opposed by those who say that eggs contain cholesterol.

When public issues are on the agenda, there are likely to be well-defined efforts on each side. Those who are environmentalists are almost certain to oppose anything that affects the environment adversely.

Regardless of which side you may be on, it will be most helpful to your cause, product, or service to keep track of what is being done by those others. A decline in their activity, a reduction in media attention, or a shift in what they are saying may indicate that your activity is causing it. If, after your campaign has been running for some time, there is a reduction in adverse publicity, it may show that you are gaining. A decline in demonstrations, a decrease in the number of hostile speeches, an increase in favorable editorials in the mass media, or the shifting of position by opinion leaders—all these are favorable signs. Again, as with other activities, it is numbers that are important. Facts like these can be very persuasive in your report.

THE REPORT

When you have finished evaluating a campaign, you must report the results to the people who paid for it. In some cases it may be necessary to report on individual events or activities immediately after they have occurred. Even if there are no special things that justify an immediate report, there must be an overall report on the entire program. Usually this is done annually. Budgets and programs are generally reviewed at least once a year and this is the time when you must convince management or the client that what you have done is worthwhile—that the program should be continued and improved.

To prepare the report, you should refer back to the original plan and state what you accomplished under each heading. The following questions should be answered:

1. *Situation.* Was the situation properly appraised? While the program was underway, did you learn anything that forced changes? What happened and what did you do?
2. *Audience.* Was it properly identified? Did you reach it? How effectively did you reach it (i.e., numbers reached, response, feedback)?
3. *Objectives.* Did you achieve what you planned to achieve? Here you should provide figures. As stated in the previous chapter, you should have set numerical goals. Now you tell how well you did in reaching those goals.
4. *Strategy.* Did it work? Did you have to modify it? Should it be continued or changed?
5. *Tactics.* Did all the tools accomplish what they were supposed to accomplish? Were changes made? Why? Here again you can give numbers: news items published, feature stories published, printed items distributed, response of readers or viewers, TV and radio appearances, and so on.
6. *Timing.* Was everything done at the right time? Should changes be made next year?
7. *Costs.* Did you stay within the budget? If not, why not? (Some organizations will accept small overruns while others absolutely refuse to approve any expenditure over budget. If you work for one of these, you must watch your expenditures and check your appropriations regularly and accurately.) This is the point at which you set the stage for the next budget and perhaps explain why more money would have permitted greater accomplishment.

SUMMARY

1. Evaluation is absolutely essential. You must tell what was done, how well it was done, and what good it did. Give numbers whenever possible.

2. Don't just count news items and features. Find out where they were used, who used them, whether they reached the right people, and whether they were effective.

3. Through research, you can find out who your advertising reached and how effectively.

4. Newsletters, house magazines, and printed materials can all be evaluated by content analysis, reader-interest surveys, article recall, and readability tests. Advisory boards and focus groups may also be used.

5. Events can be evaluated through informal study of response and post-event surveys.

6. Attainment of objectives can be measured in some cases by counting noses or studying sales figures. More often, you will use benchmark studies, feedback, pretesting, and monitoring the competition.

7. Evaluation isn't complete until you have given a comprehensive report to your management or client.

EXERCISES

1. During a one-week period, clip all articles in the community daily newspaper regarding the university, including all general news items and sports. Find out the average cost of advertising per column-inch and multiply it times the number of column-inches found. Given the "dollar value" of the publicity, do you think the coverage was actually worth this amount? Why or why not?

2. During a period of several weeks, follow the news coverage of a major company in your area. After compiling the news clippings, do a content analysis of each clipping. What percentage, in terms of the information provided, were probably company-originated? Indicate the percentage of clippings where references were made about the following: (a) the size of the company, (b) its product lines, (c) its competitive position in the marketplace, and (d) the quality of the product.

3. Design and write a short questionnaire, for use by a company or organization, to determine the attitudes of media gatekeepers about the kind of news releases and other informational material they receive from the company. The questionnaire should be designed in such a way as to gather information that will help the company do a better job of providing media gatekeepers with useful material.

4. Design and write a questionnaire to determine the readership of the campus newspaper. A second activity would be to actually conduct the readership survey.

5. Do a content analysis of a company newsletter or magazine. Articles, and the number of column-inches, should be placed in general categories: messages from management, employee features, news of departments and divisions, personals, recreational activities, retirements, and so on. Given your findings, do you think the publication is accomplishing such corporate objectives as (a) building employee loyalty and morale, (b) informing employees of opportunities for advancement, and (c) informing employees about company policies and procedures?

6. The national tourism office of Thailand has launched a major public relations campaign in the United States to promote Thailand as a vacation destination. Some of the activities include placement of travel articles in leading publications, exhibits

of Thai culture at local art museums in major cities, advertisements in leading travel publications, and demonstrations of Thai dancing on local television shows. An "800" number is widely advertised and promoted as a way for people to order booklets and brochures about vacationing in Thailand. After one year, how would you evaluate the success of this promotional program?

SUGGESTED READINGS

Chapman, R. "Measurement Is Alive and Well." *Public Relations Journal*, May 1982, pp. 28–29.

Dozier, David. "Planning Evaluation in PR Practice."*Public Relations Review*, Summer 1985, pp. 17–24.

Gadsden, Sheila. "Clipping Services: More Than a Century Old." *Communication World*, December 1987, pp. 27–29.

Larson, Mark, and Miller, Karen "Measuring Change After a Public Education Campaign." *Public Relations Review*, Winter 1984, pp. 23–32.

Leahigh, Alan K. "Marketing Communications: If You Can't Count It, Does It Count?" *Public Relations Quarterly*, Winter 1985, pp. 23–27.

Lesly, Philip. "Multiple Measurements of Public Relations." *Public Relations Review*, Summer 1986, pp. 3–8.

Lindenmann, Walter. "Content Analysis." *Public Relations Journal*, July 1983, pp. 23–27.

Reeves, Byron, and Ferguson, Mary. "Measuring the Effect of Messages about Social Responsibility." *Public Relations Review*, Fall 1980, pp. 40–55.

Ryan, Michael. "Guidelines for Proper Polling." *Public Relations Journal*, July 1983, pp. 18–19.

Wilcox, Dennis L., Ault, Phillip, and Agee, Warren. "Evaluation." *Public Relations Strategies and Tactics*; New York: Harper & Row, 1989, chap. 10.

Index